TEACHER'S EDITION

ADDISON - WESLEY

APPLYING MATHEMATICS

A CONSUMER/CAREER APPROACH

MERVIN L. KEEDY

STANLEY A. SMITH

PAUL A. ANDERSON

ADDISON - WESLEY PUBLISHING COMPANY

Menlo Park, California
Reading, Massachusetts
Wokingham, Berkshire U.K.
Amsterdam
Don Mills, Ontario
Sydney

CONTENTS

ISBN 0–201–20645–5

ABCDEFGHIJK–VH–88765

HIGHLIGHTS

1. CAREER MATHEMATICS

Author interviews with workers on the job pinpointed the math actually used in over 50 careers. These clear-cut math applications show skills needed for success in business and in industry.

2. CONSUMER MATHEMATICS

All the math skills needed to make wise consumer decisions are included here. Coverage emphasizes personal finance and taxes, banking services, credit card buying, housing and automobile costs, as well as hobbies and recreation.

3. MOTIVATIONAL LESSON DEVELOPMENT

Full-color photographs set the career or consumer theme. Examples develop step-by-step problem-solving techniques. *Try This* exercises provide immediate reinforcement. *On Your Own* and *Decision* exercises expand career awareness.

4. CONTINUING SKILL-BUILDING EMPHASIS

Two-page *Skills Review* precedes each chapter. For further help students can refer to the *Skills Bank* for detailed examples and additional exercises. Extra review is available in the **Skills Workbook.**

5. ENRICHMENT STRANDS

Problem-Solving Hints focus on useful real-life problems. *Estimation* and *Mental Calculation* strands add to students' paper and pencil skills.

6. UP-TO-DATE CONTENT IN COMPUTERS AND STATISTICS

These optional chapters introduce students to the basic ideas they will need in a computer society.

THE LESSON

Full-color photos for each lesson establish a theme and motivate learning.

Opening paragraphs introduce a career and relate it to particular mathematics applications common in that career.

Examples carefully set out the sequence of ideas needed with a *Plan* that shows steps clearly.

Try This exercises give students opportunity to check their understanding of the preceding example.

The *Example-Try This* pattern continues as new ideas are introduced throughout the lesson.

PLUMBING

Plumbers do more than repair leaky sinks and broken pipes. Large industries require complex plumbing installations.

Ginger Kwong installs water, gas, and waste disposal systems in her work as a plumber. She also repairs these systems. Ginger served several years as an apprentice plumber. She took night courses and passed a test to obtain her license as a master plumber.

Ginger explains two ways to estimate the cost of plumbing a new house.

EXAMPLE 1. Estimate the total cost of plumbing a new house at $275 per fixture. The home will have a laundry tub, a shower, a bath tub, 2 toilets, a kitchen sink, and 2 bathroom sinks.

PLAN: **Step 1.** Find the number of fixtures.
There are 8 fixtures.

Step 2. Multiply to find the cost.
$275 × 8 = $2200

The cost will be about $2200.

EXAMPLE 2. Estimate the total cost of plumbing the house by doubling the cost of materials. The materials for plumbing a new house will cost about $1800.

$1800 × 2 = $3600

The cost will be about $3600.

TRY THIS
1. Estimate the total cost of plumbing a new house at $250 per fixture. The house will have two bath tubs, a shower, a laundry tub, 2 toilets, a kitchen sink, and 3 bathroom sinks.
2. Estimate the total cost of plumbing by doubling the cost of materials. The cost of materials for a new house will be about $1950.

To estimate the length of a coil of flexible pipe, Ginger multiplies the circumference of the coil by the number of coils.

EXAMPLE 3. Estimate the length of a coil of plastic tubing. The coil has a diameter of 35 cm. It contains 18 coils.

Coil of flexible pipe

PLAN: **Step 1.** Estimate the circumference. Use the formula $C = \pi d$, where C is the circumference and d is the diameter. Since $\pi \approx 3.14$, use 3 to estimate.
$C \approx 3 \times 35$ cm
$C \approx 105$ cm

Step 2. Multiply the circumference by the number of coils.
105 × 18 = 1890 cm

The length of the tubing is about 1900 centimeters or 19 meters.

TRY THIS
3. Estimate the length of a coil of flexible pipe. The coil has a diameter of 2 feet. It contains 9 coils.

Unusual career applications maintain students' interest.

Needed mathematics review, for example, solving proportions, appears in *Skills Review* preceding chapter opener.

Exercises cover all topics developed in lesson.

On Your Own stresses need to seek out special information from local sources.

Other lessons feature *Decision* problems, where students see that a wise choice depends on correct computation.

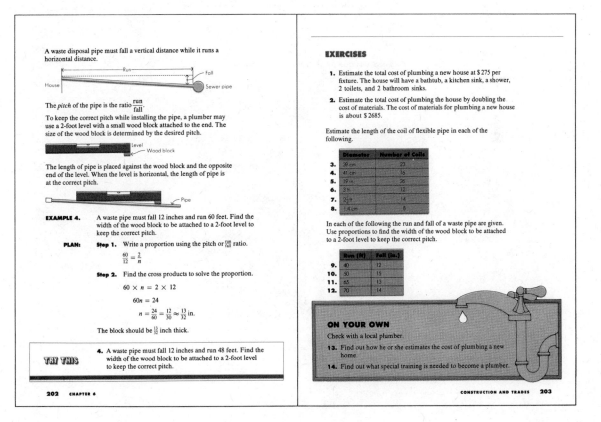

A waste disposal pipe must fall a vertical distance while it runs a horizontal distance.

The *pitch* of the pipe is the ratio $\frac{\text{run}}{\text{fall}}$.

To keep the correct pitch while installing the pipe, a plumber may use a 2-foot level with a small wood block attached to the end. The size of the wood block is determined by the desired pitch.

The length of pipe is placed against the wood block and the opposite end of the level. When the level is horizontal, the length of pipe is at the correct pitch.

EXAMPLE 4.   A waste pipe must fall 12 inches and run 60 feet. Find the width of the wood block to be attached to a 2-foot level to keep the correct pitch.

PLAN: **Step 1.**   Write a proportion using the pitch or $\frac{\text{run}}{\text{fall}}$ ratio.

$$\frac{60}{12} = \frac{2}{n}$$

Step 2.   Find the cross products to solve the proportion.

$$60 \times n = 2 \times 12$$
$$60n = 24$$
$$n = \frac{24}{60} = \frac{12}{30} \approx \frac{13}{32} \text{ in.}$$

The block should be $\frac{13}{32}$ inch thick.

TRY THIS   **4.** A waste pipe must fall 12 inches and run 48 feet. Find the width of the wood block to be attached to a 2-foot level to keep the correct pitch.

EXERCISES

1. Estimate the total cost of plumbing a new house at $275 per fixture. The house will have a bathtub, a kitchen sink, a shower, 2 toilets, and 2 bathroom sinks.

2. Estimate the total cost of plumbing the house by doubling the cost of materials. The cost of materials for plumbing a new house is about $2685.

Estimate the length of the coil of flexible pipe in each of the following.

	Diameter	Number of Coils
3.	39 cm	23
4.	41 cm	16
5.	19 in.	26
6.	3 ft	12
7.	$2\frac{1}{2}$ ft	14
8.	1.4 cm	6

In each of the following the run and fall of a waste pipe are given. Use proportions to find the width of the wood block to be attached to a 2-foot level to keep the correct pitch.

	Run (ft)	Fall (in.)
9.	40	12
10.	50	15
11.	65	13
12.	70	14

ON YOUR OWN

Check with a local plumber.

13. Find out how he or she estimates the cost of plumbing a new home.

14. Find out what special training is needed to become a plumber.

ENRICHMENT STRANDS

Full-page *Estimation, Mental Calculation,* and *Problem Solving* features add to students calculating skills.

Estimation skills add confidence in use of hand-held calculators, rough estimates.

Mental Calculation skills show that some problems can be easily worked without paper and pencil.

Problem Solving lessons develop skills for word problem attack and solution.

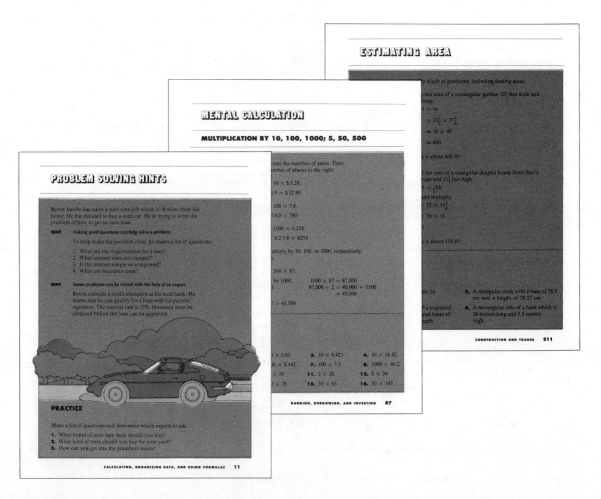

SUPPLEMENTS

A full range of extra material meets every teaching need.

Teacher's Edition has annotated answers to all problems.

Skills Workbook is keyed to the 87 basic concepts presented in the *Skills Bank.*

Projects Book provides greater practice with word problems in situations that expand on the basal text.

Test and **Quiz Book** contains ample evaluation material, including a basic skills and applications test.

EXERCISES

Dan Smith runs a janitorial service. He charges these piece rates to clean office buildings:

Service	Charge
Shampoo small rug	$20.00
Shampoo large rug	35.00
General cleaning, small office	12.50
General cleaning, large office	17.50
General cleaning, office suite	30.00
Detail cleaning, small office	22.50
Detail cleaning, large office	37.50

Find Dan Smith's charges for cleaning.

1. Detail cleaning of a large office 37.50

2. Detail cleaning of a small office, plus shampooing a small rug $42.50

3. General cleaning of a small office building containing three small offices and two large offices $72.50

4. General cleaning of a large office building containing four small offices, six large offices, and four office suites, plus shampooing three large rugs $380

Use the following table to find the charges for the jobs.

	Size	Double spaced	Single spaced	Space and one half
Typing pages	letter	$1.75	$2.30	$1.75
	legal	2.00	4.00	3.00
Duplicating copies	letter	$0.07 per page		
	legal	$0.08 per page		
Minimum charge is $5.00				

5. Typing 120 letter-sized pages, space and one half, with five copies of each page $252

6. Typing 250 legal-sized pages, double spaced, with 20 copies of each page $900

7. Typing a government report containing:

17 legal-sized pages, double spaced, with twelve copies of each,
32 letter-sized pages, single spaced, with twelve copies of each,
1 legal-sized page, space and one half, with one copy,
1 letter-sized page, space and one half, with one copy. $155.70

8. Typing an environmental impact study containing:

237 letter-sized pages, double spaced, with thirty copies of each,
15 legal-sized pages, single spaced, with thirty copies of each,
2 letter-sized pages, space and one half, with three copies of each, and
2 legal-sized pages, space and one half, with three copies of each. $876.65

Find the gross weekly pay.

9. Selma Ramsey has a pool cleaning service. She charges $17.50 for small pools and $30 for large pools. She averages twelve small and six large pools a week. How much are her average weekly earnings? $390

10. Amy Kobata does automobile tune-ups in a garage. She charges $56.75 to tune a 6-cylinder car and $69.50 to tune an 8-cylinder car. One week she tuned eighteen 6-cylinder cars and five 8-cylinder cars. Find her earnings for that week. $1369

11. Ella Goldman runs a beauty shop. She charges $12 for a haircut and $18 for a styling. Find her weekly earnings if she averages thirty haircuts and seventeen stylings per week. $666

12. Rex Carter runs a car wash. He charges $3.00 for an exterior wash, $3.75 for a wash and wax, and $4.75 for a wash, wax, and interior cleaning. He averages 13 washes, 19 wash and waxes, and 23 wash, wax, and interior cleanings per week. Find his weekly gross earnings. $219.50

DECISION

13. You are a contractor. You need a carpenter to frame houses. One carpenter charges you $14.75 per hour. Another charges you $0.40 per square foot of house floor area. Who would you hire? Why?

SKILL BUILDING

SKILLS REVIEW

Math skills needed for a chapter are reviewed just before the chapter in a two-page spread of problems. These are keyed to the *Skills Bank* for students needing more work. For additional skills work, use the supplementary **Skills Workbook**—a page of problems for each skill.

SKILLS BANK

Brief examples and related exercises for 87 basic computational skills are available in the *Skills Bank*, ready for individuals or whole classes who may need extra information.

SKILLS REVIEW

SKILL 12 Rounding decimals and money
Round to the underlined place.

1. 7.3   **2.** 8.56   **3.** $21.92   **4.** $38.07

SKILL 40 Simplifying fractions
Simplify.

5. $\frac{4}{8}$ **6.** $\frac{15}{18}$ **7.** $\frac{51}{85}$ **8.** $\frac{100}{4}$

SKILL 43 Ratio
Write the ratio. Simplify when possible.

9. 25 tires to 5 cars   **10.** 18 hits in 72 times at bat.
11. 56 baskets in 16 games   **12.** 48¢ for 2 apples

SKILL 15 Adding money
Add.

13. $5.48   **14.** $26.72   **15.** $258.17   **16.** $246.97
   + 3.21   + 18.15   + 9.49   + 579.23

SKILL 19 Subtracting money
Subtract.

17. $8.56   **18.** $6.48   **19.** $63.40   **20.** $5286.15
   − 4.32   − 1.94   − 19.65   − 3874.66

SKILL 22 Multiplying whole numbers
Multiply.

21. 80   **22.** 148   **23.** 64   **24.** 7324
   × 9   × 6   × 34   × 63

SKILL 23 Multiplying money
Multiply.

25. $4.56   **26.** $62.78   **27.** $5.98   **28.** $87.96
   × 5   × 4   × 12   × 74

184

SKILLS BANK

SKILL 1. Date Notation
Use the number of each month to write the date. Write the month first.

EXAMPLE January 15, 1983 is written 1–15–83 or 1/15/83

1. February 7, 1982   **2.** October 18, 1985
3. June 10, 1984   **4.** March 20, 1986
5. May 27, 1983   **6.** November 19, 1990

Write the date indicated.

7. 5–4–84   **8.** 3–10–90   **9.** 6–6–86   **10.** 2–3–88

SKILL 2. Time Notation
Use colons to write time notation.

EXAMPLES 4 hours 27 minutes is 4:27
7 minutes after 6 o'clock is 6:07
6 hours 12 minutes 5 seconds is 6:12:05

1. 8 hours 10 minutes   **2.** 15 minutes 30 seconds
3. 25 minutes after 4 o'clock   **4.** 1 hour 10 minutes 4 seconds

Write the time.

5. 12:15:04   **6.** 2:08:37

SKILL 3. Place Value: Whole Numbers
Give the place and value of the underlined digit.

EXAMPLE 378,194. The 7 is in the ten-thousands' place. The value is 70,000.

1. 5,397   **2.** 1,876   **3.** 345,940   **4.** 9,287,164
5. 39,278,176,400   **6.** 948,276,149,124

426   **SKILLS BANK**

SKILLS BANK

GUIDE TO SKILLS*

	Chapter 1	**Chapter 2**	**Chapter 3**	**Chapter 4**

WHOLE NUMBERS	Place value 3
	Rounding 11
	Adding 14
	Estimating sums 17
	Subtracting 18
	Multiplying 22
	Dividing 50, 51
		Place value 3
		Rounding 11
		Adding 14
		Multiplying 22
		Special
		  products 24
		Dividing 51
			Place value 3
			Word names 4
				Estimating
				  differences 21
				Dividing 51

DECIMALS	Rounding 12
	Adding 16
	Subtracting 20
	Multiplying 27
	Dividing by a
	  decimal 52
		Rounding 12
		Adding 16
		Multiplying 27
		Special
		  products 29
			Rounding 12
			Multiplying 27
				Rounding 12
				Subtracting 20
				Multiplying 27

MONEY	Rounding 12
	Adding 15
	Subtracting 19
	Multiplying 23
	Estimating
	  products 26
		Rounding 12
		Adding 15
		Multiplying 23
		Multiplying with
		  fractions 48
			Notation 6
			Rounding 12
			Adding 15
			Multiplying 23
			Multiplying with
			  fractions 48
				Rounding 12
				Adding 15
				Subtracting 19
				Multiplying 23
				Estimating
				  products 26
				Multiplying with
				  fractions 48

FRACTIONS	Multiplying 53	Multiplying 53	Writing as
			  decimals 34
			Multiplying,
			  simplifying 53, 54
			Writing mixed
			  numbers as
			  decimals 38
			Multiplying
			  mixed numbers 55
				Dividing 56
				Dividing mixed
				  numbers 57

PERCENTS	Finding a
	  percent of a
	  number 67
	Finding what
	  percent one
	  number is of
	  another 68
	Finding a number
	  given a percent 69
		Converting to
		  decimals 44
		Finding a
		  percent of a
		  number 67
			Converting to
			  decimals 44
			Finding a
			  percent of a
			  number 67
				Converting to
				  decimals 44
				Finding a
				  percent of a
				  number 67

OTHER	Date notation 1 Time notation 2	Date notation 1 Time notation 2	Date notation 1 Standard notation 5	

*The number following each skill refers to **Skills Bank.**

	Chapter 10	Chapter 11	Chapter 12

WHOLE NUMBERS	Multiplying 22
	Special
	  products 24
	Dividing 50, 51
	  products 25
	Dividing 50, 51
		Adding 14
		Subtracting 18
		Multiplying 22
		Estimating
			Adding 14
			Subtracting 18
			Multiplying 22
			Dividing 50, 51

DECIMALS	Rounding 12
	Adding 16
	Subtracting 20
	Multiplying 27
	Dividing by a
	  decimal 52
		Adding 16
		Subtracting 20
		Multiplying 27
		Dividing by a
		  decimal 52
			Adding 16

MONEY	Rounding 12 Adding 15 Subtracting 19		Adding 15 Subtracting 19
FRACTIONS			Converting to percents 47

PERCENTS	Finding a
	  percent of a
	  number 67
	Finding a
	  number given
	  a percent 69		

OTHERS		Translating
		  number
		  sentences 49
		Changing
		  metric units 72
		Evaluating
		  formulas 87
			Ratios 43
			Finding means 85
			Finding medians 86

ANSWERS

Answers are found in several places.

1. The **Teacher's Edition** contains over-printed answers for all problems, including *Try This* exercises, *Skills Reviews,* and *Skills Bank.* When answers are too long to be included on the page, they appear in the *Additional Answers* section which begins below.

2. In the **Student Text,** *Try This* answers begin on page 470. With answers provided to these exercises, students have immediate reinforcement. They can then determine if they understand the skill and are ready to go on to the exercises. Odd answers are provided for the *Skills Reviews* and *Skills Bank.*

ADDITIONAL ANSWERS

CHAPTER 1
Pages 22–23

1.

Interval	Tally	Frequency
78–80	卌 I	6
81–83	IIII	4
84–86	卌	5
87–89	卌 I	6
90–92	III	3
93–95	卌	5
96–98	卌	5
99–101	III	3
102–104	III	3

2.

Interval	Tally	Frequency
400–499	II	2
500–599	卌	5
600–699	卌 I	6
700–799	卌 I	6
800–899	卌	5
900–999	卌 II	7
1000–1099	I	1
1100–1199	I	1
1200–1299	II	2

3.

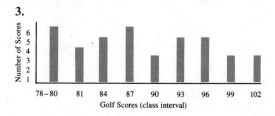

4.

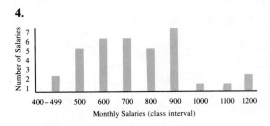

Number of Salaries / Monthly Salaries (class interval)

Page 29

55.

Interval	Tally	Frequency
25–27	|||	3
28–30	|||	3
31–33	||	2
34–36	|||	3
37–39	ⅢⅡ	5
40–42	ⅢⅡ	6
43–45	|||	3
46–48	|||	3
49–51	||	2

56.

Interval	Tally	Frequency
41–45	||	2
46–50			1
51–55	|||	3
56–60			1
61–65	ⅢⅡ	5
66–70	|||	3
71–75	||||	4
76–80	||||	4
81–85	ⅢⅡ	6
86–90	ⅢⅡ	5
91–95	||||	4
96–100	||	2

57.

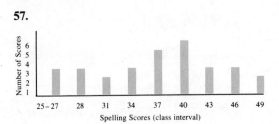

Number of Scores / Spelling Scores (class interval)

58.

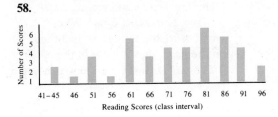

Number of Scores / Reading Scores (class interval)

CHAPTER 3
Page 70
7. Fifteen and $\frac{93}{100}$ **8.** Forty-five and $\frac{00}{100}$

9. Twenty-two and $\frac{02}{100}$ **10.** One hundred eight

and $\frac{19}{100}$ **11.** Thirty-four and $\frac{16}{100}$

12. Fifty-five and $\frac{25}{100}$ **13.** Seventy-eight and $\frac{94}{100}$

14. Two hundred twenty-six and $\frac{97}{100}$

CHAPTER 11
Pages 386–387
1. 10 Read values for X, Y, and Z from DATA
statement.
20 Add the 3 numbers, divide by 3, and
assign the average to A.
30 Print the value of A.
40 Accept 16 for X, 8 for Y, and 18 for Z.
50 Program is finished.

3. 10 Read values for length L and width W
from DATA statement.
20 Multiply length times width. Assign this
area to A.
30 Print THE AREA IS and the value of A,
1500.
40 Accept 60 for L and 25 for W.
50 Program is finished.

5. 10 Read value for F, the Fahrenheit
temperature.
20 Subtract 32 from F, multiply by 5, and
divide by 9. Assign this value to C.

30 Print THE CELSIUS TEMPERATURE IS
   and the value of C, 0.
35 Go to the READ statement.
40 Accept 32 as the first value of F.
   Following the GO TO statement, the
   READ statement accepts 100 as the second
   value and "erases" 32. The READ
   statement accepts 78 as the third value
   and "erases" 100.
50 The program ends when the READ
   statement finds no more DATA.

Page 389

13. See page 355 for DATA. Examples:
    10   READ P
    20   LET W = 0.003 * P
    30   PRINT "W = " W
    40   DATA 88, 96, 92
    50   GO TO 10
    60   END
    W = .264
    W = .288
    W = .276

    10   READ G, S
    20   LET H = 1.36 * G * S
    30   PRINT "H = " H
    40   DATA 15, .89, 14, .92, 13, .96
    50   GO TO 10
    60   END
    H = 18.156
    H = 17.5168
    H = 16.9728

Page 393

1. x + 2.25, y + 0.75   2. x − 1.5, y + 2.0
3. x − 2.5, y + 0   4. x − 1.25, y − 1.25
5. x + 1.25, y − 1.0   6. x + 2.75, y − 1.75
7. x − 2.75, y − 1.25   8. x + 1.0, y + 1.75

9–16.

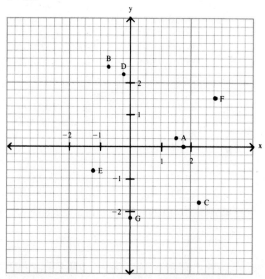

For pages 396–401, all column heads would print on one line.

Page 396

ITEM	COST	SOLD	SELLING PRICE	PROFIT
6	1.86	128	3.38	194.56
7	82	14	150	952
8	22	11	39.95	197.45
9	4	20	7.4	68
10	1.13	23	2.05	21.16

Page 397

1. 16   2. 57   3. 7   4. 22   5. 8   6. 8   7. 16
8. 64   9. 3.76   10. 365.4   11. 1620   12. 23.94
13. 404.6   14. 1989   15. 2205   16. 98.64

17.

ITEM	SOLD	SELLING PRICE	GROSS SALES	PROFIT
1	8	1.05	8.4	3.76
2	63	12.88	811.44	365.4
3	18	200	3600	1620
4	18	2.95	53.1	23.94
5	20	44.95	899	404.6
6	17	260	4420	1989
7	14	350	4900	2205
8	36	6.1	219.6	98.64

TOTAL PROFIT IS 6710.34
TOTAL SALES IS 14911.54

Page 399

TRIP	FOOD	LODGING	AUTO (MILES)	SUBTOTAL
1	19.45	26	50	55.95
2	45.78	72	150	149.28
3	35.6	84.6	300	183.2
4	50	0	75	65.75
5	39.62	45.8	220	131.62
6	24.56	29.8	180	92.16
7	97.98	250.8	450	443.28
8	65.9	75	306	205.16
9	34.67	41.8	263	131.7
10	19	0	27	24.67
11	84.5	129.8	320	281.5
12	63.85	92	408	241.53

THE MONTHLY TOTAL IS $2005.8

Page 401

1.

TRIP	FOOD	LODGING	AUTO (MILES)	SUBTOTAL
1	38.29	72	120	135.49
2	46.83	110.25	210	201.18
3	53.29	83.75	186	176.1
4	27.53	0	82	44.75
5	62.38	95	260	211.98
6	187.62	263.85	510	558.57
7	93.65	142.69	320	303.54
8	23.18	0	80	39.98
9	65.29	35.86	62	114.17
10	73.86	51.9	87	144.03

THE MONTHLY TOTAL IS $1929.79.

21.

ITEM	IN STOCK, MAR 1	SOLD IN MAR	IN STOCK, APR 1
1	60	42	18
2	110	120	40
3	21	16	7

22. 80   PRINT I, H, A, S, R
40   PRINT "ITEM", "IN STOCK, MAR 1",
"ADDED IN MAR", "SOLD IN MAR",
"IN STOCK, APR 1"

ITEM	IN STOCK, MAR 1	ADDED IN MAR	SOLD IN MAR	IN STOCK, APR 1
1	60	0	42	18
2	110	50	120	40
3	21	2	16	7

CHAPTER 12

Page 415

1. Trousers   Shirts   Outfits

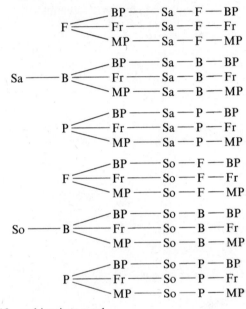

6 outfits total

2. Appetizer Main Dish Vegetable Combinations

18 combinations total

Page 420

4. The months in Graph B are listed in opposite order from those in Graph A.   **9.** The interval of the scores is greater in graph C.

ADDISON - WESLEY
APPLYING
MATHEMATICS
A CONSUMER/CAREER APPROACH

MERVIN L. KEEDY

STANLEY A. SMITH

PAUL A. ANDERSON

ADDISON - WESLEY PUBLISHING COMPANY

Menlo Park, California
Reading, Massachusetts
Wokingham, Berkshire U.K.
Amsterdam
Don Mills, Ontario
Sydney

ACKNOWLEDGMENTS

PHOTOGRAPHS

American Motors Corp.: 270
© 1981 Jim Anderson/Woodfin Camp & Associates: 408
The Bettmann Archive: 96, 303
© Ken Biggs/After-Image: 196
Elihu Blotnick*: 38, 122
Daniel Brody/Stock, Boston: 82
© 1981 Dan Budnik/Woodfin Camp & Associates: 242
Michael Collier/Stock, Boston: 228
Culver Pictures: 72, 412
© 1980 Donald Dietz/Stock, Boston: 308
© 1980 Dick Durrance II/Woodfin Camp & Associates: 390
© 1981 Dick Durrance II/Woodfin Camp & Associates: 88
© M. Durrance/Black Star: 348
© 1979 Timothy Eagan/Woodfin Camp & Associates: 147
Tom Ervin/Black Star: 274
© 1980 Jose A. Fernandez/Woodfin Camp & Associates: 268
Focus On Sports: 345, 416
George B. Fry III*: 12, 16, 50, 58, 92, 109, 112, 116, 126, 134, 138, 174, 178, 204, 208, 322, 394
Keith Gunnar/Tom Stack & Associates: 248
George Hall: 20
© 1980 George Hall/Woodfin Camp & Associates: 158, 166, 238
© 1981 George Hall/Woodfin Camp & Associates: 286
George Hall*: 4, 54, 192
Tom Hardin/Black Star: 334
© Erich Hartmann/Magnum Photos: 278
Grant Heilman Photography: 263
© Frank Lane/Bruce Coleman Inc.: 24
Andy Levin/Black Star: 100, 356
© Gregg Mancuso/After-Image: 67

Mike Mazzaschi/Stock, Boston: 162
Dan McCoy/Black Star: 384
Dan McCoy/Rainbow: 290
David McCray/Tom Stack & Associates: 314
© Ken McVey/After-Image: 330
© 1980 Peter Menzel: 170
John Running/Stock, Boston: 294
© 1980 Sepp Seitz/Woodfin Camp & Associates: 150
© Glenn Short/After-Image: 46
© Chad Slattery/After-Image: 254, 368
Tom Stack/Tom Stack & Associates: 212
© 1982 Harald Sund: 1, 33, 42, 78, 200, 234, 252
Tom Tracy: 216, 381
Mark Tuschman: 8
Univac, Division of Sperry Rand Corporation: 398
Western History Collections, University of Oklahoma: 154
© Jerry Wachter/Focus On Sports: 326
© Bruce M. Wellman/Tom Stack & Associates: 360
Andy Whipple: 318
Frank Wing/Stock, Boston: 364
*Photographs provided expressly for the publisher.

BOOK DESIGN

Design Office, San Francisco

ILLUSTRATION   TECHNICAL ILLUSTRATION
Terra Muzick   Art by Axya

ACKNOWLEDGMENT

p. 130: from the 1927 Edition of *The Sears, Roebuck Catalogue*. Copyright © 1970 by Crown Publishers, Inc. Used by permission of Crown Publishers, Inc.

AUTHORS

MERVIN L. KEEDY is Professor of Mathematics at Purdue University. He received his Ph.D. degree at the University of Nebraska, and has taught at the University of Maryland, as well as in junior and senior high schools. He is the author of many books on mathematics, and he is co-author of an algebra series and **General Mathematics**, published by Addison-Wesley.

STANLEY A. SMITH is Coordinator, Office of Mathematics (K-12), for Baltimore County Public Schools, Maryland. He earned his M.A. degree at the University of Maryland. He has taught junior and senior high school mathematics. He is co-author of an algebra series and **General Mathematics**, published by Addison-Wesley.

PAUL A. ANDERSON is a teacher in the Clark County School District, Las Vegas, Nevada. He earned his M.Ed. degree at the University of Nevada. He is a former principal and instructor of mathematics education at the University of Nevada, Las Vegas. He is a co-author of **General Mathematics**, published by Addison-Wesley.

SPECIAL THANKS

To Dr. Dennis Ortwein, William F. Oberle, Gloria Wren
and to our career advisors:

John Ahern	Wayne Hockett	Paul Nutter
Ken Ails	Kathleen Hoey	Bob O'Connell
Pat Akehurst	Dave Jackson	Charles Powers
John Anderson	Greg Jones	Charles Pumphrey
Steve Baxter	Dr. Freida Klein	David Rakowski
Dick Bissett	Ted Krautsch	Albert Smith
Lenore Byrnes	Larry Lochridge	Joyce Standish
Dan Carlson	Richard Loff	Lee Syphus
Bill Ciliax	Robert Mahood	Scott Teets
Edward Clark	Richard Masimore	Jim Thomas
Pat Coon	Gary Mathis	David Trivette
Lou Geczy	Charles McCubbin	Mitchell Twardowicz
Irv Goldstein	Colleen McHugh	Bill Wallin
Ralph Harris	Larry McKay	Christian Wild
Joe Hawk	Jay Murphy	

TO THE STUDENT

This text has been written to help you use your mathematical skills in everyday life, in the career you choose, and in your day-to-day life as a consumer.

This book is about real-world mathematics.
We went out and talked to many people at work. We asked them about the mathematics they actually use in doing their jobs. We found out about the computational skills they need and special ways they solve the kinds of problems they deal with every day. The problems in this book are like the problems that real people solve in their work.

This book will help you become a wise consumer.
Regardless of the careers we choose, we are all consumers. We constantly are making decisions—what to buy, how much to save, how to plan future purchases. This book will help you learn to deal effectively with money.

This book will build your computational skills.
In this book you will find a constant emphasis on computational skills. Working with numbers in many different situations will help you develop confidence in your ability to solve problems correctly in your job and as a consumer.

Finally, we believe that this book will help you prepare for your life after school days are over. We hope that you find enjoyment in learning about math in real life.

The Authors

TABLE OF CONTENTS

APPENDIX

1

CALCULATING,
ORGANIZING DATA,
AND USING FORMULAS

CALCULATING SUMS AND DIFFERENCES

Today's computers are able to process more calculations than ever dreamed possible 30 years ago.

An important step in solving some problems is *calculating*. Some calculations can be done mentally. Others require pencil and paper. And others are best done on a calculator.

EXAMPLE 1.

Since electronic calculators are becoming widespread, you may want to instruct students on their proper use. Of course the needs and resources of each student and each school district vary. Teaching philosophies also vary. Therefore, the use of electronic calculators is optional for every problem in this book.

Olivia Romero recorded monthly mileages of 534, 246, and 793. Find the total.

To calculate $534 + 246 + 793$, add ones, then tens, then hundreds, and so on.

Add Ones	Add Tens	Add Hundreds
$\overset{1}{5}\,3\,4$	$\overset{1}{5}\,\overset{1}{3}\,4$	$\overset{1}{5}\,\overset{1}{3}\,4$
$2\,4\,6$	$2\,4\,6$	$2\,4\,6$
$+\,7\,9\,3$	$+\,7\,9\,3$	$+\,7\,9\,3$
3	$7\,3$	$1\,5\,7\,3$

The total mileage is 1573.

EXAMPLE 2. Scott Jensen read these dimensions from a blueprint: 29.4 mm, 63.54 mm. Find the total length.

To add, line up the decimal points. A calculator does this automatically.

$$\begin{array}{r} 29.4 \\ + 63.54 \\ \hline 92.94 \text{ mm} \end{array}$$

 ② ⑨ ⊙ ④ ⊕ ⑥ ③ ⊙ ⑤ ④ ⊜ 92.94

TRY THIS

Calculate.

1. $854 + 629 + 342$ **1825**   2. $1257 + 829 + 764$ **2850**
3. $40.2 + 66.32 + 5.9$ **112.42**   4. $56.2 + 29.5 + 0.63$ **86.33**

EXAMPLE 3. Andrea Hill's garden supply store had 437 kg of fertilizer. Her records showed that 294 kg had been sold. To find how much was left she calculated $437 - 294$.

Subtract ones, tens, hundreds, and so on as needed.

Subtract Ones	Subtract Tens	Subtract Hundreds
$\begin{array}{r} 437 \\ -294 \\ \hline 3 \end{array}$	$\begin{array}{r} {}^{3}\cancel{4}{}^{13}\cancel{3}7 \\ -294 \\ \hline 43 \end{array}$	$\begin{array}{r} {}^{3}\cancel{4}{}^{13}\cancel{3}7 \\ -294 \\ \hline 143 \end{array}$

143 kg of fertilizer are left.

EXAMPLE 4. A bottle contained 54.7 mL of acid solution. Paul poured out 8.62 mL. How much was left?

When subtracting you must also line up the decimal points. Once again, a calculator does this for you.

$$\begin{array}{r} 54.7 \\ - 8.62 \\ \hline 46.08 \end{array}$$

⑤ ④ ⊙ ⑦ ⊖ ⑧ ⊙ ⑥ ② ⊜ 46.08

There are 46.08 mL of solution left.

TRY THIS

Find the difference.

5. $429 - 316$ **113**   6. $718 - 549$ **169**
7. $46.3 - 9.5$ **36.8**   8. $532.8 - 29.64$ **503.16**

EXERCISES

Calculate.

1. 84 + 13 **97**   **2.** 75 + 23 **98**   **3.** 62 + 17 **79**   **4.** 53 + 25 **78**

5. 74 + 16 **90**   **6.** 53 + 28 **81**   **7.** 42 + 39 **81**   **8.** 63 + 29 **92**

9. 235 + 465 **700**   **10.** 328 + 564 **892**   **11.** 354 + 429 **783**   **12.** 463 + 281 **744**

13. 439 + 654 + 218 **1311**   **14.** 532 + 108 + 324 **964**   **15.** 650 + 243 + 718 **1611**

16. 295 + 783 + 44 **1122**   **17.** 2.4 + 13.6 + 26.43 **42.43**   **18.** 5.8 + 16.4 + 53.29 **75.49**

19. 8.4 + 19.8 + 64.32 **92.52**   **20.** 9.2 + 21.3 + 83 **113.5**   **21.** 14.2 + 8.91 + 81.11 **104.22**

22. 94 − 22 **72**   **23.** 65 − 23 **42**   **24.** 72 − 31 **41**

25. 64 − 38 **26**   **26.** 57 − 29 **28**   **27.** 98 − 49 **49**

28. 402 − 216 **186**   **29.** 503 − 428 **75**   **30.** 747 − 351 **396**

31. 12.4 − 4.16 **8.24**   **32.** 28.2 − 9.24 **18.96**   **33.** 43.2 − 11.6 **31.6**

34. 46.28 − 5.39 **40.89**   **35.** 54.16 − 8.29 **45.87**   **36.** 78.4 − 36.5 **41.9**

37. While on a vacation, the Cohen family drove 428, 359, and 516 miles. How far did they drive? **1303 mi**

38. Find the total cost of these purchases: peanuts, $ 1.90; cheese, $ 2.43; newspaper, $ 0.25; and lettuce, $ 0.87. **$5.45**

39. A can contained 125.4 kg of grass seed. Pam Ono took out 14.9 kg. How much seed was left? **110.5 kg**

40. Clyde bought coffee for $ 4.08, canned peaches for $ 1.23, and a box of cereal for $ 0.93. He paid with a $ 20 bill. How much change did he get? **$13.76**

DECISION

For each of the following calculations decide whether you would do it mentally, with paper and pencil, or with a calculator.

41. 3 + 2   **42.** 56.4 + 29.82   **43.** 40 + 3

44. 1829 + 6243 + 19   **45.** 24 + 15   **46.** 16 + 8

47. 1829 − 564   **48.** 14 − 2   **49.** 29.35 − 1.56

50. 200 − 40   **51.** 62 − 39   **52.** 6391 − 390

ROUNDING AND ESTIMATING

Can you fill an order for 200 boards? Often a quick estimate is more important than an exact count.

Sometimes practical problems do not need an exact answer. Then you can round and estimate. The rules for rounding are arbitrary. Later various methods will be shown.

EXAMPLE 1.   Round to the nearest thousand.   534,946

| Find the place to be rounded. | The digit to the right is 5 or more. | Round up. | Change to zeros. |

5 3 4,9 4 6   5 3 5,0 0 0

EXAMPLE 2.   Round to the nearest whole number.   78.39

| Find the place to be rounded. | The digit to the right is less than 5. | Keep the digit the same. | Drop the digits to the right. |

7 8.3 9   7 8

TRY THIS

Round to the nearest thousand.

1. 51,849 52,000   **2.** 26,324 26,000   **3.** 6,523 7,000

Round to the nearest whole number.

4. 24.47 24   **5.** 7.95 8   **6.** 29.864 30

EXAMPLE 3. Round to the nearest dollar. $234.63

| Find the place to be rounded. | The place to the right is 5 or more | Round up. | Drop the digits to the right. |

$$\$ 2 \, 3 \, \overset{\nearrow}{4}.\overset{\nwarrow}{6} \, 3$$

$$\$ 2 \, 3 \, 5$$

TRY THIS

Round to the nearest dollar.

7. $4.83 **$5**   **8.** $62.21 **$62**   **9.** $739.82 **$740**

You can estimate sums or differences by rounding. Round in a way that makes calculating easy. **It is helpful to ask students for ideas about how rounding and estimating might be done.**

EXAMPLES.   Estimate.   *Some Possible Estimates*

Where estimates are called for, various answers are possible.

4.
```
   523        520        500
 +  86      +  90      +  90
            ─────      ─────
              610        590
```

5.
```
    18.2        18        18
    3.15         3         3
 +  7.463     +  7      +  7.5
             ─────     ─────
               28       28.5
```

TRY THIS

Estimate the sums or differences.

10.
```
   583
    52
 +  44
 ─────
   670
```

11.
```
  5326
 − 2245
 ─────
  3080
```

12.
```
  19.4
  4.62
 + 8.574
 ─────
    33
```

13.
```
 $ 58.19
 − 26.84
 ─────
   $31
```

An estimate of a total is often good enough for decision making.

EXAMPLE 6.   Is this meal less than $15? Estimate the cost.

Shrimp cocktail $3.55   Lasagne $5.65
Salad $2.90   Coffee $0.75

$4 + $3 + $6 + $1 = $14

This meal is less than $15.

EXERCISES

Round to the nearest thousand.

1. 3684 **4000**   **2.** 9289 **9000**   **3.** 42,503 **43,000**   **4.** 34,493 **34,000**

Round to the nearest whole number.

5. 43.92 **44**   **6.** 6.431 **6**   **7.** 26.5 **27**   **8.** 149.81 **150**

Round to the nearest dollar.

9. $ 8.94 **$9**   **10.** $ 16.53 **$17**   **11.** $ 234.50 **$235**   **12.** $ 432.95 **$433**

Estimate the sums or differences.

13.
```
    64
  + 71
```
130

14.
```
    38
  + 41
```
80

15.
```
   931
 + 472
```
1400

16.
```
   758
 + 424
```
1180

17.
```
   743
   384
  + 68
```
1190

18.
```
   427
    83
  + 96
```
610

19.
```
   618
    85
  + 62
```
770

20.
```
   853
    71
  + 30
```
950

21.
```
    3.76
   14.9
  + 2.876
```
21.6

22.
```
   1.832
   4.9
 + 6.05
```
12.8

23.
```
   18.9
    9.463
  + 2.712
```
31.1

24.
```
    82.62
     2.975
 + 125.023
```
210.6

25.
```
  $ 84.21
  -  7.16
```
$77

26.
```
  $ 125.84
  -  16.92
```
$109

27.
```
  $ 243.54
  -  64.84
```
$179

28.
```
  $ 103.21
  -  82.54
```
$20

29. Estimate the total cost of these items:

1 TV dinner at $ 2.34 **$5.00**
1 gallon of milk at $ 1.94
1 can of soup at $ 0.84

30. You have $ 20. Can you buy a blouse and two scarves? **Yes.**

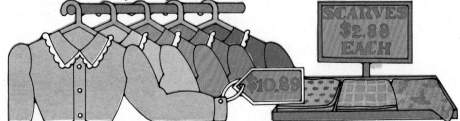

MENTAL CALCULATION

FRONT END ADDITION AND MULTIPLICATION

A quick way to add and multiply mentally is to work from left to right.

EXAMPLE 1. Add 84 + 47.

Add the tens first. $80 + 40 = 120$
Then add the ones. $4 + 7 = 11$
Then add together. $120 + 11 = 131$

EXAMPLE 2. Multiply 2 × 37.

Multiply the tens by 2. $2 \times 30 = 60$
Multiply the ones by 2. $2 \times 7 = 14$
Then add together. $60 + 14 = 74$

PRACTICE

Add mentally.

1. 92 + 38 130   **2.** 75 + 82 157   **3.** 17 + 32 49   **4.** 92 + 87 179
5. 87 + 49 136   **6.** 64 + 39 103   **7.** 43 + 85 128   **8.** 61 + 58 119
9. 72 + 68 140   **10.** 32 + 96 128   **11.** 68 + 49 117   **12.** 27 + 95 122
13. 44 + 69 113   **14.** 85 + 38 123   **15.** 79 + 83 162   **16.** 68 + 57 125

Multiply mentally.

17. 2 × 48 96   **18.** 2 × 57 114   **19.** 3 × 49 147   **20.** 3 × 193 579
21. 2 × 86 172   **22.** 2 × 63 126   **23.** 3 × 127 381   **24.** 3 × 59 177
25. 2 × 186 372   **26.** 2 × 149 298   **27.** 3 × 63 189   **28.** 3 × 74 222
29. 3 × 76 228   **30.** 3 × 42 126   **31.** 2 × 86 172   **32.** 2 × 98 196

CALCULATING PRODUCTS AND QUOTIENTS

Because they keep plants in orderly rows, greenhouse workers can use multiplication to find the quantity on hand each day.

In some practical problems we need to multiply or divide.

EXAMPLE 1. Eric Larson manages the office cafeteria. He calculates the sandwich sales each quarter. He knows they sell about 76 sandwiches each day. He multiplies this number by 65, the number of days in a quarter.

$$
\begin{array}{r}
76 \\
\times\ 65 \\
\hline
380 \\
456\ \ \\
\hline
4940 \\
\end{array}
$$

380 ⟵ *Multiply by the ones digit.*
456 ⟵ *Multiply by the tens digit.*
4940 ⟵ *Add.*

When multiplying decimals count the number of decimal places in both factors. Then count off this number of places in the product. Calculators do this automatically. **When multiplying decimals on a calculator, students should estimate the answers to see where the decimal points should go.**

EXAMPLE 2.   Gloria DeRosa bought 85 shares of utility stock at $ 123.75 a share. Find the total cost.

$$
\begin{array}{r}
1\,2\,3.7\,5 \quad \textit{2 places} \\
\times \qquad 8\,5 \\
\hline
6\,1\,8\,7\,5 \\
9\,9\,0\,0\,0 \\
\hline
1\,0\,5\,1\,8.7\,5 \quad \textit{2 places}
\end{array}
$$

①②③.⑦⑤⊗⑧⑤⊜ **10,518.75**

The cost is $ 10,518.75.

TRY THIS

Calculate.

1. 84 × 23 **1932**   **2.** 165 × 24 **3960**
3. 9.5 × 16 **152**   **4.** $ 2.14 × 12 **$25.68**

EXAMPLE 3.   Find 390.6 ÷ 18.

$$
\begin{array}{r}
2\,1.7 \\
18\overline{)3\,9\,0.6} \\
3\,6 \\
\hline
3\,0 \\
1\,8 \\
\hline
1\,2\,6 \\
1\,2\,6 \\
\hline
\end{array}
$$

Here is the paper and pencil solution.

Calculators show decimal notation. They do not show quotients with remainders. Here is the calculator solution.

③⑨⓪.⑥÷①⑧⊜ **21.7**

TRY THIS

Calculate.

5. 13.25 / 28)371   **6.** 23.41 / 32)749.12

7. 0.36 / 91)32.76   **8.** 60.63 / 8)485.04

While using a calculator, students should first estimate their answers to make sure the calculator answers are reasonable.

Calculate.

1. 75 × 19 1425　　**2.** 62 × 37 2294　　**3.** 51 × 14 714　　**4.** 92 × 48 4416

5. 49 × 58 2842　　**6.** 91 × 82 7462　　**7.** 78 × 27 2106　　**8.** 62 × 97 6014

9. 432 × 53 22,896　**10.** 629 × 84 52,836　**11.** 716 × 59 42,244　**12.** 349 × 42 14,658

13. $4.17 × 13
$54.21
14. $6.14 × 21
$128.94
15. $7.59 × 18
$136.62
16. $3.24 × 39 $126.36

17. $52.96 × 19
$1006.24
18. $64.34 × 16
$1029.44
19. $58.42 × 23
$1343.66
20. $74.83 × 62 $4639.46

21. 96 ÷ 32 3　　**22.** 105 ÷ 42 2.5　　**23.** 504 ÷ 48 10.5　　**24.** 320 ÷ 64 5

25. 357 ÷ 30 11.9　**26.** 744 ÷ 31 24　　**27.** 858 ÷ 52 16.5　　**28.** 974.4 ÷ 87 11.2

29. 1353 ÷ 41 33　**30.** 2177 ÷ 70 31.1　**31.** 3015.39 ÷ 83
36.33
32. 2139 ÷ 62 34.5

33. $45.90 ÷ 9 $5.10　**34.** $50.24 ÷ 8 $6.28　**35.** $62.37 ÷ 9
$6.93
36. $84.35 ÷ 7 $12.05

37. 26.37 ÷ 9 2.93　**38.** 38.8 ÷ 8 4.85　**39.** 62.51 ÷ 7 8.93　**40.** 84.6 ÷ 6 14.1

41. Sylvia Valdez works 8 hours a day for 10 days for $5.63 per hour. What is her gross pay? $450.40

42. For the bowling league banquet there are 54 people signed up to attend. The cost per person is $12.50. What is the total cost? $675.00

43. Bob Collins collects 384 bottles. He puts them in cartons containing 24 bottles each. How many cartons are needed? 16 cartons

44. Janet Miller buys a two-kilogram roast for $13.92. How much does the roast cost per kilogram? $6.96

45. There are 317 people signed up to go on the school picnic. The cost per person is $2.00. What is the total cost of the picnic? $634

DECISION

For each of the following calculations decide whether you would do it mentally, use paper and pencil, or use a calculator.

46. 46 × 2　　　　**47.** 23 × 18　　　　**48.** 56.5 ÷ 18.4

49. 3 × 9　　　　**50.** 1652 × 827　　**51.** 14 ÷ 7

52. 0.0356 ÷ 0.08　**53.** 97 × 100　　　**54.** 46 ÷ 23

PROBLEM SOLVING HINTS

Byron Jacobs has taken a part-time job which is 18 miles from his home. He has decided to buy a used car. He is trying to solve the problem of how to get an auto loan.

HINT   **Asking good questions can help solve a problem.**

To help make the problem clear, he makes a list of questions.

1. What are the requirements for a loan?
2. What interest rates are charged?
3. Is the interest simple or compound?
4. What are insurance costs?

HINT   **Some problems can be solved with the help of an expert.**

Byron consults a credit counselor at his local bank. He learns that he can qualify for a loan with his parents' signature. The interest rate is 17%. Insurance must be obtained before the loan can be approved.

PRACTICE

Make a list of questions and determine which experts to ask.

1. What brand of auto tape deck should you buy?
2. What kind of trees should you buy for your yard?
3. How can you get into the plumbers union?

ESTIMATING PRODUCTS AND QUOTIENTS

With seven or eight hanks of yarn in each tube, it is easy to estimate the total quantity in stock.

Products can be estimated by rounding so that the calculations are simple. **When estimating, student answers may vary. Students should be able to explain their estimating procedure.**

EXAMPLES.

Estimate.   *Some Possible Estimates*

1.
$$\begin{array}{r} 528 \\ \times\ \ 7 \\ \hline \end{array}$$
$$\begin{array}{r} 530 \\ \times\ \ 7 \\ \hline 3710 \end{array}$$
$$\begin{array}{r} 500 \\ \times\ \ 7 \\ \hline 3500 \end{array}$$

2.
$$\begin{array}{r} 3876 \\ \times\ 389 \\ \hline \end{array}$$
$$\begin{array}{r} 3900 \\ \times\ \ 400 \\ \hline 1,560,000 \end{array}$$
$$\begin{array}{r} 4000 \\ \times\ \ 400 \\ \hline 1,600,000 \end{array}$$

TRY THIS

Estimate.

1.
$$\begin{array}{r} 62 \\ \times\ \ 7 \\ \hline 420 \end{array}$$

2.
$$\begin{array}{r} 895 \\ \times\ \ 62 \\ \hline 54,000 \end{array}$$

3.
$$\begin{array}{r} 2231 \\ \times\ 552 \\ \hline 1,200,000 \end{array}$$

Estimates may involve decimals or money.

EXAMPLES.   Estimate.   *Some Possible Estimates*

3. 43.56
$\times$ 16.3

44	40
$\times$ 16	$\times$ 20
264	800
44	
704	

4. $ 16.18
$\times$ 8

$ 16	$ 20
$\times$ 8	$\times$ 8
$ 128	$ 160

5. $ 87.75
$\times$ 43

$ 90	$ 88
$\times$ 40	$\times$ 40
$ 3600	$ 3520

TRY THIS

Estimate.

4.   53.94
$\times$ 17.3
1000

5. $ 8.22
$\times$ 7
$56

6. $ 68.49
$\times$ 54
$3500

EXAMPLE 6.   Estimate $3873 \div 5$

Think: 3873 is about 4000
         Since $5 \times 8 = 40, 5 \times 800 = 4000.$

So, $3873 \div 5$ is about 800.

EXAMPLE 7.   Estimate $ 19.73 \div 4$

Think: $ 19.73 is about $ 20
         $20 \div 4 = 5$

So, $ 19.73 \div 4$ is about 5.

EXAMPLE 8.   Estimate $5892 \div 68$

Think: 5892 is about 6000
         68 is about 70
         $6000 \div 70$ is about 80.

So, $5892 \div 68$ is about 80.

EXERCISES

Estimate the products or quotients.

1. 731
  × 7
 ___
 4900

2. 668
  × 9
 ___
 6300

3. 904
  × 8
 ___
 7200

4. 443
  × 5
 ___
 2000

5. 2943
  × 524
 ___
 1,500,000

6. 3287
  × 629
 ___
 1,800,000

7. 6972
  × 149
 ___
 1,050,000

8. 7852
  × 678
 ___
 5,600,000

9. 53.27
  × 18.9
 ___
 1060

10. 83.24
  × 42.7
 ___
 4000

11. 78.62
  × 18.9
 ___
 1600

12. 67.34
  × 22.7
 ___
 1400

13. $ 7.22
  × 7
 ___
 $49

14. $ 6.94
  × 6
 ___
 $42

15. $ 8.13
  × 4
 ___
 $32

16. $ 9.79
  × 8
 ___
 $80

17. $ 3.84
  × 482
 ___
 $2000

18. $ 9.43
  × 212
 ___
 $2000

19. $ 6.84
  × 379
 ___
 $2800

20. $ 7.13
  × 684
 ___
 $4900

21. 932 ÷ 7 **130**   **22.** 7258 ÷ 6 **1200**   **23.** 6349 ÷ 9 **700**   **24.** 8214 ÷ 5
 1600

25. $ 33.56 ÷ 8 **$4.00**   **26.** $ 61.73 ÷ 9 **$7.00**   **27.** $ 64.04 ÷ 7 **$9.00**   **28.** $ 81.79 ÷ 4
 $20

DECISION

For each of the following calculations a calculator answer is given.
Estimate and decide whether you think the calculator answer is correct.

	Calculation	Calculator answer
29.	793 × 83	65,819
30.	4.82 × 16	771.2
31.	4752 ÷ 6	792

MENTAL CALCULATION

QUICK MULTIPLICATION BY 4 AND 8

You can multiply mentally by 4 and 8 by successive doubling.

EXAMPLE 1.   Multiply 4×14.

Double 14. $2 \times 14 = 28$
Double again. $2 \times 28 = 56$

$4 \times 14 = 56$

EXAMPLE 2.   Multiply 8×46.
To multiply by 8, double three times.

Double. $2 \times 46 = 92$
Double again. $2 \times 92 = 184$
Double a third time. $2 \times 184 = 368$

$8 \times 46 = 368$

PRACTICE

Multiply mentally by the doubling method.

1. 4×19 76	**2.** 4×23 92	**3.** 4×38 152	**4.** 4×46 184
5. 4×75 300	**6.** 4×53 212	**7.** 4×56 224	**8.** 4×29 116
9. 8×33 264	**10.** 8×76 608	**11.** 8×91 728	**12.** 8×37 296
13. 8×24 192	**14.** 8×17 136	**15.** 8×38 304	**16.** 8×93 744
17. 4×350 1400	**18.** 4×120 480	**19.** 4×205 820	**20.** 4×675 2700
21. 4×410 1640	**22.** 4×180 720	**23.** 4×230 920	**24.** 4×160 640
25. 8×125 1000	**26.** 8×130 1040	**27.** 8×205 1640	**28.** 8×160 1280
29. 8×250 2000	**30.** 8×550 4400	**31.** 8×175 1400	**32.** 8×270 2160

CALCULATING PERCENTS

Percent descriptions are often used. In this boot display, 20% are
light, 60% face left, and 30% are in the middle row.

Many practical problems involve percents. Recall that percent
means hundredths. $n\%$ means $n \times 0.01$.

EXAMPLE 1. In the basketball free throw contest, Mike O'Brien made 17
out of 30 attempts. What percent did he make?

17 is what percent of 30?

$17 = n \times 30$

$\frac{17}{30} = n$

$$
\begin{array}{r}
0.566 \approx 0.57 = 57\% \\
30\overline{)17.00} \\
\underline{150} \\
200 \\
\underline{180} \\
20
\end{array}
$$

*Round to the
nearest percent.
$\approx$ means "is
approximately
equal to."*

Mike made 57% of his attempts.

Calculate the percent of attempts made.

1. 16 out of 20 80%   **2.** 47 out of 50 94%

Calculators also help find percents. You can use the calculator to divide. Then change the decimal to a percent.

EXAMPLE 2.   Sally Andrews made 23 free throws out of 30 attempts. What percent did she make?

$$②③÷③⓪= \quad 0.7666666 ≈ 0.77 = 77\%$$

Sally made 77% of her attempts.

Calculate the percent of attempts made.

3. 19 out of 30 63%   **4.** 32 out of 50 64%
5. 29 out of 40 73%   **6.** 47 out of 60 78%

Have students round to the nearest percent

EXAMPLE 3.

To translate a sentence like "What is 41% of 483?" into symbols, the word "what" becomes a variable such as n. The word "is" becomes = (equal sign) and the word "of" becomes × (times).

Otis Atwood is an assistant manager of a fast food restaurant. He estimates that 35% of the daily sales are from double-burgers. One day the daily sales total was $3519. About how much of the total sales was from double-burger sales?

What is 35% of $3519?   *35% means 35 × 0.01.*
$n = 0.35 × 3519 = \$1231.65$ *So, 35% = 0.35.*

The daily sales from double-burgers was about $1231.65.

7. Otis estimates that 25% of the daily sales are from french fries. One day the daily sales total was $3760. About how much of the total sales was from french fries sales? $940

EXAMPLE 4.   Otis Atwood estimates that 15% of the daily sales are from fried fish sandwiches. Today's sales total was $3852. About how much of the total sales was from fried fish sandwich sales?

What is 15% of $3852?

You can use the calculator to find $0.15 × 3852$.

$$.①⑤×③⑧⑤②= \quad 577.8$$

The daily sales from fried fish sandwiches was about $577.80.

Some calculators have a ⓧ key. When you use this key the decimal point moves two places to the left, and the resulting number is displayed.

EXAMPLE 5. What is 8% of 16? You can use the calculator to multiply and move the decimal point.

Press. ① ⑥ ⓧ ⑧ ⑳

Display ⌐Ь. ⌐ Ь.28

8% of 16 is 1.28.

TRY THIS

Calulate.

8. What is 8% of 40? **3.2**   **9.** What is 18% of $751? **$135.18**

EXAMPLE 6. Dash is a pitcher on the school baseball team. 65% of his pitches this season have been strikes. He has pitched 221 strikes. How many pitches has Dash thrown?

221 is 65% of what number?

$221 = 0.65 \times n$

$$\frac{221}{0.65} = n$$

$$0.65 \overline{)221.00.}$$

$$\begin{array}{r} 340. \\ \underline{195} \\ 260 \\ \underline{260} \end{array}$$

Dash has thrown 340 pitches.

TRY THIS

Calculate.

10. 210 is 35% of what number? **600**

EXERCISES

Calculate. In Exercises 1–7 round to the nearest percent.

1. 3 is what percent of 8? **38%**   **2.** 5 is what percent of 6? **83%**

3. 43 is what percent of 54? **80%**   **4.** 75 is what percent of 86? **87%**

5. What percent of 63 is 18? 29%   **6.** What percent of 7 is 21? 300%

7. What percent of 15 is 25? 167%   **8.** What is 9% of 19? 1.71

9. What is 26% of 62? 16.12   **10.** What is 82% of 364? 298.48

11. What is 125% of 62? 77.50   **12.** 9.8% of 31 is what number? 3.038

13. 9.2% of 30 is what number? 2.76   **14.** 3.3% of 59 is what number? 1.947

15. 194 is 40% of what number? 485   **16.** 277 is 45% of what number? 615.5

17. In a large city the number of people using public buses has increased 25%. If 12,800 people rode buses before, how many ride now? 16,000 people

18. Ramona Pacheco was told that she scored higher than 79% of of the students who took the English test. There were 426 students who took the test. How many students had scores lower than Ramona? 337 students

19. In a basketball game the Wildcat squad scored as follows:

Clarence	18 points	Hiroshi	5 points
Anne	16 points	George	2 points
Lana	13 points	Christina	2 points

How many points did the Wildcats score? What percent of the total did Anne score? What percent did the top three scorers together make? 56 points, 29%, 84%

Questions or assignments labeled "On Your Own" are not necessarily intended to be completed by every student. A small group may be assigned to research these questions and report back to the rest of the class. Try to avoid situations in which every student contacts the same businesses or individuals.

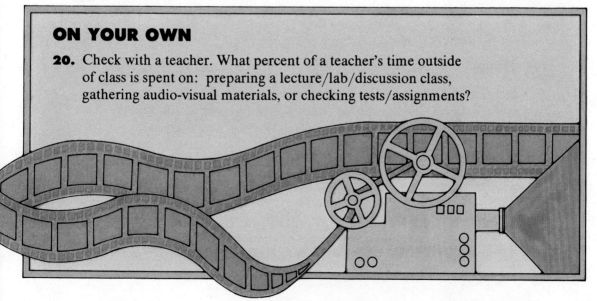

ON YOUR OWN

20. Check with a teacher. What percent of a teacher's time outside of class is spent on: preparing a lecture/lab/discussion class, gathering audio-visual materials, or checking tests/assignments?

ORGANIZING DATA

To plan office buildings, hotels, and freeways, city planners collect
data on people arriving at the city center.

To gain insight into practical problems you may need to collect data
or information. To help interpret the data we need to organize it.
One way to do this is to make a frequency table. A frequency table
shows how many times certain things occur.

EXAMPLE 1. Gary Carlson works in a light bulb factory. He picked a
random sample of 30 light bulbs to be tested. The following
shows how many hours each bulb took to burn out. Prepare
a frequency table using these data.

983	964	1214	1521	1211	1417
1084	1075	892	1322	949	1423
979	1083	1344	984	1445	975
1283	1325	1492	1246	1028	1024
1352	1562	1432	1321	1223	1359

The lowest time is 892. The highest is 1562. To prepare
the table group the data into intervals. Use an interval of 100.

Interval	Tally	Frequency
800–899	I	1
900–999	JHT	5
1000–1099	JHT	5
1100–1199		0
1200–1299	JHT	5
1300–1399	LHT I	6
1400–1499	JHT	5
1500–1599	II	2

The lowest interval includes the lowest time. The highest interval includes the highest time.

TRY THIS

1. Here are 40 reading scores. Prepare a frequency table. Use an interval of 3. Start with 16–18. **See answer section.**

20	43	17	57	39	35	36	52
21	43	18	50	29	34	58	19
21	18	24	47	30	18	29	22
22	21	56	43	27	22	30	20
25	34	52	40	30	28	40	43

A bar graph can help you visualize the data. **Sometimes called a histogram**

EXAMPLE 2. Draw a bar graph for the light bulb data of Example 1.

Draw a bar for each interval. The height of each bar shows the frequency.

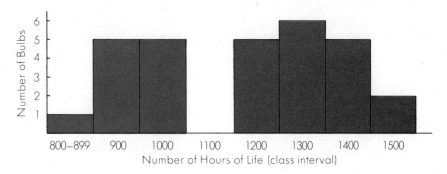

The leftmost bar shows 1 tally in the 800–899 interval. The next bar shows 5 tallies, etc.

Teachers often organize test scores by averaging. They do this by adding all the scores and dividing by the number of scores.

EXAMPLE 3.   Rita Garcia computes the final grade by averaging. She uses this scale.

90–100 A   80–89 B   70–79 C   60–69 D   Below 60 F

Don had the following test scores: 81, 76, 74, 92, 63, 95. What was his final grade?

To find the average, add the scores and divide by the number of scores.

$81 + 76 + 74 + 92 + 63 + 95 = 481$
$481 \div 6 \approx 80$

Don's grade is B.

TRY THIS

Find the average and determine the final grade.

3. 76, 63, 91, 71, 74, 65, 51 70,C   **4.** 95, 89, 82, 93, 97, 90 91,A
5. 70, 75, 68, 63, 42, 81 66,D   **6.** 72, 83, 81, 78, 91, 95 83,B

EXERCISES

1. Here are 40 golf scores. Prepare a frequency table. Use an interval of 3. Start with 78–80. See answer section.

82	79	102	89	102	84	100	89	93	94
79	79	98	101	79	89	97	92	84	81
85	81	78	100	80	85	88	89	94	86
94	88	103	96	83	91	96	94	96	90

2. Here are 35 monthly salaries. Prepare a frequency table. Use an interval of 100. See answer section.

465	845	1100	843	925	815	715	600	1025
829	900	980	680	1200	785	680	915	1200
623	560	550	490	785	980	590	900	815
755	585	650	585	915	725	725	685	

3. Draw a bar graph for the golf scores in Exercise 1. See answer section.

4. Draw a bar graph for the monthly salaries of Exercise 2. See answer section.

For Exercises 5–8 use this scale.

90–100 A   80–89 B   70–79 C   60–69 D   Below 60 F

5. Cindy Moto had the following history test scores: 93, 90, 88, 92, 97, 91, 74, 96. What was her final grade? A

6. Billy Bobb's test scores for French were: 83, 85, 91, 97, 64, 72, 73, 70. What was his final grade? C

7. Here are the mathematics test scores for Wilma Washington: 74, 83, 88, 90, 68, 84, 83, 91. What was her final grade? B

8. Lucy works on a farm. She grows two varieties of wheat. She must decide which brand grows a taller stalk. Here are some heights of stalks measured in inches:

Variety A					Variety B			
17.2	19.7	18.4	19.7		25.7	19.5	42.3	16.2
25.7	32.0	14.6	19.7		41.7	15.6	18.0	25.6
32.6	42.5	21.6	14.0		12.6	18.4	26.4	22.6
22.8	26.7	10.9	22.6		41.5	42.0	13.7	21.6

Find the average for each variety. Which brand grows taller?
22.5″, 25.2″, Variety B

ON YOUR OWN

9. Bring to class graphs from newspapers and magazines. Tell why some are easy and some are hard to understand.

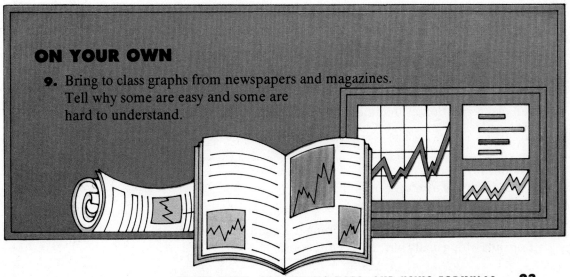

USING FORMULAS

The ability to substitute numbers into formulas is an important skill. Attractive bulletin boards may be made that show some of the many applications of formulas.

Formulas give you information quickly—when you hear thunder, a short calculation tells the distance to the lightning strike.

Nancy Baily attends the county police academy. As a cadet she is learning to be a police officer. In one of her classes she works with electronic equipment that is used to find the speed of a vehicle. Nancy learns that the equipment uses the formula:

$$r = \frac{d}{t}$$

r stands for the *rate.*
d stands for the *distance.*
t stands for the *time.*

A formula is a rule or recipe for doing a certain calculation. Formulas are usually written as equations.

EXAMPLE 1.   Nancy finds that a car travels 250 meters in 12 seconds.
She uses the formula $r = \frac{d}{t}$ to find the car's speed.

$$r = \frac{d}{t}$$
$$= \frac{250}{12}$$
$$\approx 20.8 \text{ meters per second} \qquad \textit{Round to the nearest tenth.}$$

TRY THIS   **1.** Find the speed of a car which travels 157 meters in 12
seconds. **13.1 meters per second**

The distance from a thunderstorm can be found by the formula:

$$d = \frac{1}{5}s$$

d stands for the *distance* in miles.
s stands for the *time* in seconds for the sound of thunder to reach
a person after a lightning flash is seen.

EXAMPLE 2.   Find the distance to a storm. The time elapsed between a
lightning flash and the sound of thunder is 12 seconds.

$$d = \frac{1}{5}s$$
$$= \frac{1}{5} \times 12$$
$$= \frac{12}{5}$$
$$= 2.4 \text{ miles away}$$

TRY THIS   **2.** Eight seconds after a lightning flash, Isaac hears the
thunder. How far away from Isaac is the storm? **1.6 miles**

The number of gallons in a farm gasoline tank can be found
by the formula:

$$g = 0.014\, r^2 h$$

g stands for the number of gallons.
r stands for the radius of the tank in inches.
h stands for the height of the gasoline in inches.

EXAMPLE 3.   A 4-foot radius tank contains gasoline 13 inches deep. Find the number of gallons of gasoline.

Change all numbers to inches and substitute them into the formula.

$$g = 0.014\, r^2 h$$
$$= 0.014 \times 48 \times 48 \times 13 \qquad \textit{4 feet = 48 inches}$$
$$= 419.328$$

There are about 419 gallons in the tank.

TRY THIS

3. The gasoline in a storage tank 3 feet in radius is down to a depth of only 15 inches. Find the number of gallons of gasoline in the tank. **272.2 gallons**

The area of many geometric shapes can be found by using a formula. A trapezoid is a 4-sided figure with two parallel sides. To find its area we use this formula:

$$A = \tfrac{1}{2}h(B + b)$$

EXAMPLE 4.   Mike plans to put sod on a piece of land shaped like a trapezoid. What is the area of this land?

$$A = \tfrac{1}{2}h(B + b)$$
$$= \tfrac{1}{2} \times 5 \times (17 + 12)$$
$$= 2.5 \times 29$$
$$= 72.5$$

b = 12 ft
h = 5 ft
B = 17 ft

The area is 72.5 ft²

TRY THIS

Use the formula $A = \tfrac{1}{2}h(B \times b)$ to find the area.

4. 14 cm / 9 cm / 23 cm **166.5 cm²**

5. 18 cm / 8 cm / 8 cm **104 cm²**

6. 14 in. / 10 in. / 28 in. **210 in.²**

EXERCISES

Use the formula $r = \frac{d}{t}$ to find the speed of each of these vehicles.

	Vehicle	Distance	Time	
1.	A	320 meters	14 seconds	22.9 m/sec
2.	B	195 meters	8 seconds	24.4 m/sec
3.	C	450 meters	36 seconds	12.5 m/sec
4.	D	250 meters	11 seconds	22.7 m/sec
5.	E	212 meters	12 seconds	17.7 m/sec

6. Use the formula $d = \frac{1}{5}s$ to find the distance to a storm. The time between the lightning and the sound of thunder is 15 seconds. **3 mi**

7. Use the formula $g = 0.014\, r^2 h$ to find the number of gallons of gasoline. The tank has a 4-foot radius and is holding gasoline which is 22 inches deep. **709.6 gal**

8. Use the formula $A = \frac{1}{2}h(B + b)$ to find the area.

a.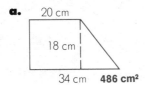
34 cm **486 cm²**

b.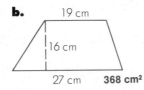
27 cm **368 cm²**

c.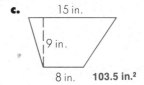
8 in. **103.5 in.²**

9. The formula $I = Prt$ tells how to calculate interest. I stands for interest in dollars, P stands for the principal in dollars, r stands for the rate of interest per year, and t stands for time in years. How much interest will $400 earn at 11% in 2 years? **$88**

10. The formula $A = Prt + P$ is used to find the amount A in dollars you will have if you invest the principal P at a rate r for t years. Find A when $5000 is invested at 12% for 3 years. **$6800**

11. The formula $S = R - \frac{W}{n-1}$ gives the score on a multiple choice test. R stands for the number of right answers, W stands for the number of wrong answers, and n stands for the number of choices per item. Find the score on a 50-item test with 4 choices per item. The number right is 38 and the number wrong is 12. **34**

CHAPTER REVIEW

Calculate.

1. $85 + 17$ 102   **2.** $93 + 18$ 111   **3.** $356 + 492$ 848   **4.** $347 + 268$
                                                                     615

5. $729 + 408$ 1137   **6.** $462 + 829$ 1291   **7.** $2.8 + 15.6$ 18.4   **8.** $3.2 + 14.9$
                                                                     18.1

9. $97 - 32$ 65   **10.** $84 - 51$ 33   **11.** $78 - 49$ 29   **12.** $85 - 37$ 48

13. $402 - 186$ 216   **14.** $207 - 194$ 13   **15.** $47.82 - 5.79$ 42.03   **16.** $56.39 - 6.82$
                                                                                  49.57

Estimate.

17. 68 **18.** 75 **19.** 5.74 **20.** 3.87 **21.** 509.16
     $+\ 97$ $+\ 84$ 16.8 14.9 214.83
      165   159 $+\ 2.759$ $+\ 3.742$ $+\ 73.15$
                                                25.3   22.5   798

22. 305.08 **23.** 508 **24.** 456 **25.** 256.27 **26.** 342.36
        182.97 $-\ 192$ $-\ 183$ $-\ 74.83$ $-\ 84.90$
     $+\ 62.17$ 300   270   181   257
         550

Calculate.

27. 78×29 2262   **28.** 83×31 2573   **29.** 622×54 33,588   **30.** 536×62
                                                                                                                                                          33,232

31. $\$8.23 \times 42$ **32.** $\$7.18 \times 31$ **33.** $\$62.83 \times 42$ **34.** $\$59.47 \times 32$
      $345.61 $222.58 $2638.86 $1903.04

35. $86 \div 42$ 2.05   **36.** $92 \div 27$ 3.41   **37.** $419 \div 53$ 7.91   **38.** $329 \div 49$
                                                                                               6.71

39. $3142 \div 74$ 42.46   **40.** $2783 \div 62$ 44.89   **41.** $\$57.83 \div 6$ $9.64   **42.** $\$64.38 \div 4$
                                                                                                      $16.10

Estimate.

43. 3846 **44.** 4256 **45.** $\$8.79$ **46.** $\$9.57$
     $\times\ \ 635$ $\times\ \ 764$ $\times\ \ 421$ $\times\ \ 318$
    2,280,000   3,187,500 $3600 $3000

47. $8497 \div 7$ 1200   **48.** $7584 \div 8$ 950   **49.** $\$56.97 \div 7$ $8.00   **50.** $\$64.83 \div 9$
                                                                                                                        $7.00

Calculate. In Exercises 51 and 52 round to the nearest percent.

51. 78 is what percent of 114? 68%

52. 64 is what percent of 97? 66%

53. What is 52% of 79? 41.1

54. 27.88 is 34% of what number? 82

55. Here are 30 spelling scores. Prepare a frequency table. Use an interval of 3. Start with 25–27. **See answer section.**

42	39	41	50	42	46
37	48	43	49	29	32
48	40	36	43	30	27
35	41	30	36	33	38
26	27	38	39	43	40

56. Here are 40 reading scores. Prepare a frequency table. Use an interval of 5. Start with 41–45. **See answer section.**

96	46	52	63	76	92	52	63
82	52	75	42	88	89	88	42
75	83	62	79	75	95	72	57
68	91	82	84	68	90	70	79
97	79	87	92	81	64	64	83

57. Draw a bar graph for the spelling scores of Exercise 55. **See answer section.**

58. Draw a bar graph for the reading scores of Exercise 56. **See answer section.**

59. Find the average of these weights: 74 kg, 62 kg, 79 kg, 86 kg, 78 kg, and 64 kg. **73.8 kg**

60. Find the average of these heights: 173 cm, 182 cm, 190 cm, 178 cm, and 162 cm. **177 cm**

61. Use the formula $r = \frac{d}{t}$ to find the speed of a vehicle which travels 78.2 meters in 5.9 seconds. **13.3 m/sec**

62. Use the formula $d = \frac{1}{5} s$ to find the distance in miles to a storm. The time between the lightning flash and the sound of thunder is 11 seconds. **2.2 mi**

SKILLS REVIEW

The skills included in each Skills Review are used prominently in the coming chapter. By reviewing the skills on these two pages, students will be ready for the new concepts that arise in Chapter 2. Skills Reviews are found immediately before each chapter throughout the text.

SKILL 14 Adding whole numbers

1.	2.	3.	4.
37	728	9428	37,487
49	479	+ 6759	+ 28,643
63	280	16,187	66,130
+ 47	+ 146		
196	1633		

SKILL 15 Adding money

5.	6.	7.	8.
$ 7.15	$ 4.17	$ 20.00	$ 5.87
+ 8.92	13.29	19.35	28.61
$16.07	+ 6.54	+ 0.78	2.99
	$24.00	$40.13	+ 0.73
			$38.20

SKILL 16 Adding decimals

9.	10.	11.	12.
8.7	8.746	7.63	6.4
+ 3.9	+ 0.943	9.87	4.295
12.6	9.689	+ 1.4	3.87
		18.90	+ 9.9
			24.465

13. $2.3 + 0.8 + 19.46$ 22.56

14. $12.4 + 6.78 + 0.39 + 0.068$ 19.638

SKILL 22 Multiplying whole numbers

15.	16.	17.	18.
482	927	798	1376
× 17	× 42	× 480	× 605
8194	38,934	383,040	832,480

SKILL 24 Special products whole numbers

19.	20.	21.	22.
80	300	900	2000
× 50	× 70	× 60	× 400
4000	21,000	54,000	800,000

SKILL 23 Multiplying money

23.	24.	25.	26.
$ 0.84	$ 3.24	$ 5.37	$ 13.99
× 6	× 18	× 24	× 17
$5.04	$58.32	$128.88	$237.83

SKILL 27 Multiplying decimals

27.	28.	29.	30.
93.6	87.1	0.03	10.04
× 7	× 0.32	× .02	× 21.8
655.2	27.872	0.0006	218.872

SKILL 29 Special products decimals

31. 10×1.52 15.2   **32.** 1000×3.417 3417   **33.** 100×4.3 430   **34.** 10×104.07
1040.7

SKILL 11 Rounding whole numbers

Round to the underlined place.

35. $\underline{4}9$ 50   **36.** $\underline{1}421$ 1000   **37.** $18,\underline{5}21$ 19,000   **38.** $\underline{7}08,121$
700,000

SKILL 12 Rounding decimals and money

Round to the underlined place.

39. $3.\underline{8}12$ 4   **40.** $\$4.\underline{7}8$ $5.00   **41.** $16.\underline{2}71$ 16   **42.** $\$\underline{4}2.07$ $40.00

43. $5.0\underline{3}1$ 5.03   **44.** $\$23.\underline{8}9$ $24.00   **45.** $14.7\underline{9}6$ 14.80   **46.** $\$\underline{2}45.82$
$200.00

SKILL 51 Dividing money

Divide. Round to the nearest cent.

47. $\overset{\$1.81}{4)\$7.24}$ **48.** $\overset{\$0.30}{9)\$2.70}$ **49.** $\overset{\$5.19}{8)\$41.50}$ **50.** $\overset{\$1.25}{12)\$15.00}$

51. $\overset{\$0.37}{80)\$29.50}$ **52.** $\overset{\$7.53}{17)\$128}$ **53.** $\overset{\$0.03}{35)\$0.90}$ **54.** $\overset{\$9.46}{54)\$511}$

SKILL 53 Multiplying fractions

55. $\frac{1}{3} \times \frac{1}{4}$ $\frac{1}{12}$ **56.** $\frac{2}{5} \times \frac{4}{9}$ $\frac{8}{45}$ **57.** $\frac{3}{4} \times \frac{1}{4}$ $\frac{3}{16}$ **58.** $4 \times \frac{1}{5}$ $\frac{4}{5}$

59. $8 \times \frac{2}{3}$ $5\frac{1}{3}$ **60.** $\frac{1}{2} \times 40$ 20   **61.** $\frac{3}{4} \times 100$ 75   **62.** $125 \times \frac{5}{8}$ $78\frac{1}{8}$

SKILL 48 Multiplying fractions and money

Multiply. Round to the nearest cent.

63. $\frac{1}{2} \times \$4.16$ $2.08   **64.** $\frac{1}{4} \times \$3.05$ $0.76   **65.** $\frac{2}{3} \times \$4.08$ $2.72   **66.** $\frac{3}{4} \times \$22.00$
$16.50

67. $\frac{3}{8} \times \$12.42$ $4.66   **68.** $\frac{4}{5} \times \$42.75$ $34.20   **69.** $\frac{3}{16} \times \$20.00$ $3.75   **70.** $\frac{5}{8} \times \$120.04$
$75.03

SKILL 44 Converting percents to decimals

71. 15% 0.15   **72.** 4% 0.04   **73.** 20% 0.2   **74.** 350% 3.5

SKILL 67 Percent of a number

75. What is 25% of 40? 10   **76.** What is 10% of 100? 10

2
EARNING MONEY

CHOOSING A JOB

When you accept a job, you need to find a way to get there. Many workers commute by automobile—alone or in car pools.

Rodney Green is an employment counselor. He works for a state employment office. He received an associate degree in counseling from a local college. Rodney helps people find jobs.

Job descriptions may list salaries by the year, the month, or by the hour. To find how salaries differ, compare them for the same time period.

EXAMPLE 1. Find the difference in yearly salary.

Job A pays $ 12,725 yearly.
Job B pays $ 1174 monthly.

PLAN: **Step 1.** Convert monthly salary to yearly salary.

$ 1174 \times 12 = $ 14,088

Step 2. Subtract to find the difference.

$ 14,088 - $ 12,725 = $ 1363

Job B pays $ 1363 more per year.

EXAMPLE 2. Find the difference in weekly salary.

Job A pays $3.75 per hour for a 42-hour week.
Job B pays $4.02 per hour for a 36-hour week.

PLAN: **Step 1.** Multiply to find each weekly salary.

Job A: $3.75 × 42 = $157.50
Job B: $4.02 × 36 = $144.72

Step 2. Subtract to find the difference.

$157.50 − $144.72 = $12.78

Job A pays $12.78 more per week.

TRY THIS

1. Find the difference in yearly salary.

Job A pays $13,792 per year.
Job B pays $1200 per month. **$608**

2. Find the difference in weekly salary.

Job A pays $5.37 per hour for a 42-hour week.
Job B pays $6.00 per hour for a 35-hour week.
$15.54

Rodney points out that you should consider the cost of commuting to and from work. If you live 20 miles from your job you will be commuting over 800 miles each month! Taking public transportation or car pooling often saves money and helps conserve energy. Your employer can help you find information on car pooling.

EXAMPLE 3.

The cost per mile of driving a car includes the purchase price, gasoline, insurance, and repairs.

Suppose it costs $0.18 per mile to drive your car to work. Compare these jobs with that in mind.

Job A pays $1144 per month. You must drive 180 miles per month.

Job B pays $1327 per month. You must drive 1170 miles per month.

PLAN: **Step 1.** Multiply to find the driving cost.

Job A: $0.18 × 180 = $32.40
Job B: $0.18 × 1170 = $210.60

Step 2. Subtract the driving cost from the salary.

Job A: $1144 − $32.40 = $1111.60
Job B: $1327 − $210.60 = $1116.40

Job B provides you with more money per month.

Rodney says the salary for some jobs increases faster than for others.
You may want to think of this as you look for a job.

EXAMPLE 4. Find the difference in salary after five years.

Job A: Starting salary $ 14,000, with raises of $ 1000 per year
Job B: Starting salary $ 12,400, with raises of $ 1500 per year

PLAN: **Step 1.** Add the increase to find each salary after five years.

Job A: $ 14,000 + $ 5000 = $ 19,000
Job B: $ 12,400 + $ 7500 = $ 19,900

Step 2. Subtract to find the difference in salary between the jobs.

$ 19,900 − $ 19,000 = $ 900

Job B pays $ 900 more after five years.

TRY THIS

4. Find each salary after five years. Compare.

Job A: $ 9820, with raises of $ 550 per year
Job B: $ 13,200, with raises of $ 450 per year
Job A: $12,570; Job B: $15,450

EXERCISES

Find the difference in yearly salary.

1. Job A: $ 9242 yearly   Job B pays
Job B: $ 790 monthly $238 more

2. Job A: $ 24,294 yearly   Job A pays
Job B: $ 1900 monthly $1494 more

Find the difference in weekly salary.

3. Job A: $ 3.81 per hour, 40-hour week
Job B: $ 4.90 per hour, 35-hour week
Job B pays $19.10 more

4. Job A: $ 8.42 per hour, 37-hour week
Job B: $ 7.25 per hour, 40-hour week
Job A pays $21.52 more

Find the travel costs per year.

5. You drive 13 miles a day, 245 days a year. Use $0.18 per mile. $573.30

6. You take the train for $17.50 per month, 11 months per year. $192.50

7. You take the bus for $0.50 a trip, 234 trips a year. $117.00

Compare these jobs with travel costs in mind. Assume that driving costs are $0.18 per mile; car pool costs are $0.10 per mile.

8. Job A pays $15,792. You must drive 21 miles per week, 48 weeks per year.

Job B pays $17,820. You must drive 237 miles per week, 50 weeks per year. **Job B pays $76.44 more**

9. Job A pays $19,240. You must drive 120 miles per week, 49 weeks per year.

Job B pays $18,900. You travel by train for $21 per month, 11 months per year. **Job B pays $487.40 more**

10. Job A pays $15,927. You must drive 110 miles per week, 50 weeks per year.

Job B pays $14,900. You ride in a car pool and drive 24 miles a week, 50 weeks per year. **Job A pays $157 more**

11. Find the difference in salary after five years.

Job A: $12,900, with raises of $1,000 per year
Job B: $15,000, with raises of $650 per year **Job B pays $350 more**

12. Compare these jobs after five years with travel costs in mind. Assume that driving costs are $0.18 per mile.

Job A pays $9200 yearly, with raises of $1100 per year. You must drive 198 miles per week, 40 weeks per year.

Job B pays $8490 yearly, with raises of $900 per year. You must drive 40 miles per week, 48 weeks per year. **Job A pays $630 more**

ON YOUR OWN

13. From newspaper ads find a job giving an hourly wage and one giving a yearly salary. Find the difference in yearly salary.

ESTIMATING

Estimates can be done mentally or with paper and pencil. As usual, round to make the calculations simpler.

EXAMPLES.   Estimate.   *Some Possible Estimates*

		Written	Mentally
1.	634	630	600
	× 8	× 8	× 8
		5040	4800

		Written	Mentally
2.	624	620	600
	63	60	100
	+ 96	+ 100	+ 100
		780	800

		Written	Mentally
3.	$ 36.23	$ 36	$ 40
	− 19.50	− 20	− 20
		$ 16	$ 20

PRACTICE

Estimate mentally or with paper and pencil.   Estimates may vary.

1.	539	**2.**	725	**3.**	522	**4.**	138
	46		693		603		206
	+ 84		+ 47		+ 158		+ 449
	670		1480		1280		800

5.	832	**6.**	649	**7.**	838	**8.**	729
	× 7		× 9		× 56		× 68
	5810		5850		50,400		51,100

9.	$ 45.82	**10.**	$ 62.18	**11.**	$ 118.46	**12.**	$ 203.46
	− 18.47		− 21.53		− 65.80		− 73.85
	$27.30		$40.70		$52.70		$126.60

HOURLY RATE AND OVERTIME

Most of the accounting is done by computer.

Many construction workers are paid an hourly rate that increases if they work more than 40 hours in one week.

Margaret King is a payroll clerk at a large department store. She keeps accounts of time and wages for all employees. Courses in bookkeeping and accounting helped her qualify for this job.

Most of the workers at the store are paid an hourly rate. Their gross pay is the number of hours worked times the hourly rate. Margaret King shows workers how their pay is calculated from a time card.

Time Card

Name _Jeff Reko_   Job Title _stock clerk_

Hourly Rate _$5.15_   Week Ending _10-21_

Day	Month–Date	Time In	Time Out	Less Lunch Time	Total Daily Hrs
Mon	10-15	9:00	5:00	1 hr.	
Tues	10-16	9:00	5:00	1 hr.	
Wed	10-17	9:00	5:00	1 hr.	
Thurs	10-18				
Fri	10-19	9:00	5:00	1 hr.	
Sat	10-20	9:00	5:00	1 hr.	
Sun	10-21				
				Total Weekly Hours	
				Gross Weekly Pay	

EXAMPLE 1.   Find the gross weekly pay for Jeff Reko.

PLAN: **Step 1.**   Subtract to find the number of hours worked each day. This is the calculation for Monday.

$$5:00 \text{ PM} \longrightarrow 17:00 \quad \textit{When passing from AM to}$$
$$- 9:00 \text{ AM} \qquad - 9:00 \quad \textit{PM add 12 to 5:00.}$$
$$8:00 = 8.0 \text{ hours at work}$$

8 hours at work − 1 hour lunch = 7 hours worked
Now calculate the number of hours Jeff worked on Tuesday, Wednesday, etc.

Step 2.   Add to find the total weekly hours.
$$7.0 + 7.0 + 7.0 + 7.0 + 7.0 = 35 \text{ hours}$$

Step 3.   Multiply to find his gross weekly pay.
$$\$5.15 \times 35 = \$180.25 \quad \textit{Hourly rate} \times \textit{total hours}$$

Minutes are converted to decimals for ease of computation:
15 min = $\frac{1}{4}$ hr = 0.25 hr
30 min = $\frac{1}{2}$ hr = 0.5 hr
45 min = $\frac{3}{4}$ hr = 0.75 hr
60 min = 1 hr = 1.0 hr

Find the gross weekly pay.

TRY THIS

1.

Time Card					
Name Sophia Conti			Job Title Dock Worker		
Hourly Rate $6.18			Week Ending 1-11		
Day	Month–Date	Time In	Time Out	Less Lunch Time	Total Daily Hrs
Mon	1-5	7:00	4:00	1 hr	
Tues	1-6	7:00	4:00	1 hr	
Wed	1-7	7:00	4:00	1 hr	
Thurs	1-8	7:00	4:00	1 hr	
Fri	1-9	7:00	4:00	1 hr	
Sat	1-10	7:00	12:00		
Sun	1-11				
				Total Weekly Hours	
				Gross Weekly Pay	$278.10

Many times an employee is asked to work overtime. Margaret King explains that the hourly rate is higher for overtime. The rate for working more than 8 hours in a day or more than 40 hours in a week is often one and a half times the usual rate. For example, if you get $4.00 an hour and receive overtime rate of 1.5 you will be earning $6.00 an hour for overtime. ($4.00 × 1.5 = $6.00)

An overtime rate can also be paid for work on Sundays and holidays. This rate is often two times your hourly rate. So, if you get $4.00 an hour and receive an overtime rate of 2.0 you will be earning $8.00 an hour for overtime.   **Overtime rate depends on employer, labor contract, laws, etc.**

EXAMPLE 2.   Find the gross weekly pay.

Regular Hours	Regular Rate	Regular Pay	Over-time Hours	Over-time Rate	Over-time Pay	Gross Pay
40	$ 4.85		5	1.5		

PLAN:

Step 1. Multiply to find the regular pay.

$ 4.85 \times 40 = $ 194.00

Step 2. Multiply the regular rate, the overtime rate, and the overtime hours to find the overtime pay.

$ 4.85 \times 1.5 \times 5 \approx $ 36.38

Step 3. Add to find the gross pay.

$ 194.00 + $ 36.38 = $ 230.38   *Regular pay + overtime*

Find the gross weekly pay.

TRY THIS

	Regular Hours	Regular Rate	Regular Pay	Over-time Hours	Over-time Rate	Over-time Pay	Gross Pay
2.	40	$ 4.50	$180.00	8	2.0	$72.00	$252.00
3.	40	$ 5.20	$208.00	5	1.5	$39.00	$247.00

EXERCISES

Find the total weekly hours.

1.

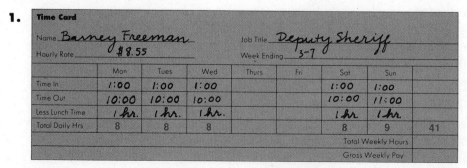

Time Card								
Name *Barney Freeman*					Job Title *Deputy Sheriff*			
Hourly Rate *$8.55*					Week Ending *3-7*			
	Mon	Tues	Wed	Thurs	Fri	Sat	Sun	
Time In	1:00	1:00	1:00			1:00	1:00	
Time Out	10:00	10:00	10:00			10:00	11:00	
Less Lunch Time	1 hr.	1 hr.	1 hr.			1 hr.	1 hr.	
Total Daily Hrs	8	8	8			8	9	41
						Total Weekly Hours		
						Gross Weekly Pay		

2.

Time Card

Name _Felicia Flores_

Hourly Rate _$7.32_

Job Title _Word Processor_

Week Ending _9-19_

	Mon	Tues	Wed	Thurs	Fri	Sat	Sun	
Time In	8:00	8:00	8:00	8:00	8:00	8:00	8:00	
Time Out	4:00	4:00	4:00	4:00	4:00	4:00	12:00	
Less Lunch Time	1 hr.	1 hr.	1 hr.	1 hr.	1 hr.	1 hr.		
Total Daily Hrs	7	7	7	7	7	7		
						Total Weekly Hours		
						Gross Weekly Pay		

Find the gross weekly pay.

	Regular Hours	Regular Rate	Regular Pay	Overtime Hours	Overtime Rate	Overtime Pay	Gross Pay
3.	40.0	$ 6.34		3.5	2.0		
4.	37.0	$ 7.98			1.5		
5.	40.0	$ 6.50			1.5		
6.	40.0	$ 9.60		3.0	2.5		
7.	40.0	$ 4.20			2.0		
8.	40.0	$10.00		4.0	1.5		
9.	40.0	$ 5.50		3.5	1.5		
10.	37.0	$10.75			1.5		
11.	40.0	$ 4.05		8.5	2.0		
12.	40.0	$ 8.63		7.5	2.0		
13.	35.0	$11.45			1.5		
14.	40.0	$ 9.83		3.5	2.5		
15.	36.0	$ 6.35			2.5		
16.	40.0	$ 5.25		3.0	1.5		
17.	40.0	$ 4.03		8.0	1.5		
18.	38.0	$ 4.95			2.0		

PAYROLL DEDUCTIONS—NET PAY

Paycheck deductions for taxes and health benefits are common to workers in small offices and those in large factories.

Allan Baker works in data processing. He is responsible for writing the computer program used to calculate deductions from gross pay. After high school he attended a computer programming school to qualify for his job.

Allan Baker says that two items are deducted or withheld from almost everyone's gross pay. They are federal income tax and FICA (social security). Sometimes deductions are made for union dues, United Fund, insurance, credit union, and so on.

The amount withheld for federal income tax depends on two things, the amount you earn and the number of allowances you claim. It can be found by using a tax table.

Here is a sample table.

Single Persons—Weekly Payroll Period					
And the wages are—		And the number of withholding allowances claimed is—				
At least	But less than	0	1	2	3	4
		The amount of income tax to be withheld shall be—				
$135	$140	$19.00	$15.30	$11.80	$ 8.40	$ 5.00
140	145	20.00	16.20	12.70	9.30	5.80
145	150	21.20	17.10	13.60	10.20	6.70
150	160	22.60	18.60	15.00	11.50	8.10
160	170	24.70	20.70	16.80	13.30	9.90
170	180	26.80	22.80	18.80	15.10	11.70
180	190	28.90	24.90	20.90	16.90	13.50
190	200	31.00	27.00	23.00	18.90	15.30
200	210	33.60	29.10	25.10	21.00	17.10
210	220	36.20	31.20	27.20	23.10	19.10
220	230	38.80	33.80	29.30	25.20	21.20
230	240	41.40	36.40	31.40	27.30	23.30
240	250	44.00	39.00	34.00	29.40	25.40
250	260	46.60	41.60	36.60	31.60	27.50
260	270	49.20	44.20	39.20	34.20	29.60
270	280	51.80	46.80	41.80	36.80	31.80
280	290	54.80	49.40	44.40	39.40	34.40
290	300	57.80	52.10	47.00	42.00	37.00
300	310	60.80	55.10	49.60	44.60	39.60
310	320	63.80	58.10	52.30	47.20	42.20
320	330	67.20	62.60	58.00	54.00	49.90
330	340	70.40	65.80	61.20	56.80	52.70
340	350	73.60	69.00	64.40	59.70	55.50

Table can change depending on current tax law.

Note that table is for a *single person, weekly payroll* period. There are different tables for different situations.

EXAMPLE 1. Find the federal withholding tax if your gross weekly pay is $ 189.26 and you claim one withholding allowance.

PLAN: **Step 1.** Find the wage interval.

$ 189.26 is at least $ 180, but less than $ 190.

Step 2. Find the column for one withholding allowance.

The amount to be withheld is $ 24.90.

TRY THIS

Find the federal withholding tax. Use the table above.

1. Gross weekly pay $ 137.50, 1 allowance **$15.30**
2. Gross weekly pay $ 137.50, 0 allowances **$19.00**
3. Gross weekly pay $ 200.00, 2 allowances **$25.10**
4. Gross weekly pay $ 270.00, 4 allowances **$31.80**

The FICA deduction can also be found from tables, but Allan Baker shows the percent method.

EXAMPLE 2.

The rate of 6.8% is used in 1982. The rate can change yearly by law.

Find the FICA deduction for the gross weekly pay of $189.26 in Example 1. The FICA rate is 6.7%.

$$6.7\% = \frac{6.7}{100} = 0.067$$

$$0.067 \times \$189.26 = \$12.68042$$

$12.68042 rounded to the nearest cent is $12.68.

TRY THIS

Find the FICA deduction.

5. Gross weekly pay $137.50, FICA rate 6.7% $9.21
6. Gross weekly pay $90.00, FICA rate 6.82% $6.14
7. Gross weekly pay $248.12, FICA rate 6.9% $17.12
8. Gross weekly pay $198.15, FICA rate 7.15% $14.17

You usually get an *earnings statement* with your pay check. It shows your gross pay, deductions, and net pay. The *net pay* is your gross pay minus deductions. It is your *take home* pay.

EXAMPLE 3.   Find the net pay for Melba Thomas.

McMendy's Whoopie Burger Co.		EARNINGS STATEMENT	
Melba Thomas Soc. Sec. No. 999-99-9999			
Pay Period Ending 10-21-83			
Hours	Amount	Deductions	
40.0 Regular	$160.00	Fed. Withholding Tax	$48.21
7.0 Overtime	42.00	FICA	16.02
Gross Pay	$202.00	United Fund	1.00
Net Pay _____		Credit Union	25.00

PLAN:

Step 1. Add to find the total deductions.

$48.21 + $16.02 + $1.00 + $25.00 = $90.23

Step 2. Subtract the deductions from the gross pay to find the net pay.

$202.00 − $90.23 = $111.77

The net pay is $111.77.

Find the net pay.

9. Gross pay $ 171.50 $132.21 **10.** Gross pay $ 284.50 $204.77

Deductions | | Deductions
Fed Withholding | | Fed Withholding
  Tax $ 22.80 | | Tax $ 28.52
  FICA   11.49 | | FICA   19.06
  Union Dues 5.00 | | Insurance   32.15

EXERCISES

Find the federal withholding tax. Use the table on page 43.

1. Gross pay $ 142.50, 0 allowances $20.00

2. Gross pay $ 165.78, 1 allowance $20.70

3. Gross pay $ 305.75, 2 allowances $49.60

4. Gross pay $ 250.00, 0 allowances $46.60

5. Gross pay $ 310.00, 3 allowances $47.20

6. Gross pay $ 239.99, 1 allowance $36.40

Find the FICA deduction.

7. Gross pay $ 174.50, FICA rate 6.7%
$11.69

8. Gross pay $ 186.25, FICA rate 6.85%
$12.76

9. Gross pay $ 227.50, FICA rate 7.0%
$15.93

10. Gross pay $ 346.90, FICA rate 7.15%
$24.80

11. Gross pay $ 180.00, FICA rate 7.25%
$13.05

12. Gross pay $ 426.57, FICA rate 7.3%
$31.14

Find the net pay.

13. Gross pay $ 185.00

Deductions
Fed Withholding
  Tax $ 24.75
FICA   12.78
$147.47

14. Gross pay $ 328.74

Deductions
Fed Withholding
  Tax $ 58.30
FICA   22.50
$247.94

15. Gross pay $ 456.00

Deductions
Fed Withholding
  Tax $ 86.64
FICA   43.79
Union Dues   10.00
Insurance   23.47
$291.10

16. Gross pay $ 678.98

Deductions
Fed Withholding
  Tax $ 132.41
FICA   62.34
Union Dues   15.67
United Fund   12.00
$456.56

WAGES AND TIPS

In many service occupations, such as cab driving, tips received for good service make up a major part of income.

Some jobs pay at a low hourly rate. Tips for good service can raise the gross income.

EXAMPLE 1.   Find the gross weekly income.

Inge Anderson is a waitress. She works a 5-day, 40-hour week. She earns $ 3.25 an hour. She also averages $ 22.00 a day in tips.

PLAN: **Step 1.**   Multiply to find Inge's weekly wages.
$ 3.25 \times 40 = $ 130.00

Step 2.   Multiply to find the weekly tips.
$ 22.00 \times 5 = $ 110.0

Step 3.   Add to find her gross weekly income.
$ 130.00 + $ 110.00 = $ 240.00

Find the gross weekly income.

1. 4-day, 30-hour week, $ 3.50 per hour, $ 15.25 daily tips $166.00
2. 5-day, 40-hour week, $ 3.15 per hour, $ 19.75 daily tips $224.75
3. 3-day, 24-hour week, $ 4.10 per hour, $ 11.50 daily tips $132.90
4. 4-day, 32-hour week, $ 3.05 per hour, $ 17.80 daily tips $168.80

EXAMPLE 2.

Total fares are determined by the meter readings.

Kathleen Gallagher is a taxi driver. Her wages are one half of the total fares she collects. Tips average one third of her total fares. Her employer requires her to pay one half of the gas bill for her cab.

In one week Kathleen collected $ 478.00 in fares. The total gas bill was $ 42.50. Find her gross weekly income.

PLAN:

Step 1. Multiply to find her weekly wages.

$$\frac{1}{2} \times \$ 478.00 = \$ 239.00$$

Step 2. Multiply to find her weekly tips. Round to the nearest cent.

$$\frac{1}{3} \times \$ 478.00 \approx \$ 159.33$$

Step 3. Add her wages and tips to find her total income.
$$\$ 239.00 + \$ 159.33 = \$ 398.33$$

Step 4. Multiply to find her share of gas costs.

$$\frac{1}{2} \times \$ 42.50 = \$ 21.25$$

Step 5. Subtract to find her gross weekly income.
$$\$ 398.33 - \$ 21.25 = \$ 377.08$$

Kathleen's gross weekly income is $ 377.08

Find the gross weekly income.

5. $ 410.50 weekly fares $291.71
$ 48.50 weekly gas
Earnings: $\frac{1}{2}$ of fares
Tips: $\frac{1}{4}$ of fares
Less gas: $\frac{1}{3}$ of weekly gas

6. $ 395.80 weekly fares $329.83
$ 47.00 weekly gas
Earnings: $\frac{1}{2}$ of fares
Tips: $\frac{1}{3}$ of fares
No gas charge

EXERCISES

Copy and complete this table of restaurant worker weekly earnings.

	Name	Title	Hours Worked	Hourly Wage	Days Worked	Average Daily Tips	Gross Weekly Income
1.	Lily	Manager	47	$7.50	5	none	? $326.50
2.	Reginald	Manager	52	$6.20	6	none	? $322.40
3.	Jake	Waiter	40	$7.10	5	$17.35	? $370.75
4.	Nick	Waiter	40	$6.25	5	? $19.45	$347.25
5.	Isabel	Waitress	47	$6.25	5	? $21.18	$399.65
6.	Craig	Busboy	40	$5.35	5	? $0.80	$214.00
7.	Judith	Waitress	45	$6.25	5	$15.20	? $357.25

Find the gross weekly income.

8. Chung Woo is a taxi driver. His wages are one half of the total fares he collects. His tips average one fifth of his total fares. His employer pays for all of the gas. One week Chung collected $379.00 in fares. The total gas bill was $37.00. Find his gross income for that week. **$265.30**

9. Laura Taylor is a taxi driver. Her wages are two thirds of the total fares she collects. Her tips average one fourth of her total fares. Her employer requires she pay two thirds of the total gas bill. One week Laura collected $641.00 in fares. The total gas bill was $64.00. Find her gross income for that week. **$544.91**

10. Leon Johnson is a skycap at the airport. He works four days per week, ten hours each day. He gets paid $3.50 per hour plus $1.70 for each service (helps passengers with their luggage). He averages 25 services each day. He receives an average of $29.00 in tips each day. Find Leon's gross weekly income. **$426.00**

ON YOUR OWN

11. List some jobs in your community that depend on tips as an important source of income.

12. Do you have to pay income tax on tips? Yes.

MENTAL CALCULATION

QUICK MULTIPLICATION BY 3

To multiply a number by 3, you can double and then add the number.

EXAMPLE 1.   Multiply 3×19.

PLAN: **Step 1.**   Double.

$2 \times 19 = 38$

Step 2.   Add.

$38 + 19 = 40 + 17 = 57$

$3 \times 19 = 57$

EXAMPLE 2.   Multiply 3×451.

PLAN: **Step 1.**   Double.

$2 \times 451 = 902$

Step 2.   Add.

$902 + 451 = 1353$

$3 \times 451 = 1353$

PRACTICE

Multiply mentally by 3.

1. 27 81	**2.** 64 192	**3.** 45 135	**4.** 88 264	**5.** 94 282	**6.** 79 237
7. 165 495	**8.** 137 411	**9.** 158 474	**10.** 183 549	**11.** 67 201	**12.** 110 330
13. 350 1050	**14.** 261 783	**15.** 345 1035	**16.** 153 459	**17.** 640 1920	**18.** 163 489
19. 35 105	**20.** 171 513	**21.** 85 255	**22.** 480 1440	**23.** 72 216	**24.** 76 228

WAGES AND COMMISSIONS

People who sell mopeds like these—or TV's, stereos, and refrigerators—receive a base salary plus commissions.

Commissions are an important source of income on some jobs. They are used as incentives for more sales and better work. Both the employer and worker benefit.

EXAMPLE 1. Lionel Archer sells and delivers ice for his employers. He earns $4.50 per hour plus 3% commission on his gross sales.

In one week he worked 40 hours and sold $820.00 of ice. Find his weekly gross earnings.

PLAN: **Step 1.** Multiply to find his weekly earnings.
$4.50 × 40 hours = $180.00

Step 2. Multiply to find his commission earnings.
0.03 × $820 = $24.60

Step 3. Add to find his total earnings.
$180.00 + $24.60 = $204.60

Find the weekly gross earnings.

1. 38 hours $166.21
   $ 3.95 per hour
   $ 402.80 gross sales
   4% commission

2. 40 hours $198.00
   $ 4.25 per hour
   $ 1400 gross sales
   2% commission

EXAMPLE 2.

Rhonda Copper is an auto mechanic. She earns $ 7.80 per hour plus a 10% commission on labor charges.

One week she worked 40 hours and her total labor charge was $ 968.00. Find her gross pay.

PLAN:

Step 1. Multiply to find her weekly wages.
$ 7.80 × 40 hours = $ 312.00

Step 2. Multiply to find her commission earnings.
0.10 × $ 968.00 = $ 96.80

Step 3. Add to find her total earnings.
$ 312.00 + $ 96.80 = $ 408.80

Rhonda's gross pay is $ 408.80.

Find the weekly gross earnings.

3. $ 6.90 per hour for 40 hours $348.00
   9% commission on $ 800 labor charges

EXAMPLE 3.

Jim Lambert is a beautician. He earns $ 4.15 an hour plus a commission of 60% on his work and sales *over* his wage.

In one week he worked 40 hours and brought in $ 725.00 for his work. Find his gross weekly earnings.

PLAN:

The difference between the amount charged to customers and the amount of his wages is called "amount over wages." Customer charges include sales on items such as hair spray.

Step 1. Multiply to find his weekly wages.
40 × $ 4.15 = $ 166.00

Step 2. Subtract to find the amount over wages.
$ 725 − $ 166 = $ 559

Step 3. Multiply to find his commission earnings.
0.60 × $ 559 = $ 335.40

Step 4. Add to find his total earnings.
$ 166.00 + $ 335.40 = $ 501.40

Jim's gross weekly earnings are $ 501.40.

Find the weekly gross earnings.

4. Wages plus 25% on $331.25 work and sales over wage
40 hours at $4.25 per hour
$815 work and sales

5. Wages plus 50% on $455.50 work and sales over wage
30 hours at $6.20 per hour
$725 work and sales

EXERCISES

Find the gross weekly earnings.

1. 40 hours
$4.10 per hour
$500.00 gross sales
3% commission $179.00

2. 32 hours
$6.25 per hour
$425.50 gross sales
4% commission $217.02

3. 40 hours
$6.50 per hour
$725.00 labor charges
15% commission $368.75

4. 24 hours
$7.15 per hour
$475.20 labor charges
12% commission $228.62

5. Wages plus 30% on work and sales over wages
40 hours at $4.65 per hour
$605.00 work and sales $311.70

6. Wages plus 55% on work and sales over wages
36 hours at $5.10 per hour
$585.00 work and sales $404.37

7. 40 hours
$5.35 per hour
$375.80 gross sales
5% commission $232.79

8. Wages plus 40% on work and sales over wages
40 hours at $4.80 per hour
$575.00 work and sales $345.20

DECISION

9. Which job would you prefer? Why?

a. Salesperson
40 hours
$6.15 per hour

b. Salesperson
$4.00 per hour
15% commission

PROBLEM SOLVING HINTS

Rafael Sanchez, an electrician, is ordering *conduit* to cover electric wires. The job calls for the following:

Length	Number of Pieces
$7\frac{1}{2}$ feet	4
$8\frac{1}{2}$ inches	2
$12\frac{1}{2}$ inches	3
$10\frac{5}{8}$ inches	2

Conduit comes in pieces 10 feet long. Rafael needs to find:

how many pieces to order, and
how to cut the conduit to decrease the waste.

Rafael decides that to get 4 pieces of $7\frac{1}{2}$ feet in length, he must order at least 4 pieces.

HINT   Drawing a picture can help solve some problems.

He then draws a picture to see how to cut the lengths with the least waste.

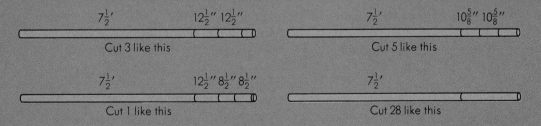

Cut 3 like this

Cut 5 like this

Cut 1 like this

Cut 28 like this

PRACTICE

1. Draw pictures to find another way Rafael can cut the lengths.

STRAIGHT COMMISSION

Examples are sales in autos, real estate, door-to-door etc.

The real estate person who sells one of the condominium homes
will receive a commission based on the sales price.

Many people in sales jobs earn a straight commission. This means
they receive no wages or salary other than their sales commission.

EXAMPLE 1. Anita Peterson sells cosmetics at shows in a person's home.
She receives a 40% sales commission on the gross sales.
At one show the gross sales were $65.50. Find her
commission.

0.40 × $65.50 = $26.20

EXAMPLE 2. Elliot Meyer sells real estate. He receives a 6% commission
on the gross sales price. He sold a home for $79,950. Find
his commission.

0.06 × $79,950 = $4797

Some salespeople earn a commission that changes as their sales increase.

EXAMPLE 3. Ethel Atkinson sells large appliances at a store. She earns weekly commissions this way:

5% on sales up to $ 500,
10% on sales from $ 500 to $ 2500,
20% on sales over $ 2500.

One week her sales were $ 4250. Find her commission.

PLAN: **Step 1.** Multiply to find her commission on the first $ 500.

$0.05 \times \$500 = \$25$

Step 2. Multiply to find her commission on sales from $ 500 to $ 2500.

$0.10 \times \$2000 = \$200$

**$2500 − $500 = $2000.
Add step if students
have trouble.**

Step 3. Subtract to find the sales over $ 2500.

$\$4250 - \$2500 = \$1750$

Step 4. Multiply to find her commission on sales over $ 2500.

$0.20 \times \$1750 = \$350$

Step 5. Add to find her total commission.

$\$25 + \$200 + \$350 = \$575$

Her total commission is $ 575.

EXERCISES

Find the commission.

1. 15% commission on sales of $4250 $637.50

2. 8% commission on sales of $18,650 $1492

3. 1% commission on sales of $650 $6.50

4. 4% commission on sales of $16,020.84 $640.83

5. Floyd Jackson sells home computers. He receives 13% commission on the gross sales. Last month he sold $12,547 worth of computer units. $1631.11

6. Becky McCoy is a real estate broker. She receives 3.5% commission on sales. She sold a house valued at $75,900. $2656.50

7. Victoria is an appliance salesperson. She receives 14% commission. Last week she sold three mixers at $45.60 each, two food processors at $68.75 each, and three lawn mowers at $102.40 each. $81.41

Find the commission on these weekly sales. Use this commission rate:

8% on sales up to $1000,
10% on sales from $1000 to $5000,
15% on sales over $5000.

8. $890
$71.20

9. $1500
$130.00

10. $3800
$360

11. $6000
$630

12. $10,900
$1365

Find the commission on these weekly sales. Use this commission rate:

3% on sales up to $2000,
6% on sales from $2000 to $15,000,
12% on sales over $15,000.

13. $1300
$39

14. $6900
$354

15. $12,400
$684

16. $20,150
$1458

17. $29,630
$2595.60

ON YOUR OWN

18. Authors and inventors are often paid on a *royalty* basis. What is a royalty?

MENTAL CALCULATION

QUICK DIVISION BY 2

To divide by 2 mentally it is best to group first.

EXAMPLE 1.   Divide $935 ÷ 2.

Think of 935 as 900 + 30 + 5.
Half of 900 is 450.
Half of 30 is 15.
Half of 5 is 2.5.

So, $935 ÷ 2 is $467.50.

QUICK DIVISION BY 4

To divide by 4 mentally you can take half and then half again.

EXAMPLE 2.   Divide $59.68 ÷ 4.

Take half of $59.68. $59.68 ÷ 2 = $25 + $4.50 + $0.34
$$= \$29.84$$

Take half of $29.84. $29.84 ÷ 2 = $10 + $4.50 + $0.42
$$= \$14.92$$

So, $59.68 ÷ 4 is $14.92.

PRACTICE

Divide by 2 mentally.

1. 1450 ÷ 2 725   **2.** 962 ÷ 2 481   **3.** 1385 ÷ 2 692.5

4. 433 ÷ 2 216.5   **5.** 1269 ÷ 2 634.5   **6.** 746 ÷ 2 373

7. 766 ÷ 2 383   **8.** 2385 ÷ 2 1192.5   **9.** 3554 ÷ 2 1777

Divide by 4 mentally.

10. $16.56 ÷ 4 $4.14   **11.** 86 ÷ 4 21.5   **12.** 3452 ÷ 4 863

13. $2492 ÷ 4 $623   **14.** 85.20 ÷ 4 21.3   **15.** 56.92 ÷ 4 14.23

16. $52.40 ÷ 4 $13.10   **17.** $39.44 ÷ 4 $9.86   **18.** $216.80 ÷ 4 $54.20

PIECEWORK

People who create and sew these down vests are paid for each
piece they finish.

Some workers are paid by the number of units they complete or
produce. This is called *piecework*.

EXAMPLE 1.   Joyce Barker has a secretarial service. She charges customers
these piece rates:

	Size	Double spaced	Single spaced	Space and one half
Typing pages	letter	$1.15	$2.30	$1.75
	legal	2.00	4.00	3.00
Duplicating copies	letter	$0.07 per page		
	legal	$0.08 per page		
Minimum charge is $5.00.				

Joyce has been asked to type a three-page report. Her customer has given her the following instructions:

double space, use letter paper, and make 20 copies of each page.

PLAN: **Step 1.**   Multiply to find the typing charge.

$\$1.15 \times 3 = \$3.45$

Step 2.   Multiply to find the copy charge.

$\$0.07 \times 3 \times 20 = \$4.20$

Step 3.   Add to find her total charges.

$\$3.45 + \$4.20 = \$7.65$

Joyce will charge a total of $\$7.65$.

TRY THIS

Find the total cost. Use the piece rates from Example 1.

1. Typing 16 pages, **$79.36** legal size, single spaced, 12 copies of each page

2. Typing 86 pages, **$162.54** letter size, space and one half, 2 copies of each page

---

EXAMPLE 2.   Richard Yoshida hangs (installs) doors. He charges $\$55$ for hanging a single door and $\$100$ for hanging a double door. In one week he hung twelve single doors and three double doors. Find his earnings for that week.

PLAN: **Step 1.**   Find his earnings for the single doors.

$\$55 \times 12 = \$660$

To hang a door means to install the door in a door frame.

Step 2.   Find his earnings for the double doors.

$\$100 \times 3 = \$300$

Step 3.   Add to find his total earnings.

$\$660 + \$300 = \$960$

Richard Yoshida's total earnings are $\$960$.

TRY THIS

3. Tony Lucero has a window cleaning service. His piece rates are: $\$0.75$ for small windows, $\$1.25$ for average size windows, and $\$2.50$ for large windows. In one week he cleaned 85 small, 150 average, and 56 large windows. How much did he earn? **$391.25**

EXERCISES

Dan Smith runs a janitorial service. He charges these piece rates to clean office buildings:

Service	Charge
Shampoo small rug	$20.00
Shampoo large rug	35.00
General cleaning, small office	12.50
General cleaning, large office	17.50
General cleaning, office suite	30.00
Detail cleaning, small office	22.50
Detail cleaning, large office	37.50

Find Dan Smith's charges for cleaning.

1. Detail cleaning of a large office 37.50

2. Detail cleaning of a small office, plus shampooing a small rug $42.50

3. General cleaning of a small office building containing three small offices and two large offices $72.50

4. General cleaning of a large office building containing four small offices, six large offices, and four office suites, plus shampooing three large rugs $380

Use the following table to find the charges for the jobs.

	Size	Double spaced	Single spaced	Space and one half
Typing pages	letter	$1.15	$2.30	$1.75
	legal	2.00	4.00	3.00
Duplicating copies	letter	$0.07 per page		
	legal	$0.08 per page		
Minimum charge is $5.00.				

5. Typing 120 letter-sized pages, space and one half, with five copies of each page $252

6. Typing 250 legal-sized pages, double spaced, with 20 copies of each page $900

7. Typing a government report containing:

17 legal-sized pages, double spaced, with twelve copies of each,
32 letter-sized pages, single spaced, with twelve copies of each,
1 legal-sized page, space and one half, with one copy,
1 letter-sized page, space and one half, with one copy. **$155.70**

8. Typing an environmental impact study containing:

237 letter-sized pages, double spaced, with thirty copies of each,
15 legal-sized pages, single spaced, with thirty copies of each,
2 letter-sized pages, space and one half, with three copies of
each, and
2 legal-sized pages, space and one half, with three copies of each. **$876.65**

Find the gross weekly pay.

9. Selma Ramsey has a pool cleaning service. She charges $ 17.50 for small pools and $ 30 for large pools. She averages twelve small and six large pools a week. How much are her average weekly earnings? **$390**

10. Amy Kobata does automobile tune-ups in a garage. She charges $ 56.75 to tune a 6-cylinder car and $ 69.50 to tune an 8-cylinder car. One week she tuned eighteen 6-cylinder cars and five 8-cylinder cars. Find her earnings for that week. **$1369**

11. Ella Goldman runs a beauty shop. She charges $ 12 for a haircut and $ 18 for a styling. Find her weekly earnings if she averages thirty haircuts and seventeen stylings per week. **$666**

12. Rex Carter runs a car wash. He charges $ 3.00 for an exterior wash, $ 3.75 for a wash and wax, and $ 4.75 for a wash, wax, and interior cleaning. He averages 13 washes, 19 wash and waxes, and 23 wash, wax, and interior cleanings per week. Find his weekly gross earnings. **$219.50**

DECISION

13. You are a contractor. You need a carpenter to frame houses. One carpenter charges you $ 14.75 per hour. Another charges you $ 0.40 per square foot of house floor area. Who would you hire? Why?

CHAPTER REVIEW

Find the difference in yearly salary.

1. Job A: $ 13,250 yearly
Job B: $ 1090 monthly **Job A pays $170 more**

Compare these jobs with travel costs considered. Use $ 0.18 per mile.

2. Job A: Salary $ 15,720, drive 19 miles per week, 50 weeks per year
Job B: Salary $ 15,900, drive 39 miles per week, 48 weeks per year
Job B pays $14.04 more

Find the difference in salary after five years.

3. Job A: Starting salary $ 15,000, with raises of $ 1100 per year
Job B: Starting salary $ 12,900, with raises of $ 1500 per year
Job A pays $100 more

Find the total weekly hours.

4.

Time Card					
Name _Alice Morris_			Job Title _Checker_		
Hourly Rate _$4.95_			Week Ending _9-19_		
Day	Month–Date	Time In	Time Out	Less Lunch Time	Total Daily Hrs
Mon	9-13	7:00	4:00	1 hr.	8
Tues	9-14	7:00	4:00	1 hr.	8
Wed	9-15	7:00	4:00	1 hr.	8
Thurs	9-16	8:00	5:00	1 hr.	8
Fri	9-17				
Sat	9-18	7:00	4:00	1 hr.	8
Sun	9-19				
				Total Weekly Hours	40
				Gross Weekly Pay	

5.

Regular Hours	Regular Hourly Rate	Regular Pay	Overtime Hours	Overtime Rate	Overtime Pay	Gross Pay
40	$ 5.35	$214.00	7	1.5	$56.18	$270.18

Find the federal withholding tax. Use the table on page 43.

6. Gross pay $ 298.50, 1 allowance **$52.10**

7. Gross pay $ 287.00, 0 allowances **$54.80**

Find the FICA deduction.

8. Gross weekly pay $ 182.50, FICA rate 6.7% **$12.23**

9. Gross weekly pay $ 298.75, FICA rate 7.15% **$21.36**

Find the net pay.

10. Gross pay $ 255.75

Deductions
Federal Withholding Tax $ 42.70
FICA $ 21.50
Union Dues $ 2.25 **$189.30**

11. Gross pay $ 327.80

Deductions
Federal Withholding Tax $ 53.25
FICA $ 26.40
Credit Union $ 25.00
$223.15

Find the gross weekly income.

12. Waiter
40-hour week
$ 3.50 per hour
5 days
$ 21.50 average daily tips **$247.50**

13. Cab Driver
$ 476.00 total fares
$ 49.50 total gas
Earnings: $\frac{1}{2}$ of fares
Tips: $\frac{1}{4}$ of fares
Less gas: $\frac{1}{2}$ of total gas **$332.25**

14. 40 hours
$ 4.15 per hr
$ 625 gross sales
4% commission **$191.00**

15. Wages plus 45% on work
and sales over wages
32 hours at $ 6.15 per hour
$ 428 work and sales **$300.84**

Find the commission.

16. Cosmetic sales $ 128.76 **$38.63**
Commission rate 30%

17. Real Estate sales $ 72,550 **$4353**
Commission rate 6%

Find the commission on these weekly sales:

7% on sales up to $ 500,
10% on sales from $ 500 to $ 1500,
16% on sales over $ 1500.

18. $ 1750 **$175**

19. $ 1275 **$112.50**

20. The Quality-Tune Garage charges $ 45.50 to tune 4-cylinder
cars, $ 52.00 for 6-cylinder cars, and $ 67.90 for 8-cylinder cars.
In one week mechanics tuned fourteen 4-cylinder cars, twenty-
four 6-cylinder cars, and nine 8-cylinder cars. What are the
charges for that week? **$2496.10**

SKILLS REVIEW

SKILL 6 Money notation

Write money notation.

1. eight cents $0.08, or 8¢

2. forty-three cents $0.43, or 43¢

3. fifteen dollars $15

4. eight dollars and fifty-eight cents $8.58

5. two hundred dollars and sixteen cents $200.16

6. five dollars and three cents $5.03

SKILL 12 Rounding decimals and money

Round to the underlined place.

7. $ 2̲8.46 $28

8. $ 137̲.92 $138

9. $ 5̲8.95 $59

10. $ 8.43̲6 $8.44

11. 5̲.973 6.0

12. 126.4̲058 126.4

13. $ 7̲65.28 $800

14. $ 929̲.50 $930

SKILL 34 Writing fractions as decimals

Convert to a decimal. Round to the nearest hundredth if necessary.

15. $\frac{4}{5}$ 0.8

16. $\frac{5}{4}$ 1.25

17. $\frac{7}{8}$ 0.875, or 0.88

18. $\frac{53}{20}$ 2.65

19. $\frac{1}{6}$ 0.17

20. $\frac{8}{3}$ 2.67

21. $\frac{4}{7}$ 0.57

22. $\frac{10}{9}$ 1.11

SKILL 38 Writing mixed numbers as decimals

Convert to a decimal.

23. $5\frac{9}{10}$ 5.9

24. $8\frac{41}{100}$ 8.41

25. $78\frac{7883}{10,000}$ 78.7883

26. $14\frac{1}{1000}$ 14.001

27. $9\frac{3}{5}$ 9.6

28. $12\frac{3}{8}$ 12.375

29. $10\frac{3}{4}$ 10.75

30. $8\frac{17}{20}$ 8.85

SKILL 44 Converting percents to decimals

Convert to a decimal.

31. 44% 0.44

32. 38% 0.38

33. 130% 1.30

34. 240% 2.40

35. 9% 0.09

36. 7% 0.07

37. 7.8% 0.078

38. 9.2% 0.092

SKILL 15 Adding money

Add.

39.
$ 14.76
+ 31.19
$45.95

40.
$ 108.91
+ 74.66
$183.57

41.
$ 8.47
0.49
+ 6.40
$15.36

42.
$ 9.87
3.68
+ 1.98
$15.53

SKILL 23 Multiplying money

Multiply. Round to the nearest cent.

43. $\begin{array}{r} \$43.60 \\ \times\ \ \ \ 7 \\ \hline \$305.20 \end{array}$ **44.** $\begin{array}{r} \$316.74 \\ \times\ \ \ \ \ 5 \\ \hline \$1583.70 \end{array}$ **45.** $\begin{array}{r} \$0.67 \\ \times\ \ \ 24 \\ \hline \$16.08 \end{array}$ **46.** $\begin{array}{r} \$63.87 \\ \times\ \ \ \ 93 \\ \hline \$5939.91 \end{array}$

47. $\begin{array}{r} \$17.30 \\ \times\ \ \ 0.6 \\ \hline \$10.38 \end{array}$ **48.** $\begin{array}{r} \$24.80 \\ \times\ \ \ 0.03 \\ \hline \$0.74 \end{array}$ **49.** $\begin{array}{r} \$178.56 \\ \times\ \ \ \ 0.08 \\ \hline \$14.28 \end{array}$ **50.** $\begin{array}{r} \$7546.00 \\ \times\ \ \ \ \ 0.11 \\ \hline \$830.06 \end{array}$

SKILL 27 Multiplying decimals

Multiply.

51. $\begin{array}{r} 2.9 \\ \times\ \ 7 \\ \hline 20.3 \end{array}$ **52.** $\begin{array}{r} 8.56 \\ \times\ \ \ 4 \\ \hline 34.24 \end{array}$ **53.** $\begin{array}{r} 9.7 \\ \times\ 0.8 \\ \hline 7.76 \end{array}$ **54.** $\begin{array}{r} 3.768 \\ \times\ \ \ \ 12 \\ \hline 45.216 \end{array}$

SKILL 53 Multiplying fractions

Multiply.

55. $5 \times \frac{7}{8}$ $\frac{35}{8}$, or $4\frac{3}{8}$ **56.** $4 \times \frac{1}{5}$ $\frac{4}{5}$ **57.** $\frac{2}{3} \times \frac{4}{5}$ $\frac{8}{15}$

58. $\frac{2}{7} \times \frac{4}{7}$ $\frac{8}{49}$ **59.** $\frac{3}{4} \times \frac{9}{10}$ $\frac{27}{40}$ **60.** $\frac{2}{5} \times \frac{4}{9}$ $\frac{8}{45}$

SKILL 54 Multiplying fractions—simplifying

Multiply and simplify.

61. $\frac{3}{4} \times \frac{1}{3}$ $\frac{1}{4}$ **62.** $\frac{3}{5} \times \frac{1}{6}$ $\frac{1}{10}$ **63.** $\frac{4}{5} \times \frac{15}{16}$ $\frac{3}{4}$ **64.** $6 \times \frac{7}{8}$ $5\frac{1}{4}$

SKILL 55 Multiplying mixed numbers

Multiply and simplify.

65. $8 \times 3\frac{1}{4}$ 26 **66.** $5 \times 2\frac{1}{2}$ $12\frac{1}{2}$ **67.** $3\frac{1}{4} \times \frac{2}{5}$ $1\frac{3}{10}$ **68.** $5\frac{2}{3} \times \frac{5}{6}$ $4\frac{13}{18}$

SKILL 67 Finding a percent of a number

69. 60% of $10 is what number? $6   **70.** What is $33\frac{1}{3}$% of $127 $42.33

SKILL 48 Multiplying fractions and money

Multiply. Round to the nearest cent.

71. $20.60 \times \frac{1}{2}$ $10.30   **72.** $10.29 \times \frac{2}{3}$ $6.86   **73.** $50.00 \times \frac{3}{4}$ $37.50   **74.** $90.47 \times \frac{1}{5}$

   $18.09

3
BANKING, BORROWING, AND INVESTING

SAVINGS ACCOUNTS

Many local banks and savings and loan associations have literature available concerning savings accounts.

Many people save up for vacation trips, like this one to the Sierra, by making regular deposits in their savings account.

Eleanor Abernathy is learning to be an electrician. Since she lives with her parents, she is able to save most of her money. Eleanor puts this money into a savings account at Bankers Trust. She knows that making regular deposits into a savings account is a good way to save money. She uses a deposit slip like this.

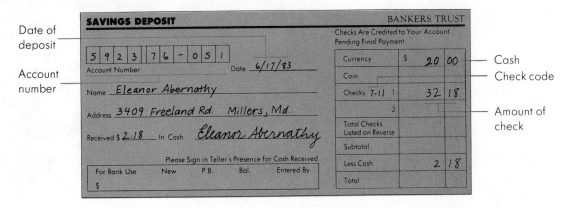

EXAMPLE 1.   Find Eleanor's net deposit.

PLAN: **Step 1.**   Add the amounts in cash and checks to find the total deposit.

$20.00 + $32.18 = $52.18

Step 2.   Subtract the cash Eleanor receives from the total deposit to find the net deposit.

$52.18 − $2.18 = $50.00

Eleanor's net deposit is $50.00.

TRY THIS

1. Find the total deposit and the net deposit.

		Dollars	Cents
Cash	Currency	10	00
	Coin		
Checks	7·15	27	19
Total		37	19
Less Cash Received		2	19
Net Deposit		35	00

You may wish to make a duplicating master of deposit and withdrawal slips. It is often possible to obtain samples from local banks.

Eleanor uses a withdrawal slip to take money out of her account.

Her account number

Amount in words

Amount in numbers

Date of withdrawal

SAVINGS WITHDRAWAL RECEIPT   BANKERS TRUST

5 9 2 3 7 6 - 0 5 1

Account Number
Received of Bankers Trust Co.

Date *Aug. 21, 1982*
$ *34.00*

Thirty-four and $\frac{00}{100}$ ————————————————— Dollars

For Bank Use	New	P.B.	Bal.	Entered By
$				
Transfer to Account Number				

Eleanor Abernathy
Customer's Signature

Eleanor Abernathy
Customer's Name—Please Print

On checks and savings withdrawal slips, the dollar amounts are written in words. Cents are written as a fraction of a dollar.

EXAMPLE 2.   Write $25.92 as you would on a check or withdrawal slip.

Twenty-five and $\frac{92}{100}$ dollars.

TRY THIS

Write these amounts as you would on a check or withdrawal slip. **See answer section.**

2. $14.82   **3.** $119.16   **4.** $64.97

Eleanor has a *passbook* for her account. It is a record of all deposits, withdrawals, and interest. It also shows the current balance.

Date	Withdrawals	Deposits	Interest	Balance
5–10–82				529.88
6–17–82		25.00		?
8–21–82	34.00			?

EXAMPLE 3.   What was Eleanor's balance on May 10, 1982?

Her balance on May 10, 1982 was $529.88

TRY THIS

5. How much was deposited on June 17, 1982? $25.00

EXAMPLE 4.   What is her balance on 6–17–82?

Add the deposit to the previous balance.

$529.88 + $25.00 = $554.88

The new balance is $554.88.

TRY THIS

6. Find Eleanor's balance on 8-21-82 after the $34 withdrawal. $520.88

EXERCISES

Find the total deposit and the net deposit.

1.

		Dollars	Cents
Cash	Currency		
	Coin		
Checks	21·86	37	19
	57·01	40	00
	Total	77	19
	Less Cash Received	15	00
	Net Deposit	62	19

2.

		Dollars	Cents
Cash	Currency	20	00
	Coin		
Checks	19~26	56	29
	Total	76	29
	Less Cash Received		
	Net Deposit	76	29

Find the net deposit.

	Currency	Checks	Less cash received	Net deposit	
3.	$ 25.00	$ 19.29	$ 10.00	?	$34.29
4.	$ 75.00	$ 24.54	$ 3.50	?	$96.04
5.	$ 120.00	$ 63.75	$ 15.00	?	$168.75
6.	$ 12.00	$ 103.19	$ 15.00	?	$100.19

Write these dollar amounts in words. See answer section.

7. $ 15.93   **8.** $ 45.00   **9.** $ 22.09   **10.** $ 108.19

11. $ 34.16   **12.** $ 55.25   **13.** $ 78.94   **14.** $ 226.97

15. Begin with a passbook balance of $ 517.19. Find the balance after each deposit or withdrawal:

a. deposit of $ 29.48 $546.67   **b.** withdrawal of $ 25.00 $521.67

c. withdrawal of $ 30.00 $491.67 **d.** deposit of $ 95.00 $586.67

e. deposit of $ 60.00 $646.67   **f.** deposit of $ 48.00 $694.67

ON YOUR OWN

16. Get an application to open a savings account. What information does it ask for? Why? Go to several banks. Are all deposit and withdrawal forms alike?

ESTIMATING PERCENTS

It is important to be able to estimate percents in solving some problems.

EXAMPLES

1. What is 11% of 59?

Think: 11% of 59 is about 10% of 60.
10% of 60 is 6.

11% of 60 ≈ 6

2. What is $3\frac{1}{2}$% of $409?

Think: $3\frac{1}{2}$% of $409 is about 4% of 400.

1% of 400 is $4.   4% of 400 is $16.

$3\frac{1}{2}$% of $409 ≈ $16

PRACTICE

Estimate.

1. 26% of 81

2. 40% of 620

3. $47\frac{1}{2}$% of 321

4. 52% of 501

5. 1.1% of 39

6. 13% of 827

7. 3% of $129.50

8. 34% of $59.64

9. 69% of 365 days

10. 73% of 4812

11. 12.2% of 81 km

12. 21.3% of 97 kg

13. 151% of 16

14. 312% of 19

15. $\frac{1}{2}$% of $96.20

16. $\frac{1}{2}$% of $16.40

17. 54% of $18.94

18. 14% of 43 lb

19. 48% of $73.15

20. 86% of 16 gal

21. $3\frac{1}{2}$% of 3852

CHECKING ACCOUNTS

Many local banks have literature available concerning checking accounts.

Compared with 1900, more people today trust banks with their money. Banks, in turn, offer many more services for their customers.

To use checks, you first deposit money into a checking account. Then you can make payments by writing checks. Most businesses accept checks as well as cash. They send your check to a bank to get the money. Your bank subtracts the amount of each check from your account.

Amount in words   Payee   Date the check was written   Check number

Eleanor Abernathy
3409 Freeland Rd
Millers, MD 21067

August 18 1983

2008

53-242
113

Federal Reserve number

Pay to the Order of *Princeton Cycle Shop* $ 98.18

Amount in numbers

Ninety-eight and 18/100 ———————— Dollars

Signature

BANKERS TRUST COMPANY
Millers, MD

Amount the bank paid

MEMO *10-speed bike*   *Eleanor Abernathy*

⑆011302425⑆ ⑆025 1299 8⑆   ⑈0000009818⑈

Eleanor's account number

CONSUMER HINTS

Through the use of computers, checks and deposits can be recorded on the same day as the transaction.

1. Write the correct date. Never date ahead.

2. Do not leave the payee blank. Always fill in a name.

3. Start at the left. Do not leave a space after the dollar sign.

4. Carefully write the amount in words. Fill the entire space.

5. Never sign checks before filling all the other blanks.

When the amount written in words does not agree with the amount in numbers, the bank will pay the amount written in words.

MARTIN ROSEN
2327 Main Street
West Valley, IN 47331

300

Oct 15 19 *83*

90–8074
3211

Pay to the Order of *The Pet Shop* $ 17 39/100

Seven and 39/100 Dollars

WEST VALLEY SAVINGS
West Valley, IN.

FOR *bird cage*

Martin Rosen

1: 3211807481: 0300   060'''061843'''

EXAMPLE 1.   How much did the bank pay The Pet Shop?

The bank paid The Pet Shop $7.39.

---

1. How much did the bank pay the Spinning Record store?
$14.87

TRY THIS

FRED SANDBORN
338 17th Street
Albany, ME 27103

332   11-35/1210

Oct. 31   19 *83*

PAY TO THE ORDER OF *Spinning Record Co.* $ 4.87

Fourteen and 87/100 DOLLARS

BANK OF MAINE

Fred Sandborn

1: 1210003521: 0332'''11806'''08778'''

Eleanor wants to withdraw some money from her checking account.
To do so she can make the check payable either to herself or cash.

EXAMPLE 2. How does Eleanor write a check so she can withdraw $ 20?

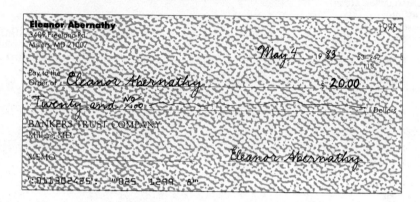

2. What does this check tell the bank to do?
Give Eleanor $14.00 in cash.

TRY THIS

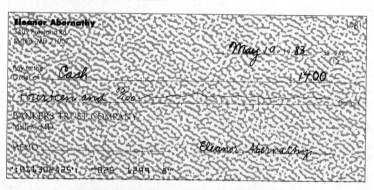

A *running balance* is a continuous record of how much is in your account. Eleanor keeps a running balance on the *check stubs* attached to her checks. Here is an example.

Date 8-18 19 83 98.18		
To Princeton Cycle Shop		
For 10-speed bike		
Balance Forward	Dollars	Cents
	782	33
Amount of Deposit	105	16
Total		
Amount of Check	98	18
Balance Carried Forward		

This check is for $ 98.18.

$ 782.33 is in the account.

Add to find the total.

Subtract to find the balance. Write this amount at the top of the next check stub.

EXAMPLE 3.   Find the balance carried forward for the previous check.

PLAN: **Step 1.**   Add the amount of the deposit to the balance forward to find the total.

$$\begin{array}{r} \$\ 782.33 \\ +\ 105.16 \\ \hline \$\ 887.49 \end{array}$$

Step 2.   Subtract the amount of the check from the total.

$$\begin{array}{r} \$\ 887.49 \\ -\ 98.18 \\ \hline \$\ 789.31 \end{array}$$

The balance carried forward is $ 789.31.

TRY THIS

3. The balance after check number 2008 is $ 789.31. Eleanor then deposits $ 105.16 and writes a check for $ 74.22. Find the balance carried forward. **$820.25**

Julie Rice prefers to use a *check register* to record her checks and deposits. It is a booklet separate from the checks. It usually fits into the checkbook.

Sample check registers often can be obtained from your local bank.

Number	Date	Description	Payment/Debit (−)	T	Fee (If any) (−)	Deposit/Credit (+)		Balance $345.54	
230	1-16	NORTHERN ACCEPTANCE	$ 83.19		$	$		262	35
	1-19	deposit				235	00	497	35
231	2-8	Nick's Sporting Goods	46.26						

RECORD ALL CHARGES OR CREDITS THAT AFFECT YOUR ACCOUNT

EXAMPLE 4.   Find Julie's balance after she writes check number 231. Subtract the amount of this check from the previous balance.

$$\begin{array}{r} \$\ 497.35 \\ -\ 46.26 \\ \hline \$\ 451.09 \end{array}$$

The balance is $ 451.09.

TRY THIS

4. The balance after check number 231 is $ 451.09. Julie then deposits $ 116.74 and writes check number 232 for $ 58.29. Find the new balance. **$509.54**

EXERCISES

Give the account number, the payee, and the amount the bank
will pay.

1.

MARY COLINS
47 Beach Drive
Deerfield FL 87032

296

Aug. 27 19 83

90–8074
8211

Pay to the
Order of Aurora Federal Savings $ 325.92

Three hundred twenty and 92/100 —————— Dollars

Florida Savings & Loan
Deerfield, Florida

For mortgage payment   Mary Colins

':821120748':0296   060'''021848'''

060 021848, Aurora Federal Savings, $325.92

2.

JOHN JACKSON
Box 4983
Fargo, TX 55515

336   11-35/1810

9/15 19 83

Pay to the Order of Now Sounds $259.63

Two hundred fifty nine and 63/100 ———— Dollars

CATTLEMEN'S TRUST CO.
Fargo, Texas

John Jackson

':181000358':0336'''11306'''08771'''

11306 08771, Now Sounds, $259.63

3.

SUSAN LARKIN
54 Apple Lane
Northridge, VT 05046

297

March 10 19 83

90–8074
7211

Pay to the
Order of Cash $ 14.87

Fourteen and 87/100 ————————— Dollars

FIRST BANK OF VERMONT

for _____   Susan Larkin

':721180748':0297   060'''061848'''

060 061848, Susan Larkin, $14.87

4.

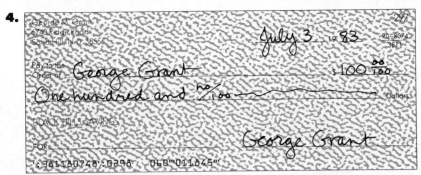

George M. Grant
8740 Ridge Road
Sand Hill, N.D. 58555

297

July 3 19 83

90-8074
3811

Pay to the
Order of George Grant $ 100 $\frac{00}{100}$

One hundred and $\frac{no}{100}$ Dollars

BLACK HILLS SAVINGS

FOR   George Grant

⑆381180748⑆ 0298   060⑈011845⑈

060 011845, George Grant, $100

Find the new balance on these check stubs.

5.

Date _____ 19 _____		
To _____		
For _____		
Balance Forward	Dollars	Cents
	825	44
Amount of Deposit		
Total	825	44
Amount of Check	325	92
Balance Carried Forward	499	52

6.

Date _____ 19 _____		
To _____		
For _____		
Balance Forward	Dollars	Cents
	658	23
Amount of Deposit		
Total	658	23
Amount of Check	187	16
Balance Carried Forward	471	07

Complete the running balance.

7.

		RECORD ALL CHARGES OR CREDITS THAT AFFECT YOUR ACCOUNT						
Number	Date	Description	Payment/Debt (−)	T	Fee (If any) (−)	Deposit/Credit (+)	Balance $85.24	
625	4-14	IRS FOR TAXES	$ 38.00		$	$	47	24
	4-17	DEPOSIT				185 —	232	24
626	4-20	DR. CASSIDY FOR CHECK-UP	40.00				192	24
627	4-27	ANDY'S AUTO REPAIR	79.18				113	06
628	4-30	ABC DEPT. STORE	58.25				54	81

ON YOUR OWN

8. Visit some local banks. Find out about different types of checking accounts. Be sure to ask about minimum balance check fees and service charges. Try to get some samples of checks, deposit slips, check stubs, and check register pages.

RECONCILING CHECKING ACCOUNTS

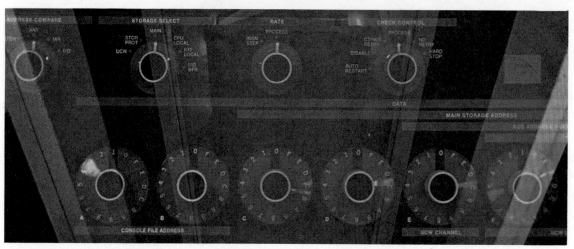

Computerized equipment makes it possible for banks to keep every customer's account up-to-date.

Each month the bank sends you information about your account. You should compare this *bank statement* with your own records to be sure they agree. This process is called *reconciling* your account.

BANKERS TRUST COMPANY
Millers, Maryland

Eleanor Abernathy
3409 Freeland Road
Millers, MD 21107

ALL ITEMS ARE RECEIVED BY THIS BANK FOR PURPOSES OF COLLECTION. ALL CREDITS FOR ITEMS ARE PROVISIONAL

ACCOUNT NUMBER	DISP CODE	PERIOD ENDING	NUMBER OF ENCLOSURES	PAGE
025-1299-8		10-02-82	5	1

Balance this statement

PREVIOUS BALANCE	CHECKS AND OTHER DEBITS NUMBER	AMOUNT	+ DEPOSITS AND OTHER CREDITS NUMBER	AMOUNT	− SERVICE CHARGE	= NEW BALANCE
426 92	5	255 92	2	405 81	4 50	572 31

Balance last statement

Service charge

The total checks shown on this statement

CHECKS AND OTHER DEBITS		CREDITS	DATE	BALANCE
		195 17	9 10	622 09
16	15		9 11	605 94
28	34		9 12	577 60
95	10		9 14	482 50
104	17		9 16	378 33
		210 64	9 21	588 97
12	16		9 24	576 81
4	50		10 02	572 31

1. Put the cancelled checks in numerical order.
2. Match the checks with your stubs or register.
3. List the checks entered in your register that have not been cancelled.
4. List the deposits that are not shown on the statement.
5. List any service charges, such as the cost of new checks.

Most banks send you a form to help reconcile your account. Eleanor Abernathy completes the form as follows. A deposit of $95.00 is not shown.

Checks Not Shown on Statement			
Number	Dollars	Cents	
516	14	82	Bank balance on statement $ 572.31
517	73	06	Add deposits not shown 95.00
525	8	29	TOTAL _____
			Subtract checks not shown _____
			BALANCE $ _____
TOTAL			(check stub or register)

EXAMPLE.　　Reconcile this account.

PLAN:　**Step 1.** Find the total after the deposit is added to the bank balance shown on the statement.

$572.31 + $95 = $667.31

Step 2. Find the total of the checks not shown on the statement.

$14.82 + $73.06 + $8.29 = $96.17

Step 3. Subtract the checks outstanding from the bank balance plus the deposit.

$667.31 − $96.17 = $571.14

Step 4. Compare the bank balance with that shown on the check stub or register.

Eleanor's next check stub shows a balance of $571.14.

The account is reconciled.

AMERICAN BANK

STATEMENT OF ACCOUNT

ACCOUNT NUMBER	STATEMENT PERIOD ENDING	PAGE
64822-1057	JUNE 5, 1982	1

AMERICAN BANK & TRUST

100 MAIN STREET

WABASH, TEXAS 75306

BRENDA HOLMES EVANS

38 Lomas Drive

Wabash, TX 75302

STATEMENT TOTALS

BEGINNING BALANCE	NO. OF CHECKS	NO. OF DEBITS	TOTAL DEBIT AMOUNT	NO. OF CREDITS	TOTAL CREDIT AMOUNT	SERVICE CHARGE	ENDING BALANCE
745.30	12		$501.62	1	100.00	1.50	342.18

Please examine your statement and items promptly. The bank shall not be liable for unauthorized signatures or alterations if not reported to bank within 15 days of receipt.

1. Reconcile the above account. Your checkbook shows a balance of $ 383.17. One deposit of $ 84.75 is not shown, and there are checks totaling $ 45.26 outstanding.

TRY THIS

Bank balance on statement	$ 342.18
Add deposits not shown	84.75
TOTAL	
Subtract checks not shown	45.26
BALANCE $	

EXERCISES

Reconcile these statements. Tell whether each account is reconciled.

	Bank Balance	Deposits Not Shown By Bank	Total Checks Not Shown On Statement	Your Checkbook Balance
1.	$627.13	$114.09	$84.26	$656.96
2.	$122.49	$63.58	$23.97	$163.10
3.	$816.08	$225.95	$422.34	$619.79
4.	$23.59	$75.00	$62.19	$36.40
5.	$508.02	$138.19	$159.27	$487.94
6.	$1408.79	$500.00	$648.22	$900.57

Reconcile the following accounts.

7. Beverly has two deposits not shown by the bank: $103.72 and $42.76. She has three checks not shown: $12.05, $21.45, and $8.43. The bank balance on the statement is $332.61 and Beverly's check register balance is $437.16. $437.16 reconciled

8. William has three deposits not shown by the bank: $1040.28, $14.37, and $82.01. All his checks are shown. The bank balance on his statement is $4.12. William's check register balance is $1151.78. $1140.78 not reconciled

ON YOUR OWN

9. Obtain forms for reconciling checking accounts from several banks. Compare them to the form shown in this book.

10. Find out what a bank does if a checking account is overdrawn.

CALCULATING INTEREST

You may wish to obtain current compound interest tables from your local bank.

At many colleges, low-interest loans help students meet expenses.
Some loans need not be repaid until after graduation.

Interest is money paid for the use of money. If you borrow money, you pay interest to the lender. If you put money in a savings account, you receive interest from the bank.

The formula used to calculate *simple interest* is

Interest = Principal $\times$ rate $\times$ time, or $I = Prt$.

I stands for the amount of interest.
P stands for the amount borrowed or in the savings account.
r stands for the rate given as a percent.
t stands for the length of time given in years.

EXAMPLE 1. Find the simple interest on $ 1000 invested for two years at a rate of 6%.

PLAN: **Step 1.** Identify $P, r,$ and t.
$P = \$ 1000, r = 0.06, t = 2$

Step 2. Use the formula to find the interest.
$I = Prt$
$\quad = \$ 1000 \times 0.06 \times 2$
$\quad = \$ 1000 \times 0.12$
$\quad = \$ 120$

EXAMPLE 2. Wade put $250 in a savings account for six months at a rate of $8\frac{1}{2}\%$. Find the simple interest.

PLAN: **Step 1.** Change the rate to decimal form.

$$8\frac{1}{2}\% = 0.085$$

Step 2. Rewrite the time in years.

$$6 \text{ months} = \frac{1}{2} \text{ year}$$

Step 3. Use the formula to find the interest.

$$I = Prt$$
$$= \$250 \times 0.085 \times \frac{1}{2}$$
$$= \$250 \times 0.0425$$
$$= \$10.625 \approx \$10.63 \text{ interest}$$

TRY THIS

1. Ludwig kept $200 in a savings account at 8% for two years. Find the simple interest. $32
2. Margo borrowed $300 from a friend at $9\frac{1}{2}\%$ for one year. Find the simple interest. $28.50

When interest on the principal is entered into your account, it also earns interest. This interest on your interest is called *compound interest*. Interest can be *compounded* annually (once a year), semiannually (twice a year), quarterly (four times a year), or daily.

EXAMPLE 3. Hector Perez has $300 in a savings account at a rate of 7% compounded semiannually. Find the amount in his account after one year.

PLAN: **Step 1.** Find the interest after the first payment period. Since interest is compounded semiannually, then $t = \frac{1}{2}$ year.

$$I = Prt$$
$$= \$300 \times 7\% \times \frac{1}{2}$$
$$= \$300 \times 0.07 \times \frac{1}{2}$$
$$= \$10.50$$

Step 2. This interest is added to the principal. Find the new principal.

$300 + \$10.50 = \$310.50$

Step 3. Find the interest after the second payment period. $t = \frac{1}{2}$

$$I = Prt$$

$$= \$310.50 \times 7\% \times \frac{1}{2}$$

$$= \$310.50 \times 0.07 \times \frac{1}{2}$$

$$= \$10.87$$

For table below:

One dollar at 2% interest compounded for 16 periods becomes $1.3728. The formula used is $T = (1 + i)^n$ where T is the interest plus principal, i is the percent of interest (written as a decimal), and n is the number of periods.
$1.3728 = (1 + 0.02)^{16}$.

Step 4. Add this interest to the principal to find the total principal after one year.

$$P = \$310.50 + \$10.87 = \$321.37$$

TRY THIS

3. Gina Cruz deposits $450 in a savings account at a rate of $7\frac{1}{2}\%$ compounded semiannually. Find the amount in her account after one year. **$484.38**

Compound interest tables can make your work easier.

No. of Periods	2%	2.5%	3%	3.5%	4%	4.5%	5%	6%	7%	8%	9%	10%
1	1.0200	1.0250	1.0300	1.0350	1.0400	1.0450	1.0500	1.0600	1.0700	1.0800	1.0900	1.1000
6	1.1262	1.1597	1.1941	1.2293	1.2653	1.3023	1.3401	1.4186	1.5007	1.5869	1.6771	1.7716
7	1.1487	1.1887	1.2299	1.2723	1.3159	1.3609	1.4071	1.5036	1.6058	1.7138	1.8280	1.9487
8	1.1717	1.2184	1.2668	1.3168	1.3686	1.4221	1.4775	1.5938	1.7182	1.8059	1.9926	2.1436
9	1.1951	1.2489	1.3048	1.3629	1.4233	1.4861	1.5513	1.6895	1.8385	1.9990	2.1719	2.3579
10	1.2190	1.2801	1.3439	1.4106	1.4802	1.5530	1.6289	1.7908	1.9672	2.1589	2.3674	2.5937
11	1.2434	1.3121	1.3842	1.4600	1.5395	1.6229	1.7103	1.8983	2.1049	2.3316	2.5804	2.8531
12	1.2682	1.3449	1.4258	1.5111	1.6010	1.6959	1.7959	2.0122	2.2522	2.5182	2.8127	3.1384
13	1.2936	1.3785	1.4685	1.5640	1.6651	1.7722	1.8856	2.1329	2.4098	2.7196	3.0658	3.4523
14	1.3195	1.4130	1.5126	1.6187	1.7317	1.8519	1.9799	2.2609	2.5785	2.9372	3.3417	3.7975
15	1.3459	1.4483	1.5580	1.6753	1.8009	1.9353	2.0789	2.3966	2.7590	3.1722	3.6425	4.1772
16	1.3728	1.4845	1.6047	1.7340	1.8730	2.0224	2.1829	2.5404	2.9522	3.4259	3.9703	4.5950
17	1.4002	1.5216	1.6528	1.7947	1.9479	2.1134	2.2920	2.6928	3.1588	3.7000	4.3276	5.0545
18	1.4282	1.5597	1.7024	1.8575	2.0258	2.2085	2.4066	2.8543	3.3799	3.9960	4.7171	5.5599
19	1.4568	1.5987	1.7535	1.9225	2.1068	2.3079	2.5270	3.0256	3.6165	4.3157	5.1417	6.1159
20	1.4859	1.6386	1.8061	1.9898	2.1911	2.4117	2.6533	3.2071	3.8697	4.6610	5.6044	6.7275

Compound Interest Table

EXAMPLE 4. $ 100 is invested at a rate of 4% per period compounded for 12 periods. Find the new principal after 12 periods.

PLAN: **Step 1.**   Find the entry on the 12-period row and the 4% column. $ 1.6010 per dollar of investment.

Step 2.   Multiply the principal by the entry to find the new principal.
$ 100 × 1.6010 = $ 160.10

$ 160.10 is the new principal.

EXAMPLE 5. $ 600 is invested at an annual rate of 8% compounded quarterly for five years. Find the new principal after five years.

PLAN: **Step 1.**   Find the total number of periods. Multiply the number of periods per year by the number of years.
4 periods per year × 5 years = 20 periods

Step 2.   Find the rate per period. Divide the annual rate by the number of times the interest is compounded in one year.
8% per year ÷ 4 periods per year = 2% per period

Step 3.   Find the entry on the 20-period row and the 2% column. $ 1.4859 per dollar of investment

Step 4.   Multiply the principal by the entry to find the new principal.
$ 600 × $ 1.4859 = $ 891.54

$ 891.54 is the new principal.

Example 5 shows that $ 600 grew to $ 891.54 in five years at a rate of 8% interest compounded quarterly. At a rate of 8% simple interest $ 600 would grow to only $ 840.

TRY THIS

Find the new principal. Use the table on page 84.
4. $ 500 at 6% per period compounded for 10 periods $895.40
5. $ 720 at 3.5% per period compounded for 17 periods $1292.18
6. $ 350 at 10% for five years compounded quarterly $573.51
7. $ 525 at 8% for six years compounded semiannually $840.53
8. $ 1750 at 7% per period compounded for 14 periods $4512.38
9. $ 2365 at 9% per period compounded for 11 periods $6102.65
10. $ 5420 at 16% for 10 years compounded semiannually $25,262.62

EXERCISES

Find the simple interest.

1. $P = \$300$, $r = 6\%$, $t = 2$ years $36

2. $P = \$875$, $r = 6\frac{1}{2}\%$, $t = 1$ year $56.88

3. $P = \$1000$, $r = 8\%$, $t = 3$ years $240

4. $P = \$425$, $r = 7\frac{1}{2}\%$, $t = 6$ months $15.94

5. $P = \$710$, $r = 7\%$, $t = 9$ months $37.28

6. $P = \$55$, $r = 6\frac{1}{4}\%$, $t = 2\frac{1}{2}$ years $8.59

7. $P = \$920$, $r = 7\frac{1}{4}\%$, $t = 3$ years $200.10

8. $P = \$2500$, $r = 8.5\%$, $t = 5$ years $1062.50

9. $P = 25$, $r = 6.5\%$, $t = 8$ years $13

10. $P = \$1625$, $r = 8.2\%$, $t = 6\frac{1}{2}$ years $866.13

Find the compound interest. Use the table on page 84.

11. $500 at 7% per period for 9 periods $919.25

12. $250 at 8% per period for 6 periods $396.73

13. $320 at 6% per period for 8 periods $510.02

14. $470 at 9% per period for 10 periods $1112.68

15. $1200 at 10% for 5 years compounded quarterly $1966.32

16. $650 at 7% for 4 years compounded semiannually $855.92

17. $45 at 8% for 12 years compounded annually $113.32

DECISION

18. Which is better: investing $500 at 8% for five years compounded quarterly or at 10% for two years compounded semiannually?

MENTAL CALCULATION

MULTIPLICATION BY 10, 100, 1000; 5, 50, 500

To multiply by 10, 100, 1000, count the number of zeros. Then move the decimal point that number of places to the right.

EXAMPLES

1. Multiply 10 × $3.29.

$$1\underline{0} \times 3.2\,9 = \$32.90$$

2. Multiply 100 × 7.8.

$$1\underline{0\,0} \times 7.8\,0 = 780$$

3. Multiply 1000 × 6.258.

$$1\underline{0\,0\,0} \times 6.2\,5\,8 = 6258$$

To multiply by 5, 50, or 500, multiply by 10, 100, or 1000, respectively, and then take half of that result.

EXAMPLE

4. Multiply 500 × 87.

Multiply by 1000. $1000 \times 87 = 87,000$
Take half. $87,000 \div 2 = 40,000 + 3500$
$= 43,500$

$$500 \times 87 = 43,500$$

PRACTICE

Multiply mentally.

1. 10 × 7.23 _72.3_   **2.** 10 × 0.83 _8.3_   **3.** 10 × 8.423 _84.23_   **4.** 10 × 56.42 _564.2_

5. 100 × 39.56 _3956_   **6.** 100 × 8.142 _814.2_   **7.** 100 × 7.3 _730_   **8.** 1000 × 46.2 _46,200_

9. 1000 × 718.03 _718,030_   **10.** 5 × 18 _90_   **11.** 5 × 26 _130_   **12.** 5 × 34 _170_

13. 5 × 234 _1170_   **14.** 50 × 78 _3900_   **15.** 50 × 63 _3150_   **16.** 50 × 143 _7150_

BORROWING MONEY

Many local banks have literature available concerning secured loans.

Wheat farmers run small businesses. Income from the crop must support the family for a year and repay the bank loan.

Frank Campbell is a grain farmer. He grows oats, wheat, and barley. To plant each new crop, Frank must buy seed and fertilizer. He usually borrows money to pay for these supplies.

At the bank Frank gets a *secured* loan. This is a loan for which something valuable is used to guarantee that he will repay the loan. He may use his land or machinery in this way as "security" for the bank. If he does not repay the loan, then he may lose his land or machinery.

EXAMPLE 1. Frank borrows $ 12,000 at 16.5% interest. He agrees to repay the loan in three years. How much money must he repay?

PLAN: **Step 1.** Find the interest.

$I = Prt$
$= \$ 12,000 \times 0.165 \times 3 \text{ years}$
$= \$ 5940$

Step 2. Find the total to be repaid.

$\$ 12,000 + \$ 5940 = \$ 17,940$

1. Yolanda Gonzalez obtains a secured loan of $8000 for repairs to her restaurant. She agrees to pay 14.25% interest and to repay the loan in $2\frac{1}{2}$ years. How much money must she repay? **$10,850**

Jim Murphy needs to borrow $1800 for some house improvements. His credit references are good, so he finds that he can get a personal loan by signing a *promissory note*. No security is required.

Sample promissory notes can be obtained from banks and savings and loan associations.

Length of loan

The lender

$ 1800.00   Westminster, MD   May 5, 19 82

90 days *after date, for value received,* I

promise to pay to   Vermont Federal Bank *, or order,*

at Vermont Federal Bank

the sum of ***One Thousand eight hundred********* *dollars* — Principal

in lawful money of the United States of America, with interest thereon, — Rate of interest

payable in like lawful money, at the rate of 18% *per cent*

per year *from date until paid.*

Jim Murphy — Signature

No. 5629 *Due* August 5, 1982 — Due date

EXAMPLE 2. How much will Jim Murphy have to repay the bank?

90 days = 3 months = $\frac{1}{4}$ year

$$I = Prt$$
$$= \$1800 \times 18\% \times \frac{1}{4}$$
$$= \$1800 \times 0.18 \times \frac{1}{4}$$
$$= \$81$$

Jim must repay $1800 plus $81, or $1881.

EXAMPLE 3. To qualify for a loan, Hilda Schmidt needs a *cosigner*. A cosigner is a person who agrees to pay the loan if Hilda defaults. Hilda borrows $600 from the National Loan Company. She agrees to repay the loan in nine months. The interest rate is 22%. How much money must Hilda repay?

$$I = Prt$$

$$= \$600 \times 22\% \times 9 \text{ months}$$

$$= \$600 \times 0.22 \times \frac{3}{4} \text{ year}$$

$$= \$99$$

Hilda will repay $600 plus $99, or $699.

TRY THIS

2. Sherman Jones borrows $675 from the Regal Loan Company. He agrees to repay the loan in 15 months. The interest rate is 23%. How much money must Sherman repay? $869.06

EXERCISES

For each of the following secured loans, tell how much money must be repaid.

	Principal	Rate	Time	
1.	$14,000	16.5%	2 years	$18,620
2.	$23,000	14%	$1\frac{1}{2}$ years	$27,830
3.	$2500	15.25%	9 months	$2785.94
4.	$7500	16.75%	$2\frac{1}{2}$ years	$10,640.63
5.	$12,750	18%	3 years	$19,635
6.	$15,000	17.5%	4 years	$25,500

7. Sharon Clark obtains a secured loan of $7500 to buy a car. She agrees to pay 15% interest and to repay the loan in three years. How much money must she repay? $10,875

8. Mitch Simpson borrows $2200 at 16% interest to buy a motorcycle. He agrees to repay the loan in two years. How much money must he repay? **$2904**

Tell how much money must be repaid on the following promissory notes.

9. $893

$ 800.00   July 17 , 19 82

9 months *after date, for value received.* I *promise to pay to*

First National Bank , *or order,*

at First National Bank, 497 Market St., Lexington, KY

the sum of ***** Eight Hundred **************** *dollars*

in lawful money of the United States of America, with interest thereon,

payable in like lawful money, at the rate of 15 1/2% *per cent*

per year *from date until paid.*

Mary Anne Wilkerson

No. 5627 *Due* April 17, 1983

10. $1456

$ 1200.00   January 7 , 19 83

1 year 4 months *after date, for value received.* I *promise to pay to*

FIRST FEDERAL BANK , *or order,*

at FIRST FEDERAL BANK, 2202 East 12th Street, Chico, CA.

the sum of ***** Twelve hundred **************** *dollars*

in lawful money of the United States of America, with interest thereon,

payable in like lawful money, at the rate of 16% *per cent*

per year *from date until paid.*

David R. Smith

No. 8356 *Due* May 7, 1984

Tell how much must be repaid on the following loans.

	Principal	Rate	Time	
11.	$500	22.5%	18 months	$668.75
12.	$750	23%	1 year	$922.50
13.	$1250	22.75%	2 years	$1818.75
14.	$650	23.25%	$1\frac{1}{2}$ years	$876.69
15.	$350	21%	9 months	$405.13

CREDIT CARD CHARGES

Develop this lesson carefully. Since the information on a credit card statement is complex, there are many opportunities for confusion. Some actual samples of credit card statements would be helpful in presenting this lesson.

With a credit card you can buy your bicycle now, and pay for it over several months without opening a charge account at the bicycle shop.

Clifford Wilcox uses a credit card for shopping expenses. When he buys something using the card, he simply signs his name. Then, each month the credit card company sends him a *statement* telling how much he owes.

Many local banks have literature available concerning credit cards.

If Clifford pays the full amount each month, there is no finance charge. If he pays less than the full amount, then he must pay a finance charge the next month on the remaining balance. This charge is $1\frac{1}{2}\%$ per month for the first $500. For any amount over $500, the finance charge is 1%.

EXAMPLE 1. Last month Clifford's credit card balance was $96.30. He paid $25 on this balance. This month he charged $38.29. How much is the finance charge? What is the new balance?

PLAN: **Step 1.** Subtract to find the amount still owed.

$$\$96.30 - \$25.00 = \$71.30$$

Step 2. Multiply to find the finance charge.
Round to the nearest cent.

$$1\tfrac{1}{2}\% \times \$71.30 = 0.015 \times \$71.30$$
$$= \$1.0695 \approx \$1.07$$

The finance charge is $ 1.07.

Step 3. Add to find the new balance.

$$\$71.30 + \$1.07 + \$38.29 = \$110.96$$

The finance charge is $ 1.07 and the new balance is $ 110.96.

TRY THIS

1. Clifford decides to pay $ 51 on the balance of $ 110.96. The following month he charges $ 27.39. How much is the finance charge? What is the new balance? $0.91, $88.96

EXAMPLE 2. Last month Rhoda Goodman made a payment of $100 on her credit card statement of $ 796.68. This month she charged $ 43.97. The finance charge is $1\tfrac{1}{2}\%$ per month on the first $500. After $ 500 the finance charge is 1%. How much must Rhoda pay in finance charges? What is Rhoda's new balance?

PLAN:

Step 1. Subtract to find the amount still owed.

$$\$796.68 - \$100.00 = \$696.68$$

Step 2. Multiply to find the finance charge on the first $ 500.

$$1\tfrac{1}{2}\% \text{ of } \$500 = 0.015 \times \$500 = \$7.50$$

Step 3. Multiply to find the finance charge on the amount over $ 500.

$$1\% \text{ of } \$196.68 = 0.01 \times \$196.68$$
$$= \$1.9668 \approx \$1.97$$

Step 4. Add to find the total finance charge.

$$\$7.50 + \$1.97 = \$9.47$$

The finance charge is $ 9.47.

Step 5. Add to find the new balance.

$$\$696.68 + \$9.47 + \$43.97 = \$750.12$$

The finance charge is $ 9.47 and the new balance is $ 750.12.

TRY THIS

2. On this new balance of $750.12, Rhoda decides to pay $75. In the following month she charges $32.16. What finance charges must she pay? What is the new balance? $9.25, $716.53

Some credit card companies require a *minimum payment*. The amount is 5% of the unpaid balance rounded to the nearest dollar.

EXAMPLE 3.   The new balance on Guido Russo's credit card is $142.89. What is the minimum amount he must pay?

5% of $142.89 = 0.05 × $142.89 = $7.1445

Rounded to the nearest dollar, the minimum payment is $7.00.

TRY THIS

3. Janet Burke has a new balance on her credit card of $322.58. What is the minimum amount she must pay? $16.00

EXERCISES

For each of the following credit card accounts, the finance charge rate is $1\frac{1}{2}\%$ on the first $500 and 1% on charges over $500. The minimum payment is 5%. Find

a. the balance after payment.   **b.** the finance charge.

c. the new balance   **d.** the minimum payment on the new balance.

	Unpaid balance	Payment	Purchases	
1.	$215.62	$50.00	$62.15	a. $165.62 b. $2.48 c. $230.25 d. $12
2.	$320.19	$100.00	$114.62	a. $220.19 b. $3.30 c. $338.11 d. $17
3.	$53.90	$25.00	$312.63	a. $28.90 b. $0.43 c. $341.96 d. $17
4.	$584.90	$150.00	$226.00	a. $434.90 b. $6.52 c. $667.42 d. $33
5.	$88.16	$20.00	$113.63	a. $68.16 b. $1.02 c. $182.81 d. $9
6.	$1055.84	$500.00	$246.00	a. $555.84 b. $8.06 c. $809.90 d. $40
7.	$64.29	$10.00	$18.48	a. $54.29 b. $0.81 c. $73.58 d. $4
8.	$158.33	$25.00	$86.14	a. $133.33 b. $2.00 c. $221.47 d. $11
9.	$630.09	$250.00	$39.40	a. $380.09 b. $5.70 c. $425.19 d. $21
10.	$414.16	$180.00	$153.26	a. $234.16 b. $3.51 c. $390.93 d. $20
11.	$107.92	$85.00	$32.04	a. $22.92 b. $0.34 c. $55.30 d. $3
12.	$62.31	$20.00	$56.52	a. $42.31 b. $0.63 c. $99.46 d. $5

PROBLEM SOLVING HINTS

When you solve problems, keep these steps in mind.

1. Understand   What must I find?
What information is given?
What other information do I need?

2. Plan   Is an approximate answer sufficient?
Can I estimate the answer?
Should I restate the problem?
What operations are needed?

3. Carry Out   Did I calculate correctly?
Did I check my work?

4. Look Back   Is my answer close to my estimate?
Does the answer fit the problem?

EXAMPLE.   Green-Up Lawn Service will cut your grass once each week for $ 15.
Or, you can agree to a 3-month contract for $ 175 plus a billing charge
of $ 12. Which is less expensive?

Understand   I must compare two amounts of money. Since I know
that 3 months is 13 weeks, I have enough information.

Plan   I must multiply and then compare.
I estimate each method to be near $ 200.

Carry Out

$$
\begin{array}{ll}
\$\ 15 & \$\ 175 \\
\times\ 13 & +\ \ 12 \\
\hline
45 & \$\ 187 \quad \textit{less expensive} \\
\underline{15\ \ } & \\
\$\ 195 &
\end{array}
$$

Look Back   The answer is close to the estimate. It makes sense
in this problem.

HINT: Use carefully planned steps to get meaningful results from your
problem solving.

BUYING AND SELLING STOCKS

The actual names of some stocks used in this lesson are the following: Aero-Flo Dynamics (AeroFlo), Aegis Corporation (AegisCp), AZL Resources (AZL), Adobe Oil and Gas (AdobeO).

The elaborate artwork on these stock certificates prevents imitations from being made.

Anna Mendoza is a stockbroker. She explains that when you buy *stock* in a company, you buy a part of the company. Profits given to stockholders are called *dividends.* When you buy stock, you get a *certificate* like the ones above. If you want to buy some stock, Anna will buy it for you at a *stock exchange.* She earns a commission for her work.

Anna shows how to read the financial section of a newspaper dealing with stocks.

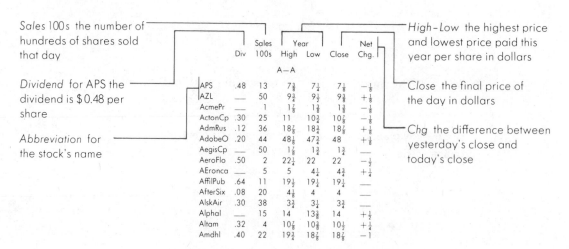

Sales 100s the number of hundreds of shares sold that day

Dividend for APS the dividend is $0.48 per share

Abbreviation for the stock's name

High-Low the highest price and lowest price paid this year per share in dollars

Close the final price of the day in dollars

Chg the difference between yesterday's close and today's close

	Div	Sales 100s	Year High	Low	Close	Net Chg.
A–A						
APS	.48	13	$7\frac{3}{8}$	$7\frac{1}{4}$	$7\frac{1}{4}$	$-\frac{1}{8}$
AZL	—	50	$9\frac{3}{4}$	$9\frac{1}{2}$	$9\frac{3}{4}$	$+\frac{1}{8}$
AcmePr	—	1	$1\frac{7}{8}$	$1\frac{3}{8}$	$1\frac{3}{8}$	$-\frac{1}{8}$
ActonCp	.30	25	11	$10\frac{3}{4}$	$10\frac{7}{8}$	$-\frac{1}{8}$
AdmRus	.12	36	$18\frac{7}{8}$	$18\frac{1}{2}$	$18\frac{7}{8}$	$+\frac{1}{8}$
AdobeO	.20	44	$48\frac{1}{8}$	$47\frac{3}{4}$	48	$+\frac{1}{8}$
AegisCp	—	50	$1\frac{7}{8}$	$1\frac{3}{4}$	$1\frac{3}{4}$	—
AeroFlo	.50	2	$22\frac{1}{4}$	22	22	$-\frac{1}{2}$
AEronca	—	5	5	$4\frac{1}{4}$	$4\frac{3}{4}$	$+\frac{1}{4}$
AffilPub	.64	11	$19\frac{1}{2}$	$19\frac{1}{4}$	$19\frac{1}{4}$	—
AfterSix	.08	20	$4\frac{1}{8}$	4	4	—
AlskAir	.30	38	$3\frac{3}{4}$	$3\frac{1}{4}$	$3\frac{3}{4}$	—
AlphaI	—	15	14	$13\frac{3}{8}$	14	$+\frac{1}{2}$
Altam	.32	4	$10\frac{7}{8}$	$10\frac{3}{8}$	$10\frac{1}{2}$	$+\frac{1}{4}$
Amdhl	.40	22	$19\frac{3}{4}$	$18\frac{7}{8}$	$18\frac{7}{8}$	-1

TRY THIS

1. What dividend is paid on AeroFlo? $0.50
2. How many hundreds of shares of AegisCp were sold? 50
3. What was the high cost per share of AZL? $9.75
4. What was the low cost per share of AfterSix? $4
5. What was the closing cost of AdobeO? $48

Anna explains that stock is bought and sold by the *share*. For instance, a stock listed at $14\frac{7}{8}$ costs $14.875 per share.

EXAMPLE 1. What is the cost of 200 shares of IBM at $52\frac{3}{8}$ per share? Multiply the cost per share by the number of shares.

$52\frac{3}{8} = \$52.375$ per share

$\$52.375 \times 200$ shares $= \$10,475$

200 shares of IBM cost $10,475.

TRY THIS

6. What is the cost of 150 shares of ATT at $53\frac{3}{4}$ per share? $8062.50

Anna's *rate of commission* depends on the number of shares bought or sold. Her rate of commission is higher for a smaller number of shares than for a larger number of shares.

EXAMPLE 2. Anna's commission on 20 shares of a stock at $15\frac{1}{4}$ per share is $25. The commission for 100 shares is $37.81. Find the rate of commission for each.

PLAN: **Step 1.** Multiply the cost per share by the number of shares to find the cost of the shares.

$15\frac{1}{4} = \$15.25$

$\$15.25 \times 20$ shares $= \$305$ $\quad$ $\$15.25 \times 100$ shares $= \$1525$

20 shares cost $305. $\qquad\qquad$ 100 shares cost $1525.

Step 2. Divide the commission by the cost of the shares to find the rate of commission for each.

$\frac{\$25}{\$305} \approx 0.082$ $\qquad\qquad\qquad$ $\frac{\$37.81}{\$1525} \approx 0.025$

$0.082 = 8.2\%$ $\qquad\qquad\qquad\qquad$ $0.025 = 2.5\%$

The rate for 20 shares is 8.2%   The rate for 100 shares is 2.5%.

7. Anna's commission on 50 shares of a stock at $16\frac{3}{4}$ per share is $27.19. The commission on 500 shares is $165.53. Find the rate of commission for each. **3.2%, 2.0%**

EXAMPLE 3. Find the total amount you must pay for 350 shares of SJuanR at $16\frac{1}{4}$ per share. The commission is $131.08.

PLAN: **Step 1.** Multiply the cost per share by the number of shares.

$$16\frac{1}{4} = \$16.25$$

$$\$16.25 \times 350 \text{ shares} = \$5687.50$$

Step 2. Add the commission to the cost of the shares to find the amount you must pay.

$$\$5687.50 + \$131.08 = \$5818.58$$

The total amount you must pay is $5818.58.

8. Find the total amount you must pay for 250 shares of PalmBc at $14\frac{3}{8}$ per share. The commission is $98.32. **$3692.07**

Anna Mendoza says annual dividends are paid by the share.
Multiply the dividend per share by the number of shares.

EXAMPLE 4. AffilPub pays an annual dividend of $0.64 per share. What dividend will be paid on 200 shares?

$0.64 \times 200 = \$128$

EXAMPLE 5. What dividend is paid on Alphal? Use the chart on page 96.
Alphal paid no dividend.

9. BlackDr pays an annual dividend of $0.72 per share. What dividend will be paid on 150 shares? **$108**

10. Use the chart on page 96. What dividend is paid by AlskAir? What would be the dividend on 125 shares? **$0.30,$37.50**

11. What dividend would be paid on 475 shares of Acme Pr? **none**

EXERCISES

	Div	Sales 100s	Year High	Low	Clos	Net Chg
			A—A			
ACF	2.50	203	$43\frac{1}{4}$	$27\frac{1}{2}$	$34\frac{1}{2}$	$+\frac{1}{8}$
AMF	1.24	100	$18\frac{1}{8}$	$11\frac{1}{2}$	$15\frac{1}{2}$	$-\frac{1}{8}$
AM Intl	.28	103	20	$12\frac{1}{2}$	$16\frac{1}{2}$	$-\frac{1}{4}$
APL	.50	44	$12\frac{1}{4}$	$7\frac{1}{2}$	10	—
ARA	1.82	242	$40\frac{1}{8}$	$24\frac{1}{2}$	$30\frac{1}{2}$	$-\frac{1}{2}$
ASA	.30	618	$54\frac{7}{8}$	$24\frac{3}{8}$	$53\frac{1}{8}$	$-\frac{3}{8}$
ATO	.60	79	$12\frac{3}{8}$	$8\frac{1}{8}$	$10\frac{1}{2}$	—
AVX	.32	143	$31\frac{3}{4}$	17	$26\frac{3}{4}$	-1
AbbtLb	1.20	253	$46\frac{1}{2}$	$32\frac{1}{2}$	$43\frac{3}{8}$	$-\frac{3}{8}$
AcmeC	1.40	123	$34\frac{1}{4}$	$18\frac{3}{4}$	$25\frac{1}{2}$	$+\frac{1}{8}$
AamDg	.04	17	$4\frac{7}{8}$	$2\frac{3}{4}$	$3\frac{3}{8}$	$-\frac{1}{4}$
AdaEx	1.49	34	$14\frac{1}{2}$	11	$13\frac{3}{8}$	$-\frac{1}{8}$
AdmMl	.20	45	$5\frac{3}{8}$	$3\frac{3}{8}$	$4\frac{3}{4}$	$+\frac{1}{2}$
AMD	—	689	$46\frac{3}{8}$	$26\frac{7}{8}$	$40\frac{3}{8}$	$+\frac{3}{4}$
AeinLf	2.12	1113	$39\frac{1}{2}$	$29\frac{1}{2}$	$38\frac{3}{8}$	$+\frac{3}{4}$
Ahmans	1.20	7	$28\frac{1}{2}$	15	$23\frac{1}{2}$	$-\frac{1}{8}$
Aileen	—	38	$3\frac{1}{4}$	2	3	$-\frac{1}{8}$
AirPrd	.80	197	$43\frac{1}{8}$	$27\frac{1}{2}$	$42\frac{3}{4}$	$+\frac{1}{4}$
AirbFrt	1.20	15	$28\frac{1}{4}$	$16\frac{1}{2}$	$17\frac{3}{4}$	$-\frac{1}{4}$
Akzona	.80	125	$17\frac{1}{2}$	$7\frac{3}{4}$	$10\frac{1}{8}$	$-\frac{1}{8}$

Give each answer in dollar amounts.

1. What was the closing cost of Akzona? $10.125

2. What dividend is paid by ARA? $1.82

3. How many hundreds of shares of Aileen were sold? 38

4. What was the high cost per share of AMIntl? $20

5. What dividend is paid by AcmeC? $1.40

6. What was the low cost per share of AVX? $17

Complete the chart using the given information.

	Shares	Cost Per Share	Cost of Shares	Commission	Rate of Commission	Total Cost
7.	100	$18\frac{7}{8}$	$1887.50	$ 43.41	2.3%	$1930.91
8.	150	$12\frac{1}{4}$	$1837.50	$58.80	3.2%	$1896.30
9.	25	$111\frac{1}{8}$	$2778.13	$ 55.84	2.0%	$2833.97
10.	75	$16\frac{1}{4}$	$1218.75	$32.91	2.7%	$1251.66
11.	350	$22\frac{3}{8}$	$7831.25	$164.46	2.1%	$7995.71
12.	225	$43\frac{1}{8}$	$9703.13	$174.66	1.8%	$9877.79

BUYING BONDS

The actual names of some bonds used in this Lesson are the following: Fairchild Industries Incorporated (Frch), First National State Bancorporation (FtNSt), First Federal Savings and Loan Association of Wisconsin (FtWis), First Federal Savings and Loan Association of Chicago (FstChi), First Security Corporation (FstSec.)

The floor of the stock exchange where stocks and bonds are bought and sold is often a scene of feverish activity.

Anna Mendoza also sells bonds. A *bond* issued by the government or a corporation is a promise to pay a certain amount of money, plus interest, at a certain time. When you buy a bond, you do not become part owner of a company. Instead, the government or corporation is borrowing money from you.

Each bond has a *par value,* an amount printed on the bond. Each also has a *maturity date,* such as 20 years in the future, when the par value will be paid to the holder. When you buy a bond, you pay the current *market price,* which may be less than the par value. Each bond earns interest based on the par value. This changes the market price each year. At *full maturity* the market price equals the par value. Since the maturity date may be several years in the future, many people sell their bonds at the current market price before they reach full maturity.

EXAMPLE 1. The Salisbury City Park is selling bonds at 86% of the $ 1000 par value. What is the market price?

86% of $ 1000 = 0.86 × $ 1000 = $ 860

The market price is $ 860.

EXAMPLE 2. The interest rate of the Salisbury City Park bonds is 4.25%. What is the annual interest paid?

4.25% of $ 1000 = 0.0425 × $ 1000 = $ 42.50

The annual interest paid is $ 42.50.

TRY THIS

1. A $ 1000 bond is selling at 79% of par value. What is the market price? $790

2. This bond pays 5.65% interest. What is the annual interest paid? $56.50

Each bond also has a *current yield*, the current rate of interest on the current market price. Since the market price is often less than the par value, the current yield may be greater than the quoted interest rate. At full maturity the current yield equals the quoted interest rate.

EXAMPLE 3. The market price of a $ 1000 bond paying 7.2% is $890. Find the current yield.

PLAN: **Step 1.** Multiply to find the annual interest paid.
0.072 × $ 1000 = $ 72

Step 2. Divide the annual interest by the market price to find the current yield.
$ 72 ÷ $ 890 ≈ 0.081 = 8.1%

The current yield is 8.1%. Note that the current yield exceeds the quoted interest rate.

TRY THIS

Find the current yield.

3. Par value $ 1000, interest rate 5.8%, market price $ 910 6.4%

4. Par value $ 5000, interest rate 9.6%, market price $ 4780 10%

The financial section of a newspaper often gives information about bonds.

Current Yield

Year of Maturity

Rate of Interest

Abbreviation for company's name

Bonds			Cur Yld	Vol	High	Low	Close	Net Chg
EasAir	4	3/493	cv	68	$54\frac{1}{2}$	54	54	$-\frac{1}{2}$
EasAir	14	1/299	cv	183	94	$93\frac{1}{2}$	94	—
ElPas	6	93	cv	11	140	139	140	+4
Exxon	6	97	9.7	46	$62\frac{1}{8}$	$61\frac{1}{4}$	$61\frac{3}{8}$	$-\frac{3}{8}$
Exxon	6	1/298	10.	75	64	$63\frac{7}{8}$	64	$+\frac{1}{8}$
ExxP	9	04	11.	20	$80\frac{1}{2}$	$78\frac{3}{4}$	$80\frac{1}{2}$	$-\frac{1}{4}$
ExxP	8.05	80	8.1	10	$99\frac{5}{8}$	$99\frac{5}{8}$	$99\frac{5}{8}$	
ExxP	8	7/800	11.	20	79	79	79	$+\frac{7}{8}$
ExxP	8	1/401	11.	10	75	75	75	+2
Frch	9	3/498	14.	10	$70\frac{1}{4}$	69	69	−2
Farah	5	94	cv	6	50	49	50	+1
Feddr	5	96	cv	10	$39\frac{1}{4}$	39	$39\frac{1}{4}$	$+\frac{1}{8}$
FedN	4	3/496	cv	1	79	79	79	−4
Filmwy	11	98	16.	19	$67\frac{1}{2}$	$67\frac{1}{2}$	$67\frac{1}{2}$	—
Firest	8	1/283	9.9	6	$86\frac{1}{2}$	86	86	−2
FstChi	7	3/486	9.7	19	$79\frac{1}{2}$	$79\frac{1}{2}$	$79\frac{1}{2}$	—
FtNSt	8	7/888	11.	10	80	80	80	−14
FtPenn	5	93	cv	4	46	45	45	$+\frac{3}{8}$
FstSec	10	99	10.	45	$99\frac{3}{4}$	$99\frac{1}{2}$	$99\frac{3}{4}$	$+\frac{3}{8}$
FtWis	8	1/296	12.	1	70	70	70	−1
FishF	6	1/294	cv	8	$60\frac{1}{8}$	$60\frac{1}{8}$	$60\frac{1}{8}$	$-\frac{1}{8}$

High-Low the highest and lowest price shown as the percent of par value

Close the final price of the day shown as the percent of par value

Chg the difference between yesterday's close and today's close

EXAMPLE 4. What is the year of maturity for Frch?

The year of maturity is 1998.

EXAMPLE 5. Suppose the par value of a FtNSt bond is $1000. How much interest does the bond pay per year?

PLAN: **Step 1.** Find the rate of interest.

The paper shows that the rate is $8\frac{7}{8}\%$.

Step 2. Multiply to find the interest.

$$8\frac{7}{8}\% \text{ of } \$1000 = 0.08875 \times \$1000$$

$$= \$88.75 \text{ per year}$$

EXAMPLE 6. Suppose the par value of FtWis is $ 1000. What is the market value?

The closing price is 70% of the par value. The market value is 70% of $ 1000, or $ 700.

EXAMPLE 7. What is the current yield on FstChi?

The current yield is 9.7%.

5. Suppose the par value of a FstSec bond is $ 1000. How much interest does the bond pay per year? $100

6. Suppose the par value of FishF is $ 1000. What is the market value? $60.13

EXERCISES

1. The Hanford County Government is selling bonds at 91% of the $ 1000 par value. What is the market price? $910

2. The interest rate on the Hanford County bonds is 6.25%. What is the annual interest paid? $62.50

Find the current yield.

	Par Value	Interest Rate	Market Price	
3.	$ 1000	6.3%	$ 860	7.3%
4.	$ 1000	8.5%	$ 770	11%
5.	$ 2000	$11\frac{1}{2}$%	$ 1005	22.9%
6.	$ 5000	$4\frac{1}{4}$%	$ 4300	4.9%
7.	$ 10,000	7.5%	$ 9650	7.8%
8.	$ 25	6.3%	$ 18	8.8%
9.	$ 50	7.2%	$ 30	12%
10.	$ 100	8.5%	$ 85	10%

11. What is the rate of interest for MohD? 5%

12. What is the year of maturity of MonyM? 1990

13. What is the current yield of Mobil? 11%

14. Suppose the par value of a MoPtC is $ 1000. How much interest does the bond pay per year? $100

15. Suppose the par value of NCNB is $ 1000. What is the market value? $725

Bonds			Cur Yld	Vol	High	Low	Close	Net Chg
MPac	4	1/405	9.7	1	44	44	44	—
MPac	5	45	—	46	$42\frac{1}{4}$	$42\frac{1}{4}$	$42\frac{1}{4}$	$+\frac{1}{4}$
MoPtc	10	97	13.	9	79	79	79	$-\frac{1}{2}$
Mobil	8	1/201	11.	72	75	$74\frac{3}{4}$	$74\frac{3}{4}$	$+\frac{5}{8}$
MohD	5	1/294	cv	2	$57\frac{1}{8}$	$57\frac{1}{8}$	$57\frac{1}{8}$	$+\frac{5}{8}$
MntWC	6	1/287	10.	5	64	64	64	$-7\frac{1}{4}$
MntWC	13	5/887	13.	34	$103\frac{1}{4}$	103	103	$+\frac{1}{2}$
MonyM	7	90	cv	20	85	85	85	$+1\frac{5}{8}$
Morgn	4	3/498	cv	62	$64\frac{1}{2}$	$63\frac{3}{4}$	$63\frac{3}{4}$	$-\frac{1}{4}$
Morgn	8	86	9.7	8	83	$82\frac{1}{2}$	$82\frac{1}{2}$	$-1\frac{1}{2}$
MtSTI	7	3/413	12.	26	67	66	66	$+\frac{5}{8}$
MtSTI	9	3/412	12.	15	82	82	82	$-\frac{5}{8}$
MtSTI	9	5/815	12.	7	81	81	81	$-\frac{1}{2}$
MtSTI	8.7	81	8.9	15	$97\frac{1}{2}$	$96\frac{3}{4}$	$97\frac{1}{2}$	$+\frac{3}{4}$
MtSTI	7	7/8	12.	5	$65\frac{7}{8}$	$65\frac{5}{8}$	$65\frac{5}{8}$	$+\frac{3}{4}$
MtSTI	8	5/818	12.	5	$72\frac{5}{8}$	$72\frac{5}{8}$	$72\frac{5}{8}$	$-1\frac{3}{8}$
NCNB	8.4	95	12.	23	$72\frac{1}{2}$	$72\frac{1}{2}$	$72\frac{1}{2}$	$+\frac{3}{8}$

CHAPTER REVIEW

1. Find the total deposit and the net deposit.

		Dollars	Cents
Cash	Currency	20	00
	Coin		
Checks	21-93	46	87
	Total	66	87
	Less Cash Received	12	00
	Net Deposit	54	87

2. Begin with a $612.96 passbook balance. Find the successive balances after each deposit or withdrawal.

a. Deposit of $18.16 **$631.12**
b. Withdrawal of $150.00 **$481.12**
c. Withdrawal of $86.00 **$395.12**
d. Deposit of $25.96 **$412.08**

3. Identify the account number, the payee, and the amount the bank will pay. **0277 523460, Cherie Rosen, $46.71**

Memo:	NORTH FLORIDA SAVINGS 11-24/277 1210(8) 200

March 17 19 82

Pay to the Order of _Cherie Rosen_ $ 36.$\frac{17}{100}$

Forty-six and $\frac{7}{100}$ _____ Dollars

David R. Smith

⑈121000 248⑈: 200   0277   523460⑈

4. Find the simple interest on a principal of $800 at 8% for 3 years. **$192**

5. Find the new principal after ten years. Use the table on page 84. **$10,955.50**
$P = \$5000, r = 8\%, t = 10$ years, compounded semiannually.

6. Find the balance carried forward on this check stub written in Exercise 3.

	Dollars	Cents
Date _3/17_ 19 _82_ To _Cherie Rosen_ For _sweater for Dad_		
Balance Forward	532	63
Amount of Deposit	50	25
Total	582	88
Amount of Check	46	71
Balance Carried Forward	536	17

7. Reconcile this account. Your checkbook shows a balance of $ 472.16; one deposit of $ 195.74 is not shown, and there are checks totaling $ 36.37 outstanding. **$789.40 not reconciled**

Checking Account Summary				
Balance Last Statement	Amount of Checks and Debits	Amount of Deposits and Credits	Service Charge	Balance This Statement
1383.95	1026.50	274.08	1.50	630.03

8. A secured loan of $ 12,500 was obtained at 14% interest for 2 years. How much must be paid back? **$16,000**

9. A credit card account has an unpaid balance of $ 354.97. A payment of $ 100 was made and additional purchases were $ 75.18. The finance charge is $1\frac{1}{2}$% and the minimum payment is 5%. Find a) the balance of the payment, b) the finance charge, c) the new balance, d) the minimum payment. **a) $254.97, b) $3.82, c) $333.97, d) $17.00**

10. Find the total cost of 150 shares of stock costing $12\frac{1}{2}$ per share. The commission is $ 56.22. **$1931.22**

11. The commission on 350 shares of stock costing $22\frac{3}{8}$ per share is $ 162.10. Find the rate of commission. **2.1%**

12. Find the current yield on a corporate bond with a par value of $ 1000, paying 8.4%, and having a market value of $ 890. **9.4%**

SKILLS REVIEW

SKILL 12 Rounding decimals and money

Round to the underlined place.

1. $4.92 $5   **2.** $15.81 $16   **3.** $1.769 $1.77   **4.** 46.35¢ 46.4¢

SKILLS 26 Reciprocals

Find the reciprocal.

5. $\frac{2}{3}$ $\frac{3}{2}$, or $1\frac{1}{2}$ **6.** $\frac{1}{4}$ 4   **7.** $\frac{6}{11}$ $\frac{11}{6}$, or $1\frac{5}{6}$ **8.** 15 $\frac{1}{15}$

SKILL 44 Converting percents to decimals

Convert to a decimal.

9. 16% 0.16   **10.** 97% 0.97   **11.** 5% 0.05   **12.** 1% 0.01

SKILL 15 Adding money

Add.

13. $ 10.68   **14.** $ 273.58   **15.** $ 4.93   **16.** $ 9.48
     +   8.43   + 356.92   0.29   7.04
       $19.11 $630.50   + 6.34   + 0.09
                                                  $11.56 $16.61

SKILL 19 Subtracting money

Subtract.

17. $ 48.36   **18.** $ 182.87   **19.** $ 50.05   **20.** $ 38.00
     − 19.28   −   94.38   − 27.86   − 17.59
      $29.08 $88.49 $22.19 $20.41

SKILL 20 Subtracting decimals

Subtract.

21.   8.6   **22.**   7.38   **23.**   6.071   **24.**   8.7
     − 1.9   − 1.29   − 4.268   − 1.93
      6.7   6.09   1.803   6.77

SKILL 21 Estimating differences: Whole numbers—decimals

Estimate the difference.

25.   4.7   **26.**   15.3   **27.**   27.6   **28.**   6.482
     − 3.87   − 6.1   − 19.4   − 1.39
       1   9   9   5

106

SKILL 23 Multiplying money

Multiply. Round to the nearest cent.

29. $89.47
$\times$ 8
$715.76

30. $8.76
$\times$ 60
$525.60

31. $46.50
$\times$ 75
$3487.50

32. $19.05
$\times$ 490
$9334.50

SKILL 27 Multiplying decimals

Multiply.

33. 374
$\times$ 0.4
149.6

34. 32.6
$\times$ 16
521.6

35. 8.76
$\times$ 5.3
46.428

36. 0.08
$\times$ 0.6
0.048

SKILL 51 Dividing money

Divide. Round to the nearest cent.

37. $\overset{\$0.19}{7)\overline{\$1.33}}$

38. $\overset{\$0.07}{5)\overline{\$0.35}}$

39. $\overset{\$1.50}{4)\overline{\$6}}$

40. $\overset{\$4}{38)\overline{\$178}}$

41. $\overset{\$0.43}{92)\overline{\$39.60}}$

42. $\overset{\$15.42}{28)\overline{\$431.66}}$

43. $\overset{\$10.58}{526)\overline{\$5565.08}}$

44. $\overset{\$300.10}{321)\overline{\$96,332.10}}$

SKILL 56 Dividing fractions

45. $\frac{3}{5} \div \frac{3}{4}$ $\frac{4}{5}$

46. $\frac{2}{3} \div \frac{3}{4}$ $\frac{8}{9}$

47. $\frac{3}{5} \div \frac{9}{4}$ $\frac{4}{15}$

48. $10 \div \frac{2}{3}$ 15

SKILL 57 Dividing: Mixed numbers

49. $6 \div 4\frac{1}{2}$ $1\frac{1}{3}$

50. $9 \div 2\frac{1}{4}$ 4

51. $4\frac{3}{4} \div 1\frac{1}{3}$ $3\frac{9}{16}$

52. $1\frac{7}{8} \div 1\frac{2}{3}$ $1\frac{1}{8}$

SKILL 67 Finding a percent of a number

Solve. Round to the nearest cent.

53. 97% of $500 is what number? $485 **54.** What is 49% of $7? $3.43

55. What is 1% of $73? $0.73 **56.** What is 128% of $150? $192

SKILL 48 Multiplying fractions and money

Multiply. Round to the nearest cent.

57. $27 \times \frac{2}{3}$ $18 **58.** $1.50 \times \frac{2}{5}$ $0.60 **59.** $10.50 \times 2\frac{1}{2}$ $26.25 **60.** $\frac{5}{8} \times \$15.85$ $9.91

61. $35 \times \frac{3}{5}$ $21 **62.** $20 \times 2\frac{1}{4}$ $45 **63.** $\frac{3}{8} \times \$49.28$ $18.48 **64.** $5\frac{1}{3} \times \$0.87$ $4.64

4
SPENDING
WISELY

BUDGETING

Everyone's budget must begin with a look at costs for housing, food, utilities, and transporation.

Lynn Barnes is a financial counselor. She helps people with their budget and investment problems. She liked business and economics courses in high school. After graduating she took other business courses to qualify for her work.

Explain to students that most budgets are done on a monthly basis.

A *budget* is a plan for managing your money. It is the key to spending wisely. Lynn Barnes prepares a budget for a family of four. Their *gross income* each month is $ 1562.

Remind students that gross income is income before deductions.

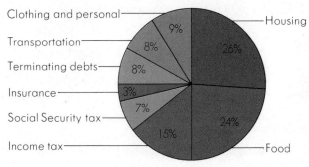

Clothing and personal
Transportation
Terminating debts
Insurance
Social Security tax
Income tax

Housing
9%
8%
8%
3%
7%
26%
24%
15%
Food

Terminating debts are debts that end. Car payments are an example.

EXAMPLE 1.   Find the amount for terminating debts.

PLAN: **Step 1.**   Change the percent to a decimal.
$$8\% = 0.08$$

Step 2.   Multiply the gross monthly income by the decimal.
$$\$1562 \times 0.08 = \$124.96$$

$124.96 is the amount for terminating debts.

TRY THIS

Find the amount for each item in Lynn's budget.

1. Insurance $46.86
2. Food $374.88
3. Housing $406.12
4. Taxes (Income + Social Security) $343.64

Lynn Barnes helps Leonard make his budget. He is single with a *net income* of $900 a month. Net income is income after taxes.

Expense	Amount	Percent
Rent and Utilities	$350.00	39%
Food	160.00	
Transportation	90.00	
Clothing	85.00	
Personal Expenses	55.00	
Savings	110.00	
Terminating debts	50.00	
Total	$900.00	100%

EXAMPLE 2.   Find the percent of income for rent and utilities.

$350 out of $900 $= \dfrac{\$350}{\$900}$.   *Find the fraction.*

$\$350 \div \$900 = 0.388 \approx 39\%$ *Divide and change to a percent.*

TRY THIS

Find the percent of Leonard's income for each budget item.

5. Food 18%
6. Transportation 10%
7. Savings 12%
8. Terminating debts 6%

EXERCISES

Find the amount for each budget item.

1. Housing $537.00

2. Food and clothing $483.30

3. Terminating debts $143.20

4. Transportation $107.40

5. Taxes $519.10

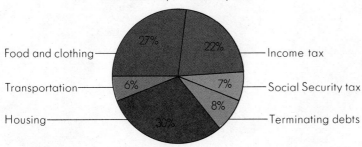

Jefferson Budget

Gross Monthly Income – $1790

Food and clothing — 27%

22% — Income tax

Transportation — 6%

7% — Social Security tax

8% — Terminating debts

Housing — 30%

Find the percent for each item.

	Expense	Amount	Percent
6.	Rent and utilities	$330.00	30%
7.	Food and clothing	$275.00	25%
8.	Transportation	$155.00	14%
9.	Savings	$90.00	8%
10.	Terminating debts	$100.00	9%
11.	Other	$150.00	14%
12.	Total	$1100.00	100%

ON YOUR OWN

13. List your total monthly income. List your typical monthly expenses. Make a budget for yourself.

Students should list income from all sources, i.e., allowances, jobs, etc. If none, they should make up some.

14. Find a pie chart of your local or federal government's budget. Which is the largest budget item? Which is the smallest? Which do you think is the most important?

SHOPPING FOR FOOD

Define impulse buying for students.

Delicatessens provide shoppers with prepared foods as well as products not available in supermarkets.

Andy Billings is an experienced shopper. He also reads consumer articles published by the government and the Better Business Bureau. He has these hints for you about food shopping.

1. Spend no more than you budget.
2. Plan weekly menus and make shopping lists.
3. Compare prices. Check ads.
4. Resist impulse buying.

Robin Silverstein has a net monthly income of $903. She budgets 25% for food.

EXAMPLE 1. How much of her monthly income should Robin spend per week for food?

PLAN: **Step 1.** Multiply to find the amount per month for food.

$0.25 \times \$903 = \$225.75$ *Use 0.25 for 25%.*

Step 2. Divide to find the weekly amount.

$\$225.75 \div 4.3 = \$52.50$ *Use 4.3 weeks in one month.*

Given the following incomes and percents for food, find the weekly amounts for food in these budgets. Use 4.3 weeks in one month.

1. $780 net monthly income, 22% $39.91
2. $1000 net monthly income, 27% $62.79
3. $850 net monthly income, 25% $49.41
4. $740 net monthly income, 28% $48.19
5. $930 net monthly income, 23% $49.74
6. $640 net monthly income, 32% $47.63

Robin makes a weekly shopping list. She reads the ads for weekly specials.

Item	Amount Needed	Regular Price	Sale Price	Cost
Eggs	1 dozen	$0.98 per dozen	$0.77 per dozen	$0.77
Milk	2 half gallons	0.93 per half gallon	none	
Bread	2 loaves	1.09 per loaf	none	
Cereal	2 boxes	0.75 per box	0.69 per box	
Butter	1 pound	1.22 per pound	none	
Hamburger	2 pounds	1.49 per pound	1.19 per pound	

EXAMPLE 2. Find Robin's cost for milk this week.

$\$0.93 \times 2 = \$1.86$ *Item price times amount needed*

$1.86 is Robin's cost for milk this week.

Find Robin's cost this week for each item.

7. Bread $2.18 **8.** Cereal $1.38
9. Butter $1.22 **10.** Hamburger $2.38

Andy Billings says you should compare prices at several stores. Also, compare prices of different brands and look for sales.

EXAMPLE 3. You need three cans of corn for a recipe. Find the difference in cost between two brands.

Brand A $0.47 per 16-oz can, Brand B $0.41 per 16-oz can

PLAN: **Step 1.** Subtract to find the cost difference for one can.

$$\$0.47 - \$0.41 = \$0.06$$

Step 2. Multiply the difference per can by the number of cans to find the difference for three cans.

$$\$0.06 \times 3 = \$0.18$$

EXAMPLE 4. Which is the better buy: Brand A, 1 can for 65¢ or Brand B, 3 cans for $2.00?

PLAN: **Step 1.** Multiply to find the cost of 3 cans of Brand A.

$$\$0.65 \times 3 = \$1.95$$

Step 2. Compare.

Brand A is cheaper.

Find the difference in cost.

TRY THIS

11. 2 lb of hamburger $0.76   Store A, $1.57 per lb
Store B, $1.19 per lb

12. 3 lb of melons $0.16   Store A, $0.28 per lb
Store B, 3 lb for $1.00

EXERCISES

Find the amounts for food, given the percents per week in these budgets. Use 4.3 weeks in one month.

1. $825 monthly net income, 23% $44.13   **2.** $1312 monthly net income, 21% $64.07

3. $950 monthly net income, 24% $53.02   **4.** $1125 monthly net income, 26% $68.02

5. $798 monthly net income, 28% $51.96

Use this shopping list. Find the cost for each item.

	Item	Amount Needed	Regular Price	Sale Price	Cost
6.	Eggs	2 dozen	$1.25 per dozen	$1.09 per dozen	$2.18
7.	Milk	3 half gallons	$0.98 per half gallon	none	$2.94
8.	Bread	2 loaves	$1.03 per loaf	$0.59 per loaf	$1.18
9.	Cereal	3 boxes	$0.84 per box	none	$2.52
10.	Tomatoes	2 pounds	$0.63 per pound	$0.59 per pound	$1.18
11.	Soap	1 box	$2.49 per box	none	$2.49

Find the difference in cost.

12. 3 lb of peaches   Store A, $0.98 per lb $1.17
                            Store B, $0.59 per lb

13. 5 lb of potatoes   Regular Price, $0.29 per lb $0.40
                            Sale Price, $0.21 per lb

14. 4 cans of applesauce   Brand A, $0.39 per can $0.24
                             Brand B, $0.45 per can

ON YOUR OWN

15. Plan a weekly menu. Prepare a shopping list. Include the amount needed, the regular price, and any advertised sale price.

16. Pick six items from your list. Compare the cost between regular prices and sale prices at different stores.

UNIT PRICE AND SHOPPING TRIPS

Comparing prices is easy when groceries post the unit price, that is,
the cost for exactly one ounce or one pound.

Andy Billings has some more shopping hints for you.

1. Compare unit prices.   **2.** Use coupons wisely.   **3.** Plan your shopping trips.

A *unit price* is a price for *one* unit of an item, such as, one ounce of
soup. Unit prices help you compare costs. If a store does not display
unit prices, then you need to calculate them.

> It is customary to
> change quantities to
> the smaller unit (oz),
> although it would
> be mathematically
> accurate to change
> to any common unit.

EXAMPLE 1.   A 1-lb 4-oz box of soap costs $ 1.37.
Find the unit price (price per ounce).

PLAN: **Step 1.**   Change to the smaller unit. 16 oz = 1 lb
1 lb 4 oz = 16 oz + 4 oz = 20 oz

Step 2.   Divide the total cost by the number of ounces to
find the price per ounce.
$ 1.37 ÷ 20 = $ 0.0685

Step 3.   Round to the nearest tenth of a cent.
$ 0.0685 ≈ $ 0.069

The unit price is $ 0.069 per oz.

Find the unit price.

1. Tuna, 6.5 oz for $0.58 $0.089 per oz
2. Instant breakfast drink, 1 lb 8 oz for $1.09 $0.045 per oz
3. Flour, 5 lb 8 oz for $1.89 $0.021 per oz
4. Stewed tomatoes, 454 grams for $0.49 $0.001 per gram
5. Chopped olives, 4.2 oz for $0.41 $0.098 per oz

Products are sold under various brand names. Containers come in many sizes. You can use unit prices to compare costs.

EXAMPLE 2. Find the lowest unit price among these three brands of corn.

Brand A	Brand B	Brand C
Regular price	Sale price	Regular price
10 oz for $0.47	10 oz for $0.39	12 oz for $0.42

PLAN: **Step 1.** Divide to find the unit prices.

$0.47 ÷ 10 = $0.047 per oz   *Brand A regular price*
$0.39 ÷ 10 = $0.039 per oz   *Brand B sale price*
$0.42 ÷ 12 = $0.035 per oz   *Brand C regular price*

Step 2. Compare to find the lowest unit price.

Brand C at $0.035 per oz is the lowest unit price.

Find the lowest unit price.

6.
Store A	Store B	Store C Store C at
Brand X	Brand X	Brand X $0.068 per oz
Cereal	Cereal	Cereal
13 oz for $0.95	20 oz for $1.39	13 oz for $0.89

7.
Brand A	Brand A	Brand A Store B at
Peanut butter	Peanut butter	Peanut butter $0.0595
Regular price	Sale price	Regular price per oz
10 oz for $0.63	20 oz for $1.19	28 oz for $1.69

8.
Brand A	Brand B	Brand C
Orange juice	Orange juice	Orange juice Brand A
12 oz for $0.59	12 oz for $0.68	20 oz for $1.19 at $0.049 per oz

9.
Brand A	Brand B	Brand C
Tomato sauce	Tomato sauce	Tomato sauce Brand C
8 oz for $0.19	16 oz for $0.39	24 oz for $0.56 at $0.023 per oz

You can use coupons to lower unit prices. It is wise to use them only for items on your shopping list.

EXAMPLE 3. Find the lower unit price.

Brand A Brand B
Peanut Butter Peanut Butter
12 oz for $1.75 16 oz for $2.00
Coupon 25¢ off No coupon

PLAN: **Step 1.** Find unit price for Brand A.

$1.75 − $0.25 = $1.50 *Subtract coupon saving.*

$1.50 ÷ 12 oz = $0.125 *Divide cost by number of ounces.*

= $0.125 per oz

Step 2. Find unit price for Brand B.

$2.00 ÷ 16 oz = $0.125 *No coupon to subtract*

= $0.125 per oz

Step 3. Compare unit prices. They are equal.

TRY THIS

10. Find the lower unit price. Syrup Brand A, 20 oz for $1.29, no coupon Brand B at $0.055 per oz
Syrup Brand B, 10 oz for $0.65, coupon 10¢ off

You can save time and money by planning your shopping trips. Travel costs also affect your total bill.

Planning helps to avoid unnecessary and impulse buying.

EXAMPLE 4. You need one dozen eggs. Store A sells eggs for $0.90, Store B sells eggs for $0.69. You must drive one mile round-trip if you go to Store A. If you go to Store B, then you must drive five miles round-trip. It costs you $0.17 per mile to drive your car. At which store will your total cost be less?

Explain to students that even with good planning sometimes they may need only one item.

PLAN: **Step 1.** Multiply to find the travel costs.

Store A: 1 × $0.17 = $0.17
Store B: 5 × $0.17 = $0.85

Step 2. Add the cost of travel to the cost of eggs to find your total cost.

Store A: $0.17 + $0.90 = $1.07
Store B: $0.85 + $0.69 = $1.54

Your total cost is less at Store A.

11. Pedro Freitas drives three miles round-trip for a half gallon of milk. His travel costs are 12¢ a mile. The milk is $1.05. What is the total cost? **$1.41**

12. Florence Johnston needs ten pounds of hot dogs for a party. At Store A they are $0.89 per pound. At Store B they are $0.69 per pound. Store A is a two-mile round trip. Store B is a seven-mile round trip. Her travel costs are $0.14 a mile. Which store gives her the lower total cost? **Store B at $7.88**

EXERCISES

Find the unit price.

1. 32 oz for $1.95 **$0.061**

2. 8 oz for $0.56 **$0.070**

3. 10 oz for $0.41 **$0.041**

4. 2 liters for $2.89 **$1.445**

5. 16 oz for $3.27 **$0.204**

6. 18 oz for $0.49 **$0.027**

7. 90 grams for $4.05 **$0.045**

8. 8 oz for $0.74 **$0.093**

9. 640 grams for $6.81 **$0.011**

10. 12 oz for $2.55 **$0.213**

11. 6 oz for $1.35 **$0.225**

12. 3.2 kg for $0.99 **$0.309**

Find the travel cost.

13. 2 miles × $0.41 per mile **$0.82**

14. 10 miles × $0.37 per mile **$3.70**

15. 4.5 kilometer × $0.22 per kilometer **$0.99**

16. 57 miles × $0.52 per mile **$29.64**

17. 25 miles × $0.49 per mile **$12.25**

18. 182 miles × $0.29 per mile **$52.78**

19. 0.7 miles × $0.32 per mile **$0.22**

20. 9.7 miles × $0.68 per mile **$6.60**

21. 4.3 kilometers × $0.18 per kilometer **$0.77**

22. 0.3 miles × $0.38 per mile **$0.11**

23. 280 miles × $0.56 per mile **$156.80**

24. 1580 miles × $0.56 per mile **$884.80**

Find the unit price.

25. Stuffed olives, 7-oz can for $1.19 **$0.17 per oz**

26. Hamburger, 3 lb for $4.88 **$1.627 per lb**

27. Chunk chili, 15-oz can for $0.89 **$0.059 per oz**

28. Soap, 2-lb 5-oz box for $3.98 **$0.108 per oz**

29. Peanut butter and jelly mix, 12 oz jar for $2.19 **$0.1825**

Find the lowest unit price.

30. Hash browns   32-oz package for $0.89   1-lb 8-oz package for $0.027 per oz.
                          16-oz package for $0.49
                          1-lb 8-oz package for $0.65

31. Mustard   Store A, 24-oz jar for $0.59   Store A at $0.025 per oz.
              Store B, 24-oz jar for $0.70
              Store C, 12-oz jar for $0.39

32. Pickles   Brand A, 225-gram jar for $0.38, coupon 5¢ off   Store A at
            Brand B, 140-gram jar for $0.75, no coupon $0.001 per gram
            Brand C, 675-gram jar for $1.09, coupon 5¢ off

33. Soda   Store A, 2 liters for $1.49, no coupon   Store B at $0.298 per liter
         Store B, 750-mL cans, 6-pack for $1.29, no coupon
         Store C, 1-liter bottles, 6-pack for $1.89, coupon 10¢ off

Solve.

34. Simon needs one package of hamburger buns. He drives three miles round-trip to the store for them. His travel costs are $0.13 a mile. The buns cost $1.19. What is the total cost? $1.58

35. You need three pounds of hamburger. Your travel costs are $0.18 a mile. Store A has hamburger at $1.19 per lb. It is a four-mile round trip. Store B has hamburger at $0.99 per lb. It is a six-mile round trip. Which store gives you the lower total cost? Store B, $4.05

DECISION

36. When would you buy a product with the higher unit price?

37. Sometimes buying in large amounts is wise. If you found these items at a very low cost, which would you buy in large amounts? Paper towels? Tomatoes? Meat? Lettuce?

38. By law, ingredients are listed on a label. The ingredient with the largest portion is listed first. The one with the smallest portion is listed last. Which would you buy? Why?

ESTIMATING SUMS BY ROUNDING UP

When estimating meal prices, it is best to round up. When you do this you get a price that will include sales tax.

EXAMPLE.   Estimate the price of this restaurant meal. Round up so that your estimate includes sales tax.

Onion soup	$1.15 ≈ $	1.50
Chef's salad	1.85 ≈	2.00
Roast chicken	7.65 ≈	8.00
Coffee	.80 ≈	1.00
Cheesecake	2.30 ≈	2.50
		$15.00

The bill will be no more than $15.

PRACTICE

Estimate these sums by rounding up.

1. $ 2.20
    3.40
    1.86
+ .73
$9

2. $15.16
    2.39
    6.64
+ 18.42
$43.50

3. $ 1.34
  12.15
   6.75
+ .86
$22

4. $23.19
   1.78
   2.53
   6.10
+ .93
$36

5. $14.16
   8.20
   1.62
   5.84
+ 10.74
$42

6. $14.13
   2.37
   8.19
   6.14
+ 8.76
$41

7. $5.63 + $6.10 + $0.98 + $0.18 $14

8. $0.76 + $3.19 + $0.85 + $9.10 $15

9. $17.32 + $5.18 + $0.32 + $8.06 $32

10. $2.15 + $15.26 + $2.08 + $1.82 $22.50

11. $4.26 + $2.92 + $7.41 + $0.95 $16

12. $8.63 + $9.08 + $1.65 + $3.15 $24

EATING OUT

Eating out can be costly, but with the great variety of restaurants in most cities, you can find a place you can afford.

Your food budget should include the cost of meals at restaurants. You should estimate the cost of a meal before you order. As you estimate, round up. Your estimate will then cover both the price of the meal and the sales tax.

Do not have the students find the exact cost.

EXAMPLE 1. Estimate the cost of this dinner. Use the following menu. Chef's salad, garlic bread, spaghetti with meatballs, milk, and cheesecake.

Exact: $ 2.70 + $ 1.00 + $ 4.90 + $ 0.60 + $ 1.10

Estimate: $ 3 + $ 1 + $ 5 + $ 1 + $ 2 = $ 12
The exact cost of the dinner comes to $ 10.30. A 10% tip would be $ 1.00. Dinner plus tip, $10.30 plus $ 1.00, is $ 11.30. So the estimate of $ 12 is close enough to include the sales tax.

Estimate the cost. Use the menu below.

1. Tossed salad, linguine with white clam sauce, coffee, mint chip ice cream **$9.00**

2. 12-inch sausage and mushroom pizza, delivered **$8.00**

3. Minestrone soup, lasagna dinner, soft drink **$9.00**

4. Child—ravioli with meat sauce, milk, vanilla ice cream **$5.00**

ANGELA'S ITALIAN GARDEN
EAT IN — TAKE OUT — DELIVERY SERVICE ($1.10 CHARGE)

APPETIZERS

Pizza Bread	$1.50
Garlic Bread	$1.00
Tossed Salad	$0.90
Chef's Salad	$2.70
Minestrone Soup	$1.30

PASTA

Spaghetti with	
Meat Sauce	$3.70
Meatballs	$4.90
Linguine with	
White Clam Sauce	$5.30
Mushrooms and Garlic Butter	$4.00

DRINKS

Milk	$0.60
Coffee-Tea	$0.70
Soft Drinks	$0.50

DESSERTS

Cheesecake	$1.10
Vanilla Ice Cream	$0.60
Mint Chip Ice Cream	$0.80

DINNERS

Lasagna	$5.90
Fettuccine Alfredo	$6.50
Ravioli with Meat Sauce	$5.80
Eggplant Parmesan	$5.30
Scampi	$8.90

PIZZA — 1 ITEM PRICE

8 inch	$2.50	10 inch	$3.40
12 inch	$4.70	15 inch	$5.80

$0.90 charge for each extra item

Pepperoni	Mushrooms
Hamburger	Green Peppers
Sausage	Olives

SANDWICHES

Ham and Cheese	$2.50
Italian Sausage	$2.80

Children under 12:
Half price on all items

After your meal the waitress or waiter gives you the total bill, including sales tax. You decide how much of a tip to leave. Restaurants suggest about 10% for average service and 15% for excellent service.

EXAMPLE 2.   You decide to tip about 10% for average service. Your bill is $ 18.15. Estimate the bill mentally.

PLAN: **Step 1.**   Round the bill to the nearest dollar.

$ 18.15 ≈ $ 18.00

Step 2.   Take 10% of this amount by moving the decimal point one place to the left.

10% of $ 18.00 = $ 1.80

The tip should be about $ 1.80.

EXAMPLE 3.   You decide to tip about 15% for excellent service. Your bill is $ 10.92. Estimate the tip mentally.

PLAN: **Step 1.**   Take 10% of the bill to the nearest dollar.

10% of $ 11.00 = $ 1.10

Step 2.   Divide $ 1.10 by 2 to find 5% of $ 11.00.

$ 1.10 ÷ 2 = $ 0.55

Step 3.   Add 10% of $ 11.00 to 5% of $ 11.00 to find 15% of $ 11.00.

$ 1.10 + $ 0.55 = $ 1.65

The tip should be about $ 1.65.

TRY THIS

Find the approximate tip.

5. $ 9.87 bill, average service $1.00
6. $ 21.91 bill, excellent service $3.30
7. $ 16.04 bill, average service $1.60

Angela Rubino is the owner of the Italian Garden Restaurant. To determine each menu price, she multiplies the cost of the ingredients by 2.5. Then she rounds up to the next ten cents.

EXAMPLE 4.   Angela's cost for a 12-inch sausage pizza is $ 1.87. What will be her menu price?

PLAN: **Step 1.**   Multiply Angela's cost by 2.5.

$ 1.87 × 2.5 = $ 4.675

Step 2.   Round up to nearest 10 cents.

$ 4.675 ≈ $4.70

TRY THIS

Find Angela's menu prices.

8. Small salad and dressing, Angela's cost $0.35 $0.90
9. Pizza bread, Angela's cost $0.60 $1.50
10. Scampi dinner, Angela's cost $3.53 $8.90
11. Ravioli with meat sauce, Angela's cost $2.30 $5.80

EXERCISES

Estimate the cost. Use the menu on page 123.

1. Pizza bread, spaghetti with meat sauce, coffee, mint chip ice cream $7.00

2. 15-inch pizza (hamburger, mushrooms, and olives), 2 soft drinks $9.00

3. Eggplant parmesan dinner, milk, cheesecake $9.00

4. Milk, Italian sausage sandwich, vanilla ice cream $5.00

5. 12-inch pizza (pepperoni, sausage, mushrooms, green peppers, and olives), delivered $11.00

Find the approximate tip.

6. $12.15 bill, average service $1.20   **7.** $14.85 bill, average service $1.50

8. $19.75 bill, excellent service $3.00   **9.** $15.10 bill, excellent service $2.25

The Tops is an expensive restaurant. Its menu prices are set by multiplying the cost of ingredients by 4.5 and rounding up to the next 10 cents. Find the menu prices.

10. Steak dinner; ingredient costs are $5.40. $24.30

11. Chef's salad; ingredient costs are $0.85. $3.90

12. Soup; ingredient costs are $0.39. $1.80

ON YOUR OWN

13. Obtain or look at a menu from your favorite restaurant. Estimate the cost of your favorite meal.

BUYING ON SALE

Garden tools at sale prices are just what the careful shopper hopes
to find to keep home maintenance costs low.

Carlos Dias is the manager of Clark's Department Store. His job
is to see that everything is done well and on time. Carlos started
working at Clark's after graduating from high school. He started as
a sales clerk. Carlos earned several promotions. After 12 years he
became manager.

Carlos gives you these hints for spending wisely:

1. Do not buy on impulse. Buy only what you need or have thought
about.

2. Compare prices. A competitor's price or another sale price may
be lower.

3. Compare quality. Know what you are buying.

Prices can change from season to season. They also vary from store
to store.

EXAMPLES.   Find the sale price.

1. Men's suits regularly $ 175, summer sale 20% off

PLAN: **Step 1.** Take 20% of the regular price to find the amount
off.   Encourage students to do mental
                         arithmetic by finding 10% and doubling to
$0.20 \times \$175.00 = \$35$ get 20%. Note that the sale price can also
                         be found by taking 80%.

Step 2. Subtract the amount off from the regular price to
find the sale price.

$\$175 - \$35 = \$140$

The sale price is $ 140.

2. Women's coats regular price $ 178, now $\frac{1}{3}$ off

PLAN: **Step 1.** Take $\frac{1}{3}$ of the regular price.   *Round to*
                                                nearest cent.
$\frac{1}{3}$ of $ 178 $\approx$ $ 59.33

Step 2. Subtract to find the sale price.

$\$178 - \$59.33 = \$118.67$

The sale price is $ 118.67.

TRY THIS   Find the sale price.

1. Dress shoes regular price $ 22.95, fall sale 25% off **$17.21**

2. Swim suit regular price $ 27.69, now 1/4 off **$20.77**

Sometimes the sale price is given. You can calculate the percent of
decrease.

EXAMPLE 3.   Hats regularly $ 15, now $ 12

Find the percent of decrease.

PLAN: **Step 1.** Subtract to find the amount off.

$\$15 - \$12 = \$3$

Step 2. Divide the amount off by the regular price to find
the percent of decrease.

$\$3 \div \$15 = 0.20 = 20\%$

The percent of decrease is 20%.

These are some other sales options commonly used.

Sale	Result
2-for-1 sale	You get $\frac{1}{2}$ off.
Buy 2, get 1 free	You get $\frac{1}{3}$ off.
Buy 3, get 1 free	You get $\frac{1}{4}$ off.

EXAMPLES. Find the sale price per item.

4. Soap regular price, $ 0.39 per bar, 2-for-1 sale

$\frac{1}{2} \times \$ 0.39 \approx \$ 0.20$ per bar

5. Pens regular price, $ 1.29 each, buy 2, get 1 free

PLAN: **Step 1.** Take $\frac{1}{3}$ of the regular price,

$\frac{1}{3} \times \$ 1.29 = \$ 0.43$

Step 2. Subtract to find the sale price.

$\$ 1.29 - \$ 0.43 = \$ 0.86$ each

TRY THIS

Find the sale price per item.

4. Comb sets regular price, $ 1.76 per set, buy 3, get 1 free **$1.32**

5. Socks, $ 2.10 a pair, buy 4 pair, get 1 pair free **$1.68**

EXERCISES

Find the sale price.

1. Calculators regular price $ 14, clearance sale 20% off **$11.20**

2. Jogging shoes regularly $ 12.95, sale 30% off **$9.07**

3. Tennis rackets regularly $ 24.50, fall sale $\frac{1}{4}$ off **$18.38**

Find the sale price. How much lower is the sale price than the competitor's price?

4. Luggage regular price $92, now $\frac{1}{5}$ off, competitor's price $95 **$21.40**

5. Aluminum cookware regular price $120, now 25% off, competitor's price $142 **$52.00**

6. Moonstone pendant regular price $16.50, now $\frac{1}{3}$ off, competitor's price $19 **$8.00**

Find the percent of decrease.

7. Multiband portable radio regular price $80, now $60 **25%**

8. Cassette recorder regularly $30, now $20 **33%**

9. 35 mm camera regularly $82, now $70 **15%**

10. Binoculars regular price $70, now $54 **23%**

Find the sale price per item.

11. Records regular price $3.98 each, 2-for-1 sale **$1.99**

12. Hair spray regularly $0.89 each, buy 2, get 1 free **$0.59**

13. Shock absorbers regular price $12.50 each, buy 3, get 1 free **$9.38**

14. Tires regularly $72 each, buy 3, get 1 free **$54**

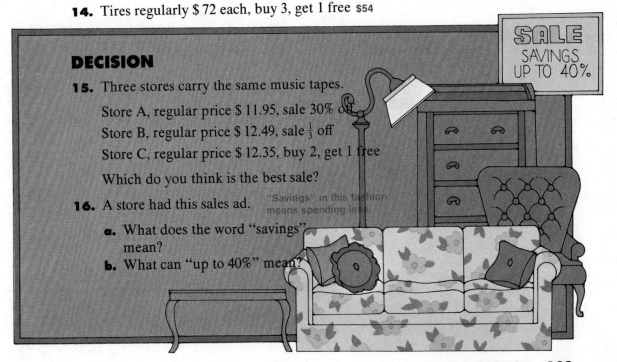

DECISION

15. Three stores carry the same music tapes.

Store A, regular price $11.95, sale 30% off
Store B, regular price $12.49, sale $\frac{1}{3}$ off
Store C, regular price $12.35, buy 2, get 1 free

Which do you think is the best sale?

16. A store had this sales ad.

"Savings" in this fashion means spending less.

a. What does the word "savings" mean?

b. What can "up to 40%" mean?

SALE
SAVINGS
UP TO 40%

BUYING FROM A CATALOG

Catalog buying has progressed from the 1920's, when it was a necessity for many, until today, when it is mostly a convenience.

Naomi Sanyo is the catalog sales supervisor for a mail order company. She started as a stock clerk for the company. By maintaining good work habits and building good working relationships with people, she earned several promotions. She now supervises the work of many stock clerks and sales clerks.

Naomi gives you these facts about catalog buying:

1. Some companies limit their merchandising to catalog sales.

2. In some areas of the country, catalog buying can give you more selection than local stores.

3. Though a company may not be located in your area, you may be able to make a purchase by catalog.

4. Catalog prices are usually cheaper than store prices.

5. When ordering by catalog, be careful to specify size, measurement, and color.

6. Remember to add shipping costs to the catalog price.

7. Allow time for the shipping of your order.

Weight in Pounds	Charge	Weight in Pounds	Charge
Up to 0.5	$1.50	Up to 10	$3.10
1	1.62	15	3.78
2	1.84	20	4.27
3	1.99	25	4.99
4	2.20	30	5.48
5	2.31	35	6.08
6	2.48	40	6.81
7	2.61	45	7.41
8	2.80	50	7.90
9	3.00	Each extra pound	$0.14

EXAMPLES. Use the table above to find the shipping charge.

1. 3 Blouses, weight 0.25 lb each
8 Skirts, weight 0.50 lb each

PLAN:

Step 1. Multiply to find the total weight of each.

3 blouses $\times$ 0.25 = 0.75

8 skirts $\times$ 0.50 = 4.00

Step 2. Add to find the total weight of both.

0.75 lb + 4.00 lb = 4.75 lb

Step 3. Find the shipping charge for 4.75 lb from the table. 4.75 lb is nearly 5 lb.

The total shipping charge is $2.31.

2. One room air conditioner weighs 68 lb.

PLAN:

Step 1. Find the shipping charge for 50 lb from the table.

$7.90

Step 2. Subtract to find the weight over 50 lb.

68 lb − 50 lb = 18 lb

Step 3. Multiply the result by $0.14 per lb to find the additional shipping charge.

$0.14 $\times$ 18 = $2.52

Step 4. Add to find the total shipping charge.

$7.90 + $2.52 = $10.42

The total shipping charge is $10.42.

TRY THIS

Find the shipping charge.

1. 1 Baseball jacket, weight 1.40 lb
1 Baseball mit, weight 1.60 lb $1.99

2. 1 Running shoes, weight 2.80 lb
2 Shirts, weight 0.40 lb each $2.20

3. 1 Easy chair, weight 116 lb
1 Sofa, weight 237 lb
1 Love seat, weight 194 lb $77.48

To find the total cost of an order, add the item prices and the shipping charge.

EXAMPLE 3. Find the total cost.

3 Denim overalls at $ 17.99 each, weight 2.10 lb each

PLAN: **Step 1.** Multiply to find the total item cost.

$ 17.99 $\times$ 3 = $ 53.97

Step 2. Multiply to find the total weight.

3 $\times$ 2.10 = 6.30

From the table the shipping charge for 6.30 lb is $ 2.61.

Step 3. Add the total item cost and shipping charge to find the total cost.

$ 53.97 + $ 2.61 = $ 56.58

The total cost of the three denim overalls is $ 56.58.

TRY THIS

Find the total cost.

4. 1 Workshirt $ 8.99, weight 0.90 lb
1 Workpants $ 10.99, weight 1.50 lb
1 Denim overalls $ 17.99, weight 2.10 lb $40.28

5. 1 Suitcase $ 24.99, weight 1.40 lb
2 Sweaters $ 17.99 each, weight 0.50 lb each
2 Skirts $ 13.99 each, weight 0.60 lb each
2 Blouses $ 14.99 each, weight 0.20 lb each
1 Dress $ 24.99, weight 0.80 lb $146.23

6. 3 Pants $ 15.99 each, weight 1.80 lb each
2 Belts $ 10.99 each, weight 0.80 lb each
3 Dress shirts $12.99 each, weight 0.20 lb each
2 Ties $ 5.99 each, weight 0.05 lb each $123.70

EXERCISES

Find the shipping charges. Use the table on page 131.

1. 1 Pullover sweater, weight 0.60 lb $1.62

2. 1 Digital watch, weight 0.20 lb $1.50

3. 1 Full-length coat, weight 4.25 lb $2.31
1 Pair leather gloves, weight 0.40 lb

4. 2 Shoes, weight 2.75 lb each $3.00
1 Western-style boots, weight 3.25 lb

5. 1 Coffee table, weight 1.18 lb $5.48
1 Desk, weight 25 lb

6. 2 End tables, weight 7.30 lb each $5.48
2 Lamps, weight 5.80 lb each
2 Pillows, weight 0.35 lb each

Find the total cost.

7. 1 Infant's car seat $38.99, weight 15 lb $51.25
1 Infant's car seat cover $7.99, weight 0.60 lb

8. 2 Turtleneck sweaters $8.49 each, weight 0.65 lb each $27.21
1 V-neck sweater $8.39, weight 0.60 lb

9. 3 Denim jeans $14.99 each, weight 1.50 lb each $66.45
1 Belt $6.50, weight 0.50 lb
1 Sweat shirt $5.59, weight 1.20 lb
1 Sweat pants $6.59, weight 1.30 lb

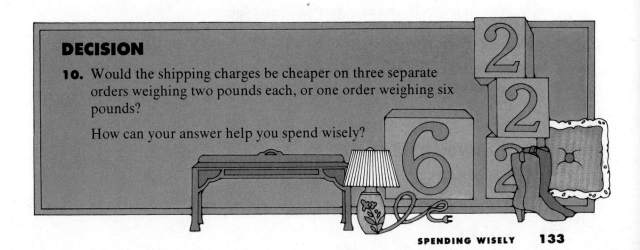

DECISION

10. Would the shipping charges be cheaper on three separate orders weighing two pounds each, or one order weighing six pounds?

How can your answer help you spend wisely?

BUYING VERSUS MAKING

By finishing this new furniture themselves, buyers can have the beauty of handsome antiques at a fraction of the cost.

Sometimes you can spend less by "doing it yourself." For example, you can grow your own fruits and vegetables, finish your own furniture, or sew your own clothes. It is often wise to make what you need.

David Brennan owns Sew-It, a sewing store. He sells patterns, fabrics, and sewing machines. David says you can spend less by making your own clothes.

EXAMPLE 1. The patterns, fabric, and supplies to make a dress cost $ 17.75. A similar dress at a store costs $ 29.95. Find the difference in cost.

$ 29.95 - $ 17.75 = $ 12.20

You spend $ 12.20 less by making the dress.

EXAMPLE 2. About how many dresses like the one above would you have to make to pay for a $298.95 sewing machine?

PLAN: **Step 1.** Round the numbers.

$$\$298.95 \approx \$300 \quad \$12.20 \approx \$10$$

Step 2. Divide the cost of the machine by the savings per dress.

$$\$300 \div \$10 = 30$$

You have to make 30 dresses to pay for the sewing machine.

TRY THIS

"Earn" here implies value of sewing time, i.e., how much your time is worth.

1. Find the difference in cost.

Make a jacket. **$20.15**
Costs: Pattern $2.90
 Material $12.50
 Buttons, thread, etc. $7.25

Buy a similar jacket.
Cost: $42.80

2. You spend about $125 less by making your own winter clothes. If sewing the clothes takes you 20 hours of work, how much do you "earn" per hour? **$6.25**

Paulette Jordan is a salesperson at The Home Center. She sells lumber, building supplies, and unfinished wood furniture. Paulette explains that by doing some work yourself you can spend less.

Unfinished furniture is constructed, but not sanded or painted. To finish it is to do the latter.

EXAMPLE 3. How much less would this bookcase cost if you finished it yourself?

Finished bookcase $139.50

Unfinished bookcase $79.95
Sandpaper $0.95   Varnish $8.50
Stain $4.78   Brushes $5.00

PLAN: **Step 1.** Add to find the total cost for the unfinished bookcase.

$$\$79.95 + \$0.95 + \$4.78 + \$8.50 + \$5.00 = \$99.18$$

Step 2. Subtract to find the difference in costs.

$$\$139.50 - \$99.18 = \$40.32$$

This bookcase would cost $40.32 less if you finished it yourself.

EXAMPLE 4. It took three hours to finish the bookcase. How much did you "earn" per hour?

$$\$40.32 \div 3 = \$13.44$$

You "earned" $13.44 per hour.

TRY THIS

3. Find the difference in cost. **$51.10**

Build your own cabinet   Buy an unfinished cabinet

Costs: Lumber $ 28.50   Cost: $ 95.80

        Nails and glue   7.25

        Hinges   8.95

4. You decide to build your own cabinet. It takes you ten hours. How much did you "earn" per hour by doing it yourself? **$5.11**

EXERCISES

Add.

1. $ 7.30
     8.21
     2.45
  + 6.92   **$24.88**

2. $ 5.63
     2.98
     3.05
  + 8.72   **$20.38**

3. $ 9.85
     6.49
     7.83
  + 2.56   **$26.73**

4. $ 4.73
     8.45
     1.35
  + 9.87
  $24.40

5. $ 6.54
     7.98
     9.81
  + 3.45
  $27.78

6. $ 8.45
     3.81
     6.92
  + 4.08
  $23.26

Subtract.

7. $ 4.23
  − 2.95   **$1.28**

8. $ 7.41
  − 3.86   **$3.55**

9. $ 23.89
  − 16.45   **$7.44**

10. $ 32.61
  − 28.30
  $4.31

11. $ 14.99
  − 7.43
  $7.56

12. $ 4.95
  − 1.76
  $3.19

Divide.

13. $ 35.81 ÷ 5   **$7.16**   **14.** $ 52.03 ÷ 7   **$7.43**   **15.** $ 21.52 ÷ 3   **$7.17**

16. $ 63.82 ÷ 9   **$7.09**   **17.** $ 71.45 ÷ 6   **$11.91**   **18.** $ 47.21 ÷ 4   **$11.80**

Solve.

19. You can make a sweater for $ 10.98. A similar sweater in a store costs $ 28.50. How much less would you spend by making it? **$17.52**

20. A dress shirt costs $ 19.25 at a store. You can make it. The costs are pattern $ 3.10, 2 yards of cloth at $ 4.12 per yard, thread $ 0.85, and 8 buttons at $ 0.28 each. How much less would you spend by making it? $4.82

21. You saved $ 150 by sewing your spring clothes. It took you 25 hours. How much did you "earn" an hour? $6

22. A finished end table costs $ 93.50. An unfinished one costs $ 17.50. The costs to finish it are sandpaper $ 1.30, stain $ 3.80, varnish $ 7.60, and brushes $ 4.25. How much less would you spend by finishing it yourself? $59.05

23. It took two hours to finish the end table in Exercise 22. How much did you "earn" an hour? $29.53

24. A new coffee table costs $ 285.95. You find an old but similar table at an auction. It costs $ 100. The costs to refinish it are paint remover $ 5.65, sandpaper $ 2.50, stain $ 3.50, varnish $ 7.00, and brushes $ 3.75. How much less would you spend by refinishing it? $163.55

25. You can 40 pints of peaches. The costs are bushel of peaches $ 10.00, 40 jars at $ 0.32 each, and 3 lb of sugar at $ 0.27 per lb. Find the total cost. $23.61

26. At the neighborhood market you can buy 16-ounce cans (1 pint) of peaches for $ 1.09. How much less would you spend by canning instead of buying 40 pints of peaches? Use the prices for canning peaches in the previous problem. $19.99

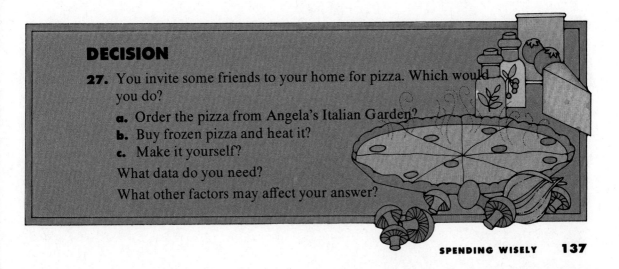

DECISION

27. You invite some friends to your home for pizza. Which would you do?

   a. Order the pizza from Angela's Italian Garden?
   b. Buy frozen pizza and heat it?
   c. Make it yourself?

What data do you need?

What other factors may affect your answer?

RENTING VERSUS BUYING

When you need a special tool, or machine—but only for a short
time—renting can be far less expensive than buying it.

Ruby is a high school student. She works after school and on
weekends at Ahren's Rental Center. Ruby can help you spend
wisely. She explains that sometimes it is better to rent than to buy.

When To Rent It
1. You need to use it only for a short time.
2. You need to use it only once or twice a year.
3. You have limited storage space.
4. You want to try one out before buying.
5. You can rent a better one than you can afford to buy.

EXAMPLE 1.   A new carpet steam cleaner costs about $950. It rents for
$20 a day. How many times could it be rented for the cost
of buying?

$950 \div \$20 \approx 48$ times   *Round your answer.*

EXAMPLE 2. Assume that it takes one day to steam clean your carpets. You do it twice a year, as recommended. How many years can they be cleaned for the cost of buying the steam cleaner?

$48 \div 2 = 24$ years

It is probably wiser to rent than buy.

How many times could you rent for the cost of buying?

TRY THIS

1. Furniture dolly 20 times
Cost $80   Rent $4 per day

2. Boat trailer 40 times
Cost $470   Rent $12 per day

3. Pickup truck 250 times
Cost $10,000   Rent $40 per day

This is a small part of the rate chart that Ruby uses to figure customer's bills.

Item	Charge Per Hr	Minimum Hours	Day	Week	4 Weeks
Air drill—$\frac{1}{2}$ in.	—	—	$10	$30	$90
Bike (exercise)	—	—	$10	$20	—
Bike (tandem)	$4	—	$14	$36	$65
Canoe	—	—	$10	$20	—
Chain saw	$8	3	$36	$140	$220
Concrete mixer	—	—	$25	$100	$300
Forklift	$22.50	2	$90	$360	$1,080
Fork (salad)	—	—	$0.12	—	—
Horse trailer (single)	—	—	$24	$96	$288
Popcorn machine	—	—	$14	—	—
Post hole digger	—	—	$5	$16	$25
Punch bowl (3 gal)	—	—	$12.50	—	—
Scooter (motor)	$6	2	$18	—	—
Skis (water)	—	—	$6	$16	$32
Snow blower	$10	2	$50	—	—
Stereo (8-track)	—	—	$10	—	—
Stump cutter	—	—	$200	$1,000	—
TV (19-in. color)	—	—	$12	$24	$35
Wheelbarrow	—	—	$6	$18	$45

EXAMPLES. Use the chart on page 139 to find the rental fee.

3. Snow blower for three hours

$3 \times \$10 = \$30$ *Hours times hourly rate*

4. Post hole digger for six days

$6 \times \$5 = \$30$ *Days times rate per day*

The weekly rate is $\$16$. The lower weekly rate will be charged.

5. Bike (tandem) for one day plus three hours

PLAN: Step 1. Find the cost for one day.

$\$14.00$

Step 2. Multiply to find the cost for three hours.

$\$4 \times 3 = \$12$

Step 3. Add to find total fee.

$\$14 + \$12 = \$26.00$

TRY THIS

Find the rental fee.

4. Air drill for four days $30.00
5. Wheelbarrow for one week plus two days $30.00
6. Ten forks (salad) for two days $2.40
7. Forklift for one hour $45.00

Along with the rental fee, you must also make a deposit as a guarantee that you will return the rental item in good condition. When you return the rental item, you get your deposit back. At Ahren's the deposit is 1.5 times the rental fee, rounded up to the next $5.

EXAMPLE 6. Find the deposit on a scooter (motor) rental for three hours.

PLAN: Step 1. Multiply to find the rental fee.

$\$6 \times 3 = \$18$ *Hourly rate times hours*

Step 2. Multiply the rental fee by 1.5 to find the deposit.

$\$18 \times 1.5 = \$27 \approx \$30$ *Round up to the next $5.*

The deposit on a scooter is $30.

EXERCISES

How many times could you rent for the cost of buying an item?

1. Boat trailer
Cost $600, rent $12 per day **50 times**

2. Horse trailer
Cost $1100, rent $30 per day
37 times

3. Crutches
Cost $25, rent $5 per week **5 times**

4. Tent
Cost $150, rent $9 per day
17 times

5. Hand saw
Cost $10, rent $4 per day **3 times**

6. Bicycle
Cost $200, rent $20 per day
10 times

Find the rental fee. Use the rates from page 139.

7. Concrete mixer for two days $50

8. Popcorn machine for three days
$42

9. Skis (water) for five days $16

10. Stereo for four hours $10

11. Stump cutter for one day plus 4 hours $400

12. TV for four days $24

13. Scooter for five days $90

14. Snow blower for eight hours $50

Find the deposit.

15. Post hole digger for one day $5

16. Wheelbarrow for two days $12

17. Canoe for one week $20

18. Chain saw for three days $108

19. Stereo for two days $20

20. TV for two months $70

21. Popcorn machine for three days $42

22. Bike (tandem) for six hours $14

DECISION

23. A new lawn mower costs $180. It rents for $6 an hour or $36 a day.

Should you rent or buy?
What other data do you need?

CHAPTER REVIEW

Find the amount for each item.

1. Food
$429

2. Savings
$165.00

3. Housing
$495

4. Transportation
$181.50

5. Clothing
$148.50

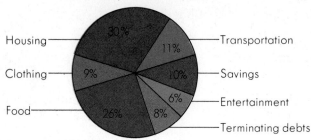

Gunderson Budget
Net Monthly Income – $1650

Housing — 30%
Clothing — 9%
Food — 26%
Transportation — 11%
Savings — 10%
Entertainment — 6%
Terminating debts — 8%

Find the difference in cost.

6. 2-lb beef rib roast
Store A, $2.74 per lb; Store B, $2.19 per lb **$1.10**

7. 3 cans of orange juice
Brand A, $0.79 per can; Brand B, $0.87 per can **$0.24**

Find the lowest unit price.

8. Bread   Brand A, 24 oz for $1.09 **Brand A at $0.045 per oz**
Brand B, 16 oz for $0.62
Brand C, 1 lb 6 oz for $0.98

9. Mayonnaise   Store A, 24 fl oz for $1.45, no coupon **Store B at $0.055 per oz**
Store B, 16 fl oz for $0.88, no coupon
Store C, 24 fl oz for $1.75, coupon 20¢ off

Estimate the cost. Use the menu on page 123.

10. Tossed salad, spaghetti with meatballs, soft drink, cheesecake **$9.00**

11. 15-inch pizza (hamburger, mushrooms, green peppers, olives), delivered **$11.00**

Find the sale price.

12. Auto speakers regular price $125, sale 20% off **$100**

13. Digital clock radio regular price $39, sale $\frac{1}{3}$ off **$26**

Find the total catalog price. Use the following shipping charge rates.

Weight in Pounds	Charge	Weight in Pounds	Charge
Up to 0.5	$1.50	Up to 10	$3.10
1	1.62	15	3.78
2	1.84	20	4.27
3	1.99	25	4.99
4	2.20	30	5.48
5	2.31	35	6.08
6	2.48	40	6.81
7	2.61	45	7.41
8	2.80	50	7.90
9	3.00	Each extra pound	$0.14

14. 1 Pair roller skates $44.95, weight 9.25 lb
   1 Roller skates trunk case $12.50, weight 6.50 lb
   3 Pair socks $3.49 each, weight 0.30 lb each
   1 Pair knee pads $12.99, weight 0.50 lb **$85.18**

15. 1 Lawn mower $207.50, weight 64 lb **$240.31**
   1 Grass catcher $22.39, weight 4 lb

Solve.

16. A dress costs $49.95 at a store. To make it the costs are pattern
   $3.10, thread $0.85, buttons $1.25, and 4 yards of cloth at
   $4.75 per yard. How much less would you spend by making it? **$25.90**

How many times could you rent for the cost of buying each item?

17. Battery charger,
   Cost $200, rent $7 per day **29 times**

18. Pipe wrench,
   Cost $13, rent $2 per day **7 times**

Find the rental cost. Use the rates from page 139.

19. Bike (tandem) for five hours **$14**

20. Chain saw for one day and four hours **$68**

21. Snow blower for one hour **$20**

SKILLS REVIEW

SKILL 12 Rounding decimals and money

Round to the underlined place.

1. 8.7<u>3</u>2¢ 8.73¢   **2.** 27.4<u>6</u>9¢ 27.47¢   **3.** $48.2<u>9</u>5 $48.30   **4.** $107.6<u>0</u>2 $107.60

SKILL 35 Writing mixed numbers as fractions

Convert to a fraction.

5. $1\frac{1}{2}$ $\frac{3}{2}$ **6.** $2\frac{3}{5}$ $\frac{13}{5}$ **7.** $1\frac{7}{8}$ $\frac{15}{8}$ **8.** $8\frac{11}{12}$ $\frac{107}{12}$

SKILL 44 Converting percents to decimals

Convert to a decimal.

9. 18% 0.18   **10.** 4.7% 0.047   **11.** 316% 3.16   **12.** $8\frac{3}{4}$% 0.0875

SKILL 45 Converting decimals to percents

Convert to a percent.

13. 0.86 86%   **14.** 0.9 90%   **15.** 2 200%   **16.** 0.045 4.5%

SKILL 15 Adding money

Add.

17. $85.98
   + 37.68
   $123.66

18. $1.23
     4.56
   + 0.10
    $5.89

19. $8.95
     6.87
   + 0.78
   $16.60

20. $37.48
     26.49
   + 5.97
   $69.94

SKILL 19 Subtracting money

Subtract.

21. $9.38
   − 2.50
   $6.88

22. $6.74
   − 3.81
   $2.93

23. $80.04
   − 56.28
   $23.76

24. $486.79
   − 87.80
   $398.99

SKILL 23 Multiplying money

Multiply. Round to the nearest cent.

25. $82.91
   × 7
   $580.37

26. $80.56
   × 30
   $2416.80

27. $42.81
   × 81
   $3467.61

28. $43.70
   × 0.8
   $34.96

SKILL 51 Division: 2- and 3-digit divisors

Divide. Round to the nearest hundredth.

29. $76\overline{)608}$ 8

30. $52\overline{)780}$ 15

31. $37\overline{)925}$ 25

32. $96\overline{)743}$ 7.74

SKILL 52 Dividing a decimal by a decimal

Divide. Round to the nearest hundredth.

33. $4.7\overline{)98.7}$ 21

34. $0.4\overline{)16}$ 40

35. $7.1\overline{)610.6}$ 86

36. $5.1\overline{)6.7}$ 1.31

SKILL 55 Multiplying mixed numbers

Multiply and simplify.

37. $6 \times 2\frac{1}{2}$ 15

38. $10 \times 1\frac{2}{5}$ 14

39. $3 \times 1\frac{1}{2}$ $4\frac{1}{2}$

40. $4\frac{3}{8} \times 3\frac{2}{5}$ $14\frac{7}{8}$

SKILL 63 Subtracting mixed numbers

Subtract. Simplify when possible.

41. $9\frac{1}{12} - 6\frac{7}{12}$ $2\frac{1}{2}$

42. $4\frac{4}{5} - 3\frac{9}{10}$ $\frac{9}{10}$

43. $9 - 2\frac{1}{2}$ $6\frac{1}{2}$

44. $6 - 3\frac{3}{4}$ $2\frac{1}{4}$

SKILL 67 Finding a percent of a number

Solve.

45. What is 63% of $90? $56.70

46. What is 16% of $360? $57.60

47. What is $66\frac{2}{3}$% of $36? $24

48. What is $62\frac{1}{2}$% of $400? $250

49. What is 0.4% of $56.25? $0.225

50. What is 18.5% of $1500? $277.50

SKILL 68 Finding what percent a number is of another

Solve.

51. $7 is what percent of $8? 87.5%

52. What percent of $40 is $32? 80%

53. What percent of $125 is $80? 64%

54. $200 is what percent of $50? 400%

SKILL 74 Adding measurements

Add.

55.
  6 ft
+ 3 ft 4 in.
 9 ft 4 in.

56.
  4 ft 3 in.
+ 7 ft 6 in.
 11 ft 9 in.

57.
  11 ft 8 in.
+ 3 ft 9 in.
 15 ft 5 in.

58.
  12 ft 6 in.
+ 14 ft 6 in.
 27 ft

5
HOUSING

HOUSING COSTS

Many cities contain a large variety of housing—some of it old, some
of it new, some high rises, and some single-family homes.

When you rent a house or apartment, how much money should you
spend? Ann Garcia is an advisor at the Housing Counseling Agency
where she advises people making economic decisions on housing.
Ann suggests that you spend a monthly amount no more than one
week's gross pay.

EXAMPLE 1. Fred earns $6.85 an hour as a road maintenance worker.
He works 40 hours a week. Fred's wife, Amy, averages
$1204 a month in salary and commissions as a salesperson.
How much should they budget for their monthly housing
costs?

PLAN: **Step 1.** Multiply to find Fred's gross weekly earnings.

$\$6.85 \times 40 = \$274$ *Hourly rate $\times$ hours per week*

Step 2. Divide to find Amy's gross weekly earnings.

$\$1204 \div 4.3 = \$280$ *Use 4.3 weeks per month.*

Step 3. Add to find their gross pay for one week.

$\$274 + \$280 = \$554$

They should budget a maximum of $554 for monthly
housing costs.

TRY THIS

1. Ed earns $ 7.80 per hour, 40 hours per week. $312

2. Pat and Mike share rent. Pat earns $ 4.85 an hour for a 40-hour week. Mike earns $ 6.25 per hour in wages and tips for a 30-hour week. $381.50

3. Kathy, Ruth, and Sue share a 3-bedroom house. Kathy averages $ 325 per week in commissions, Ruth earns $ 415 per week in salary, and Sue earns $ 1375 per month in wages and tips. $1059.77

When buying a house, you are advised by the housing counselor to pay no more than 2.5 times one year's gross income.

EXAMPLE 2. Find the maximum amount Carl and Sally Bond should pay for a house.

Carl earns $ 8.75 an hour, 40 hours a week, 52 weeks a year, as a truck driver.

Sally earns $ 525 per month, 12 months a year, as a salesclerk.

PLAN: **Step 1.** Multiply to find Carl's gross yearly earnings.
$ 8.75 \times 40 \times 52 = $ 18,200

Step 2. Multiply to find Sally's gross yearly earnings.
$ 525 \times 12 = $ 6300

Step 3. Add to find their total gross yearly earnings.
$ 18,200 + $ 6300 = $ 24,500

Step 4. Multiply by 2.5 to find the suggested maximum.
$ 24,500 \times 2.5 = $ 61,250

EXAMPLE 3. The Shields earn $ 1250 per month. Should they buy a condominium for $ 50,000?

PLAN: **Step 1.** Find the gross yearly earnings.
$ 1250 \times 12 = $ 15,000

Step 2. Multiply by 2.5.
$ 15,000 \times 2.5 = $ 37,500

Step 3. Compare.
$ 50,000 > $ 37,500

They should not buy the condominium.

4. Find the maximum Sheila Frey should pay for a house. She earns $ 1825 a month. **$54,750**

5. Joe Edwards earns $ 11.50 per hour, 40 hours a week, 52 weeks a year. Should he buy a house for $ 58,900? **yes**

EXERCISES

How much should be budgeted for monthly housing costs?

1. Joe earns $ 8.75 per hour, 40 hours per week. **$350.00**

2. Allan earns $ 5.25 per hour, 40 hours per week. Yvonne earns $ 278 per week. **$488.00**

3. Susan earns $ 350 per week. Her roommate, Bea, earns $ 4.25 per hour, 35 hours per week. **$498.75**

4. Rochelle Strand has a yearly teaching contract of $ 21,800. **$422.48**

Find the maximum amount to pay for a house.

5. Mike and Cindy Ondy have an income of $ 24,500 per year. **$61,250**

6. Carla Hatfield earns $ 1750 per month. **$52,500**

7. Sally Martin gets $ 7.15 per hour, 40 hours per week, 52 weeks per year. **$37,180**

8. Bob Soule makes $ 1850 per month in commissions. Nicole Soule earns $ 8.75 per hour, 30 hours per week, 40 weeks per year. **$81,750**

9. Alba Jones makes $ 2400 per month. Carl Jones makes $ 10.75 per hour, 40 hours per week, 52 weeks per year. **$127,900**

10. The Carsons earn $ 19,750 a year. Should they buy a house for $ 75,000? **no**

11. Barbara averages $ 725 per week in wages and tips. She works 50 weeks a year. Should she buy a condominium for $ 63,000? **yes**

ON YOUR OWN

12. List some factors other than price to consider in renting or buying a house.

RENTING

Every community has some rental units. But in this neighborhood
of New York, almost everyone lives in a rented apartment.

Janice and Guy Bork are the apartment managers at The Meadows.
They keep the records on rents and expenses. They rent the
apartments and also do minor repairs. Janice and Guy are college
students. This job helps pay their expenses and gives them business
experience. The owner worked with them for several months to train
them for the job.

Janice and Guy give these suggestions for renting.

Shop to find the best place for you. Consider both cost and location.

Ask about utility costs, such as water, electricity, and heat. They
may or may not be included in the rent.

Ask if any fee or deposit is required.

EXAMPLE 1.   Utilities average $45 per month. Find the monthly cost for a 2-bedroom apartment.

$$\$375 + \$45 = \$420$$
$$\uparrow \qquad \uparrow \qquad \uparrow$$
rent   utilities   total monthly cost

THE MEADOWS

Fully carpeted   Quiet, safe
Pool   All Electric
Tennis Courts

1 BR — $325, plus utilities
2 BR — $375

OPEN DAILY, 9–5
Equal Housing Opportunity

Find the monthly cost.

HARMONY ARMS
$425
1 Bedroom
Close to shops
Side access
Plush carpets, drapes

THE PALMS
$520
2 Bedrooms
New paint
2 Baths
Panoramic view

ORANGE HILL
3BR-$630
Includes utilites
Fireplace
Easy commute to town
Large lawn

TRY THIS

1. Harmony Arms, 1 bedroom, unfurnished, utilities average $42.50 per month **$467.50**
2. The Palms, 2 bedroom, furnished, utilities average $51 per month **$571.00**
3. Orange Hill, 3 bedroom, furnished, utilities included in the rent **$630.00**

Your landlord may require you to sign a monthly or a yearly lease agreement. You must read leases carefully to understand their conditions.

Your landlord may also ask for fees or deposits before you move in. The most common fees are first month's rent, cleaning deposit, and security deposit. Less common fees or deposits are last month's rent, application fee, pet deposit, and key deposit.

Some common amounts and general reasons for such fees are listed.

cleaning deposit	$25 and up	landlord's cleaning costs
security deposit	one month's rent	to pay for any damage you cause
application fee	$10 to $25	to check your personal and credit references
pet deposit	$25 to $150	to pay pet damage costs
key deposit	$5 and up	to pay for lost keys

Utility companies may also ask for a deposit of $ 25 and up if you have not established any previous credit with them.

Some fees and deposits are refundable. Others are partly refundable. Sometimes you get nothing back. Be sure you know what is in your rental agreement.

EXAMPLE 2. Find the move-in cost.
First month's rent $ 240, application fee $ 10, security deposit $ 240, cleaning deposit $ 50, electricity $ 45, phone $ 50

$ 240 + $ 10 + $ 240 + $ 50 + $ 45 + $ 50 = $ 635

TRY THIS

Find the total move-in cost.

4. First month's rent $ 410, cleaning deposit $ 35, security deposit $ 400, last month's rent $ 410, pet deposit $ 50, electricity $ 50, gas $ 35, phone $ 40 **$1430**

EXERCISES

Find the monthly cost.

SPARTAN ARMS $670	CAMPUS LIFE $425	EASY WAY $455
1 Bedroom	1 Bedroom	2 Bedrooms
Furnished	Furnished	Garden area
RV parking	Walk-in closets	Close to schools
Inside laundry	Fully landscaped	Cable TV
New kitchens	Heated pool	We pay utilities.

EAST SIDE $395 for 2-BR	FRIENDLY ARMS $405	GENTLE BREEZE $490 includes utilities
Family room	Studio	2 Bedrooms
Pets welcome	Deluxe kitchen	Formal dining room
New carpet	Breakfast bar	Large yard
	Custom drapes	Covered patio

1. Spartan Arms: 1 bedroom, furnished, utilities average $ 60 per month **$730**

2. Campus Life: large 1 bedroom, furnished, utilities paid in rent **$425**

3. Easy Way Apartments: 2 bedroom, unfurnished, utilities average $ 42 per month **$497**

4. East Side Townhouses: large 2-bedroom, utilities average $ 55 per month **$450**

5. Friendly Arms Apartments: studio, utilities average $ 70 per month **$475**

6. Gentle Breeze: 2-bedroom apartments, utilities paid in rent **$490**

Find the total move-in cost.

7. Spartan Arms: first month's rent, cleaning deposit of $ 25, **$795** security deposit of $ 100

8. Campus Life: first and last month's rent, key deposit of $ 10, **$870** application fee of $ 10

9. Easy Way Apartments: first and last month's rent, cleaning **$1035** deposit of $ 75, pet deposit of $ 50

10. East Side Townhouses: first month's rent, application fee of **$567.50** $ 12.50, security deposit of $ 150, key deposit of $ 10

11. Friendly Arms Apartments: first and last month's rent, cleaning deposit of $ 100 **$910**

12. Gentle Breeze: first month's rent, application fee of $ 15, pet deposit of $ 50, key deposit of $ 7.50 **$562.50**

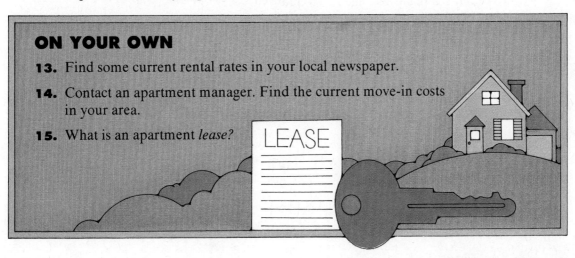

ON YOUR OWN

13. Find some current rental rates in your local newspaper.

14. Contact an apartment manager. Find the current move-in costs in your area.

15. What is an apartment *lease?*

BUYING

15,000 people arrived in one day to find new homesites after the Oklahoma territory was opened to settlers in 1889.

Lois Rodman is a real estate agent. To qualify for her job, she took real estate classes and passed the state real estate examination. If you want to buy a house, Lois can help you arrange for a loan and handle the details of the purchase.

The loan does not cover the entire cost of the house. The buyer must have some money for a *down payment*. Lois says that the amount of the down payment depends on the amount of the loan and the company making the loan.

EXAMPLE 1. The Browns want to buy a house for $72,500. Their loan company requires 20% down. Find their down payment.

$0.20 \times \$72,500 = \$14,500$ *Use 0.20 for 20%.*

They need $14,500 for a down payment.

EXAMPLE 2.   Elsa Cushing wants to buy a house for $72,500. Her loan requires a down payment of 3% of the first $25,000, 5% of the next $42,500, and 100% of the remaining balance. Find her down payment.

PLAN: **Step 1.**   Multiply to find the down payment on the first $25,000.

$$0.03 \times \$25,000 = \$750$$

Step 2.   Multiply to find the amount required on the next $42,500.

$$0.05 \times \$42,500 = \$2125$$

Step 3.   Subtract the sum of $25,000 and $42,500 from the price of the house to find the remaining balance.

$$\$72,500 - \$67,500 = \$5000$$

Step 4.   Add to find the total down payment.

$$\$750 + \$2125 + \$5000 = \$7875$$

Find the down payment.

TRY THIS

1. House cost $68,750
down payment 15% **$10,312.50**

2. House cost $82,250
down payment 25% **$20,562.50**

3. House cost $70,000
down payment 3% on first $25,000, plus
5% on balance to $67,500, plus
cash for amount over $67,500 **$5375.00**

In addition to the down payment, the buyer must pay *closing costs*. Closing costs vary in different regions. Some include loan fee, deed recording fee, credit report, prepaid insurance, prepaid taxes, lawyer's fee, and escrow fee. Escrow fee is a charge made by the company that handles the paper work for selling your house.

EXAMPLE 3.   The loan on a new house is $47,850. The loan fee is 1%. Find the loan fee.

$$0.01 \times \$47,850 = \$478.50$$

The loan fee is $478.50

EXAMPLE 4. The buyer and the seller usually each pay half of the escrow fee. Find the buyer's share of a $325 escrow fee.

$325 \div 2 = \$162.50$

The buyer and the seller must each pay $162.50 toward the escrow fee.

TRY THIS

4. Find the total closing costs. **$1615.00**

Purchase price $60,000 Prepaid insurance $660
loan $54,000 prepaid taxes $175
loan fee 1% of loan lawyer's fee $20
deed recording fee $15 escrow fee (half to buyer) $310
credit report $50

Suppose you have found a house that you would like to buy. Lois computes the amount of cash you need by adding the required down payment and the closing costs. Next she must see whether you "qualify" for a loan. That is, your monthly income must be large enough to make regular payments on your loan.

Lois uses this formula:

(Monthly income − terminating debts) ÷ 4 = maximum payment

If the monthly payment needed is greater than this number, your loan request will probably be denied.

EXAMPLE 5. Does Mr. Green qualify for monthly loan payments of $360? His gross monthly income is $1280. His terminating debts total $135.

$\$1280 - \$135 = \$1145$
$\$1145 \div 4 = \$286.25$

He does not qualify.

TRY THIS

Does the buyer qualify? All figures are monthly amounts.

	Loan payment	Gross income	Terminating debts
5.	$252	$1300	$125 yes
6.	$485	$1650	$80 no

EXERCISES

Find the down payment.

	House cost	Down payment rate	Down payment
1.	$72,000	15%	$10,800.00
2.	$49,000	20%	$9800.00
3.	$68,750	25%	$17,187.50
4.	$59,000	35% of first $5000, plus 5% of balance	$4450.00
5.	$82,400	3% of first $5000, plus 5% of next $42,000 plus 100% of balance	$37,650

Find the total closing costs.

6. Purchase price $72,000
  loan fee   1% of loan
  deed recording fee $20
  credit report $60
  Loan $64,500
  prepaid insurance $780
  prepaid taxes $160
  lawyer $15
  escrow ($\frac{1}{2}$ to buyer) $340 **$1925**

7. Purchase price $81,450
  loan fee   1.5% of loan
  deed recording fee $20
  credit report $65
  Loan $72,000
  prepaid insurance $925
  prepaid taxes $225
  lawyer $15
  escrow ($\frac{1}{2}$ to buyer) $340 **$2641.75**

Find whether the buyer qualifies. All figures are monthly amounts.

8. Loan payment $375, gross income $1660, terminating debts $45 **yes**

9. Loan payment $474, gross income $2150, terminating debts $195 **yes**

10. Loan payment $526, gross income $2400, no terminating debts **yes**

11. Loan payment $725, gross income $3200, terminating debts $650 **no**

ON YOUR OWN

12. The seller of a house must also pay closing costs. Contact a real estate agent. Find the seller's closing costs.

13. Find out what escrow means and how it is handled in your area.

MORTGAGE PAYMENTS

Explain to the students that (cost/thousands) × thousands = cost.

For many people, a new home is the most expensive purchase they will ever make, but it often proves to be the most satisfying.

Robert Applewhite is a loan officer at MacKay Mortgage Company. Robert graduated from college with a degree in finance. He then spent two years as a management trainee. If you buy a house, you will probably need a *mortgage loan.* Robert can help you find the loan best suited to your needs.

Robert uses a table to find monthly payments on loans.

This sort of table is called a loan amortization table.

Monthly Payment Per $1000

Interest Rate	20-year term	25-year term	30-year term		Interest Rate	20-year term	25-year term	30-year term
7.5%	$8.06	$7.39	$6.99		15.0%	$13.17	$12.81	$12.64
8.0	8.36	7.72	7.34		15.5	13.54	13.20	13.05
8.5	8.68	8.05	7.69		16.0	13.91	13.59	13.45
9.0	9.00	8.39	8.05		16.5	14.29	13.98	13.85
9.5	9.32	8.74	8.40		17.0	14.67	14.38	14.26
10.0	9.65	9.08	8.78		17.5	15.05	14.78	14.66
10.5	9.98	9.44	9.15		18.0	15.40	15.17	15.07
11.0	10.32	9.80	9.52		18.5	15.82	15.57	15.48
11.5	10.66	10.16	9.90		19.0	16.21	15.98	15.89
12.0	11.01	10.53	10.29		19.5	16.60	16.38	16.30
12.5	11.36	10.90	10.67		20.0	16.99	16.78	16.71
13.0	11.72	11.28	11.06		20.5	17.38	17.19	17.12
13.5	12.07	11.66	11.45		21.0	17.78	17.60	17.53
14.0	12.44	12.04	11.85		21.5	18.17	18.00	17.94
14.5	12.80	12.42	12.25		22.0	18.57	18.41	18.36

EXAMPLE 1. Find the monthly payment on a mortgage loan of $42,500 at 19% for a 30-year term.

PLAN: **Step 1.** From the table find the amount per $1000 at 19% for 30 years.

$15.89

Step 2. Write $42,500 as 42.5 thousand dollars.

Step 3. Multiply to find the monthly payment.

$15.89 × 42.5 = $675.325

The monthly payment to the nearest cent is $675.33.

TRY THIS

Find the monthly payment.

1. $50,000 mortgage at 18% for 25 years $758.50
2. $82,500 mortgage at 22% for 30 years $1514.70
3. $75,750 mortgage at 13.5% for 20 years $914.30

Part of each monthly payment is *interest*. The rest is *principal*. The principal amount reduces the loan. This payment process is often shown to the customer as a table.

Loan Table

Smith Loan—$75,000 at 11.75% for 30 years—Monthly Payment $757.06

Payment Number	Loan Balance	Payment Amount	Interest Amount	Principal Amount	New Loan Balance
1	$75,000.00	$757.06	$734.38	$22.68	$74,977.32
2	74,977.32	757.06	734.15	22.91	$74,954.41
3	74,954.41	757.06	733.93	23.13	$74,931.28
4	74,931.28	757.06	733.70	23.36	$74,907.92
.					
.					
.					
356	3676.56	757.06	36.00	721.06	$ 2955.50
357	2955.50	757.06	28.94	728.12	$ 2227.38
358	2227.38	757.06	21.81	735.25	$ 1492.13
359	1492.13	757.06	14.61	742.45	$ 749.68
360	749.68	757.06	7.38	749.68	$ 0.00

EXAMPLE 2. Find the principal amount on payment 3.
From the table the amount is $23.13.

EXAMPLE 3.   About what percent of payment 1 was interest?

PLAN: **Step 1.**   Round the amounts.

$ 734 out of $ 757 was interest.

Step 2.   Divide to find the percent.

$$\frac{\$ 734}{\$ 757} \approx 0.9696 \approx 97\%$$

About 97% of payment 1 was interest.

TRY THIS

4. Find the loan balance before and after payment 2. **$74,977.32, $74,954.41**

5. About what percent of payment 4 was interest? **97%**

6. What percent of payment 4 was used to reduce the loan? **3%**

In addition to principal and interest, the mortgage company may collect money to pay taxes and insurance on the house.

EXAMPLE 4.   Find the total monthly payment.

Principal and interest $ 343.13, taxes and insurance $ 98.00

$ 343.13 + $ 98.00 = $ 440.13

TRY THIS

Find the total monthly payment.

7. Principal and interest $ 773.41, taxes and insurance $ 128.00 **$901.41**

EXERCISES

Find the monthly payment. Use the table on page 158.

1. $ 70,000 mortgage loan at 20.5% for 30 years **$1198.40**

2. $ 52,500 mortgage loan at 12.0% for 25 years **$552.83**

3. $ 67,750 mortgage loan at 11.5% for 30 years **$670.73**

4. $ 79,000 mortgage loan at 16.5% for 25 years **$1104.42**

5. $ 82,500 mortgage loan at 18.0% for 30 years **$1243.28**

6. $ 75,000 mortgage loan at 15.0% for 30 years **$948**

Use the loan table on page 159.

7. Find the interest amount on payment 1. $734.38

8. Find the amount used to reduce the loan on payment 3. $23.13

9. Find the loan balance on payment 3. $74,931.28

10. Find the interest amount on payment 3. $733.93

11. Find the amount used to reduce the loan on payment 356. $721.06

12. Find the loan balance on payment 356. $2955.50

13. What percent of payment 3 is interest? 97%

14. What percent of payment 356 is interest? 5%

15. What percent of payment 1 is used to reduce the loan? 5%

16. What percent of payment 356 is used to reduce the loan? 95%

Find the total monthly payment.

17. Principal and interest $ 289.42, taxes and insurance $ 82.00 $371.42

18. Principal and interest $ 419.36, taxes and insurance $ 92.00 $511.36

19. Principal and interest $ 437.28, taxes and insurance $ 137.50 $574.78

20. Principal and interest $ 621.04, taxes and insurance $ 154.25 $775.29

Use the loan table on page 159 (optional).

21. How much of the loan is reduced by the first four payments? $92.08

22. By how much does the principal amount change for payments 2, 3, and 4? increase of $0.23, $0.22, $0.23

23. By how much does the interest amount change for payments 2, 3, and 4? decrease of $0.23, $0.22, $0.23

24. How much of the loan is reduced by the last four payments? $2955.50

ON YOUR OWN

25. Find the meaning of each term: prepayment penalty, FHA loan, VA loan, conventional loan.

MORTGAGE INTEREST RATES

When mortgage interest rates are high, the increased cost of buying houses or undeveloped land is too great for most people.

Robert Applewhite, a mortgage loan officer, can show you some other facts about mortgage interest rates.

EXAMPLE 1. Find the total interest.

Loan principal $60,000, rate $12\frac{3}{8}\%$,
term 30 years (360 months), monthly principal
and interest payment of $634.55

PLAN: **Step 1.** Find the total amount paid. The total principal paid is equal to the loan principal amount.

$634.55 \times 360 = $228,438

Step 2. Subtract the principal from the total amount paid to find the interest paid.

$228,438 - $60,000 = $168,438

Find the total interest.

1. Loan principal $40,000, rate 19%, term 20 years (240 months), monthly principal and interest payment of $648.40 **$115,616**

2. Loan principal $75,000, rate 13%, term 30 years (360 months), monthly principal and interest payment of $829.65 **$223,674**

A change in the loan percentage rate affects the total interest. A lower rate is less expensive.

EXAMPLE 2. Find the difference in total interest paid. Loan $50,000, 25 years (300 months), monthly principal and interest payments of $490.06 at 11.0% *or* $436.85 at 9.5%

PLAN: **Step 1.** Multiply to find the total amount paid at 11.0%.
$490.06 × 300 = $147,018

Step 2. Multiply to find the total amount paid at 9.5%.
$436.85 × 300 = $131,055

Step 3. Subtract to find the difference.
$147,018 − $131,055 = $15,963

The lower rate saves $15,963.

Find the difference in total interest paid.

3. Loan $20,000, term 10 years (120 months), monthly principal and interest payments of $132.16 at 10% *or* $161.34 at 15% **$3501.60**

4. Loan $80,000, term 30 years (360 months), monthly principal and interest payments of $784.62 at $11\frac{3}{8}$% *or* $995.59 at $14\frac{3}{4}$% **$75,949.20**

A change in the term (length) of a loan also affects the total interest. A shorter term is less expensive. **The word "savings" is sometimes used in the same manner as less expensive.**

EXAMPLE 3. Find the difference in total interest paid.

Loan $60,000, rate $12\frac{3}{4}$%,

monthly principal and interest payments of $652.02 for 30 years (360 months) *or* $692.29 for 15 years (180 months)

PLAN:

Step 1. Multiply to find the total amount paid for 30 years.
$$\$652.02 \times 360 = \$234,727.20$$

Step 2. Multiply to find the total amount paid for 15 years.
$$\$692.29 \times 180 = \$124,612.20$$

For a 15-year loan, the borrower will pay $40.27 per month more, for a total of $7,248.60 more after 15 years, but in the end will save $110,005 over the 30-year term.

Step 3. Subtract to find the difference.
$$\$234,727.20 - \$124,612.20 = \$110,115.00$$

The shorter loan saves $110,115.

Find the difference in total interest paid.

TRY THIS

5. Loan $50,000, rate 11%, monthly principal and interest payments of $476.17 for 30 years (360 months) *or* $516.10 for 20 years (240 months) $47,557.20

6. Loan $70,000, rate $11\frac{3}{4}$%, monthly principal and interest payments of $758.60 for 20 years (240 months) *or* $697.06 for 35 years (420 months) $110,701.20

This table shows the rate at which mortgages are paid off (retired).

Percent of original loan amount still owed after 30-year term at different rates of interest						
Interest rate	After 5 years	After 10 years	After 15 years	After 20 years	After 25 years	After 30 years
Life of mortgage—30 years						
10%	97	91	82	66	41	0
11	97	92	84	69	44	0
12	98	93	86	72	46	0
13	98	94	87	74	49	0
14	98	95	89	76	51	0
15	99	96	90	78	53	0
16	99	97	92	80	55	0
17	99	97	93	82	57	0
18	99	97	94	84	59	0

EXAMPLE 4. Find the amount still owed on a 30-year mortgage after 20 years, with an original loan of $50,000, and a 10% rate.

PLAN:

Step 1. Find the percent of the loan still owed.
66%

Step 2. Multiply to find the amount still owed.
$$\$50,000 \times 0.66 = \$33,000$$

Find the amount still owed.

7. After 15 years, loan $ 63,000, rate 10.0% $51,660.00

8. After 25 years, loan $ 58,000, rate 15% $30,740.00

EXERCISES

Find the total interest.

1. Loan $ 52,000, term 30 years (360 months), monthly principal and interest payment of $ 446.77 $108,837.20

2. Loan $ 61,000, term 25 years (300 months), monthly principal and interest payment of $ 767.50 $169,250

Find the difference in the total interest paid.

3. Term 30 years (360 months), monthly principal and interest payments of $ 403.62 at 9.5% *or* $ 421.24 at 10.0% $6343.20

4. Term 25 years (300 months), monthly principal and interest payments of $ 570.43 at 10.0% *or* $ 821.89 at 15.0% $75,438

5. Monthly principal and interest payments of $ 495.46 for 20 years (240 months) *or* $ 457.12 for 30 years (360 months) $45,652.80

6. Monthly principal and interest payments of $ 955.37 for 25 years (300 months) *or* $ 932.46 for 35 years (420 months) $105,022.20

Find the amount still owed. Use the table on page 164.

7. After 10 years, loan $ 72,000, rate 11% $66,240

8. After 5 years, loan $ 65,750, rate 18% $65,092.50

ON YOUR OWN

9. Find the approximate current mortgage rate on new houses in your area.

10. Ask house owners why they may take longer term loans rather than shorter term loans.

11. Find out about mortgage loans having a variable interest rate.

for Sale

UTILITIES

Hoover Dam and other federally-funded projects provide electrical power to keep our homes and factories operating.

After high school Tim Schultz got a job as a meter reader for the Central Power Company. There he learned about electric meters and how to read them. Each month he reads all the meters in his territory. He goes to houses and businesses. Tim sometimes uses a telescope to read meters that are hard to reach.

Tim explains that electrical energy is measured in kilowatt hours (kWh). One kWh is 1000 watts of power used for one hour. For example, ten 100-watt bulbs lighted for one hour uses 1 kWh.

Tim shows you how to read an electric meter. A meter has four or five dials. Begin reading with the dial on the left. If the pointer is between numbers, read the lower number (except if between 0 and 9, read 9).

EXAMPLE 1. Read the meter.

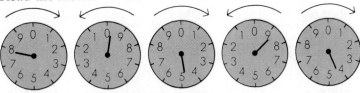

The meter reads 79,484.

Read the meter.

1.

58915

2.

59502

To find your electric energy cost, multiply the number of kWh used by the cost per kWh. The cost per kWh varies in different regions.

EXAMPLE 2. Find the cost.

Present meter reading 79484
previous meter reading 77495
rate $ 0.054 per kWh

Other charges may be added, such as, deferred energy, service charge, fuel adjustment, minimum charge, tax surcharge.

PLAN: **Step 1.** Subtract to find the number of kWh used.

79484 − 77495 = 1989 kWh

Step 2. Multiply to find the cost. Round to the nearest cent.

$ 0.054 × 1989 = $ 107.406 ≈ $ 107.41

Find the cost.

3. Present meter reading 09492,
previous meter reading 08814,
rate $ 0.0536 per kWh **$36.34**

The average yearly use in kWh for some common appliances has been estimated. From these figures you can estimate the yearly cost. The formula is

These estimates were based on U.S. industry statistics for 1980. They may vary by region and individual use.

Estimated cost per kWh × yearly kWh = yearly cost

EXAMPLE 3. A clothes dryer is estimated to use 1410 kWh yearly. Using the rate of $0.0619 per kWh, find the estimated yearly cost.

Multiply to find the yearly cost.
$0.0619 × 1410 = $87.2790 ≈ $87.28

Note that the yearly cost is rounded to the nearest cent.

The cost of using the dryer for a year is about $87.28.

TRY THIS

Find the estimated yearly cost.

4. Refrigerator-freezer
12 cubic feet, frostless
yearly kWh 1600
rate $0.056 per kWh **$89.60**

5. Electric blanket
yearly kWh 147
rate $0.0529 per kWh **$7.78**

Other utility costs are calculated in about the same way:

Cost per unit × number of units used = cost

Each kind of utility may have additional charges, as with electricity.

EXAMPLE 4. The unit for natural gas is usually 100 cubic feet. Find the cost for 215 units of natural gas at $0.32 per unit.

$0.32 × 215 = $68.80

Natural gas is also sold by 1000 cubic feet units to large users. It is also sold by "therm units" in some regions; 1 therm = 100,000 Btu; 100 cubic feet ≈ 1 therm.

EXAMPLE 5. The unit for heating oil is the gallon. Find the cost for 126 gallons of heating oil at $1.07 per gallon.

$1.07 × 126 = $134.82

EXAMPLE 6. The unit for water is 1000 gallons. Find the cost of 118 units at $0.48 per unit.

$0.48 × 118 = $56.64

TRY THIS

Find the cost.

6. 187 units of natural gas at $0.48 per unit **$89.76**
7. 78 gallons of heating oil at $1.15 per gallon **$89.70**
8. 87 units of water at $0.76 per unit **$66.12**

EXERCISES

Read the meter.

1.

80279

2.

60922

Find the cost.

3. Electricity
present meter reading 14,879
previous meter reading 14,192
rate $ 0.0675 per kWh **$46.37**

4. Electricity
present meter reading 87,194
previous meter reading 86, 289
rate $ 0.078 per kWh **$70.59**

5. Water heater
yearly kWh 4219
rate $ 0.0595 per kWh **$251.03**

6. Toaster
yearly kWh 3
rate $ 0.0603 per kWh **$0.18**

7. Natural gas
85 units at $ 0.43 per unit **$36.55**

8. Heating oil
78 gallons at $ 1.12 per gal **$87.36**

9. Water
38 units at $ 0.67 per unit **$25.46**

10. Natural gas
130 units at $ 0.52 per unit **$67.60**

ON YOUR OWN

11. Read your electric meter. Read it again exactly one month later.
Find your monthly kWh usage.

12. Call your local electric, natural gas, heating oil, and water
companies. Find their current rates.

13. Find the wattage rating of some of the appliances around your
home. Calculate the cost of running them for one hour.

ENERGY CONSERVATION

Hundreds of mirrors focus sunlight on the tower in this experiment
to find inexpensive ways to generate electricity.

Jerri Snyder is an energy specialist for the Central Power Company.
Jerri is a high school graduate. She applied to the power company,
passed their application test, and took their courses in energy
calculations and customer relations.

She inspects customers' houses and gives tips on how to conserve
energy and cut costs. The greatest utility expense for most houses is
for heating and cooling. There are many ways to conserve and save
money.

This is true whether you
use electricity, gas, oil,
etc.

EXAMPLE 1. Four college students share an apartment. Their monthly bill
for heating and cooling is $ 48. Find their yearly saving.

Option	Saving	Cost
Winter: set thermostat at 68°. Summer: set thermostat at 78°.	25%	None

PLAN: **Step 1.** Multiply to find the yearly cost of heating and cooling.

48×12 months $= \$576$

Step 2. Multiply to find the yearly saving.

$0.25 \times \$576 = \$144$

The yearly saving is $\$144$.

1. The average monthly heating and cooling bill for Bill and Celia is $\$60$. Find their yearly saving. **$57.60**

Option	Saving	Cost
Change filters once a month.	8%	$10 per yr

The second highest utility expense is usually for hot water.

EXAMPLE 2. The Baskins' bill for hot water averages $\$42$ per month. About how long will it take for the saving to pay for the cost of improvement?

Option	Saving	Cost
Wrap hot water heater with insulated blanket.	10%	$30

PLAN:

Explain to the students that dollars ÷ (dollars/months) = months. After 7 months, all savings can be applied to utility costs.

Step 1. Multiply to find the monthly saving.

$0.10 \times \$42 = \$4.20$

Step 2. Divide to find how long it will take for the saving to pay for the cost of improvement.

$\$30 \div \$4.20 \approx 7$ months   *Cost of improvement ÷ monthly saving*

2. Ruby and George's bill for hot water averages $\$58$ per month. About how long will it take for the saving to pay for the cost of improvement? **74 months**

Option	Saving	Cost
Convert to passive solar heating.	75%	$3200

The percent of savings is based on a national average.

EXERCISES

Find the yearly saving.

1. Maria and Charles Greene's average monthly heating and cooling cost is $ 60. $79.20

Option	Saving	Cost
Summer: close drapes on sunny side. Winter: open drapes on sunny side.	11%	None

2. Ellie and Carla's average monthly cost for running their refrigerator is $ 8. $6.72

Option	Saving	Cost
Clean coils twice a year.	7%	None

3. Jose, Jason, and Steve's hot water bill averages $ 52 per month. $74.88

Option	Saving	Cost
Lower setting from 165° to 120°.	12%	None

4. Thelma, Grace, and Margaret's hot water bill averages $ 48 per month. $190.08

Option	Saving	Cost
Take showers instead of baths.	33%	None

5. Stan and Jenny's hot water bill averages $ 58 per month. $34.80

Option	Saving	Cost
Operate dishwasher only when full.	5%	None

6. The Millers pay $ 23 extra during June, July and August for air conditioning. $13.80

Option	Saving	Cost
Set thermostat 5° higher.	20%	None

7. The Hamilton's average heating bill is $ 70. $151.20

Option	Saving	Cost
Set thermostat 5° lower.	18%	None

About how long will it take for the saving to pay for the cost of improvement?

8. Claire's hot water bill averages $25 per month. **1 month**

Option	Saving	Cost
Fix leaking hot water faucet.	20%	$2.50 for do-it-yourself washer kit.

9. The Fong's average heating bill is $50 per month. **39 months**

Option	Saving	Cost
Install wood burning stove.	80%	Stove $900, wood $200 per year

10. The Sylvan Apartments pay $65 extra each month to heat their hot tub. **45 months**

Option	Saving	Cost
Install solar heating.	$40	$1800

11. Don and Mardell Fields pay $300 a year to heat their pool. **20 years**

Option	Saving	Cost
Install solar panels.	$300	$6000

12. The Coach House Restaurant pays $400 extra each year to heat their garden room. **38 years**

Option	Saving	Cost
Build a greenhouse wall.	$225	$8500

DECISION

13. A long distance call to a relative will cost $2.60 for three minutes at the daytime rate (8 AM to 5 PM). The evening rate (5 PM to 11 PM) is 35% off. The night rate (11 PM to 8 AM) is 60% off. When should you call your relative?

CARPET

Carpet layers learn to cut and fit these large rolls of carpeting in order to have as little waste as possible.

Irv Goldstein works for Mabel's Carpet Company. He installs carpet. He went to work for the company after graduating from high school. He worked with more experienced people to learn his job. Irv tells how to estimate the costs for carpet.

Carpet is sold by the square yard (yd²). To find the number of square yards, compute the area to be covered. Area is length in yards multiplied by width in yards ($A = l \times w$). You often need to change measures to yards.   **Explain to students how to convert feet to yards.**

EXAMPLE 1.   Find the area of this room in square yards.

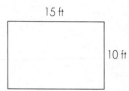

15 ft

10 ft

PLAN: **Step 1.**   Change feet to yards. (Use 3 feet = 1 yard)

15 ft = 5 yd

10 ft = $3\frac{1}{3}$ yd

Step 2. Find the area. $A = l \times w$

$$A = 5 \times 3\tfrac{1}{3}$$
$$= \tfrac{5}{1} \times \tfrac{10}{3}$$
$$= \tfrac{50}{3} = 16\tfrac{2}{3} \text{ yd}^2$$

The area is $16\tfrac{2}{3}$ square yards.

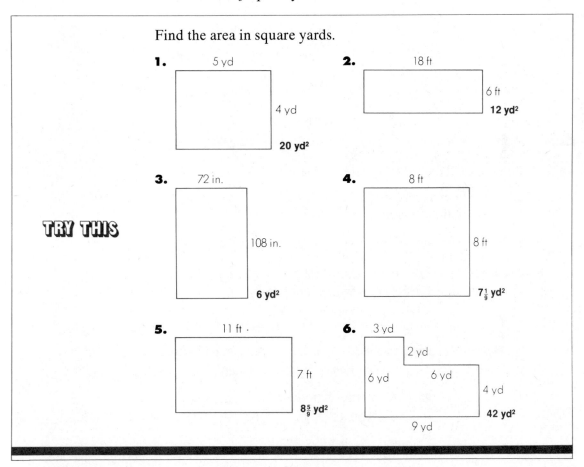

TRY THIS

Find the area in square yards.

1.
5 yd
4 yd
20 yd²

2.
18 ft
6 ft
12 yd²

3.
72 in.
108 in.
6 yd²

4.
8 ft
8 ft
7$\frac{1}{9}$ yd²

5.
11 ft ·
7 ft
8$\frac{5}{9}$ yd²

6.
3 yd
2 yd
6 yd   6 yd
4 yd
9 yd
42 yd²

Irv also says that carpet is made in 12 ft (4 yd) widths. He must often cut and sew carpet to fit a floor. Even then some carpet is wasted.

Tack strip is placed around a room to secure the carpet. To find how much tack strip is needed, compute the perimeter of the room. The perimeter is the distance around the room. It is the sum of the lengths of the sides.

EXAMPLE 2. Find out how much tack strip is needed. Add lengths of sides.

12 ft 5 in.
12 ft 5 in.
 9 ft 8 in.
 9 ft 8 in.
42 ft 26 in. = 44 ft 2 in.

You need 44 feet 2 inches of tack strip.

Find how much tack strip is needed.

TRY THIS

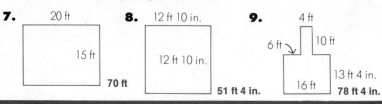

7. 20 ft / 15 ft / 70 ft

8. 12 ft 10 in. / 12 ft 10 in. / 51 ft 4 in.

9. 4 ft / 6 ft / 10 ft / 13 ft 4 in. / 16 ft / 78 ft 4 in.

To find the total cost of carpeting:

Add the costs per square yard of carpet, padding (goes under carpet), installation (includes labor and tack strip).

Multiply the total cost per square yard by the number of square yards.

EXAMPLE 3. Find the total cost for a 15-square-yard room.
Carpet costs $ 12.95 per yd².
Padding costs $ 2.50 per yd².
Installation costs $ 4.40 per yd².

PLAN: **Step 1.** Add to find the total cost per square yard.
$ 12.95 + $ 2.50 + $ 4.40 = $ 19.85

Step 2. Multiply to find the total cost.
$ 19.85 × 15 = $ 297.75

The total cost is $ 297.75.

Find the total cost.

TRY THIS

10. Room 20 yd² **$307.00**
carpet $ 9.85 per yd²
padding $ 2.00 per yd²
installation $ 3.50 per yd²

11. House 125 yd² **$2968.75**
carpet $ 14.50 per yd²
padding $ 4.25 per yd²
installation $ 5.00 per yd²

EXERCISES

Find the area in square yards.

1.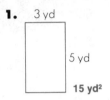

3 yd

5 yd

15 yd²

2.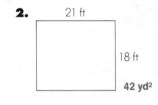

21 ft

18 ft

42 yd²

3.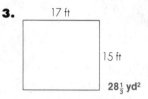

17 ft

15 ft

28⅓ yd²

Find how much tack strip is needed.

4.

10 ft

7 ft

34 ft

5.

8 ft 9 in.

14 ft 3 in.

46 ft

6.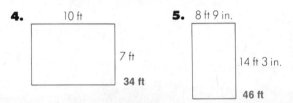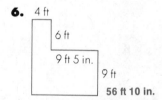

4 ft

6 ft

9 ft 5 in.

9 ft

56 ft 10 in.

Find the total cost.

	Area	Carpet	Padding	Installation	
7.	15 yd²	$9.25 per yd²	$2.00 per yd²	$3.25 per yd²	$217.50
8.	18 yd²	10.90 per yd²	3.50 per yd²	4.00 per yd²	$331.20
9.	24 yd²	15.60 per yd²	2.75 per yd²	3.75 per yd²	$530.40
10.	8 yd²	14.80 per yd²	3.15 per yd²	4.50 per yd²	$179.60
11.	30 yd²	21.40 per yd²	2.90 per yd²	3.90 per yd²	$846.00
12.	19 yd²	16.00 per yd²	3.00 per yd²	4.15 per yd²	$439.85

ON YOUR OWN

13. Measure and compute to find the number of square yards in a room.

14. Call a carpet store. Find the cost per square yard of
   a. their least expensive carpet.   **b.** their most expensive carpet.
   c. their least expensive padding.   **d.** their most expensive padding.
   e. their installation charges.

15. Calculate the lowest cost to carpet the room.

16. Calculate the highest cost to carpet the room.

WALLPAPER

Wallpaper designers create a great variety of patterns and colors suitable for any room or any house style.

Charles Humphrey is a paperhanger. He learned his skill by helping experienced workers. His work must be precise, so his job requires patience.

To calculate prices, Charles estimates how many rolls of wallpaper he will need. Most wallpaper comes in rolls 27 inches wide. This is called a width. A single roll is 16 feet long. If the wallpaper pattern is striped or has only a small pattern, Charles uses the following method to estimate how much is needed.

Explain to students that most wallpaper must be hung vertically only, and will not match if turned to cover more area.

EXAMPLE 1.   Estimate the number of rolls needed for this wall.

12 ft 2 in. width

9 ft height

PLAN: **Step 1.** Multiply and add to find the width of the wall in inches.
12 ft 2 in. = (12 × 12) + 2 = 146 in.

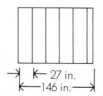

Step 2. Divide to find the number of widths needed.

146 in. ÷ 27 in. ≈ 5.4 widths
Since you cannot buy part of a width, 6 widths are needed.

Step 3. Multiply to find the total length of the six widths.
The wall is 9 ft high.

6 × 9 = 54 ft

Step 4. Divide to find the number of rolls needed.

Each roll is 16 ft long.
54 ÷ 16 ≈ 3.4   4 rolls are needed

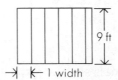

Estimate the number of rolls needed.

TRY THIS

1. 14 ft width
8 ft height
4 rolls

2. 21 ft 10 in. width
10 ft height
7 rolls

To estimate the amount of wallpaper needed for an entire room,
Charles uses the following method.

a. Add to find the perimeter in inches.

b. Divide by 27 inches to find the number of widths needed.

c. Multiply by the height in feet to find the total length of the widths.

d. Divide by 16 feet to find the number of rolls.

e. Subtract one roll for every two openings (doors, windows).

EXAMPLE 2. Estimate the number of rolls needed for a room 17 feet wide by 20 feet long by 8 feet high. There are two doors and three windows.

PLAN: **Step 1.** Add and multiply to find the perimeter in inches.
$$17 + 17 + 20 + 20 = 74 \text{ ft or } 888 \text{ inches}$$

Step 2. Divide to find the number of widths needed.
$$888 \div 27 \approx 32.8 \text{ widths or } 33 \text{ widths}$$

Step 3. Multiply to find the total length of the 33 widths.
$$33 \times 8 = 264 \text{ ft}$$

Step 4. Divide to find the number of rolls needed.
$$264 \div 16 = 16.5 \approx 17 \text{ rolls}$$

Step 5. For 5 openings deduct $2\frac{1}{2}$ rolls
$$17 - 2\frac{1}{2} = 14\frac{1}{2} \approx 15 \text{ rolls}$$

TRY THIS

Estimate the number of rolls needed.

3. Room 12 ft $\times$ 12 ft, 8 ft height, 2 openings **10 rolls**
4. Room 15 ft $\times$ 21 ft, 9 ft height, 3 openings **17 rolls**

To hang wallpaper, Charles brings tools such as razor blades, straightedge, ladder, and brushes. He charges for installation by the roll.

EXAMPLE 3. Find the total cost of 11 rolls of wallpaper at $ 5.95 per roll. The installation fee is $ 9.00 per roll.

PLAN: **Step 1.** Add to find the cost per roll.
$$\$ 5.95 + \$ 9.00 = \$ 14.95 \text{ per roll}$$

Step 2. Multiply to find the total cost.
$$\$ 14.95 \times 11 = \$ 164.45 \text{ total cost}$$

TRY THIS

Find the total cost.

5. 9 rolls
$ 8.40 per roll
$ 7.25 per roll installation **$140.85**

6. 6 rolls
$ 17.80 per roll
$ 9.50 per roll installation
$163.80

EXERCISES

Estimate the number of rolls of wallpaper needed. Use 27-inch widths.

1. Wall 10 ft × 8 ft, no openings **3 rolls**

2. Wall 10 ft 10 in. × 9 ft, no openings **3 rolls**

3. Wall 14 ft × 12 ft, no openings **6 rolls**

4. Wall 6 ft 7 in. × 9 ft 2 in., 1 opening **2 rolls**

5. Wall 15 ft × 8 ft, 2 openings **3 rolls**

6. Wall 20 ft 6 in. × 9 ft, 2 openings. **5 rolls**

7. Room 10 ft × 10 ft, 8 ft height, 2 openings **8 rolls**

8. Room 12 ft × 15 ft, 8 ft height, 3 openings **11 rolls**

9. Room 20 ft × 20 ft, 9 ft height, 7 openings **18 rolls**

10. Room 15 ft × 18 ft, 8 ft height, 8 openings **11 rolls**

11. Room 20 ft × 40 ft, 10 ft height, 10 openings **29 rolls**

Find the total cost.

12. 6 rolls
$ 10.95 per roll
$ 8 per roll for installation **$113.70**

13. 4 rolls
$ 9.90 per roll
$ 8.75 per roll for installation. **$74.60**

14. 10 rolls
$ 12.50 per roll
$ 9.50 per roll for installation **$220.00**

15. 12 rolls
$ 11.75 per roll
$ 8.50 per roll for installation **$243.00**

ON YOUR OWN

16. Measure to find the dimensions of a room (perimeter and height).

17. Estimate the number of rolls of wallpaper needed to do the room.

18. Call a wallpaper store. Find the cost per roll of
   a. their least expensive wallpaper.
   b. their most expensive wallpaper.
   c. their cost for installation.

19. Calculate the installed cost of the least expensive wallpaper and the most expensive.

CHAPTER REVIEW

How much should be budgeted for monthly housing costs?

1. Bill earns $ 11.50 per hour in a
40-hour week. **$460**

2. Mrs. Yee earns $ 8.75 per hour in a
40-hour week. Mr. Yee makes $ 300
per week in wages and tips. **$650**

3. Barbara earns $ 1800 per month. **$418.60**

Find the maximum amount to spend for a house, given these salaries.

4. $ 21,500 per year **$53,750**

5. $ 1675 per month **$50,250**

Find the monthly apartment cost.

6.

Lush Acres
$435

1 bedroom, furnished
utilities average $52 per month.

$487

7.

The Seasons
$575

2 bedroom, furnished
utilities included in rent

$575

Find the total apartment move-in cost.

8. First month's rent $ 360, cleaning
deposit $ 50, security deposit $ 225 **$635**

9. First month's rent $ 425, cleaning
deposit $ 75, security deposit $ 300
$800

Find the down payment.

10. House cost $ 72,500, 30% down **$21,750**

11. House cost $ 79,750, 25% down
$19,937.50

Find the total closing costs.

12. Purchase price $ 69,800
loan $ 52,000
loan fee   1%
deed recording fee $ 30
credit report $ 50
prepaid insurance $ 250
and taxes **$850**

13. Purchase price $ 102,500
loan $ 73,500
loan fee   1.5%
deed recording fee $ 100
credit report $ 75
prepaid insurance $ 825
and taxes **$2102.50**

Does the buyer qualify? All figures are monthly amounts.

14. Loan payment $ 380, gross income
$ 1800, terminating debts $ 125 **yes**

15. Loan payment $ 580, gross income
$ 2400, terminating debts $ 150 **no**

Find the monthly payment. Use the table on page 158.

16. $60,000 mortgage at 20.5% for 30 years $1027.20

17. $72,500 mortgage at 18.0% for 25 years $1099.83

Find the difference in total interest paid.

18. Term 25 years (300 months), monthly principal and interest payments of $684.60 at 12% *or* $986.33 at 18% $90,519

19. Monthly principal and interest payments of $663.53 for 25 years (300 months) *or* $648.03 for 30 years (360 months) $19,440.90

Find the cost.

20. Electricity
present meter reading 24186
previous meter reading 22948
rate $0.076 per kWh $94.09

21. Color TV (solid state)
yearly kWh 350
rate $0.0695 per kWh $24.33

Find the yearly saving.

22. The McCartney's average heating bill is $48 per month. $103.68

Option	Saving	Cost
Set thermostat 5° lower.	18%	None

23. Find the area in square yards. $18\frac{8}{9}$ yd²

17 ft

10 ft

24. Find the total carpet cost. $420
20 yd²
carpet $12.50 per yd²
padding $3.75 per yd²
installation $4.75 per yd²

Estimate the number of wallpaper rolls needed. Use 27-inch widths.

25.

11 ft 6 in. width

8 ft height

3 rolls

26. Room 12 ft × 9 ft, 9 ft height, 4 openings 9 rolls

SKILLS REVIEW

SKILL 12 Rounding decimals and money

Round to the underlined place.

1. 7.3 7   **2.** 8.5̲6 8.6   **3.** $ 2̲1.92 $22   **4.** $ 38̲.07 $38

SKILL 40 Simplifying fractions

Simplify.

5. $\frac{4}{8}$ $\frac{1}{2}$ **6.** $\frac{15}{18}$ $\frac{5}{6}$ **7.** $\frac{51}{85}$ $\frac{3}{5}$ **8.** $\frac{100}{4}$ 25

SKILL 43 Ratio

Write the ratio. Simplify when possible.

9. 25 tires to 5 cars $\frac{5}{1}$ **10.** 18 hits in 72 times at bat. $\frac{1}{4}$

11. 56 baskets in 16 games $\frac{7}{2}$ **12.** 48¢ for 2 apples $\frac{24}{1}$

SKILL 15 Adding money

Add.

13. $ 5.48
$\underline{+\ 3.21}$
$8.69

14. $ 26.72
$\underline{+\ 18.15}$
$44.87

15. $ 258.17
$\underline{+\ \ \ 9.49}$
$267.66

16. $ 246.97
$\underline{+\ 579.23}$
$826.20

SKILL 19 Subtracting money

Subtract.

17. $ 8.56
$\underline{-\ 4.32}$
$4.24

18. $ 6.48
$\underline{-\ 1.94}$
$4.54

19. $ 63.40
$\underline{-\ 19.65}$
$43.75

20. $ 5286.15
$\underline{-\ 3874.66}$
$1411.49

SKILL 22 Multiplying whole numbers

Multiply.

21. 80
$\underline{\times\ \ 9}$
720

22. 148
$\underline{\times\ \ 6}$
888

23. 64
$\underline{\times\ 34}$
2176

24. 7324
$\underline{\times\ \ \ 63}$
461,412

SKILL 23 Multiplying money

Multiply.

25. $ 4.56
$\underline{\times\ \ \ 5}$
$22.80

26. $ 62.78
$\underline{\times\ \ \ 4}$
$251.12

27. $ 5.98
$\underline{\times\ 12}$
$71.76

28. $ 87.96
$\underline{\times\ 74}$
$6509.04

SKILL 26 Estimating products: Money

Estimate.

29. $\begin{array}{r} \$4.98 \\ \times \quad 8 \\ \hline \$40 \end{array}$ **30.** $\begin{array}{r} \$38.74 \\ \times \quad 5 \\ \hline \$200 \end{array}$ **31.** $\begin{array}{r} \$4.78 \\ \times \quad 38 \\ \hline \$200 \end{array}$ **32.** $\begin{array}{r} \$59.48 \\ \times \quad 69 \\ \hline \$4200 \end{array}$

SKILL 50 Division: 1-digit divisors, decimals in dividend and quotient

Divide.

33. $3\overline{)9.3}$ → 3.1 **34.** $6\overline{)31.44}$ → 5.24 **35.** $23\overline{)89.7}$ → 3.9 **36.** $4\overline{)7}$ → 1.75

SKILL 51 Division: 2- and 3-digit divisors

Divide. Round to the nearest hundredth.

37. $6\overline{)438}$ → 73 **38.** $7\overline{)68,794}$ → 9827.71 **39.** $74\overline{)1702}$ → 23 **40.** $78\overline{)47,156}$ → 604.56

SKILL 52 Dividing a decimal by a decimal

Divide. Round to the nearest hundredth.

41. $0.2\overline{)6}$ → 30 **42.** $3.3\overline{)23.84}$ → 7.22 **43.** $1.2\overline{)4.9}$ → 4.08 **44.** $6.3\overline{)24.57}$ → 3.9

SKILL 64 Solving proportions

Solve.

45. $\frac{7}{8} = \frac{x}{16}$ 14   **46.** $\frac{5}{4} = \frac{25}{x}$ 20   **47.** $\frac{12}{16} = \frac{6}{x}$ 8   **48.** $\frac{x}{5} = \frac{1}{2}$ $2\frac{1}{2}$

SKILL 78 Area: Rectangles — squares

Find the area.

49. 16 in.²   4 in.   **50.** 7 m²   3.5 m   2 m   **51.** 48 yd²   6 yd   8 yd

52. Rectangle

$l = 9.8$ cm 39.2 cm²
$w = 4$ cm

53. Square

$x = 6.3$ m 39.69 m²

54. Square

$s = 5\frac{3}{4}$ ft $33\frac{1}{16}$ ft²

6
CONSTRUCTION
AND TRADES

BUILDING COSTS

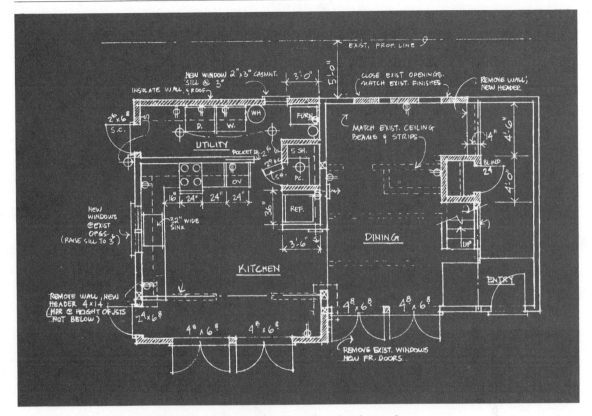

Blueprints show the location and sizes for all work to be done when
a house is being built or remodeled.

Aldo Ortega is a general contractor. He arranges for the construction
of buildings. He hires carpenters, plumbers, electricians, and other
skilled workers. They complete different parts of the construction.

Aldo started working as a carpenter. After eight years of construction
experience he formed his own contracting business.

To estimate the cost of a new house, Aldo multiplies the total living
area by a *cost factor,* which is the cost per square foot.

EXAMPLE 1. Estimate the cost of a new house. The total area is 1800
square feet and the cost factor is $ 39 per square foot.

$ 39 × 1800 = $ 70,200

The house will cost about $ 70,200 to build.

EXAMPLE 2.   Estimate the cost of this ranch house. The cost factor is $41 per square foot.

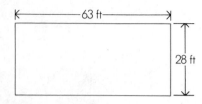

PLAN:

Step 1. Multiply to find the area.

$A = lw$
$= 63 \times 28$
$= 1764 \text{ ft}^2$

Step 2. Multiply the cost factor by the area to find the total cost.

$\$41 \times 1764 = \$72{,}324$

The ranch house will cost about $72,324 to build.

---

1. Estimate the cost of building a new house containing 1950 square feet. The cost factor is $42 per square foot. **$81,900**

2. Estimate the cost of this small house. The cost factor is $40 per square foot. **$30,720**

TRY THIS

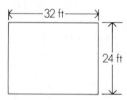

Another way to make an estimate is to compare the new house to a recently built house of similar quality.

EXAMPLE 3.   Estimate the building cost of a 2200 square foot house. Its quality is similar to that of a 2000 square foot house costing $98,000. Construction will begin in three months. (Add 1% for inflation for each month before construction begins.)

PLAN:

Step 1. Write a proportion.

$$\begin{array}{l} \text{cost of new house} \quad \rightarrow \\ \text{area of new house} \quad \rightarrow \end{array} \dfrac{h}{2200} =$$

$$\dfrac{\$98{,}000}{2000} \quad \begin{array}{l} \leftarrow \quad \text{cost of recently built house} \\ \leftarrow \quad \text{area of recently built house} \end{array}$$

Step 2. Find the cross products to solve the proportion.

$$2000 \times h = 2200 \times \$98,000$$
$$2000 \times h = \$215,600,000$$
$$h = \frac{\$215,600,000}{2000}$$
$$h = \$107,800$$

Step 3. Find the additional cost for three months delay. 1% per month for three months is 3%.

$$3\% \text{ of } \$107,800 = 0.03 \times \$107,800 = \$3234$$

Step 4. Add to find the total cost.

$$\$107,800 + \$3234 = \$111,034$$

The house will cost about $111,034 to build.

EXERCISES

Estimate the cost of building each house.

	House	Living Area (ft²)	Cost Factor (amount per ft²)	
1.	A	1800	$38	$68,400
2.	B	2100	$44	$92,400
3.	C	2450	$41	$100,450
4.	D	1900	$40	$76,000
5.	E	2300	$45	$103,500
6.	F	3000	$51	$153,000

7.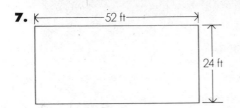

$43 per square foot **$53,664**

8.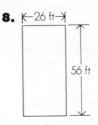

$39 per square foot **$56,784**

9.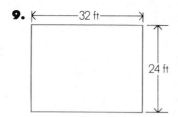

two floors, $ 37 per
square foot **$56,832**

10.

two floors, $ 40 per square foot
$80,640

11.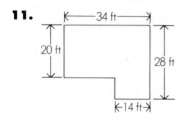

$ 45 per square foot **$35,640**

12.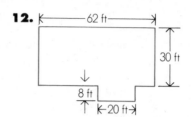

$ 40 per square foot **$80,800**

13. Estimate the cost of a 2200 square foot house. Its quality is similar to that of a 2000 square foot house costing $ 85,000. **$93,500**

14. Estimate the cost of a 2400 square foot house. Its quality is similar to that of a 2200 square foot house costing $ 102,000. **$111,273**

15. Estimate the cost of a 2500 square foot house. Its quality is similar to that of a 2300 square foot house costing $ 95,000. Construction will not begin for three months, so add 1% per month. **$106,359**

16. Estimate the cost of an 1800 square foot house. Its quality is similar to that of a 2000 square foot house costing $ 80,000. Construction will not begin for four months, so add 1% per month. **$74,880**

ON YOUR OWN   This On Your Own can make a good group activity.

17. Talk to a general contractor to find the current cost factor. Use it to estimate the cost of building a house.

18. How would you become a general contractor?

19. Find out how you get a contractor's license.

20. Find out which skilled workers would help complete the construction of a building.

MENTAL CALCULATION

QUICK CALCULATIONS WITH 25

To multiply by 25, you can multiply by 100 and then divide the result by 4.

EXAMPLE 1.　　Multiply 48 by 25.

Multiply by 100.　　48×100　　　　　　$= 4800$
Divide by 4.　　　　Take half.　　$4800 \div 2 = 2400$
　　　　　　　　　Take half again. $2400 \div 2 = 1200$

$48 \times 25 = 1200$

To divide by 25, you can multiply by 4 and then divide the result by 100.

EXAMPLE 2.　　Divide 284 by 25.

Multiply by 4.　　Double.　　$2 \times 284 = 400 + 160 + 8$
　　　　　　　　　　　　　　　$= 568$
　　　　　　Double again. $2 \times 568 = 1000 + 120 + 16$
　　　　　　　　　　　　　　　$= 1136$

Divide by 100.　　　　　　　$1136 \div 100 = 11.36$

$284 \div 25 = 11.36$

PRACTICE

1. 52×25 1300　　**2.** 63×25 1575　　**3.** 43×25 1075　　**4.** 86×25 2150

5. 95×25 2375　　**6.** 72×25 1800　　**7.** 23×25 575　　**8.** 124×25 3100

9. $38 \div 25$ 1.52　　**10.** $42 \div 25$ 1.68　　**11.** $68 \div 25$ 2.72　　**12.** $123 \div 25$ 4.92

13. $129 \div 25$ 5.16　　**14.** $213 \div 25$ 8.52　　**15.** $96 \div 25$ 3.84　　**16.** $56 \div 25$ 2.24

CARPENTRY

After being cut, trees float downriver to the lumber mill. Here they are lifted from the water to begin the final processing.

Linda Kay Cash is a carpenter. She constructs the walls, floors, ceilings, and roof of a house. She also does the trim work, such as window and floor molding.

Linda Kay learned her skills by working for several years with an experienced carpenter. Then she formed her own business.

Sometimes Linda Kay needs to build rafters for a roof. To do this, she needs to know the dimensions of the roof. **Make sure students understand these terms. They are very important in this lesson.**

The *span* is the width of the building. The *run* is half the span. The *rise* is the distance from the top of the ceiling to the peak of the roof. The *pitch* is the ratio of the rise to the span.

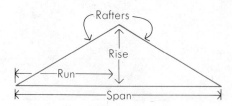

EXAMPLE 1. Find the pitch of a roof with a rise of 8 feet and a run of 12 feet.

PLAN: **Step 1.** Multiply to find the span.

$$2 \times 12 \text{ ft} = 24 \text{ ft}$$

Step 2. Find the ratio of rise to span.

$$\frac{8}{24} = \frac{1}{3}$$

The pitch is $\frac{1}{3}$.

TRY THIS

1. Find the pitch of a roof with a rise of 8 feet and a run of 10 feet. $\frac{2}{5}$

Linda Kay uses a carpenter's square to find the length of a rafter. Here is a portion of the rafter table on the square. Look under the 6-inch mark. The number 13.42 can be used to find the length of any rafter which rises 6 inches for every foot of run. Similarly, the number 14.42 under the 8-inch mark would be used to find the length of any rafter which rises 8 inches for every foot of run.

Students may be interested in seeing an actual carpenter's square that has this same information on it.

8	7	6	5	4	3	2	1
14.42	13.89	13.42	13.00	12.65	12.37	12.16	

16	15	14	13	12	11	10	9
20.00	19.21	18.44	17.69	16.97	16.28	15.62	15.00

EXAMPLE 2. Find the length of a rafter. The roof has a span of 18 feet 8 inches. It rises 6 inches for every foot of run.

PLAN: **Step 1.** Take half the span to find the run.

$$\frac{1}{2} \times 18 \text{ ft } 8 \text{ in.} = 9 \text{ ft } 4 \text{ in.} = 9\frac{1}{3} \text{ ft}$$

Step 2. Change $9\frac{1}{3}$ to a decimal. Multiply that decimal by 13.42, the number under 6 in.

$$9.33 \times 13.42 \approx 125.21 \text{ in.}$$

Students might like to try this other method:
$(9 \times 13.42) + (13.42 \div 3)$.

Step 3. Divide by 12 to find the rafter length in feet.

$$125.21 \div 12 \approx 10.43 \text{ ft}$$

The rafter should be about 10.43 feet long.

2. Find the length of a rafter. The roof has a span of 20 feet. It rises 8 inches for every foot of run. **12.02 ft**

Linda Kay also builds stairs. Building codes require that the rise be about 8 inches. The *tread* should be 10 or more inches.

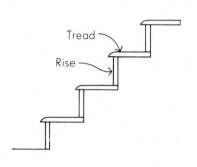

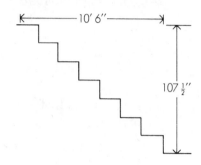

EXAMPLE 3. Find the height of each rise and the width of each tread. The stairway is to be built into an opening 10 feet 6 inches long. The distance from floor to floor is $107\frac{1}{2}$ inches.

PLAN:

Step 1. Divide to find the number of rises.

$107.5 \div 8 \approx 13.4 \approx 13$ rises

Step 2. Divide to find the height of each rise.

$107.5 \div 13$ rises ≈ 8.27 *Round to the*

$8.27 \approx 8.25 = 8\frac{25}{100} = 8\frac{1}{4}$ in.   *nearest $\frac{1}{4}$ inch.*

Step 3. Find the number of treads.

There are 13 rises. So there must be 12 treads.

Step 4. Divide to find the width of each tread.

10 ft 6 in. = 10 ft $\times$ 12 in. per ft + 6 in. = 126 in.

126 $\div$ 12 treads = 10.5

The width of each tread is $10\frac{1}{2}$ inches.

3. Find the height of each rise and the width of each tread. The stairway is to be built into an opening 12 feet 6 inches long. The distance from floor to floor is 110 inches. $7\frac{3}{4}''$, $11\frac{1}{2}''$

EXERCISES

1. Find the pitch of a roof with a rise of 10 feet and a run of 10 feet. $\frac{1}{2}$

2. Find the pitch of a roof with a rise of 6 feet and a run of 12 feet. $\frac{1}{4}$

3. Find the pitch of a roof with a rise of 8 feet and a run of 11 feet. $\frac{4}{11}$

4. Find the pitch of a roof with a rise of 12 feet and a run of 9 feet. $\frac{2}{3}$

Find the length of each rafter. Use the portions of the carpenter's square on page 193.

	Span	Distance Rafter Rises Per Foot of Run (in.)	Rafter Length (ft)
5.	20 ft	6	11.18
6.	14 ft	2	7.09
7.	36 ft	12	25.46
8.	40 ft	16	33.33
9.	28 ft	3	14.43
10.	42 ft	9	26.25
11.	36 ft 8 in.	13	27.03
12.	42 ft 3 in.	15	33.82

13. Find the height of each rise and the width of each tread. The stairway is to be built into an opening 13 feet long. The distance from floor to floor is 114 inches. $8\frac{1}{4}''$, $12''$

14. Find the height of each rise and the width of each tread. The stairway is to be built into an opening 12 feet 8 inches long. The distance from floor to floor is 109 inches. $7\frac{3}{4}''$, $11\frac{3}{4}''$

15. Find the height of each rise and the width of each tread. The stairway is built into an opening 14 feet long. The distance from floor to floor is 118 inches. $7\frac{3}{4}''$, $12''$

16. Find the height of each rise and the width of each tread. The stairway is built into an opening 15 feet long. The distance from floor to floor is 120 inches. $8''$, $12\frac{3}{4}''$

ON YOUR OWN

17. Find out what is meant by a building code.

ROOFING

You may wish to have students discuss other roofing materials that are used in your area.

A roofer's world is strong on geometry—triangles and trapezoids, parallelograms and rectangles.

Wendell Watts is a roofer. He prepares estimates for roofing jobs. Then, with his crew, he lays the roofing. Wendell learned his trade by working with an experienced roofer.

Wendell explains that roofing shingles are sold by the *square*. A square of shingles covers 100 square feet of roof. To make an estimate, Wendell finds the area of the roof in square feet. He divides by 100 to find the number of squares needed. Then he multiplies this number by the cost of one square. Labor costs are also a part of the estimate.

EXAMPLE 1. Estimate the cost of roofing this building. Shingles cost $ 32 per square. The labor charge is $ 29 per square.

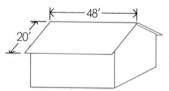

PLAN: **Step 1.** Multiply to find the area of the roof.

$$A = lw \times \text{number of sides}$$
$$= 48 \times 20 \times 2$$
$$= 960 \times 2$$
$$= 1920 \text{ ft}^2$$

Step 2. Divide to find the number of squares. Round up to the nearest square.

$$1920 \div 100 = 19.2$$
$$\approx 20 \text{ squares}$$

Step 3. Add to find the total cost per square.

$$\$32 + \$29 = \$61 \text{ per square}$$

Step 4. Multiply to find the cost of the roof.

$$\$61 \times 20 = \$1220$$

TRY THIS

1. Estimate the cost of roofing this building. Shingles cost $35 per square. The labor charge is $31 per square.

$1452

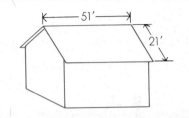

EXAMPLE 2.

Estimate the cost of roofing this garage. Shingles cost $29 per square. The labor charge is $35 per square.

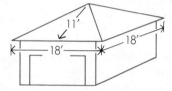

PLAN:

Step 1. Find the area of the roof. Note that there are four triangles. The area of a triangle is the base times the height divided by 2.

$$A = \frac{bh}{2}$$

$$= \frac{18 \times 11}{2}$$
$$= 99 \text{ ft}^2 \text{ for one side.}$$

Total area = 4 sides $\times$ 99 = 396 ft²

Step 2. Divide to find the number of squares.

$$396 \div 100 = 3.96 \approx 4 \text{ squares}$$

Step 3. Multiply to find the cost. The shingle cost per square is $29, the labor cost per square is $35, so the total cost is $64 per square.

$$\$64 \times 4 = \$256$$

2. Estimate the cost of roofing this building. Shingles cost $38 per square and the labor charge is $32 per square.

$420

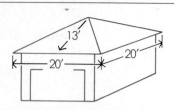

TRY THIS

EXERCISES

Estimate the cost of roofing these buildings.

1.

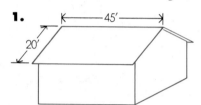

Shingle cost is $34 per square.
Labor cost is $30 per square. $1152

2.

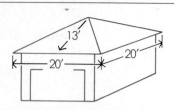

Shingle cost is $35 per square.
Labor cost is $32 per square. $1407

3.

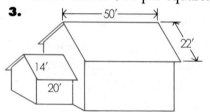

Shingle cost is $35 per square.
Labor cost is $37 per square. $2016

4.

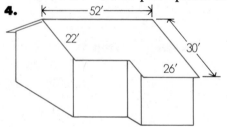

Shingle cost is $30 per square.
Labor cost is $35 per square. $1625

5.

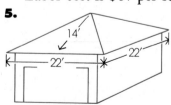

Shingle cost is $38 per square.
Labor cost is $37 per square. $525

6.

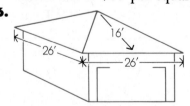

Shingle cost is $34 per square.
Labor cost is $30 per square. $576

ESTIMATING PERCENTS AGAIN

We can also estimate what percent one number is of another.

EXAMPLE 1. 12 is what percent of 25?

Think $\frac{12}{25}$ is about $\frac{12}{24}$ or $\frac{1}{2}$.

12 is about 50% of 25.

EXAMPLE 2. 3.7 is what percent of 350?

Think 3.7 is about 3.5.
350 is 100 times 3.5.

3.7 is about 1% of 350.

EXAMPLE 3. 93 is what percent of 47?

Think 93 is about 90 and 47 is about 45
90 is twice 45.

93 is about 200% of 47.

PRACTICE

Estimate. Answers will vary.

1. 12 is what percent of 37? 33%

2. 18 is what percent of 39? 50%

3. 26 is what percent of 260? 10%

4. 17 is what percent of 75? 25%

5. 82 is what percent of 400? 20%

6. 97 is what percent of 500? 20%

7. 4.3 is what percent of 790? 0.5%

8. 6.2 is what percent of 614? 1%

9. 900 is what percent of 1012? 90%

10. 638 is what percent of 812? 75%

11. 4.2 is what percent of 355? 1%

12. 5.1 is what percent of 43? 12%

13. 38 is what percent of 120? 30%

14. 46 is what percent of 239? 16%

15. 74 is what percent of 2.5? 3000%

16. 96 is what percent of 34? 300%

PLUMBING

Please inform students that plumbers use the term "lavoratory bowl" for bathroom sink.

Plumbers do more than repair leaky sinks and broken pipes. Large industries require complex plumbing installations.

Ginger Kwong installs water, gas, and waste disposal systems in her work as a plumber. She also repairs these systems. Ginger served several years as an apprentice plumber. She took night courses and passed a test to obtain her license as a master plumber.

Ginger explains two ways to estimate the cost of plumbing a new house.

EXAMPLE 1.   Estimate the total cost of plumbing a new house at $275 per fixture. The home will have a laundry tub, a shower, a bath tub, 2 toilets, a kitchen sink, and 2 bathroom sinks.

PLAN: **Step 1.**   Find the number of fixtures.

There are 8 fixtures.

Step 2.   Multiply to find the cost.

$275 \times 8 = 2200

The cost will be about $2200.

EXAMPLE 2. Estimate the total cost of plumbing the house by doubling the cost of materials. The materials for plumbing a new house will cost about $ 1800.

$ 1800 × 2 = $ 3600

The cost will be about $ 3600.

TRY THIS

1. Estimate the total cost of plumbing a new house at $ 250 per fixture. The house will have two bath tubs, a shower, a laundry tub, 2 toilets, a kitchen sink, and 3 bathroom sinks. **$2500**

2. Estimate the total cost of plumbing by doubling the cost of materials. The cost of materials for a new house will be about $ 1950. **$3900**

To estimate the length of a coil of flexible pipe, Ginger multiplies the circumference of the coil by the number of coils.

EXAMPLE 3. Estimate the length of a coil of plastic tubing. The coil has a diameter of 35 cm. It contains 18 coils.

Coil of flexible pipe

PLAN: **Step 1.** Estimate the circumference. Use the formula $C = \pi d$, where C is the circumference and d is the diameter. Since $\pi \approx 3.14$, use 3 to estimate.

$C \approx 3 × 35$ cm
$C \approx 105$ cm

Step 2. Multiply the circumference by the number of coils.
$105 × 18 = 1890$ cm

The length of the tubing is about 1900 centimeters or 19 meters.

TRY THIS

3. Estimate the length of a coil of flexible pipe. The coil has a diameter of 2 feet. It contains 9 coils. **54 ft**

A waste disposal pipe must fall a vertical distance while it runs a horizontal distance.

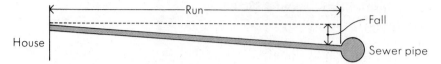

The *pitch* of the pipe is the ratio $\dfrac{\text{run}}{\text{fall}}$.

To keep the correct pitch while installing the pipe, a plumber may use a 2-foot level with a small wood block attached to the end. The size of the wood block is determined by the desired pitch.

Level
Wood block

The length of pipe is placed against the wood block and the opposite end of the level. When the level is horizontal, the length of pipe is at the correct pitch.

Pipe

EXAMPLE 4. A waste pipe must fall 12 inches and run 60 feet. Find the width of the wood block to be attached to a 2-foot level to keep the correct pitch.

PLAN: **Step 1.** Write a proportion using the pitch or $\frac{\text{run}}{\text{fall}}$ ratio.

$$\frac{60}{12} = \frac{2}{n}$$

Step 2. Find the cross products to solve the proportion.

For practical use, the thickness should be found to the nearest $\frac{1}{32}$ inch. To find how many 32nds, multiply the fraction by 32. Note that $32 \times \frac{12}{30} = 12.8 \approx 13$. Therefore, $\frac{12}{30} \approx \frac{13}{32}$.

$$60 \times n = 2 \times 12$$

Note the following shortcut:
60' pipe ÷ 30 = 2' level thus,
12" fall ÷ 30 = width of wood block.

$$60n = 24$$

$$n = \frac{24}{60} = \frac{12}{30} \approx \frac{13}{32} \text{ in.}$$

The block should be $\frac{13}{32}$ inch thick.

TRY THIS

4. A waste pipe must fall 12 inches and run 48 feet. Find the width of the wood block to be attached to a 2-foot level to keep the correct pitch. $\frac{1}{2}''$

EXERCISES

1. Estimate the total cost of plumbing a new house at $275 per fixture. The house will have a bathtub, a kitchen sink, a shower, 2 toilets, and 2 bathroom sinks. **$1925**

2. Estimate the total cost of plumbing the house by doubling the cost of materials. The cost of materials for plumbing a new house is about $2685. **$5370**

Estimate the length of the coil of flexible pipe in each of the following.

	Diameter	Number of Coils	
3.	39 cm	23	27 m
4.	41 cm	16	20 m
5.	19 in.	26	123 ft
6.	3 ft	12	108 ft
7.	$2\frac{1}{2}$ ft	14	105 ft
8.	1.4 cm	8	34 cm

In each of the following the run and fall of a waste pipe are given. Use proportions to find the width of the wood block to be attached to a 2-foot level to keep the correct pitch.

	Run (ft)	Fall (in.)	
9.	40	12	$\frac{3}{5}$ in.
10.	50	15	$\frac{3}{5}$ in.
11.	65	13	$\frac{2}{5}$ in.
12.	70	14	$\frac{7}{10}$ in.

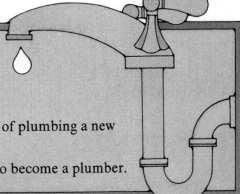

ON YOUR OWN

Check with a local plumber.

13. Find out how he or she estimates the cost of plumbing a new home.

14. Find out what special training is needed to become a plumber.

INSTALLING INSULATION

Insulation comes in rolls 16 inches wide, so it fits exactly between the studs—the vertical boards—of a wall being built.

Jim Thomas works for the Harford Insulation Company. He estimates insulation costs. He also helps with the installation. Jim began work at Harford after high school. He learned the trade from experienced workers.

Jim says that insulation comes in various R-ratings. As the R-rating increases, the insulation is more effective.

Some students may not know that a ranch house is a one-story house.

EXAMPLE 1. Estimate the cost of insulating the ceiling of a new 27′ × 43′ ranch house. A package of R-30 insulation covers 64 square feet and costs $23.68.

PLAN: **Step 1.** Round dimensions to the nearest ten feet. Multiply to find the area of the ceiling.

27 ft ≈ 30 ft, 43 ft ≈ 40 ft
30 × 40 = 1200 ft²

Step 2. Divide to find the number of packages needed.

64 ft² ≈ 60 ft²

1200 ÷ 60 = 20 packages

Step 3. Round the price to the nearest dollar. Multiply to find the cost.

$23.68 ≈ $24.00

$24.00 × 20 = $480.00

The cost of insulating the ceiling is about $480.

TRY THIS

1. Estimate the cost of insulating the ceiling of a new 49′ × 38′ house. A package of R-38 insulation covers 48 square feet and costs $27.36. **$1080**

EXAMPLE 2. Estimate the cost of insulating the 8-foot-high walls of the 27′ × 43′ ranch house. A package of R-11 insulation covers 88 square feet and costs $15.86.

PLAN: **Step 1.** Multiply the perimeter of the house by the height of the walls to find the area of the walls.

27 + 27 + 43 + 43 = 140 ft

140 × 8 = 1120 ft²

Step 2. Allow for doors and windows. Jim says doors and windows take up about 20% of the area. Therefore 80% of the area will need insulation.

0.80 × 1120 = 896 ≈ 900 ft²

Step 3. Divide to find the number of packages needed.

88 ft² ≈ 90 ft²

900 ÷ 90 = 10 packages

Step 4. Multiply to find the cost.

$15.86 ≈ $16

$16 × 10 = $160.

TRY THIS

2. Estimate the cost of insulating the 8-foot-high walls of a new 33′ × 43′ one-story house. A package of R-13 insulation covers 78 square feet and costs $16.45. Allow 20% of the area for doors and windows. **$208**

You can add insulation to existing houses by blowing a material called "blowing wool" into the attic or into the walls. Each inch of blowing wool increases the R-rating by about 2.2 units.

	BLOWING WOOL	
R-rating	**Minimum Thickness (in.)**	**Maximum Coverage per Bag (ft²)**
R–30	$13\frac{3}{4}$	33
R–26	12	37
R–22	10	45
R–19	$8\frac{3}{4}$	51
R–11	5	90

EXAMPLE 3.   Here is the floor plan of a house. How many bags of blowing wool will have to be blown into the attic to give an R-rating of R-22?

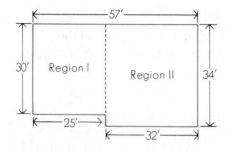

PLAN: **Step 1.**   Multiply to find the area of the ceiling.

Region I $\quad A = lw$
$= 30 \times 25$
$= 750 \text{ ft}^2$

Region II $\quad A = lw$
$= 34 \times 32$
$= 1088 \text{ ft}^2$

Total area $= 750 + 1088 = 1838 \text{ ft}^2$

Step 2.   Find the number of bags. From the chart above we see that to obtain an R-22 rating, each bag must cover 45 square feet. Divide the area by 45 to find the number of bags needed.
$1838 \div 45 = 40.84$

41 bags will be needed.

3. Here is the floor plan of a house. How many bags of insulation should be blown into the attic to give an R-rating of R-22? **26 bags**

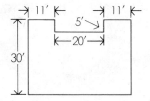

EXERCISES

1. Estimate the cost of insulating the ceiling of a new 29′ × 44′ ranch house. A package of R-30 insulation covers 64 square feet and costs $23.68. **$480**

2. Estimate the cost of insulating the ceiling of a new 32′ × 48′ house. A package of R-38 insulation covers 48 square feet and costs $27.36. **$810**

3. Estimate the cost of insulating the 8-foot-high walls of a new 35′ × 46′ one-story house. A package of R-30 insulation covers 64 square feet and costs $23.68. Allow 20% of the area for doors and windows. **$432**

4. Estimate the cost of insulating the 8-foot-high walls of a new 40′ × 52′ one-story house. A package of R-38 insulation covers 48 square feet and costs $27.36. Allow 20% of the area for doors and windows. **$648**

5. Here is the floor plan of a house. How many bags of insulation should be blown into the attic to give an R-rating of R-22? Use the chart on page 206. **43 bags**

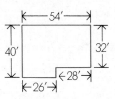

6. Here is the floor plan of a house. How many bags of insulation will have to be blown into the attic to give an R-rating of R-30? Use the chart on page 206. **56 bags**

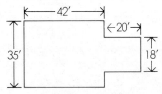

TILE LAYING

Each piece of tile has the same design. By arranging the tiles in different ways, tile layers create larger designs.

Liz Ames works for the Rudolf Floor Covering Company. She helps customers pick out floor covering. She also helps with the installation. Liz got her job after high school. She worked with experienced people to learn the trade.

Liz explains that tile is bought by the carton. A carton covers 45 sq ft.

EXAMPLE 1.   Desmond and Wanda Bates want to retile a small kitchenette. The dimensions of the floor are 8′ × 9′. How many cartons of tile are needed?

PLAN: **Step 1.**   Multiply to find the area of the room.

$$A = lw$$
$$= 9 \times 8$$
$$= 72 \text{ ft}^2$$

Step 2.   Divide to find the number of cartons.

$$72 \div 45 = 1.6 \text{ cartons}$$

Since you cannot buy part of a carton, two cartons are needed.

EXAMPLE 2.   Mariam Saroyan plans to tile her basement. Tile costs $ 19.95 per carton for up to 10 cartons and $ 18.85 per carton for each carton beyond 10. Find the cost of the tile.

PLAN: **Step 1.** Find the area of this room.

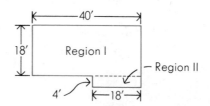

Think of the room as two rectangles, one 40 feet by 18 feet and the other 4 feet by 18 feet.

Region I

$A = lw$
$\quad = 40 \text{ ft} \times 18 \text{ ft}$
$\quad = 720 \text{ ft}^2$

Region II

$A = lw$
$\quad = 18 \text{ ft} \times 4 \text{ ft}$
$\quad = 72 \text{ ft}^2$

Total area: $720 + 72 = 792 \text{ ft}^2$

Step 2. Divide to find the number of cartons needed.

$792 \div 45 = 17.6$
18 cartons are needed.

Step 3. Multiply to find the cost for the first 10 cartons.
$\$19.95 \times 10 = \$199.50$

Step 4. Multiply to find the cost of the remaining cartons.
$\$18.85 \times 8 = \$150.80$

Step 5. Add to find the total cost.
$\$199.50 + \$150.80 = \$350.30$

TRY THIS

1. One carton of tile covers 45 square feet. Find the number of cartons needed for a laundry room whose dimensions are 6 feet by 8 feet. **2 cartons**

2. Find the cost of tile for a game room with this floor plan. The cost of tile is the same as in example 2. **$293.75**

EXERCISES

Find the cost of tiling each room. Tile costs $19.95 per carton for up to 10 cartons and $18.85 per carton for each carton beyond 10.

	Room	Dimensions (in ft)	
1.	Kitchen	18 × 32	$256.05
2.	Laundry Room	6 × 11	$39.90
3.	Bathroom	10 × 14	$79.80
4.	Clubroom	38 × 22	$369.15
5.	Workshop	22 × 18	$179.55
6.	Porch	28 × 16	$199.50

7. Kitchen $274.90

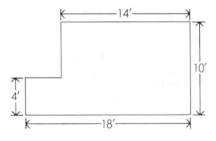

8. Laundry room $59.85

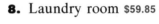

9. Bathroom $79.80

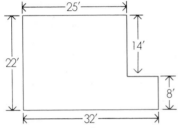

10. Clubroom $369.15

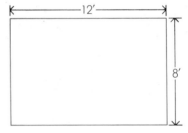

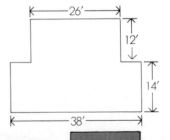

ON YOUR OWN

Contact a local floor-covering dealer.

11. Find out about various kinds of floor coverings and their costs.

12. Ask about linoleum. How is it purchased?

ESTIMATING AREA

Estimating is useful in many kinds of problems, including finding areas.

EXAMPLE 1. Estimate the area of a rectangular garden $12\frac{1}{2}$ feet wide and $37\frac{1}{4}$ feet long.

Think: $A = lw$

$$= 12\frac{1}{2} \times 37\frac{1}{4}$$

$$\approx 10 \times 40$$

$$\approx 400$$

The area is about 400 ft².

EXAMPLE 2. Estimate the area of a triangular-shaped house front that is 32 feet wide and $11\frac{3}{4}$ feet high.

Think: $A = \frac{1}{2}bh$

Round and multiply.

$A = \frac{1}{2} \times 32 \times 11\frac{3}{4}$

$$\approx \frac{1}{2} \times 30 \times 10$$

$$\approx 150$$

The area is about 150 ft².

PRACTICE

Estimate the area. Answers will vary.

1. A rectangular floor 12 feet by $28\frac{1}{4}$ feet 300 ft²

2. A triangular cloth with a base of 56.5 cm and a height of 38.25 cm 1200 cm²

3. A canvas in the shape of a trapezoid with a height of $5\frac{1}{2}$ feet and bases of 7 feet and $9\frac{3}{4}$ feet in length 48 ft²

4. A rectangular side of a barn which is 24 meters long and 5.5 meters high 125 m²

HOUSE PAINTING

In many communities, the house-painter's art has turned older homes into attractive and desirable shelter.

Lou Ferrari is a house painter. Lou learned his trade by working with his father. Because his work is high quality and because he offers his customers good follow-up service, his painting business has grown. Now Lou employs four paint crews. They paint both the inside and the outside of houses and offices. Much of Lou's time is spent in supervising and training his workers.

Before he can begin a new painting job, Lou estimates the amount of paint needed and the time it will take to do the job. Then he can give the customer an estimate of the total cost.

To estimate the amount of paint that will be needed on a job, Lou uses a chart like the one on the next page. Windows and doors are estimated to take up 15 square feet each.

Color of Paint	Coverage Per Gallon (ft²)	Coverage Per Quart (ft²)
Same color or dark over light	400	100
Light over dark (needs 2 coats)	200	50

EXAMPLE 1. Estimate the amount of paint needed to paint a $10' \times 12'$ bedroom with an 8-foot-high ceiling. The new paint is darker than the old paint. There are 2 windows and 2 doors.

PLAN:

Step 1. Multiply to find the area of the ceiling.

$10 \times 12 = 120$ ft²

Step 2. Find the perimeter and then multiply to find the area of the walls.

$10 + 12 + 10 + 12 = 44$ ft
$44 \times 8 = 352$ ft²

Step 3. Add to find the total area.

$120 + 352 = 472$ ft²

Step 4. Multiply to find the area of the doors and windows.

$4 \times 15 = 60$ ft²

Step 5. Subtract to find the area to be painted.

$472 - 60 = 412$ ft²

Step 6. From the table find the amount of paint needed.

One gallon and one quart of paint is needed.

TRY THIS

1. Estimate the amount of paint needed for a $16' \times 18'$ living room with 3 doors and 4 windows. The ceiling is 8 feet high. The paint is a light color over dark. 3 gal 3 qt

2. Estimate the amount of paint needed for an $8' \times 12'$ room with 2 doors and 4 windows. The ceiling is 10 feet high. The paint is dark over light. 1 gal 1 qt

---

The cost of painting depends on the labor charge. Lou knows the speed of his crew and can estimate the time needed. Doors, windows, and sanding require extra time. Lou says latex paint is easy to use. He explains how you can estimate labor costs.

Latex paint brushes and rollers can be easily cleaned with water.

EXAMPLE 2. Estimate the labor cost for painting a two-story house using latex paint. It has 4 doors and 16 windows. A crew of three painters will do the job. It takes them 24 hours to paint the walls. It takes an additional hour to paint the trim for each door or window. The labor cost is $7.00 per hour for each painter.

PLAN: **Step 1.** Find the time needed for windows and doors.

16 windows $\times$ 1 hr per window = 16 hr
4 doors $\times$ 1 hr per door = 4 hr

Step 2. Add to find the total time.

24 hr + 16 hr + 4 hr = 44 hr

Step 3. Find the labor cost for each painter.

$7 $\times$ 44 = $308

Step 4. Find the total labor cost.

$308 $\times$ 3 = $924

The labor cost is $924.

TRY THIS

3. Estimate the labor cost for painting the exterior of a ranch house with latex paint. It has 3 doors and 8 windows. A crew of 2 painters will do the job. They take about 7 hours to paint each side. It takes an additional hour for each door or window. Include 2 extra hours for sanding and cleaning. The labor cost is $8 per hour for each painter. **$656.00**

Oil base paint is more difficult to work with than latex paint. The labor cost is increased by about 20%.

EXAMPLE 3. Find the labor cost to paint the two-story house in example 2 with oil base paint. The cost for painting with latex paint is $924. **Example 3 can also be done by multiplying the latex cost by 120% or 1.2.**

20% of $924 = 0.20 $\times$ $924 = $184.80

The total labor cost will be $924 plus $184.80, or $1108.80.

TRY THIS

4. Find the labor cost to paint the ranch house of the previous Try This with oil base paint. **$787.20**

EXERCISES

Use the chart on page 213.

1. How many gallons of paint are needed to cover 1200 ft² with two coats of paint? **6 gal**

2. Enrique plans to cover 2800 ft² with one coat of paint. How many gallons of paint will he need? **7 gal**

3. How many gallons of paint will Barbara need to cover 4400 ft² with two coats of paint? **22 gal**

4. To cover 20,000 ft² with one coat of paint, how many gallons of paint are needed? **50 gal**

5. How many gallons of paint are needed to cover 11,600 ft² with two coats of paint? **58 gal**

6. Pearl plans to cover 2720 ft² with one coat of paint. How many gallons of paint will she need? **7 gal**

Estimate the amount of paint needed for the following rooms:

	Room	Dimensions (in ft)	Ceiling Height (ft)	Paint	Doors and Windows	
7.	Dining room	12 × 12	8	Dark over light	2 doors 1 window	1 gal 1 qt
8.	Living room	18 × 14	9	Light over dark	2 doors 3 windows	4 gal
9.	Kitchen	10 × 12	8	New—2 coats	1 door 1 window	2 gal 1 qt
10.	Bedroom	16 × 14	8	Light over dark	1 door 3 windows	3 gal 1 qt

Estimate the labor cost for painting the exterior of these four houses with latex paint.

	Room	Doors and Windows	Time	Labor Cost (amount per hour)	
11.	Ranch house	3 doors 9 windows	3 painters, 5 hours per side	$7.50	$720
12.	Two-story house	4 doors 12 windows	4 painters, 4 hours per side	$7.00	$896
13.	Bungalow	2 doors 5 windows	2 painters, 5 hours per side	$8.00	$432
14.	Beach house	2 doors 2 windows	3 painters, 6 hours per side	$9.50	$798

15–18. Find the labor cost for painting each house in exercises 7–10 with oil base paint. **$864; $1075.20; $518.40; $957.60**

ALUMINUM SIDING

Aluminum siding has been used in many communities to give a
bright new appearance to both old and new homes.

Dave Friedman works as an aluminum-siding contractor. He makes
estimates for customers and helps in the installation. Dave began
work as a helper. After learning the trade he started his own
business.

Dave explains that one square of siding covers 100 square feet. The
total cost of siding depends on the number of squares used. The
trim around windows and doors is an extra cost. Windows take
up 10% of the area.

EXAMPLE 1.   Estimate the cost of applying aluminum siding to this wall
at $ 160 per square. Trim around windows costs $ 15 per
window.

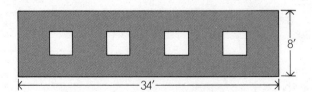

PLAN:

Step 1. Multiply to find the area.

$A = lw$
$= 34 \times 8$
$= 272 \text{ ft}^2$

Step 2. Multiply the area by 10% to find the area of the windows.

$272 \times 0.1 = 27.2 \text{ ft}^2$

Step 3. Subtract the area of the windows from the total area to find the area to be covered.

$272 - 27.2 = 244.8 \text{ ft}^2$

Step 4. Divide to find the number of squares.

$244.8 \div 100 \text{ per square} = 2.448 \text{ squares}$

About 2.5 squares are needed.

Step 5. Multiply to find the cost of the siding. You can buy part of a square.

$\$160 \times 2.5 = \$400.$

Step 6. Multiply to find the cost of the trim for the windows.

$\$15 \times 4 = \$60$

Step 7. Add to find the total cost.

$\$400 + \$60 = \$460$

The cost of applying aluminum siding to this wall is about $460.

TRY THIS

1. Estimate the cost for applying siding to this wall. Window trim costs $18 per window. Siding costs $160 per square.

$1100

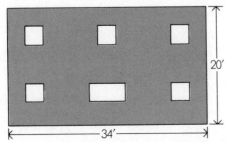

EXAMPLE 2.   Estimate the cost of applying aluminum siding to this wall at $160 per square. Allow 10% for waste because part of the wall is not rectangular.

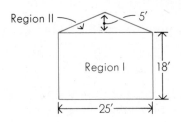

PLAN:

Step 1. Multiply to find the area of the rectangle.

$$A = lw$$
$$= 25 \times 18$$
$$= 450 \text{ ft}^2$$

Step 2. Multiply to find the area of the triangle.

$$A = \frac{bh}{2}$$
$$= \frac{25 \times 5}{2}$$
$$= \frac{125}{2}$$
$$= 62.5 \text{ ft}^2$$

Step 3. Add to find the total area.

$$450 + 62.5 = 512.5 \text{ ft}^2$$

Step 4. Take 10% of the area to find the amount for waste.

$$0.10 \times 512.5 \approx 51 \text{ ft}^2$$

Step 5. Add the amount for waste to the area to find the total amount needed.

$$51 + 512.5 = 563.5 \text{ ft}^2$$

Step 6. Divide to find the number of squares needed.

$$563.5 \div 100 = 5.6 \approx 6$$

Six squares are needed because .6 is more than half a square.

Step 7. Multiply to find the cost of the siding.

$$\$160 \times 6 = \$960$$

The total cost will be about $960.

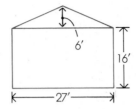

EXERCISES

These are the four walls of a house. Estimate the cost of applying aluminum siding. Subtract 10% per wall with windows or doors. For each non-rectangular wall add 10% for waste. The trim around windows and doors costs $ 17 per opening. Siding costs $ 160 per square.

1. Front $1171

2. Rear $1171

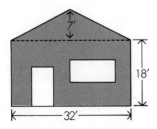

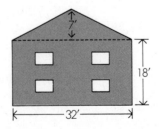

3. Side 1. $1314

4. Side 2. $1331

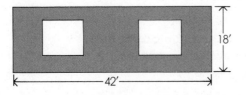

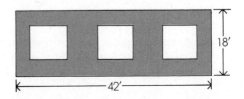

CHAPTER REVIEW

1. Estimate the building cost of this house. $40,560

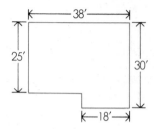

2. Estimate the cost of a 2300-square-foot house. It is of similar quality to a 2500-square-foot house costing $95,000. $87,400

3. Find the pitch of a roof with a rise of 9 feet and a run of 15 feet. $\frac{3}{10}$

4. Find the length of a rafter. The roof has a span of 22 feet. It rises 7 inches for every foot of run. Use the portion of the carpenter's square on p. 193. 12.73 ft

5. A stairway is to be built into an opening 11 feet 9 inches long. The distance from floor to floor is 112 inches. Find the height of each rise and the width of each tread. $8''$, $10\frac{3}{4}''$

6. Estimate the cost of roofing this building. $690

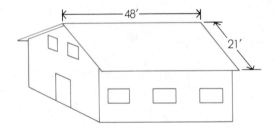

Shingles cost $36 per square. The labor charge is $33 per square.

7. Estimate the length of a coil of flexible pipe. The coil has a diameter of $2\frac{1}{2}$ feet. It contains 12 coils. 90 ft

8. A waste pipe is to be run 64 feet while falling 16 inches. Find the width of the wood block to be attached to a 2-foot level to keep the correct pitch. $\frac{1}{2}''$

9. Estimate the cost of insulating the ceiling of a new 30′ × 40′ house. A package of R-30 insulation covers 64 square feet and costs $26.88. **$510**

10. Here is the floor plan of a house. How many bags of insulation should be blown into its ceiling to give an R-rating of R-26. Use the chart on p. 206. **27 bags**

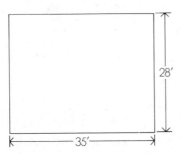

11. Find the cost of tiling a kitchen which is 19′ × 33′. Tile costs $19.95 per carton for the first 10 cartons and $18.85 for any cartons greater than 10. **$274.90**

12. Estimate the amount of paint needed for a 14′ × 18′ room with 3 windows and 2 doors. The ceiling is 8 ft high. The paint is light over dark. Use the chart on p. 213. **3 gal 2 qt**

13. Estimate the labor cost for painting the exterior of four walls with latex paint. The house has 4 doors and 10 windows. A crew of three painters will do the job. It takes them four hours to paint each wall. Each window and door takes an additional hour. The labor cost is $8 per hour for each painter. **$496**

14. Estimate the cost of applying aluminum siding to this wall. Allow 10% for waste. Siding costs $160 per square. **$1440**

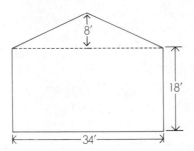

SKILLS REVIEW

SKILL 11 Rounding whole numbers

Round to the underlined place.

1. 4̲8 50   **2.** 141̲2 1410   **3.** 5̲52 600   **4.** 8̲498 8000

5. 32,8̲50 32,900   **6.** 43,9̲87 44,000   **7.** 428,0̲99 428,000   **8.** 870,9̲91 871,000

SKILL 12 Rounding decimals and money

Round to the underlined place.

9. 8̲.9 9   **10.** 9.4̲3 9.4   **11.** 9̲.88 10   **12.** 7.49̲82 7.50

13. $17̲.45 $17   **14.** $29̲.51 $30   **15.** $7.9̲2 $7.90   **16.** $14.25̲8 $14.26

SKILL 44 Converting percents to decimals

Convert to a decimal.

17. 43% 0.43   **18.** 120% 1.20   **19.** 8% 0.08   **20.** 6.3% 0.063

SKILL 46 Converting percents to fractions

Convert to a fraction, mixed number, or whole number.

21. 49% $\frac{49}{100}$ **22.** 24% $\frac{6}{25}$ **23.** 145% $1\frac{9}{20}$ **24.** $33\frac{1}{3}$% $\frac{1}{3}$

SKILL 14 Adding whole numbers

Add.

25. 74 + 96 = 170   **26.** 746 + 298 = 1044   **27.** 7284 + 3796 = 11,080   **28.** 347,821 + 981,294 = 1,329,115

SKILL 15 Adding money

Add.

29. $8.46 + 7.39 = $15.85   **30.** $3.78 + 9.65 = $13.43   **31.** $8.78 + 23.22 = $32.00   **32.** $478.97 + 923.75 = $1402.72

SKILL 16 Adding decimals

33. 8.7 + 9.2 = 17.9   **34.** 6.43 + 8.76 = 15.19   **35.** 0.918 + 6.942 = 7.860   **36.** 37.485 + 18.08 = 55.565

SKILL 18 Subtracting whole numbers

Subtract.

37.   97
          − 28
         ———
           69

38.   824
          − 673
         ———
           151

39.   3498
          − 2719
         ———
            779

40.   326,145
          − 198,087
         ————
           128,058

SKILL 22 Multiplying whole numbers

Multiply.

41.   898
          ×   4
         ———
          3592

42.   56
          × 47
         ———
          2632

43.   3784
          ×   86
         ———
          325,424

44.   798
          × 642
         ———
          512,316

SKILL 23 Multiplying money

Multiply.

45. $ 0.87
          ×   2
         ———
          $1.74

46. $ 18.78
          ×   8
         ———
          $150.24

47. $ 7.25
          ×   30
         ———
          $217.50

48. $ 0.98
          ×   21
         ———
          $20.58

SKILL 26 Estimating products — money

Estimate the product.

49. $ 6.85
          ×   7
         ———
           $49

50. $ 29.15
          ×   4
         ———
           $120

51. $ 38.76
          ×   29
         ———
          $1200

52. $ 42.16
          ×   58
         ———
          $2400

SKILL 27 Multiplying decimals

Multiply.

53.   6.42
          ×   7
         ———
          44.94

54.   9.8
          × 3.4
         ———
          33.32

55.   2.76
          × 3.8
         ———
          10.488

56.   8.14
          × 92.3
         ———
          751.322

SKILL 51 Division: 2- and 3-digit divisors

Divide. Round to the nearest hundredth.

57. $48\overline{)288}$ — 6

58. $62\overline{)3241}$ — 52.27

59. $827\overline{)4135}$ — 5

60. $225\overline{)1350}$ — 6

SKILL 53 Multiplying fractions

Multiply.

61. $\frac{1}{2} \cdot 8$ 4

62. $\frac{3}{8} \cdot \frac{2}{3}$ $\frac{1}{4}$

63. $\frac{1}{2} \cdot \frac{8}{9}$ $\frac{4}{9}$

64. $\frac{8}{3} \cdot \frac{7}{4}$ $4\frac{2}{3}$

SKILL 67 Finding a percent of a number

Solve.

65. What is 83% of 100? 83

66. What is 25% of 40? 10

7
TAXES
AND INSURANCE

SALES TAX   Some consumer items are exempted from tax.

Kathy Chan is a cashier at the Port Tack Restaurant. She calculates all customer bills, adds sales tax, receives payment, and gives change. Kathy uses a chart to find the amount to charge for sales tax.

6% SALES TAX REIMBURSEMENT SCHEDULE

Transaction	Tax	Transaction	Tax	Transaction	Tax
.01 – .10	.00	8.42 – 8.58	.51	16.92 – 17.08	1.02
.11 – .22	.01	8.59 – 8.74	.52	17.09 – 17.24	1.03
.23 – .39	.02	8.75 – 8.91	.53	17.25 – 17.41	1.04
.40 – .56	.03	8.92 – 9.08	.54	17.42 – 17.58	1.05
.57 – .73	.04	9.09 – 9.24	.55	17.59 – 17.74	1.06
.74 – .90	.05	9.25 – 9.41	.56	17.75 – 17.91	1.07
.91 – 1.08	.06	9.42 – 9.58	.57	17.92 – 18.08	1.08
1.09 – 1.24	.07	9.59 – 9.74	.58	18.09 – 18.24	1.09
1.25 – 1.41	.08	9.75 – 9.91	.59	18.25 – 18.41	1.10
1.42 – 1.58	.09	9.92 – 10.08	.60	18.42 – 18.58	1.11
1.59 – 1.74	.10	10.09 – 10.24	.61	18.59 – 18.74	1.12
1.75 – 1.91	.11	10.25 – 10.41	.62	18.75 – 18.91	1.13
1.92 – 2.08	.12	10.42 – 10.58	.63	18.92 – 19.08	1.14
2.09 – 2.24	.13	10.59 – 10.74	.64	19.09 – 19.24	1.15
2.25 – 2.41	.14	10.75 – 10.91	.65	19.25 – 19.41	1.16
2.42 – 2.58	.15	10.92 – 11.08	.66	19.42 – 19.58	1.17
2.59 – 2.74	.16	11.09 – 11.24	.67	19.59 – 19.74	1.18
2.75 – 2.91	.17	11.25 – 11.41	.68	19.75 – 19.91	1.19
2.92 – 3.08	.18	11.42 – 11.58	.69	19.92 – 20.08	1.20
3.09 – 3.24	.19	11.59 – 11.74	.70	20.09 – 20.24	1.21
3.25 – 3.41	.20	11.75 – 11.91	.71	20.25 – 20.41	1.22
3.42 – 3.58	.21	11.92 – 12.08	.72	20.42 – 20.58	1.23
3.59 – 3.74	.22	12.09 – 12.24	.73	20.59 – 20.74	1.24
3.75 – 3.91	.23	12.25 – 12.41	.74	20.75 – 20.91	1.25
3.92 – 4.08	.24	12.42 – 12.58	.75	20.92 – 21.08	1.26
4.09 – 4.24	.25	12.59 – 12.74	.76	21.09 – 21.24	1.27
4.25 – 4.41	.26	12.75 – 12.91	.77	21.25 – 21.41	1.28
4.42 – 4.58	.27	12.92 – 13.08	.78	21.42 – 21.58	1.29
4.59 – 4.74	.28	13.09 – 13.24	.79	21.59 – 21.74	1.30
4.75 – 4.91	.29	13.25 – 13.41	.80	21.75 – 21.91	1.31
4.92 – 5.08	.30	13.42 – 13.58	.81	21.92 – 22.08	1.32
5.09 – 5.24	.31	13.59 – 13.74	.82	22.09 – 22.24	1.33
5.25 – 5.41	.32	13.75 – 13.91	.83	22.25 – 22.41	1.34
5.42 – 5.58	.33	13.92 – 14.08	.84	22.42 – 22.58	1.35
5.59 – 5.74	.34	14.09 – 14.24	.85	22.59 – 22.74	1.36
5.75 – 5.91	.35	14.25 – 14.41	.86	22.75 – 22.91	1.37
5.92 – 6.08	.36	14.42 – 14.58	.87	22.92 – 23.08	1.38
6.09 – 6.24	.37	14.59 – 14.74	.88	23.09 – 23.24	1.39
6.25 – 6.41	.38	14.75 – 14.91	.89	23.25 – 23.41	1.40
6.42 – 6.58	.39	14.92 – 15.08	.90	23.42 – 23.58	1.41
6.59 – 6.74	.40	15.09 – 15.24	.91	23.59 – 23.74	1.42
6.75 – 6.91	.41	15.25 – 15.41	.92	23.75 – 23.91	1.43
6.92 – 7.08	.42	15.42 – 15.58	.93	23.92 – 24.08	1.44
7.09 – 7.24	.43	15.59 – 15.74	.94	24.09 – 24.24	1.45
7.25 – 7.41	.44	15.75 – 15.91	.95	24.25 – 24.41	1.46
7.42 – 7.58	.45	15.92 – 16.08	.96	24.42 – 24.58	1.47
7.59 – 7.74	.46	16.09 – 16.24	.97	24.59 – 24.74	1.48
7.75 – 7.91	.47	16.25 – 16.41	.98	24.75 – 24.91	1.49
7.92 – 8.08	.48	16.42 – 16.58	.99	24.92 – 25.08	1.50
8.09 – 8.24	.49	16.59 – 16.74	1.00	25.09 – 25.24	1.51
8.25 – 8.41	.50	16.75 – 16.91	1.01	25.25 – 25.41	1.52

EXAMPLE 1. Find the sales tax on a bill of $ 21.45.
$ 21.45 is betweeen $ 21.42 and $ 21.58.

The tax is $ 1.29.

TRY THIS

Find the sales tax. Use the table on page 225.

1. $ 7.25 $0.44 **2.** $ 25.00 $1.50 **3.** $ 15.75 $0.95 **4.** $ 19.86 $1.19

Sometimes a large group of people eat together. If the bill is larger than $ 25.41, then Kathy cannot find the sales tax on the chart. In this case she multiplies to find the correct tax or she uses a calculator.

EXAMPLE 2. Find the sales tax on a bill of $ 75.52.

PLAN:

Another method to find the sales tax on items over $25.41 is to use the tax chart more than once. For example, to find the tax on $37, think of $37 as $20 + $17.

Step 1. Change 6% to a decimal.

$$6\% = 6 \times 0.01 = 0.06$$

Step 2. Multiply to find the tax.

$$0.06 \times \$75.52 = \$4.5312$$

Step 3. Round to the nearest cent.

$$\$4.5312 \approx \$4.53$$

The tax is $ 4.53.

TRY THIS

Find the sales tax. Use the 6% rate.

5. $ 65.15 $3.91 **6.** $ 87.25 $5.24

7. $ 100.20 $6.01 **8.** $ 250.35 $15.02

Most states and some counties and cities have sales taxes. The rate varies. It can be changed by voter or government actions. Here are some examples. **Based on 1980 figures**

Place	State	County	City	Total
Helena, Montana	0	0	0	0%
Rutland, Vermont	3%	0	0	3%
Dallas, Texas	4%	0	1%	5%
Los Angeles, California	$4\frac{3}{4}\%$	$1\frac{1}{4}\%$	1%	7%
New York, New York	4%	Combined 4%		8%

EXAMPLE 3.   Find the sales tax on a sale of $25.86. Use $4\frac{1}{4}\%$.

PLAN: **Step 1.**   Change $4\frac{1}{4}\%$ to a decimal.

$$4\frac{1}{4}\% = 4.25\% = 0.0425$$

Step 2.   Multiply to find the tax.

$$0.0425 \times \$25.86 = \$1.099 \approx \$1.10$$

TRY THIS

Find the sales tax.

9. Amount $42, rate $4\frac{1}{2}\%$ $1.79   **10.** Amount $72, rate 7% $5.04

EXERCISES

Find the sales tax. Use the table on page 225.

1. $19.25 $1.16   **2.** $24.40 $1.46   **3.** $5.00 $0.30   **4.** $16.98 $1.02

5. $8.90 $0.53   **6.** $2.50 $0.15   **7.** $9.25 $0.56   **8.** $10.00 $0.60

Given the following amounts, find the sales tax.

9. $27.50, rate $3\frac{1}{2}\%$ $0.96   **10.** $31.99, rate $3\frac{3}{4}\%$ $1.20   **11.** $34.80, rate 4% $1.39

12. $38.45, rate $4\frac{1}{2}\%$ $1.73   **13.** $42.65, rate $4\frac{1}{4}\%$ $1.81   **14.** $45.63, rate 5% $2.28

15. $50.00, rate 5% $2.50   **16.** $53.81, rate $4\frac{1}{4}\%$ $2.29   **17.** $58.75, rate $5\frac{3}{4}\%$ $3.38

18. $70.32, rate $6\frac{1}{4}\%$ $4.40   **19.** $72.50, rate 6% $4.35   **20.** $76.89, rate $6\frac{1}{2}\%$ $5.00

21. $78.80, rate 7% $5.52   **22.** $84.26, rate $7\frac{3}{4}\%$ $6.53   **23.** $98.40, rate 8% $7.87

ON YOUR OWN

24. Find the sales tax rate in your area. Calculate the sales tax on $25.

25. What items are not subject to a sales tax in your area?

FEDERAL INCOME TAX

Tax money collected by the government is spent on many things—
such as new construction for the interstate highway system.

Gerald Hayes works part time preparing income tax returns. He
took courses at a community college to qualify for his work. Gerald
can help you with your tax return.

You must file an income tax return once a year. Gerald says that it
is important to keep records of your earnings.

Gerald shows you two common forms, the W–2 and the 1040A. The
W–2 form is given to you by your employer. You attach it to your
tax return.

Some people
(for example,
self-employed) may
pay taxes by different
methods. One way is
to estimate your yearly
income and pay
quarterly.

← 2 Employer's State number				Wage and Tax Statement **1982**
	4 Subtotal ☐ Correction ☐ Void ☐			Copy B To be filed with employee's FEDERAL tax return
	5 Employer's identification number			This information is being furnished to the Internal Revenue Service.
3 Employer's name, address, and ZIP code	6 Advance EIC payment			7
8 Employee's social security number	9 Federal income tax withheld	10 Wages, tips, other compensation	11 FICA tax withheld	12 Total FICA wages
13 Employee's name (first, middle, last)		14 Pension plan coverage Yes/No	15 *	16 FICA tips
17 Employee's address and ZIP code		18 State income tax withheld	19 State wages, tips, etc	20 Name of State
		21 Local income tax withheld	22 Local wages, tips, etc	23 Name of locality
For W–2 13-2678063 Department of the Treasury—IRS App. 6/18/82				

The Form 1040A is commonly called the short form. Many people
use it when filing their federal income tax return. Form 1040A is to be completed and filed
by April 15 of each year. You need to file only one, regardless of how many employers you had.

Form **1040A**   Department of the Treasury—Internal Revenue Service
U.S. Individual Income Tax Return   19**82**

Use IRS label. Otherwise, please print or type.	Your first name and initial (if joint return, also give spouse's name and initial)		Last name	Your social security number
	Present home address (Number and street, including apartment number, or rural route)			Spouse's social security no.
	City, town or post office, State and ZIP code		Your occupation ▶	
			Spouse's occupation ▶	

Presidential Election Campaign Fund ▶

Do you want $1 to go to this fund? .... | Yes | No
If joint return, does your spouse want $1 to go to this fund? | Yes | No

Note: Checking "Yes" will not increase your tax or reduce your refund.

For Privacy Act Notice, see page 14 of Instructions

Filing Status
Check Only
One Box.

1 ☐ Single
2 ☐ Married filing joint return (even if only one had income)
3 ☐ Married filing separate return. Enter spouse's social security number above and full name here ▶
4 ☐ Head of household. (See page 8 of Instructions.) If qualifying person is your unmarried child, enter child's name ▶

Exemptions
Always check the box labeled Yourself. Check other boxes if they apply.

5a ☐ Yourself   ☐ 65 or over   ☐ Blind | Enter number of boxes checked on 5a and b ▶
b ☐ Spouse   ☐ 65 or over   ☐ Blind | Enter number of children listed ▶
c First names of your dependent children who lived with you ▶ ....

d Other dependents: (1) Name	(2) Relationship	(3) Number of months lived in your home	(4) Did dependent have income of $1,000 or more?	(5) Did you provide more than one-half of dependent's support?	
					Enter number of other dependents ▶
					Add numbers entered in boxes above ▶

6 Total number of exemptions claimed . . . .

7 Wages, salaries, tips, etc. (Attach Forms W–2. If you do not have a W–2, see page 10 of Instructions) . . . . | **7** |
8 Interest income (See pages 4 and 10 of Instructions) . . . . | **8** |
9a Dividends (See pages 4 and 10 of Instructions)   9b Exclusion   Subtract line 9b from 9a | **9c** |
10a Unemployment compensation. Total amount received
b Taxable part, if any, from worksheet on page 11 of Instructions . . . . | **10b** |
11 Adjusted gross income (add lines 7, 8, 9c, and 10b). If under $10,000, see page 2 of Instructions on "Earned Income Credit" . . . . . | **11** |
12a Credit for contributions to candidates for public office. (See page 11 of Instructions) . . . . . | **12a** |
IF YOU WANT IRS TO FIGURE YOUR TAX, PLEASE STOP HERE AND SIGN BELOW.
b Total Federal income tax withheld (If line 7 is more than $22,900, see page 12 of Instructions) . . . . . | **12b** |
c Earned income credit (from page 2 of Instructions) . . . . | **12c** |
13 Total (add lines 12a, b, and c) . . . . | **13** |
14a Tax on the amount on line 11. (See Instructions for line 14a on page 12; then find your tax in the Tax Tables on pages 15–26.) . . . . . | **14a** |
b Advance earned income credit payments received (from Form W–2) . . . . | **14b** |
15 Total (add lines 14a and 14b) . . . . | **15** |
16 If line 13 is larger than line 15, enter amount to be **REFUNDED TO YOU** . . . . . . ▶ | **16** |
17 If line 15 is larger than line 13, enter **BALANCE DUE.** Attach check or money order for full amount payable to "Internal Revenue Service." Write your social security number on check or money order ▶ | **17** |

Under penalties of perjury, I declare that I have examined this return, including accompanying schedules and statements, and to the best of my knowledge and belief it is true, correct, and complete. Declaration of preparer (other than taxpayer) is based on all information of which preparer has any knowledge.

Your signature   Date ▶   Spouse's signature (if filing jointly, BOTH must sign even if only one had income)

Paid Preparer's Information
Preparer's signature and date ▶ | Check if self-employed ☐ | Preparer's social security no.
Firm's name (or yours, if self-employed) and address ▶ | E.I. No. | ZIP code ▶

☆ U.S. GPO:1979-283-262/80-0220-906

Form **1040A**

(left margin: Please Attach Copy B of Forms W-2 Here | Attach Payment Here | Please Sign Here)

Line 11 on Form 1040A asks for the adjusted gross income. Adjusted
gross income is the money you have received from all sources. This
is your taxable income.

EXAMPLE 1. Find the adjusted gross income for Fred Lewis. Add income from all sources.

W–2 from Al's Bakery	$7798.85
W–2 from Kim's Diner	6735.48
Interest from savings	74.87
	$14,609.20

Interest earned is reported on Form 1099

The adjusted gross income is $14,609.20.

Find the adjusted gross income.

TRY THIS

1. Alice Mayer $10,886.15

W–2 from Ace Hardware	$7284.00
W–2 from Wonder Cosmetics	3498.75
Interest from savings	103.40

2. Marcia Reyes, $14,495.00

W–2 from Bob's Trucking	$14,170.00
Interest from credit union	325.00

For Line 12B enter your Federal Income Tax Withholding from your W–2 form.

For Line 14a use the tax tables from the 1040A instruction booklet. Here is part of a table. Gerald explains that you receive one exemption for yourself and one for each member of your family dependent upon you. The table automatically gives you a deduction based on the number of your exemptions. If you have no dependents then list one exemption for yourself.

EXAMPLE 2. Find the tax on an income of $14,609.20 with 1 exemption.

Find the row containing your income. Look to the right under the column marked 1 exemption.

The tax is $2248.

Withholding helps you pay your income tax. It is automatically deducted from each of your paychecks.

Tax Table A
Single Filing Status

If Form 1040A, line 11, is—		And the total number of exemptions claimed on line 6 is—		
Over	But not over	1	2	3
		Your tax is—		
14,300	14,350	2,170	1,921	1,681
14,350	14,400	2,183	1,933	1,693
14,400	14,450	2,196	1,945	1,705
14,450	14,500	2,209	1,957	1,717
14,500	14,550	2,222	1,969	1,729
14,550	14,600	2,235	1,981	1,741
14,600	14,650	2,248	1,993	1,753
14,650	14,700	2,261	2,005	1,765
14,700	14,750	2,274	2,017	1,777
14,750	14,800	2,287	2,029	1,789
14,800	14,850	2,300	2,041	1,801
14,850	14,900	2,313	2,053	1,813
14,900	14,950	2,326	2,066	1,825
14,950	15,000	2,339	2,079	1,837
15,000	15,050	2,352	2,092	1,849
15,050	15,100	2,365	2,105	1,861
15,100	15,150	2,378	2,118	1,873
15,150	15,200	2,391	2,131	1,885
15,200	15,250	2,404	2,144	1,897
15,250	15,300	2,417	2,157	1,909

Find the tax.

3. Income $ 15,248
Exemptions 1 $2404

4. Income $ 14,340
Exemptions 2 $1921

5. Income $ 14,350
Exemptions 3 $1681

6. Income $ 15,150
Exemptions 1 $2378

After you have found the amount of taxes due (line 15), you must compare this amount with the total amount of taxes already paid (line 13). If the amount of taxes due is greater than the amount of taxes paid, subtract to find the *balance due*. If the amount of taxes paid is greater than the amount of taxes due, subtract to find your *refund*.

EXAMPLE 3. Find the difference. Will you get a refund or is there a balance due?

Line 13 $ 2164 taxes paid
Line 15 $ 2248 taxes due

PLAN: **Step 1.** Subtract these two amounts.

$ 2248 - $ 2164 = $ 84

Step 2. Compare lines 13 and 15.

Line 15 is greater so a balance of $ 84 is due.

TRY THIS

Find the difference. Will there be a refund or is there a balance due?

7. Line 13 $ 2380 taxes paid
Line 15 $ 2170 taxes due
$210 refund

8. Line 13 $ 1993 taxes paid
Line 15 $ 2076 taxes due
$83 balance due

EXERCISES

Find the adjusted gross income.

1. Bobby Allen
W–2 from Best Electric $ 8948.72
W–2 from Al's Plumbing $ 2496.88
$11,445.60

2. Roger Story
W–2 from Acme
Garage $ 13,926
Interest from credit
union $ 1040 $14,966.00

3. Ricardo Manos
W–2 from Slayton Steel
Co. $ 16,276.50
W–2 from Data Financial
Service $ 4268.50
Interest from savings $ 480.70
$21,025.70

4. Paula Ryder
W–2 from Earl's
Carpet $ 10,287.50
Interest from credit
union $ 98.70 $10,386.20

Tax Table B	Married Filing Joint Return							
If Form 1040A, line 11, is—		And the total number of exemptions claimed on line 6 is—						
	But not	2	3	4	5	6	7	8
Over	over	Your tax is—						
11,200	11,250	923	743	570	410	256	116	0
11,250	11,300	932	752	578	418	263	123	0
11,300	11,350	941	761	586	426	270	130	0
11,350	11,400	950	770	594	434	277	137	0
11,400	11,450	959	779	602	442	284	144	4
11,450	11,500	968	788	610	450	291	151	11
11,500	11,550	977	797	618	458	298	158	18
11,550	11,600	986	806	626	466	306	165	25
11,600	11,650	995	815	635	474	314	172	32
11,650	11,700	1,004	824	644	482	322	179	39
11,700	11,750	1,013	833	653	490	330	186	46
11,750	11,800	1,022	842	662	498	338	193	53
11,800	11,850	1,031	851	671	506	346	200	60
11,850	11,900	1,040	860	680	514	354	207	67
11,900	11,950	1,049	869	689	522	362	214	74
11,950	12,000	1,058	878	698	530	370	221	81
12,000	12,050	1,067	887	707	538	378	228	88
12,050	12,100	1,076	896	716	546	386	235	95
12,100	12,150	1,085	905	725	554	394	242	102
12,150	12,200	1,094	914	734	562	402	249	109
12,200	12,250	1,103	923	743	570	410	256	116
12,250	12,300	1,112	932	752	578	418	263	123
12,300	12,350	1,121	941	761	586	426	270	130
12,350	12,400	1,130	950	770	594	434	277	137
12,400	12,450	1,139	959	779	602	442	284	144
12,450	12,500	1,148	968	788	610	450	291	151
12,500	12,550	1,157	977	797	618	458	298	158
12,550	12,600	1,166	986	806	626	466	306	165
12,600	12,650	1,175	995	815	635	474	314	172
12,650	12,700	1,184	1,004	824	644	482	322	179
12,700	12,750	1,193	1,013	833	653	490	330	186
12,750	12,800	1,202	1,022	842	662	498	338	193
12,800	12,850	1,211	1,031	851	671	506	346	200
12,850	12,900	1,220	1,040	860	680	514	354	207
12,900	12,950	1,229	1,049	869	689	522	362	214
12,950	13,000	1,238	1,058	878	698	530	370	221
13,000	13,050	1,247	1,067	887	707	538	378	228
13,050	13,100	1,256	1,076	896	716	546	386	235
13,100	13,150	1,265	1,085	905	725	554	394	242
13,150	13,200	1,274	1,094	914	734	562	402	249
13,200	13,250	1,283	1,103	923	743	570	410	256
13,250	13,300	1,292	1,112	932	752	578	418	263
13,300	13,350	1,301	1,121	941	761	586	426	270
13,350	13,400	1,310	1,130	950	770	594	434	277

Use Tax Table B to find the tax due.

5. Income $ 12,876.25
Exemptions 2 $1220

6. Income $ 13,065.25
Exemptions 5 $716

7. Income $ 11,498.17
Exemptions 3 $788

8. Income $ 11,420.12
Exemptions 2 $959

9. Income $ 11,649.50
Exemptions 4 $635

10. Income $ 11,521.40
Exemptions 3 $797

11. Income $ 11,950.00
Exemptions 5 $522

12. Income $ 12,500.10
Exemptions 4 $797

13. Income $ 12,948.27
Exemptions 2 $1229

14. Income $ 13,291.92
Exemptions 5 $752

15. Income $ 13,378.60
Exemptions 3 $1130

16. Income $ 12,205.21
Exemptions 2 $1103

Find the difference. Will there be a refund or is there a balance due?

17. Line 13 $ 1746 taxes paid
Line 15 $ 1067 taxes due $679 refund

18. Line 13 $ 1079 taxes paid
Line 15 $ 1549 taxes due $470 due

19. Line 13 $ 1009 taxes paid
Line 15 $ 1022 taxes due $13 due

20. Line 13 $ 987 taxes paid
Line 15 $ 736 taxes due $251 refund

21. Line 13 $ 1180 taxes paid
Line 15 $ 1076 taxes due $104 refund

22. Line 13 $ 1049 taxes paid
Line 15 $ 1192 taxes due $143 due

23. Line 13 $ 328 taxes paid
Line 15 $ 425 taxes due $97 due

24. Line 13 $ 579 taxes paid
Line 15 $ 406 taxes due $173 refund

25. Line 13 $ 826 taxes paid
Line 15 $ 779 taxes due $47 refund

26. Line 13 $ 794 taxes paid
Line 15 $ 903 taxes due $109 due

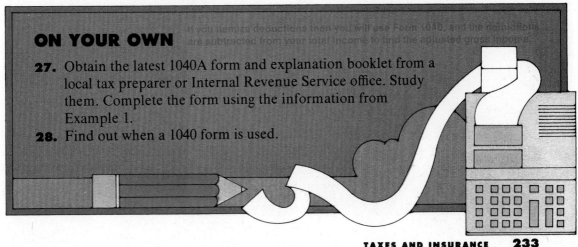

ON YOUR OWN

If you itemize deductions then you will use Form 1040, and the deductions are subtracted from your total income to find the adjusted gross income.

27. Obtain the latest 1040A form and explanation booklet from a local tax preparer or Internal Revenue Service office. Study them. Complete the form using the information from Example 1.

28. Find out when a 1040 form is used.

STATE AND CITY INCOME TAX
A few counties also have an income tax.

These World's Fair buildings were built with state and local taxes.
Now they form Seattle's cultural and convention center.

Jefferson Rollins lives in Alpena, Michigan. He works summers and part time at a farm machine shop while finishing high school. His mother helped him fill out his first tax forms. She explained that many states and some cities also have an income tax. Here are some rates:

These tax rates are based on 1980 figures.

State Income Tax Rates	
Texas	None
Michigan	4.6 % of adjusted gross income
Nebraska	17% of federal income tax paid
Alabama	$1\frac{1}{2}$% of first $ 1000 of adjusted gross income 3% of next $ 2000 of adjusted gross income $4\frac{1}{2}$% of next $ 2000 of adjusted gross income 5% of adjusted gross income over $ 5000
City Income Tax Rates	
Cincinnati, Ohio	2% of adjusted gross income
Louisville, Kentucky	2.2% of adjusted gross income for residents 1.45% of adjusted gross income for nonresidents who work inside the Louisville city limits.

EXAMPLE 1.   Jefferson had an adjusted gross income of $4786.
Find his Michigan state income tax.
Multiply the rate times the income.

$0.046 \times \$4785 = \$220.11$ *Use 0.046 for 4.6%.*

His state tax is $220.11.

EXAMPLE 2.   Patsy Ellis lives in Alabama. She earned an adjusted gross
income of $14,780 as a sales person. Find her state income tax.

PLAN: **Step 1.**   Multiply to find the tax on the first $1000 of her
adjusted gross income.

$0.015 \times \$1000 = \$15$

Step 2.   Multiply to find the tax on her next $2000.

$0.03 \times \$2000 = \$60$

Step 3.   Multiply to find the tax on her next $2000.

$0.045 \times \$2000 = \$90$

Step 4.   Subtract to find the amount over $5000.

$\$14,780 - \$5000 = \$9780$

Step 5.   Multiply to find the tax on the amount over $5000.

$0.05 \times \$9780 = \$489$

Step 6.   Add to find her total tax.

$\$15 + \$60 + \$90 + \$489 = \$654$

Her state tax is $654.

TRY THIS

Find the state income tax.

Place:	Facts:
1. Nebraska	Federal income tax paid $2746 **$466.82**
2. Alabama	Adjusted gross income $13,230 **$576.50**

EXAMPLE 3.   Mary Beth had an adjusted gross income of $19,450. She
lives and works in Louisville, Kentucky. Find her city
income tax.

Multiply the resident tax rate by her adjusted gross income.

$0.022 \times \$19,450 = \$427.90$

Mary Beth's city income tax is $427.90.

Find the city income tax.

TRY THIS

Place:

Facts:

3. Cincinnati, Ohio — Adjusted gross income $ 10,490 $209.80

4. Louisville, Kentucky — Nonresident, adjusted gross income $ 15,060 $218.37

EXERCISES

Find the state income tax.

Place:

Facts:

1. Michigan — Adjusted gross income $ 12,000 $552.00

2. Texas — Adjusted gross income $ 24,870 none

3. Alabama — Adjusted gross income $ 12,053 $517.65

4. Nebraska — Federal income tax paid $ 1,740 $295.80

5. Alabama — Adjusted gross income $ 12,249 $527.45

6. Michigan — Adjusted gross income $ 18,748 $862.41

7. Texas — Federal income tax paid $ 4,632 none

8. Nebraska — Federal income tax paid $ 2,497 $424.49

9. Alabama — Adjusted gross income $ 38,532 $1841.60

Find the city income tax.

Place:

Facts:

10. Cincinnati, Ohio — Adjusted gross income $ 24,175 $483.50

11. Louisville, Kentucky — Resident, adjusted gross income $18,345 $403.59

12. Louisville, Kentucky — Nonresident, adjusted gross income $ 19,862 $288

13. Cincinnati, Ohio — Adjusted gross income $ 32,900 $658

14. Cincinnati, Ohio — Adjusted gross income $ 6,532 $130.64

15. Louisville, Kentucky — Nonresident, adjusted gross income $ 7,435 $107.81

16. Cincinnati, Ohio — Adjusted gross income $ 36,942 $738.84

ESTIMATING MULTIPLE CALCULATIONS

Sometimes calculations require more than one step. When estimating such calculations we take one step at a time.

Estimate the following.

EXAMPLE 1. $(381 + 75) \times 12$

PLAN: **Step 1.**   Round the numbers.

$(381 + 75) \times 12 \approx (400 + 100) \times 10$

Step 2.   Do the work in the parentheses first.

$(400 + 100) \times 10 = 500 \times 10 = 5000$

$(381 + 75) \times 12 \approx 5000$

EXAMPLE 2. $\dfrac{23 + 41}{18}$

PLAN: **Step 1.**   Round the numbers.

$\dfrac{23 + 41}{18} \approx \dfrac{20 + 40}{20}$

Step 2.   Add first.

$\dfrac{20 + 40}{20} = \dfrac{60}{20}$

$= 3 \qquad \dfrac{23 + 41}{18} \approx 3$

PRACTICE

Estimate.

1. $(295 + 86) \times 14$ 4000

2. $(162 + 321) \times 23$ 10,000

3. $(645 + 131) \times 21$ 14,000

4. $(359 + 405) \times 33$ 24,000

5. $(414 + 609) \times 47$ 50,000

6. $(239 + 483) \times 54$ 35,000

7. $\dfrac{27 + 92}{58}$ 2

8. $\dfrac{47 + 92}{72}$ 2

9. $\dfrac{159 + 84}{37}$ 7

10. $\dfrac{68 + 21}{27}$ 3

11. $(305 + 294 + 608) \times 31$ 36,000

PROPERTY TAX

Assessors can also be hired outright or appointed. Taxing entities can be the state, county, city, school district, etc.

Local property taxes provide local services, such as police and fire protection, schools, and libraries.

Barbara Conners is a tax assessor. She was elected to that public office by the voters. She assesses property according to the laws of her county. Property taxes are established from her assessments. Property taxes help pay for many local services, such as schools, police, and fire protection.

Barbara explains that property taxes are based on the following:

The *market value* is the selling price of the property on the open market.

The *assessed value* is the value used for tax purposes. It is usually some percent of the market value.

The *rate of assessment* is the percent used to determine the assessed value.

The *tax rate* is the rate used to determine the amount of property tax to be paid on the assessed value.

Market values, assessed values, rates of assessment, and tax rates vary from region to region. Therefore, property taxes also vary from region to region.

EXAMPLE 1.

Find the assessed value and the property tax.

Market value	Rate of assessment	Assessed value	Tax rate	Property tax
$ 50,000	15%		$ 8 per $ 100	

PLAN:

Step 1. Multiply to find the assessed value.

$0.15 \times \$ 50,000 = \$ 7500$ *Rate of assessment × market value = assessed value*

Step 2. Multiply to find the property tax.

$\$ 7500 \times \dfrac{\$ 8}{\$ 100} = \dfrac{60,000}{100}$ *Assessed value*

$= \$ 600$ *× tax rate = property tax*

Find the assessed value and the property tax.

TRY THIS

	Market value	Rate of assessment	Assessed value	Tax rate	Property tax
1.	$ 46,000	35%	$16,100	$ 5 per $ 100	$805
2.	$ 74,000	25%	$18,500	$ 4 per $ 100	$740
3.	$ 50,000	100%	$50,000	$ 0.50 per $ 100	$250
4.	$ 72,000	40%	$28,800	$ 2 per $ 100	$576

EXAMPLE 2.

Tax rates are often given as a percent of assessed value.

Find the assessed value and the property tax.

Market value	Rate of assessment	Assessed value	Tax rate	Property tax
$ 55,000	20%		2.3%	

PLAN:

Step 1. Multiply to find the assessed value.

$0.20 \times \$ 55,000 = \$ 11,000$ *Rate of assessment × market value = assessed value*

Step 2. Multiply to find the property tax.

$\$ 11,000 \times 0.023 = \$ 253$ *Assessed value × tax rate = property tax*

EXAMPLE 3.

A 1980 Michigan rate

Mill corresponds to "milli . . ." as in millisecond, meaning one thousandth of a second.

In some areas the tax rate is given in mills per $1. A mill is one tenth of a cent. One mill = $0.001 Find the assessed value and the property tax.

Market value	Rate of assessment	Assessed value	Tax rate	Property tax
$40,000	50%		15 mills per $1	

PLAN:

Step 1. Multiply to find the assessed value.

$0.50 \times \$40,000 = \$20,000$ *Rate of assessment $\times$ market value = assessed value*

Step 2. Change mills to dollars.

15 mills = $15 \times \$0.001 = \$0.015$

Multiply to find the property tax.

$\$20,000 \times \dfrac{\$0.015}{\$1} = \$300$ *Assessed value $\times$ tax rate = property tax*

Find the assessed value and the property tax.

TRY THIS

		Market value	Rate of assessment	Assessed value	Tax rate	Property tax
5.		$90,000	20%	$18,000	3.6%	$648
6.		$75,000	50%	$37,500	2.25%	$843.75
7.		$70,000	35%	$24,500	20 mills per $1	$490

EXERCISES

Given the market value and the rate of assessment, find the assessed value.

1. $95,000 at 25% $23,750

2. $47,000 at 40% $18,800

3. $62,000 at 30% $18,600

4. $71,000 at 90% $63,900

5. $58,000 at 20% $11,600

6. $45,000 at 60% $27,000

7. $108,000 at 50% $54,000   **8.** $130,000 at 10% $13,000

9. $120,000 at 75% $90,000   **10.** $192,000 at 15% $28,800

11. $145,000 at 100% $145,000   **12.** $138,000 at 45% $62,100

13. $160,000 at 35% $56,000   **14.** $100,000 at 95% $95,000

15. $104,500 at 63% $65,835   **16.** $120,200 at 55% $66,110

Given the assessed value and the tax rate find the property tax.

17. $11,800 at $5 per $100 $590   **18.** $14,000 at $3 per $100 $420

19. $65,420 at $0.20 per $100 $130.84   **20.** $13,500 at $4 per $100 $540

21. $14,100 at 2.5% $352.50   **22.** $11,800 at 5% $590

23. $13,050 at 4.2% $548.10   **24.** $12,000 at 6% $720

25. $21,000 at 26 mills per $1 $546   **26.** $19,400 at 14 mills per $1 $271.60

27. $25,000 at 17 mills per $1 $425   **28.** $28,500 at 20 mills per $1 $570

Find the assessed value and the property tax.

	Market value	Rate of assessment	Assessed value	Tax rate	Property tax
29.	$48,000	40%	$19,200	$2.25 per $100	$332.00
30.	$82,000	25%	$20,500	$6 per $100	$1230.00
31.	$97,000	35%	$33,950	$7.25 per $100	$2461.38
32.	$64,000	20%	$12,800	4.4%	$563.20
33.	$28,000	50%	$14,000	2.3%	$322.00
34.	$39,000	30%	$11,700	5.4%	$631.80
35.	$57,000	35%	$19,950	36 mills per $1	$718.20
36.	$75,000	25%	$18,750	15 mills per $1	$281.25
37.	$84,000	40%	$33,600	12 mills per $1	$403.20

ON YOUR OWN

38. Call your assessor's office in your area.

    a. Find the rate of assessment.   **b.** Find the tax rate.

39. Calculate the property tax on an $80,000 home in your area.

CAR INSURANCE

Old or damaged cars are stripped of salvageable parts. Then they are sold for scrap to an auto junk yard.

Lee Morgan is an insurance agent. He sells car, home, health, and life insurance. Lee started as a trainee. After six months of training, he took tests to get his state license.

The contract that the insurance company gives you is called a *policy*. Lee advises you to shop for the best policy. These terms are used.

Liability coverage will pay the cost for any injury and damage for which you are liable (at fault).

Uninsured motorist coverage will help pay your costs if the other driver is liable but does not have insurance.

Collision coverage will pay for damage to your car due to an accident.

Comprehensive coverage will pay for damages to your car due to fire, theft, vandalism, or acts of nature.

The *deductible* is the amount you must pay on a claim before the insurance company begins to pay.

The *basic rate* is the starting cost for coverage.

The *driver rating factor* is a multiplier based on your age, your sex, where you live, and your driving record. It ranges from 1 to 4.5. The lower the number, the less you pay.

A young person may lower the driver rating factor by 25% by taking *driver training*. Having a B average or higher in school lowers the rate another 25%.

Most states have laws that require every driver to have liability insurance. Here are some typical amounts:

$ 20,000 maximum $ 40,000 maximum $ 10,000 maximum
to each person   to all persons   for property
you injure   you injure   you damage

20 / 40 / 10

The yearly *liability premium* is figured on a *basic rate* for the amount of coverage and the driver rating factor.

basic rate × driver rating factor = premium

EXAMPLE 1.

Note that higher coverage does *not* have a proportionally higher rate

The basic rate for 15 / 30 / 15 coverage is $ 110. Find the yearly liability premium for a driver with a 1.8 rating factor.

$ 110 × 1.8 = $ 198

basic   driver   yearly
rate   rating   premium
         factor

Coverage	Basic rate
10 / 20 / 10	$ 100
15 / 30 / 15	$ 110
20 / 40 / 15	$ 120
25 / 50 / 25	$ 126
50 / 100 / 50	$ 140
100 / 300 / 50	$ 150

TRY THIS

Find the yearly liability premium.

1. 10 / 20 / 10 coverage, 2.3 driver rating factor $230
2. 20 / 40 / 15 coverage, 2.0 driver rating factor $240
3. 25 / 50 / 25 coverage, 2.5 driver rating factor $315

The basic rate for uninsured motorist protection varies only with the amount of coverage. It can cost from $ 20 to $ 60 yearly. The premium for this coverage has no driver rating factor.

The basic rate for collision and comprehensive coverage is affected by the car class rating and the deductible. The premium for this coverage includes the driver rating factor.

Car class ratings range from 1 to 12. Cars with higher resale values are in the higher-rated classes. Cars with lower resale values are in the lower-rated classes.   Class 12 may be a new, large, expensive car. Class 8 may be an old, large, expensive car, or a new, small, cheaper car.

Increasing the *deductible* amount lowers the basic yearly rate.

Basic Rate Yearly Premiums						
	Collision deductible			Comprehensive deductible		
Car Class	$50	$100	$200	$0	$50	$100
1-5	$100	$85	$70	$25	$20	$15
6	125	110	95	30	22	17
7	150	135	125	35	25	20
8	175	160	145	40	32	26
9	195	180	165	45	36	29

EXAMPLE 2. Find the total yearly collision and comprehensive premium.

Driver rating factor 2.7, car class 6, collision deductible $50, comprehensive deductible $0

PLAN: **Step 1.** Use the table to find the basic rate yearly premiums for collision and comprehensive for a class-6 car.
Collision $125
Comprehensive $30

Step 2. Multiply by the rating factor to find the collision premium.
$125 \times 2.7 = $337.50   *Basic rate × rating factor = premium*

Step 3. Multiply to find the comprehensive premium.
$30 \times 2.7 = $81   *Basic rate × rating factor = premium*

Step 4. Add to find the yearly premium.
$337.50 + $81 = $418.50

Find the total yearly collision and comprehensive premium. Use the table above.

TRY THIS

	Driver rating factor	Car class	Collision deductible	Comprehensive deductible
4.	1.9	8	$100	none $380
5.	3.2	4	$200	$100 $272

Liability coverage is usually required for obtaining a car license.
Other coverages are optional.   **Some policies may include towing.**

EXAMPLE 3.   Find the total yearly car insurance premium. Liability $ 178,
uninsured motorist $ 25, collision $ 320, comprehensive $ 70
Add to find total.

$ 178 + $ 25 + $ 320 + $ 70 = $ 593

TRY THIS

Find the total yearly car insurance premium.

6. Liability $ 224, uninsured motorist $ 30 $254

7. Liability $ 189, uninsured motorist $ 25,
collision $ 345, comprehensive $ 82 $641

EXERCISES

Given the basic rate and the driver rating factor, find the liability
premium.

1. $ 100 at 1.8 $180   **2.** $ 125 at 1.2 $150

3. $ 107 at 3.7 $395.90   **4.** $ 136 at 1.7 $231.20

5. $ 112 at 2.9 $324.80   **6.** $ 150 at 4.2 $630

7. $ 135 at 4.5 $607.50   **8.** $ 145 at 3.2 $464

9. $ 109 at 2.6   **10.** $ 127 at 2.8 $355.60
$283.40

Find the yearly liability premium. Use the chart on page 243.

11. 10 / 20 / 10 coverage, 3.1 driver rating factor $310

12. 15 / 30 / 15 coverage, 4.2 driver rating factor $462

13. 15 / 30 / 15 coverage, 1.3 driver rating factor $143

14. 20 / 40 / 15 coverage, 2.7 driver rating factor $324

15. 50 / 100 / 50 coverage, 3.3 driver rating factor $462

16. 100 / 300 / 50 coverage, 1.3 driver rating factor $195

17. 25 / 50 / 25 coverage, 3.7 driver rating factor $466.20

Find the total yearly collision and comprehensive premium. Use the table on page 244.

	Driver rating factor	Car class	Collision deductible	Comprehensive deductible	
18.	1.3	3	$ 50	none	$162.50
19.	1.8	5	$100	$ 50	$189.00
20.	2.4	8	$200	$100	$410.40
21.	3.5	7	$100	$100	$542.50
22.	4.1	9	$200	$ 50	$824.10
23.	2.7	6	$ 50	none	$418.50
24.	4.2	4	$100	$ 50	$441.00
25.	3.1	8	$200	$100	$530.10

Find the total yearly car insurance premium.

26. Liability $ 182.40, comprehensive $ 82.15, collision $ 236.50 **$501.05**

27. Liability $ 247.80, uninsured motorist $ 17.50 **$265.30**

28. Liability $ 398.80, comprehensive $ 150.15, collision $ 475.80, uninsured motorist $ 18.25. **$1043**

29. Liability $ 225.30, comprehensive $ 125.15, collision $ 307.40 **$657.85**

30. Liability $ 294.20, uninsured motorist $ 19.75. **$313.95**

31. Liability $ 307.40, comprehensive $ 175.15, collision $ 385.40 **$867.95**

32. Liability $ 254.60, uninsured motorist $ 16.45. **$271.05**

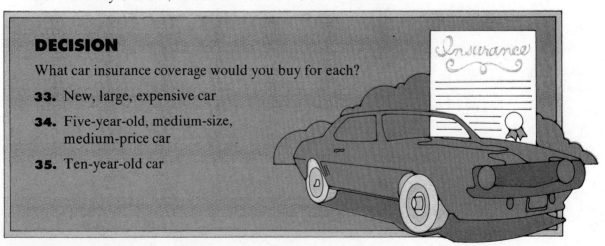

DECISION

What car insurance coverage would you buy for each?

33. New, large, expensive car

34. Five-year-old, medium-size, medium-price car

35. Ten-year-old car

MENTAL CALCULATION

SPECIAL ADDITION AND SUBTRACTION

Sometimes you can add or subtract by rounding and then adjusting.

EXAMPLE 1.　　Add: 56 + 19.
　　　　　　　　　Round 19 to 20.　56 + 20 = 76
　　　　　　　　　Then subtract 1.　76 − 1 = 75

EXAMPLE 2.　　Add: 35 + 78.
　　　　　　　　　Round 78 to 80.　　35 + 80 = 115
　　　　　　　　　Then subtract 2.　115 − 2 = 113

EXAMPLE 3.　　Add: 83 + 52.
　　　　　　　　　Round 52 to 50.　　83 + 50 = 133
　　　　　　　　　Add 2.　　　　　　133 + 2 = 135

EXAMPLE 4.　　Subtract: 532 − 180.
　　　　　　　　　Round 180 to 200.　532 − 200 = 332
　　　　　　　　　Add 20.　　　　　　332 + 20 = 352

PRACTICE

Add or subtract mentally. Use a procedure like those in the examples.

1. 97 + 19 116   **2.** 62 + 19 81   **3.** 42 + 78 120

4. 29 + 78 107   **5.** 43 + 59 102   **6.** 29 + 48 77

7. 85 + 32 117   **8.** 74 + 61 135   **9.** 63 + 22 85

10. 493 − 180 313   **11.** 357 − 180 177   **12.** 832 + 190 1022

13. 62 + 29 91   **14.** 123 + 49 172   **15.** 275 + 83 358

16. 138 + 790 928   **17.** 652 + 47 699   **18.** 243 + 91 334

HOMEOWNER'S AND RENTER'S INSURANCE

Because this damage is caused by a natural disaster, homeowners insurance may provide money for repair or replacement.

Sandi Beck is an insurance *broker*. She has about the same background and training as Lee Morgan. In addition, she passed her state's broker examination. Brokers are free to select policies from many insurance companies, not just one. They can choose a policy that best meets the needs of their customers.

Sandi says that renters and homeowners need insurance to cover possible loss by fire, theft, or natural disasters. Many renters want their personal property insured. Homeowners also need to insure the house itself.

Homeowner's insurance is based on the replacement cost of the house. The *premium* (cost of insurance) can vary due to the age, type of construction, location, and condition of the house.

EXAMPLE 1. Find the monthly premium for a house with a replacement cost of $ 70,000.

Replacement cost	Typical yearly premium
$ 50,000	$ 243
60,000	284
70,000	329
80,000	376
90,000	425
100,000	474

PLAN: **Step 1.** Find the yearly premium.
$ 329

Step 2. Divide by 12 to find the monthly payment.
$ 329 ÷ 12 = $ 27.416   *Round to the*
$ \approx $ 27.42   *nearest cent.*

Find the monthly insurance payment.

TRY THIS

1. Replacement cost $ 50,000 $20.25

2. Replacement cost $ 90,000 $35.42

Homeowner's insurance often covers additional items as well as the house itself. It usually includes personal property and liability insurance. Liability covers claims that could arise if visitors are injured on your property. This chart shows some coverages.
Note that coverage is not 100%.

Item	Amount of coverage (percent of replacement cost)
Additional structures	10%
Personal property inside of house	50%
Personal property outside of house	10%
Living expenses while house is being repaired or replaced	30%
Liability against injury or damage to persons or property	specific dollar amounts

Personal property outside of house might be a suitcase from your car or a wheelbarrow from your yard.

EXAMPLE 2. Find the amount of coverage for personal property inside a house insured for $ 75,000.

Multiply rate times replacement cost.

0.50 × $ 75,000 = $ 37,500

Find the amount of coverage.

3. Additional structures, insured home replacement cost $69,000 $6900

4. Contents away from home, insured home replacement cost $82,000 $8200

Renters may want to insure their personal property against losses due to fire or theft. Sandi explains how to calculate the amount of the coverage. **This calculation applies to renters and homeowners.**

EXAMPLE 3.   Find the amount covered by insurance.

Policies vary. Check carefully when buying insurance.

Item lost	Replacement cost	Useful years	Age in years	Deductible
Stereo	$535	15	2	$50

PLAN: **Step 1.** Divide the replacement cost by the number of useful years to find the cost per useful year.

$535 ÷ 15 ≈ $35.67 per useful year

Step 2. Subtract the age in years from the number of useful years.

15 − 2 = 13 useful years remaining

Step 3. Multiply the cost per useful year by the remaining number of useful years.

$35.67 × 13 = $463.71 current value

Step 4. Subtract the deductible from the current value to find the amount covered.

$463.71 − $50 = $413.71

Find the amount covered by insurance.

	Item lost	Replacement cost	Useful years	Age in years	Deductible
5.	TV	$400	10	3	none $250
6.	Couch	$350	15	4	$50 $206.67

EXERCISES

Find the monthly homeowner payment. Use the table on page 249.

1. Replacement cost $60,000 $23.67

2. Replacement cost $80,000 $31.33

3. Replacement cost $100,000 $39.50

Find the amount of coverage. Use the table on page 249.

4. Additional structures, insured home replacement cost $63,000 $6300

5. Personal property, insured home replacement cost $73,000 $36,500

6. Contents away from home, insured home replacement cost $58,000 $5800

7. Living expenses, insured home replacement cost $84,000 $36,150

Find the amount covered by insurance.

	Item lost	Replacement cost	Useful years	Age in years	Deductible	
8.	Desk	$650	20	5	$50	$437.50
9.	Clock	$180	15	10	$100	none
10.	Chair	$725	10	8	$100	$45
11.	TV	$810	10	new	$50	$760

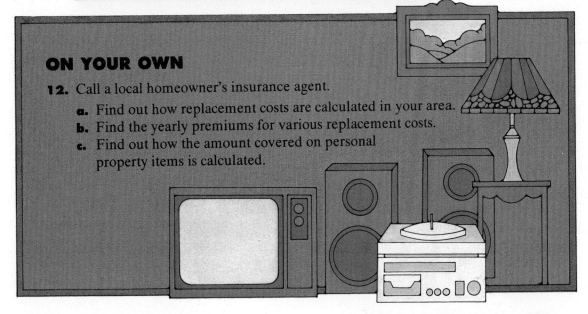

ON YOUR OWN

12. Call a local homeowner's insurance agent.
    a. Find out how replacement costs are calculated in your area.
    b. Find the yearly premiums for various replacement costs.
    c. Find out how the amount covered on personal property items is calculated.

HEALTH INSURANCE

Medical insurance can help to pay for expensive laboratory tests
and to diagnose your illness.

William Durin is a claims adjuster for a health insurance company.
He joined the company after serving in the Navy. The insurance
company gave him a special training course. He had to pass a state
examination to be licensed.   **About 3 out of 4 states require licensing.**

William can help you with your health insurance claims. He says
many policies require you to pay the first $ 100 toward your yearly
medical costs. This amount is called the deductible. The insurance
company then pays a percent of the remaining costs. The deductible
and rate of coverage can vary.

EXAMPLE.

Note that the insured
pays the deductible.

Find the amounts paid by the insurance company and by
the insured.

Covered medical expense	Deductible	Rate paid by insurance company
$ 825	$ 100	80%

PLAN: **Step 1.** Find the amount paid by the company.

a. Subtract the deductible.

$825 - $100 = $725

b. Multiply by the rate.

$0.80 \times $725 = $580

Step 2. Subtract to find the amount paid by the insured.

$825 - $580 = $245

Find the amount paid by insurance and by the insured.

	Covered medical expense	Deductible	Rate paid by insurance company	
1.	$1375	$50	85%	$1126.25, $248.75
2.	$987	none	70%	$690.90, $296.10

EXERCISES

Find the amount paid by insurance and by the insured.

	Covered medical expense	Deductible	Rate paid by insurance company	
1.	$740	$100	90%	$576, $164
2.	$2140	$50	80%	$1672, $468
3.	$7236	none	70%	$5065.20, $2170.80
4.	$1745	$200	85%	$1313.25, $431.75
5.	$3470	$250	75%	$2415, $1055
6.	$4500	$1000	100%	$3500, $1000
7.	$5195	$100	95%	$4840.25, $354.75
8.	$6245	$500	50%	$2872.50, $3372.50
9.	$10,000	none	80%	$8000, $2000
10.	$10,000	$250	80%	$7800, $2200

LIFE INSURANCE

People of all ages, from all walks of life, invest in life insurance to pay family expenses in case they die.

Connie Simpson is a life insurance agent. After graduating from high school she attended junior college. She took courses to prepare for the state insurance examination. She passed the test and received her license to sell life insurance.

Connie explains how life insurance works. You pay premiums to the company. If you die, the insurance company pays money to the person you have chosen as your *beneficiary*. Many family wage earners buy life insurance. Then if they die, their dependents will have some money for support. Some life insurance policies also pay money when a person retires.

There are four main types of life insurance. They are term life, straight or whole life, limited-pay life, and endowment.

Type	Length of coverage	Premiums	Comments
Term life insurance	Provides coverage for a given period of time, usually 5 or 10 years	You must pay premiums as long as you keep the insurance. At the end of the term, you may renew your policy. However, it will cost you more since the premiums increase as you get older.	This type of insurance gives temporary protection at a low cost. Of the four types, term insurance has the lowest premiums.
Straight or whole life insurance	Provides coverage for your whole lifetime, or until you cancel the policy	You must pay premiums as long as you keep the insurance. The premiums never increase.	If you decide to cancel the policy, you will get back some of the money you have put into it. Of the four types, straight or whole life insurance has the second lowest premiums.
Limited-pay life insurance	Provides coverage for your whole lifetime	You must pay premiums for a certain amount of time, usually 20 or 30 years. The premiums never increase.	After the 20 or 30 years, you no longer pay premiums but your coverage continues. Of the four types, limited-pay life insurance has the second highest premiums.
Endowment insurance	Provides coverage for a certain amount of time, usually 20 or 30 years	You must pay premiums for that same amount of time, 20 or 30 years. The premiums never increase.	After the 20 or 30 years, you receive money. Of the four types, endowment insurance has the highest premiums.

Connie says the premiums vary depending on the premium pay period, your sex, your age, the type of policy, and the amount of coverage.

Premiums are calculated from tables like this.

Annual Premium for Each $1000 of Insurance							
Age purchased	Term		Straight life	Limited pay		Endowment	
	5 Year	10 Year		20 Year	30 Year	20 Year	30 Year
M F							
15 18	–	–	$11.20	$28.10	$22.10	$49.50	$31.90
20 22	$4.75	$5.10	$12.10	$30.60	$24.00	$49.80	$32.40
25 28	$5.50	$6.10	$13.80	$33.30	$26.25	$50.30	$33.20
30 33	$6.70	$7.60	$15.80	$36.50	$28.90	$51.10	$34.40
35 38	$8.50	$9.80	$19.40	$40.15	$32.15	$52.30	$36.20

EXAMPLE 1.   Find the premium. Use the table on page 255.

Premium pay period	Sex	Age purchased	Type	Amount
annual	Male	20	10-yr term	$20,000

PLAN: **Step 1.**   Find the annual rate per $1000 from the table.
$5.10

Step 2.   Multiply that amount by the number of thousands to find the premium.

$5.10 × 20 = $102   *$20,000 = 20 thousands*

The annual premium for this policy is $102.

Sometimes the annual premium is too great to pay all at one time. Many people prefer to make several payments of a lesser amount each year. If you decide to do this, you will pay more for your coverage. The following table is used to compute semiannual, quarterly, and monthly payments. Shorter installment payments are more expensive—to cover costs, such as paperwork and billing.

Period	Percent of annual premiums
semiannual	51%
quarterly	26%
monthly	9%

EXAMPLE 2.   Find the premium.

Premium pay period	Sex	Age purchased	Type	Amount
monthly	F	18	straight life	$25,000

PLAN: **Step 1.**   Find the annual rate per $1000 from the table.
$11.20

Step 2.   Multiply that amount by the number of thousands to find the premium.
$11.20 × 25 = $280

Step 3.   To find the monthly payment, take 9% of the annual premium.
0.09 × $280 = $25.20

TRY THIS

		Premium pay period	Sex	Age purchased	Type	Amount
	1.	annual	M	25	5-yr term	$ 30,000
	2.	semiannual	F	18	20-yr limited pay	$ 18,000
	3.	quarterly	M	30	20-yr endowment	$25,000
	4.	monthly	F	28	straight life	$ 15,000

Find the premium. Use the tables on pages 255 and 256.

	Premium pay period	Sex	Age purchased	Type	Amount	
1.	annual	F	38	straight life	$ 30,000	$582
2.	semiannual	F	33	straight life	$ 30,000	$241.74
3.	quarterly	M	20	20-yr endowment	$ 25,000	$323.70
4.	monthly	M	25	30-yr endowment	$ 20,000	$59.76
5.	monthly	F	22	20-yr limited pay	$ 30,000	$75.87
6.	quarterly	M	15	30-yr limited pay	$ 35,000	$201.11
7.	annual	F	22	straight life	$ 50,000	$605.00
8.	monthly	M	20	10-yr term	$ 25,000	$11.48

ON YOUR OWN

9. Call a life insurance agent. Find the annual premium for a $ 20,000 policy for yourself for each of the four types of life insurance.

DECISION

10. Do you need life insurance now? Explain. If yes, which of the four types of policies and what amount would you choose? Explain.

CHAPTER REVIEW

Find the sales tax. Use the table on page 225.

1. $2.31 $0.14 **2.** $13.89 $0.83 **3.** $12.95 $0.78 **4.** $18.24 $1.09

Find the sales tax.

5. Amount $24.25, rate 4% $0.97

6. Amount $214.65, rate 6% $12.88

7. Amount $85.25, rate 5% $4.26

8. Amount $150, rate 5.5% $8.25

Find the federal income tax. Use the table on page 230.

9. Income $14,380, exemptions 1 $2183 **10.** Income $14,873, exemptions 1 $2313

11. Income $15,076, exemptions 2 $2105 **12.** Income $15,275, exemptions 3 $1909

Find the state or city income tax. Use the table on page 226.

Place: Facts:

13. Nebraska   Federal income tax paid $1430 $243.10

14. Cincinnati, Ohio   Adjusted gross income $14,750 $295.00

Find the assessed value and the property tax.

	Market value	Rate of assessment	Assessed value	Tax rate	Property tax
15.	$75,000	20%	$15,000	4.1%	$615
16.	$80,000	50%	$40,000	$2.75 per $100	$1100
17.	$65,000	100%	$65,000	13 mills per $1	$845

Find the yearly liability premium. Use the table on page 243.

18. 20 / 40 / 15 coverage, 2.9 driver rating factor $348

19. 25 / 50 / 25 coverage, 3.7 driver rating factor $466.20

Find the yearly collision and comprehensive premium. Use the table on page 244.

20. Driver rating factor 2.8,
car class 9,
collision $50 deductible,
comprehensive with no deductible $672

21. Driver rating factor 3.3,
car class 6,
collision $100 deductible,
comprehensive $50 deductible
$435.60

Find the monthly homeowner's insurance payment. Use the table on page 249.

22. Replacement cost $60,000 $23.67   **23.** Replacement cost $100,000 $39.50

Find the amount of homeowner's coverage. Use the table on page 249.

24. Personal property, insured home replacement cost $87,000
$43,500

25. Living expenses, insured home replacement cost $72,000
$21,600

Find the amount covered by personal property insurance.

	Item cost	Replacement cost	Average useful years	Age in years	Deductible	
26.	camera	$300	10	2	$50	$190
27.	bed	$450	15	5	$100	$200

Find the costs paid by health insurance and the costs paid by the insured.

	Medical expense	Deductible	Rate paid by insurance company	
28.	$845	$100	90%	$670.50, $174.50
29.	$1375	$50	80%	$1060, $315

Find the life insurance premium. Use the tables on pages 255 and 256.

	Premium pay period	Sex	Age purchased	Type	Amount	
30.	annual	M	20	straight life	$20,000	$242
31.	monthly	F	22	10-yr term	$30,000	$13.77

SKILLS REVIEW

SKILL 12 Rounding decimals and money

Round to the underlined place.

1. $\underline{4}$.6 5

2. $\$\underline{9}$.35 $9

3. $7.$\underline{86}$ $7.90

4. 29.4\underline{38}$ $29.44

SKILL 33 Writing decimals as fractions

Convert to a fraction.

5. 0.9 $\frac{9}{10}$

6. 0.04 $\frac{1}{25}$

7. 1.07 $\frac{107}{100}$

8. 0.013 $\frac{13}{1000}$

SKILL 44 Converting percents to decimals

Convert to a decimal.

9. 73% 0.73

10. 140% 1.40

11. 6% 0.06

12. 37% 0.37

SKILL 46 Converting percents to fractions

Convert to a fraction, mixed number, or whole number.

13. 27% $\frac{27}{100}$

14. 35% $\frac{7}{20}$

15. 80% $\frac{4}{5}$

16. $66\frac{2}{3}$% $\frac{2}{3}$

SKILL 14 Adding whole numbers

Add.

17. 298
      $+$ 472
      770

18. 6497
      $+$ 8585
      15,081

19. 398,108
      $+$ 169,942
      568,050

20. 473,493
      $+$ 787,875
      1,261,368

SKILL 15 Adding money

Add.

21. $7.93
      $+$ 0.08
      $8.01

22. $7.49
      $+$ 0.87
      $8.36

23. $9.47
      $+$ 3.68
      $13.15

24. $8.76
      $+$ 4.29
      $13.05

SKILL 16 Adding decimals

Add.

25. 8.7
      $+$ 3.9
      12.6

26. 7.32
      $+$ 9.48
      16.80

27. 8.746
      $+$ 0.943
      9.689

28. 8.69
      $+$ 6.738
      15.428

SKILL 22 Multiplying whole numbers

Multiply.

29.
$$\begin{array}{r} 46 \\ \times\ 5 \\ \hline 230 \end{array}$$

30.
$$\begin{array}{r} 4287 \\ \times\ 9 \\ \hline 38,583 \end{array}$$

31.
$$\begin{array}{r} 88 \\ \times\ 24 \\ \hline 2112 \end{array}$$

32.
$$\begin{array}{r} 729 \\ \times\ 67 \\ \hline 48,843 \end{array}$$

SKILL 23 Multiplying money

Multiply.

33.
$$\begin{array}{r} \$7.49 \\ \times\ 7 \\ \hline \$52.43 \end{array}$$

34.
$$\begin{array}{r} \$64.89 \\ \times\ 5 \\ \hline \$324.45 \end{array}$$

35.
$$\begin{array}{r} \$8.40 \\ \times\ 98 \\ \hline \$823.20 \end{array}$$

36.
$$\begin{array}{r} \$21.68 \\ \times\ 32 \\ \hline \$693.76 \end{array}$$

SKILL 27 Multiplying decimals

Multiply.

37.
$$\begin{array}{r} 93.6 \\ \times\ 7 \\ \hline 655.2 \end{array}$$

38.
$$\begin{array}{r} 89.43 \\ \times\ 6 \\ \hline 536.58 \end{array}$$

39.
$$\begin{array}{r} 6.34 \\ \times\ 12 \\ \hline 76.08 \end{array}$$

40.
$$\begin{array}{r} 4.287 \\ \times\ 35 \\ \hline 150.045 \end{array}$$

SKILL 50 Dividing whole numbers: 1-digit divisor, remainders

Divide.

41. $5\overline{)328}$ 65r3

42. $4\overline{)321}$ 80r1

43. $7\overline{)8241}$ 1177r2

44. $6\overline{)9487}$ 1581r1

SKILL 50 Division: 1-digit divisor, decimals in dividend and quotient

Divide. Round to the nearest hundredth.

45. $5\overline{)138}$ 27.6

46. $8\overline{)526}$ 65.75

47. $9\overline{)281}$ 31.22

48. $7\overline{)486}$ 69.43

SKILL 51 Division: 2- and 3-digit divisors

Divide. Round to the nearest hundredth.

49. $16\overline{)1000}$ 62.5

50. $65\overline{)228}$ 3.51

51. $62\overline{)3241}$ 52.27

52. $827\overline{)27,291}$ 33

SKILL 67 Finding a percent of a number

Solve.

53. What is 70% of 200? 140

54. What is 75% of 20? 15

55. 3.1% of 10 is what number? 0.31

56. What is 0.6% of 52? 0.312

57. What is $137\frac{1}{2}$% of 120? 165

58. What is 140.3% of 6000? 8418

8
TRANSPORTATION
AND TRAVEL

BUYING A CAR

It would be illustrative to obtain an actual car sticker from a local dealer and show this to the students.

Trainloads of new cars speed on their way from assembly plants to dealer showrooms in every part of the country.

Edward Brewer sells new and used cars. He got his job by answering an ad in the newspaper. The company he works for trained him as a salesperson. Edward has always liked cars, and he is successful at his job.

Edward is paid a commission on each car he sells. The commission depends on whether the car is new or used. For new cars, it also depends on the model of the car.

The *base price* of a new car is set by the manufacturer. The *sticker price* is the base price plus the cost of any extra equipment added to the car. Sometimes cars are sold for less than the sticker price. But how much less depends on many things—the dealer, how popular the car is, and the number of cars in stock.

This chart shows some base prices and the costs of "extras."

	Hatchback Coupe	Coupe	Sedan	Sports Model
Base price	$4700	$4999	$7759	$14,959
Custom interior	161	standard	standard	standard
Deluxe exterior	112	137	standard	standard
Air conditioning	531	564	647	standard
Tinted glass	64	70	90	standard
AM radio	81	81	92	standard
AM-FM radio	94	143	156	standard
CB radio	195	210	250	279
Power brakes	76	76	standard	standard
Power steering	148	148	standard	standard
Wheel covers	56	63	75	standard
Rear window defogger	95	103	109	109
Automatic transmission	275	300	300	325
Sun roof	375	400	425	425

EXAMPLE 1. Lynda Fritz bought a new coupe with air conditioning, tinted windows, AM radio, and power brakes. Find the sticker price.

Base price	$4999
Air conditioning	564
Tinted glass	70
AM radio	81
Power brakes	76
Sticker price	$5790

TRY THIS

1. Le Roy Bloomberg wants to buy a sedan with air conditioning, tinted glass, AM–FM radio, and rear window defogger. Find the sticker price. $8761.00

Edward explains that sales tax, local dealer preparation charges, and a license fee must be added to the sticker price. The resulting amount is the total cost or *cash price* of the car.

Dealer preparation costs include wash and wax, undercoating, and a general maintenance check. These costs vary with the car and the dealer. Dealer preparation charges are considered labor and are not subject to sales tax.

EXAMPLE 2. Marion Reesey is buying a new hatchback coupe. It has an AM–FM radio, power brakes, and an electric rear window defogger. The sales tax is 5%. The dealer preparation costs are $139. The license fee is $20. Find the cash price.

PLAN:

Step 1. Add to find the sticker price.

Base price	$4700.00
AM–FM radio	94.00
Power brakes	76.00
Rear window defogger	95.00
Sticker price	$4965.00

Step 2. Multiply to find the sales tax.

Sales tax is paid only on the sticker price. It is not paid on dealer preparation costs or license fees.

$0.05\% \times \$4965 = \$248.25$

Step 3. Add to find the cash price.

Sticker price	$4965.00
Sales tax	248.25
Dealer prep. cost	139.00
License fee	20.00
Cash price	$5372.25

TRY THIS

2. Harriet Horowitz is buying a new sedan. It has air conditioning, tinted glass, AM–FM radio, CB radio, and wheel covers. The sales tax is 4%. The dealer preparation costs are $146. The license fee is $25. Find the cash price. $9507.00

EXERCISES

Use the table on page 264 to help find the sticker price.

1. Sports model
Custom interior
Air conditioning
Tinted glass
CB radio
AM–FM radio $15,238

2. Sedan
Deluxe exterior
AM radio
Power brakes
Power steering $7851

3. Sedan
Air conditioning
Tinted glass
AM–FM radio
CB radio
Power brakes $8902

4. Coupe
  Deluxe exterior
  Air conditioning
  Tinted glass
  Wheel covers
  AM–FM radio $5976

5. Coupe
  AM–FM radio
  Deluxe exterior
  Power brakes
  Power steering $5503

6. Hatchback coupe
  AM radio
  Rear window defogger
  Power brakes $4952

Find the cash price of each of the following. Use the table on page 264.

7. Hatchback coupe
  AM–FM radio
  Air conditioning
  Tinted glass
  Power brakes
  Sales tax 5%
  Dealer preparation $ 163
  License fee $ 25 $5926.25

8. Sedan
  AM radio
  Wheel covers
  Deluxe exterior
  Power steering
  Sales tax 4%
  Dealer preparation $ 170
  License fee $ 30 $8443.04

9. Sports model
  Power brakes
  Rear window defogger
  Sales tax 6%
  Dealer preparation $ 159
  License fee $ 28 $16,159.08

10. Coupe
  Custom interior
  Power brakes
  Sales tax 7%
  Dealer preparation $ 146
  License fee $ 20 $5596.25

DECISION

11. Select a car with the desired options. Visit several dealers to find the costs involved. Determine the cash prices and decide where you would buy a car.

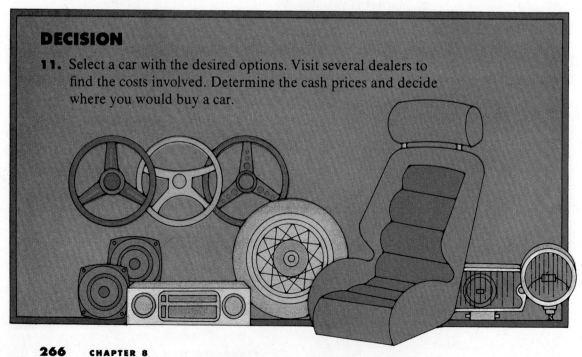

ESTIMATING MEASURES

Estimating measures can be a very useful skill. To estimate measures, you can use your experience and common sense.

EXAMPLE.   Estimate the height of a flagpole.
Reason this way.

The pole is higher than 3 meters because it is taller than the distance to a basketball hoop, which is about 3 meters. The pole is shorter than 10 meters because it is not as tall as a highway light pole, which is about 10 meters high. In fact, the pole is a little higher than the school roof, which is about 6 meters high. So, estimate that the flagpole is about 8 meters high.

PRACTICE

Make two marks 3 meters apart on the floor. Try to remember this distance. Estimate in meters.

1. the length of your classroom   **2.** the length of a bus

3. the width of your classroom   **4.** the length of your school building

5. the height of your classroom   **6.** the width of your school gym

7. the length of a car

The width of your little finger is about 1 centimeter. Try to remember this distance. Estimate in centimeters.

8. the thickness of your desk   **9.** the height of your teacher

10. the length of your desk   **11.** the length of your notebook

12. your height

BUYING A MOTORCYCLE

Suggest students bring in literature dealing with the various brands of motorcycles.

Motorcycles are popular for sport and recreation, but many people use them for day-to-day transportation.

Eileen Lowman sells motorcycles at Bontwell's Cycle Shop. After high school she began working there as a filing clerk. As she learned the business, she became a part-time salesperson.

Street bikes are used for ordinary travel, off-road bikes for racing, mopeds for traveling short distances at slow speeds.

EXAMPLE.   Vaughn and Eloise Weiss bought a large motorcycle for a vacation trip. The base price was $7200. They added a radio system which cost $289.15. The sales tax was 5%. The dealer preparation fee was $120. The license fee was $50. Find the cash price.

PLAN: **Step 1.**   Add to find the sticker price.

$$\$7200.00 + \$289.15 = \$7489.15$$

Step 2.   Multiply to find the sales tax.

$$0.05 \times \$7489.15 \approx \$374.46$$

Step 3.   Add to find the cash price.

Sticker price	$7489.15
Sales tax	374.46
Dealer preparation fee	120.00
License fee	50.00
Cash price	$8033.61

1. Doris Standish bought a street bike for $1799, with a luggage rack which cost $85. The sales tax was 7%. The dealer preparation fee was $116. The license fee was $50. Find the cash price. $2181.88

EXERCISES

Find the cash price for each of the following vehicles.

1. Street bike $1850
Saddlebags $80
Sales tax 4%
Dealer preparation fee $95
License fee $35 $2137.20

2. Moped $385
Sales tax 5%
Dealer preparation fee $89
Title fee $20 $513.25

3. Off-road cycle $2051
CB radio $190
Sales tax 6%
Dealer preparation fee $108
License fee $39 $2522.46

4. Street bike $1960
Sound system $308
Saddlebags $95
Sales tax $5\frac{1}{2}$%
Dealer preparation fee $116
License fee $40 $2648.97

5. Street bike $2280
CB radio $195
Sales tax $4\frac{1}{2}$%
Dealer preparation fee $95
License fee $45 $2818.34

6. Street bike $2015
CB radio $186
Sales tax 7%
Dealer preparation fee $92
License fee $55 $2502.07

7. Moped $415
Saddlebags $55
Sales tax 6%
Dealer preparation fee $75
Title fee $25 $598.20

8. Off-road bike $239
Special tire $35
Sales tax $6\frac{1}{2}$%
Dealer preparation fee $115
License fee $45 $451.81

ON YOUR OWN

Visit a local motorcycle shop.

9. Find out about the various types of cycles available.

10. What is the difference between a moped and a motorcycle?

FINANCING YOUR PURCHASE

If any students in the class have purchased their own car, they might describe their financing arrangements.

Financing a new car that cost less than $ 800 was not easy in the 1920s, because many people earned less than $ 20 a week.

If you finance a car or motorcycle, you will first need to make a *down payment*. The down payment may be in the form of a trade-in, cash payment, or some combination of these two. The remaining amount is the *amount financed*.

EXAMPLE 1. Sal Calleri is buying a sports car which costs $ 14,952. A down payment of at least 20% is required. What is the required down payment? What is the amount financed?

PLAN: **Step 1.** Multiply to find the down payment.

$$0.20 \times \$ 14,952 = \$ 2990.40$$

Step 2. Subtract the down payment from the cash price to find the amount financed.

$$\$ 14,952 - \$ 2990.40 = \$ 11,961.60$$

The required down payment is $ 2990.40.
The amount financed is $ 11,961.60.

Find the down payment and the amount financed.

1. A down payment of at least 20% is required on the purchase of a moped which costs $ 149. $29.80, $119.20

2. A down payment of at least one third is required on a sedan which costs $ 8946. $2982.00, $5964.00

Marilyn Fisher is buying a new compact car. It costs $ 6243. Her down payment and trade-in total is $ 2243. Marilyn decides to *finance* the remaining $ 4000. ($ 6243 − $ 2243 = $ 4000.)

To finance a car means to borrow the money. Marilyn borrows the $ 4000 from her credit union. She plans to repay the loan over a period of three years in equal monthly payments.

When you finance a car or motorcycle, you must pay a *finance charge.* The finance charge is the difference between the total of the monthly payments and the amount financed.

The *deferred payment price* is the sum of the monthly payments, the trade-in, and the down payment. This is what the car actually costs Marilyn.

EXAMPLE 2.   If Marilyn borrows $ 4000 to be paid back in three years, the monthly payments will be $ 132.82. Find the total of the monthly payments, the finance charge and the deferred payment price.

PLAN: **Step 1.**   Multiply to find the total of the monthly payments.

$ 132.82 × 36 = $ 4781.52   *Monthly payment times number of payments*

Step 2.   Subtract to find the finance charge.

$ 4781.52 − $ 4000 = $ 781.52   *Total of the monthly payments minus amount financed*

Step 3.   Add to find the deferred payment price.

$ 4781.52 + $ 2243 = $ 7024.52   *Total of the monthly payments plus trade-in and down payment of $2243*

The total of the monthly payments is $ 4781.52.
The finance charge is $ 781.52.
The deferred payment price is $ 7024.52.

TRY THIS

3. Flora Chester bought a racing motorcycle for $2100. Her down payment was $600. She financed the cycle at a finance company. She agreed to repay the loan in two years with monthly payments of $78.42. **$1882.08, $382.08. $2482.08**

The loan officer at Marilyn's credit union tells her she can repay the loan over a period of two years at $193.95 a month or three years at $132.82 a month.

EXAMPLE 3. Find how much Marilyn can save by repaying the loan in two years rather than three years.

PLAN: **Step 1.** Multiply to find the total of the monthly payments.

Two year: $193.95 × 24 = $4654.80

Three year: $132.82 × 36 = $4781.52

Step 2. Subtract to find the difference.

$4781.52 − 4654.80 = $126.72

She can save $126.72 by repaying the loan in two years.

Find the difference in the total amounts to be repaid.

TRY THIS

4. Jack Wittman financed $6000 at his bank at a rate of 17.5%. If he repays the loan in three years, the monthly payments will be $215.41. If he repays the loan in four years, the monthly payments will be $174.69. **$630.36**

EXERCISES

Find the down payment and the amount financed.

1. Ramon Alvarez is buying a sedan which costs $7980. A down payment of 20% is expected. **$1596, $6384**

2. Penny Booth is buying a street bike. It costs $2275. A down payment of one third is required. **$758.33, $1516.67**

3. Connie Atherton is buying a van which costs $8354. A down payment of 30% is expected. $2506.20, $5847.80

4. Terrance Grant is buying a pickup truck which costs $9183. A down payment of one fourth is required. $2295.75, $6887.25

Find the total of the monthly payments, the finance charge, and the deferred payment price.

5. Gail Haag bought a sports car for $12,850. Her trade-in was $6000. She financed the difference at her bank and agreed to repay it in 4 years. Her monthly payment was $156.20. $7497.60, $647.60, $13,497.60

6. Alfonso Ortiz bought a new moped for $612. His trade-in was $100. He financed the difference at his credit union and agreed to repay it in 2 years. His monthly payment was $24.12. $578.88, $66.80, $678.88

7. Mel Feldman bought a hatchback coupe for $4965. His trade-in was $1250, with a down payment of $500. He financed the difference at a finance company and agreed to repay it in 3 years. His monthly payment was $126.50. $4554.00, $1339.00, $6304.00

8. Agnes Rodriguez bought a new street bike for $2585. Her trade-in was $850, with a down payment of $200. She financed the difference with the dealer and agreed to repay it in 3 years. Her monthly payment was $51.53. $1855.08, $320.08, $2905.08

Find the difference in the total amounts to be repaid.

9. Samuel Brown financed $5000 with the car dealer at a rate of 16.5%. If he repays the loan in two years, the monthly payments will be $246.01. If he repays the loan in four years, the monthly payments will be $142.99. $959.28

10. Carmela Mendoza financed $3500 at her bank at a rate of 17%. If she repays the loan in two years, the monthly payments will be $173.05. If she repays the loan in three years, the monthly payments will be $125.78. $374.88

11. Ken Fujii financed $1250 at his savings and loan association at a rate of 15.2%. If he repays the loan in two years, the monthly payments will be $60.73. If he repays the loan in three years, the monthly payments will be $43.45. $106.68

12. Roslyn Gibson financed $675 at her credit union at a rate of 14.6%. If she repays the loan in one year, the monthly payments will be $60.80. If she repays the loan in two years, the monthly payments will be $32.60. $52.80

MAINTENANCE AND REPAIRS

Auto collectors and hobbyists keep their antique cars in tiptop
shape with daily maintenance and service.

Monroe Anderson works as an auto mechanic. He does major
repairs and basic maintenance service. Monroe studied auto
mechanics at a vocational school.

He says that regular maintenance checks can improve your gas
mileage and may prevent costly repairs. He advises people who
pump their own gas to remember to check their oil and tire pressure
regularly.

Monroe works for Gardeners Auto Repair. For each job, Monroe
completes a work order form. He first adds the cost of parts, gas,
oil, and grease. These costs for parts and materials are computed
separately from the labor costs of installing the parts. This is
because the costs for materials and parts are subject to state and local
sales taxes, but labor costs are not.

EXAMPLE 1. Find the total cost of the taxable items used for work done on Elsie Bell's van. Use 6% tax.

Quantity	Part Number	Name of Part	Price		Gas, Oil, Grease	
1	4–234	Oil filter	$ 6	70	Gasoline	
4	3–765	Spark plugs	11	86	6 qt oil	$6 00
1	900–A	Points	5	67	Grease	

PLAN:

Step 1. Add to find the taxable charges.

$$\$6.70 + \$11.86 + \$5.67 + \$6.00 = \$30.23$$

Step 2. Multiply to find the tax of 6%.

$$0.06 \times \$30.23 \approx \$1.81$$

Step 3. Add to find the total cost of the taxable items.

$$\$30.23 + \$1.81 = \$32.04$$

TRY THIS

1. Find the total cost of taxable items used in this repair job. Use 6% tax. **$67.59**

Quantity	Part Number	Name of Part	Price		Gas, Oil, Grease	
1	7–3R	Air filter	$ 5	78	Gasoline	
4	3–765	Spark plugs	12	00	4 qt oil	5 00
1	3–489	Gasket	1	98	Grease	3 00

Monroe says labor costs are not taxed and are added to your bill after the mechanic is finished.

EXAMPLE 2. Find the total repair bill for Jim Wilson's car. His taxable charges are $ 76.98. Labor costs are $ 45.00.

PLAN:

Step 1. Multiply to find the tax of 6%.

$$0.06 \times \$76.98 \approx \$4.62$$

Step 2. Add the subtotal (taxable items), tax, and labor.

$$\$76.98 + \$4.62 + \$45.00 = \$126.60$$

TRY THIS

2. Find the total repair bill for this automobile. At 6%, the taxable charges are $ 67.90. Labor costs are $ 123. **$194.97**

Monroe's cashier must total up several bills like these each day.

GARDNERS AUTO REPAIR Name _Joan Kiefer_ Job Number _4291_
Date _8-21-82_ Address _____ Phone _235-8970_

Quantity	Part Number	Name of Part	Price
1	4-021-5	Oil filter	5.00
1		Hose clamp	.95
1	8-024-6	Fuel filter	2.85
4		Spark plugs	8.64

Year _80_ Make _Coupe_ License _DEL-412_
Mileage _21,925_ Promised _4:30_
Description of Work   Amount
20,000 mile service   35.00

Total Parts _____ Total Labor _____ 35.00

Accessories   Gas, Oil, Grease Amount   Oil Changes etc. (✓) Totals
Gasoline _____   Engine _____   Parts _____
Quarts of Oil (4) _7.00_   Transmission _____   Accessories _____
Grease _____   Differential _____   Gas, Oil, Grease _____
Brake Fluid _____   Wash _____   Subtotal _____
Other _____   Wax _____   Tax _____
Total Accessories _____   Total _____   Other _____   Labor _____
TOTAL _____

EXAMPLE 3.   Find the total repair bill for Joan's car. Use 6% tax.

PLAN: **Step 1.**   Add charges for parts and oil to find taxable charges.
$5.00 + $0.95 + $2.85 + $8.64 + $7.00 = $24.44

Step 2.   Multiply to find the tax.
$0.06 \times $24.44 = 1.47

Step 3.   Add the subtotal, tax, and labor costs.
$24.44 + $1.47 + $35.00 = $60.91

The total bill is $60.91.

3. Find the total repair bill for this automobile. Use 6% tax. **$264.24**

TRY THIS

GARDNERS AUTO REPAIR Name _EVITA LOPEZ_ Job Number _4731_
Date _9-30-82_ Address _____ Phone _237-9142_

Quantity	Part Number	Name of Part	Price
1	37-2A	Water pump	44.80
1	4-6135	Rocker arm	29.00
1	3-9192	Headlamp	25.51

Year _76_ Make _Coupe_ License _BXS-311_
Mileage _42,700_ Promised _____
Description of Work   Amount

Total Parts _____ Total Labor _____ 146.25

Accessories   Gas, Oil, Grease Amount   Oil Changes etc. (✓) Totals
Gasoline _10.00_   Engine _____   Parts _____
Quarts of Oil (5) _____   Transmission _____   Accessories _____
Grease _2.00_   Differential _____   Gas, Oil, Grease _____
Brake Fluid _____   Wash _____   Subtotal _____
Other _____   Wax _____   Tax _____
Total Accessories _____   Total _____   Other _____   Labor _____
TOTAL _____

EXERCISES

Find the subtotal, the tax, the labor, and the total repair bill. Use 6% tax.

1.

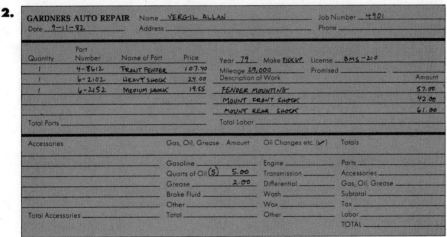

| GARDNERS AUTO REPAIR | Name _Phil Spies_ | Job Number _4296_ |

Date _9-24-82_ Address _____ Phone _235-7462_

Quantity	Part Number	Name of Part	Price
1	5-234	Oil filter	6.00
1	3-2956	Ignition key	4.50
6		Spark plugs	12.50
1	8-3975	Tail pipe	24.00

Total Parts _____

Year _80_ Make _Sedan_ License _AK6-612_
Mileage _36,483_ Promised _____
Description of Work

	Amount
Tune-up	24.00
Replace tail pipe	25.00
Lubricate: oil change	6.00

Total Labor _____

Accessories		Gas, Oil, Grease	Amount	Oil Changes etc. (✓)	Totals
		Gasoline ____		Engine ____	Parts ____
		Quarts of Oil (5)	9.00	Transmission ____	Accessories ____
		Grease	1.00	Differential ____	Gas, Oil, Grease ____
		Brake Fluid ____		Wash ____	Subtotal ____
		Other ____		Wax ____	Tax ____
Total Accessories ____		Total ____		Other ____	Labor ____
					TOTAL ____

$57, $3.42, $55, $115.42

2.

| GARDNERS AUTO REPAIR | Name _VERGIL ALLAN_ | Job Number _4901_ |

Date _9-11-82_ Address _____ Phone _____

Quantity	Part Number	Name of Part	Price
1	4-8612	FRONT FENDER	107.40
1	6-2102	HEAVY SHOCK	24.00
1	6-2152	MEDIUM SHOCK	19.55

Total Parts _____

Year _79_ Make _PICK UP_ License _BMS-210_
Mileage _29,000_ Promised _____
Description of Work

	Amount
FENDER MOUNTING	57.00
MOUNT FRONT SHOCK	42.00
MOUNT REAR SHOCK	61.00

Total Labor _____

Accessories		Gas, Oil, Grease	Amount	Oil Changes etc. (✓)	Totals
		Gasoline ____		Engine ____	Parts ____
		Quarts of Oil (5)	5.00	Transmission ____	Accessories ____
		Grease	2.00	Differential ____	Gas, Oil, Grease ____
		Brake Fluid ____		Wash ____	Subtotal ____
		Other ____		Wax ____	Tax ____
Total Accessories ____		Total ____		Other ____	Labor ____
					TOTAL ____

$157.95, $9.48, $160, $327.43

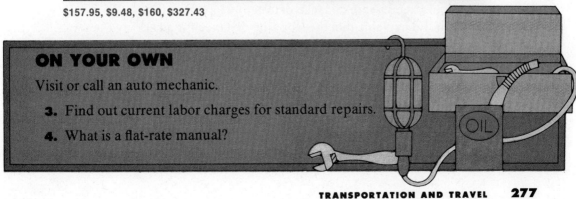

ON YOUR OWN

Visit or call an auto mechanic.

3. Find out current labor charges for standard repairs.

4. What is a flat-rate manual?

Use this lesson to emphasize the importance of safe driving and observing the speed limit. Assign some students to prepare a bulletin board containing a graph of speed vs. stopping distance.

Sensible speed limits, clearly marked exits, and correctly phased signal lights help to make commuting safe and enjoyable.

Ed Stone is a highway patrol officer. To get the job, Ed had to be a high school graduate. He passed a physical exam and attended a six-month training course at the police academy.

Ed helps to keep the highways safe. He helps people who are stopped by the side of the road with car problems. He also assists people involved in accidents.

Ed says you should keep a safe distance between your car and the car ahead of you. Ed explains that the stopping distance for a car is affected by the rate of speed and the type of road surface.

This formula gives a good estimate of a car's stopping distance.

$$D = \frac{S^2}{30f}$$

D stands for distance in feet.
S stands for speed in miles per hour.
f stands for the drag factor of the road.

This table shows drag factors for various road surfaces.

Road Surface	Drag Factor
Dry concrete	0.8
Dry asphalt or tar	0.75
Dry brick	0.7
Wet asphalt	0.6
Wet or dry gravel	0.55
Wet or dry cinders	0.53
Oiled gravel	0.5
Wet tar	0.46
Wet concrete	0.44
Wet brick	0.4
Snow	0.3
Ice	0.1

EXAMPLE 1. Find the stopping distance for a car going 40 miles per hour on a dry concrete road.

From the table the drag factor is 0.8.

$$D = \frac{S^2}{30f}$$
$$= \frac{40^2}{30 \times 0.8}$$
$$= \frac{40 \times 40}{24}$$
$$= \frac{1600}{24}$$
$$\approx 66.7 \text{ ft}$$

TRY THIS

1. Find the stopping distance for a car going 35 mph on a wet asphalt road. 68 ft

The actual nomogram used by police officers is more sophisticated than the one pictured here.

When checking an accident, Ed uses a *nomogram*. He measures the length of the skid marks. He also finds the drag factor for the road surface. Then he estimates how fast the car was traveling.

EXAMPLE 2. Ed measures skid marks of 120 feet on a dry concrete road. About how fast was the car traveling?

PLAN:

Step 1. Locate the length of the skid marks in Column I.
Read 120 ft.

Step 2. Locate the drag factor in Column II.
Read 0.80.

Step 3. Connect these two points with a straightedge.

Step 4. Read the speed of the car in Column III.
Read 54 mph.

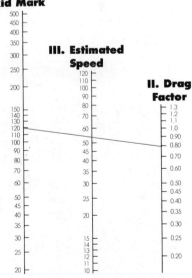

2. A skid mark is 150 feet long on an oiled gravel road. About how fast was the car traveling? 45 mph

EXERCISES

1. Use the formula $D = \dfrac{S^2}{30f}$ to find the stopping distance on snow when traveling

    a. 30 mph 100 ft   **b.** 40 mph 177.8 ft **c.** 50 mph 277.8 ft

Find the stopping distance for each. Use the formula $D = \dfrac{S^2}{30f}$.

	Speed (mph)	Road Surface	Stopping Distance (ft)
2.	35	Dry brick	?
3.	50	Wet asphalt	?
4.	40	Wet tar	?
5.	55	Oiled gravel	?
6.	30	Snow	?
7.	55	Dry concrete	?
8.	25	Ice	?
9.	60	Dry concrete	?
10.	50	Dry brick	?

Use the nomogram on page 279. Estimate how fast the car was traveling.

	Length of Skid Mark (ft)	Road Surface	Speed (mph)
11.	200	Dry concrete	?
12.	160	Wet asphalt	?
13.	250	Dry asphalt	?
14.	180	Wet brick	?

ON YOUR OWN

15. Call your local state police. Ask if they could give a demonstration of stopping distance at your school.

PROBLEM SOLVING HINTS

Fred Rheinhardt found a combination lock that he hadn't used for several years. He had lost the combination but thought that the first number was 28 and the last number was 17. He felt certain that the middle number had only one digit.

HINT: Some problems can be solved by trial and error.

Fred tried 28 - 1 - 17
            28 - 2 - 17
            28 - 3 - 17

Finally, 28 - 4 - 17 opened the lock.

HINT: Some problems can be solved by guessing and checking.

Fred also found a key ring with twelve keys on it. Some of the keys looked familiar. Fred picked several of the keys and tried them in his front door. One of them worked.

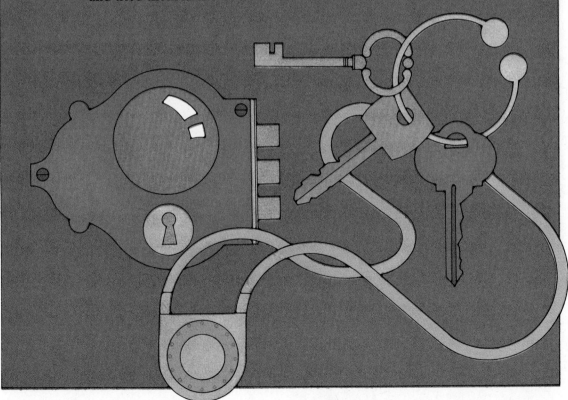

PLANNING A TRIP

Have students obtain copies of local state maps and complete similar exercises using locations more familiar to them.

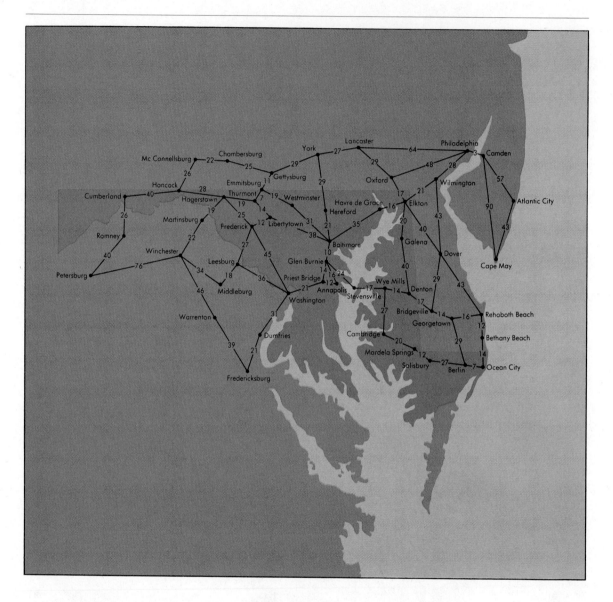

The Zaliner family is planning a vacation trip to Ocean City, Maryland. They live in Hagerstown, Maryland. They use this map to estimate the distance to be traveled. The distance between cities is shown.

The distance between Hagerstown and Thurmont, the next town shown on the map, is 19 miles.

EXAMPLE 1. Find the distance between Hagerstown and Baltimore.

PLAN: **Step 1.** List the distance along the route.

To Thurmont 19 miles
To Libertytown 14 miles
To Baltimore 38 miles

Step 2. Add the distances.
19 + 14 + 38 = 71 miles

The distance between Hagerstown and Baltimore is 71 miles.

TRY THIS

1. Find the shortest distance from Baltimore to Ocean City. **132 miles**

2. Find the total distance from Hagerstown, Maryland, to Ocean City, Maryland. **203 miles**

3. Find the distance from Annapolis, Maryland, to Gettysburg, Pennsylvania. **87 miles**

EXAMPLE 2. Brenda Yabut averages 45 miles per hour on a 180-mile trip. Allowing one hour for lunch, about how long will the trip take? She averages 27 miles per gallon. About how many gallons of gasoline will she use on the trip?

PLAN: **Step 1.** Divide to find the driving time.
180 miles ÷ 45 mph = 4 hr   *Distance divided by rate*

Step 2. Add one hour for lunch.
4 hr + 1 hr = 5 hr

Step 3. Divide to find the number of gallons she will use.
180 miles ÷ 27 miles per gallon ≈ 6.7 gallons

The trip will take about five hours.

She will use about 6.7 gallons of gasoline.

TRY THIS

4. Fred Griesinger averages 50 miles per hour on a 230-mile trip. Allowing one and one-half hours for lunch and rest, about how long will the trip take? He averages 24 miles per gallon. About how many gallons of gasoline will he use on the trip? **6 hr, 9.6 gallons**

EXAMPLE 3. To estimate expenses for a six-day trip, Brenda lists the costs. Find the total expenses and the cost per day of the trip.

Hotel	$325
Food	200
Tolls	2
Gasoline	20
Miscellaneous + entertainment	50

PLAN: **Step 1.** Add to find the total.

$$\$325 + \$200 + \$2 + \$20 + \$50 = \$597$$

Step 2. Divide to find the cost per day.

$$\$597 \div 6\ \text{days} = \$99.50\ \text{per day}$$

TRY THIS

5. To estimate expenses for an eight-day trip, Fred Griesinger lists his costs. Find the total expenses and the approximate cost per day of the trip. $955, $119.38 per day

Hotel	$540
Food	290
Tolls	5
Gasoline	40
Miscellaneous	80

EXERCISES

Find the shortest distance. Use the map on page 282.

1. Baltimore, Maryland to Washington, D.C. 45 mi

2. Baltimore, Maryland to Frederick, Maryland 50 mi

3. Dover, Delaware to Wilmington, Delaware 43 mi

4. Chambersburg, Pennsylvania to Cumberland, Maryland 88 mi

5. Philadelphia, Pennsylvania to Atlantic City, New Jersey 60 mi

6. Fredericksburg, Virginia to Winchester, Virginia 85 mi

7. Salisbury, Maryland to Dover, Delaware 99 mi

8. Cape May, New Jersey to Camden, New Jersey 90 mi

9. Annapolis, Maryland to Hereford, Maryland 47 mi

10. Gettysburg, Pennsylvania to Leesburg, Virginia 61 mi

11. Stanford Watkins estimates that he will average 40 miles per hour on a trip from Philadelphia, Pennsylvania to Cape May, New Jersey via Atlantic City. About how long will the trip take? $2\frac{1}{2}$ hr

12. Stanford also knows that his car averages about 21 miles per gallon. About how many gallons of gasoline will be used on the trip? 4.9 gal

13. Gina Diehl is planning a trip from Georgetown, Delaware to Lancaster, Pennsylvania via Dover, Delaware and Elkton, Maryland. She estimates that she will average 45 miles per hour. Allowing one hour for lunch, about how long will the trip take? $3\frac{3}{4}$ hr

14. Gina's car averages about 30 miles per gallon. About how many gallons of gasoline will she use on the trip? 4 gal

15. To estimate expenses for a seven-day trip to Yellowstone Park, Terry McDonald lists the costs.

Motel	$280
Food	$175
Gasoline	$150
Miscellaneous	$100

Find the total expenses and the approximate cost of the trip per day. $705.00, $100.71

16. Glenda Ambrose is planning a ten-day car trip to Florida. She estimates the following expenses:

Motel	$460
Food	$300
Gasoline	$225
Entertainment	$100
Miscellaneous	$150

Find the total expenses and the approximate cost of the trip per day. $1235, $123.50

ON YOUR OWN

17. Obtain a map of your state. Plan several trips. Estimate distances, gasoline requirements, and expenses.

RENTING A CAR

An increasingly popular way to travel for business or pleasure is to fly—and then rent a car at the airport.

Rick and Martha Held spent their vacation in California. They rented a car for two days. They drove from San Francisco through the Napa Valley and returned to San Francisco.

EXAMPLE 1. The Helds rented a full-size car for $ 49.95 per day. They also paid $ 0.45 per mile driven. They kept the car two days and drove 125 miles. Find the cost of renting the car.

PLAN: **Step 1.** Multiply to find the cost for 2 days.

$ 49.95 × 2 days = $ 99.90

Step 2. Multiply to find the mileage cost.

$ 0.45 per mile × 125 miles = $ 56.25

Step 3. Add to find the total cost.

$ 99.90 + $ 56.25 = $ 156.15

		Car cost per day	Number of days	Cost per mile	Number of miles driven
TRY THIS	**1.**	$48.75	3	$0.44	208
	2.	$35.95	2	$0.41	186
	3.	$50.35	4	$0.45	322
	4.	$49.75	2	$0.46	139

Sara Rosenberg plans to rent a car on a business trip. Her company has an arrangement with the car rental agency which gives Sara a discount.

EXAMPLE 2. Sara plans to rent an economy car which costs $34.85 per day and $0.41 per mile. She will keep the car three days and drive about 113 miles. She receives a 25% discount. Find the discounted cost of renting the car.

PLAN:

Step 1. Multiply to find the cost for the 3 days.
$34.85 per day × 3 days = $104.55

Step 2. Multiply to find the mileage cost.
$0.41 per mile × 113 miles = $46.33

Step 3. Add to find the total cost before discount.
$104.55 + $46.33 = $150.88

Step 4. Multiply to find the discount price.
Since there is a 25% discount, Sara pays 75%.
0.75 × $150.88 = $113.16

Find the discounted rental cost for each.

		Car cost per day	Number of days	Cost per mile	Number of miles driven	Discount
TRY THIS	**5.**	$35.25	2	$0.41	194	15%
	6.	$42.60	4	$0.48	225	30%
	7.	$50.25	3	$0.49	168	20%
	8.	$34.75	5	$0.42	304	45%

EXERCISES

Find the rental cost for each.

	Car cost per day	Number of days	Cost per mile	Number of miles
1.	$49.50	6	$0.48	522
2.	$51.25	5	$0.50	329
3.	$48.95	8	$0.45	615
4.	$46.85	7	$0.49	239
5.	$52.25	10	$0.47	685
6.	$53.80	9	$0.48	339

Find the discounted rental cost for each.

	Car cost per day	Number of days	Cost per mile	Number of miles	Discount
7.	$38.32	2	$0.42	86	20%
8.	$42.80	3	$0.48	182	25%
9.	$46.00	5	$0.51	165	15%
10.	$50.25	4	$0.48	203	25%
11.	$35.95	3	$0.43	411	40%
12.	$41.50	6	$0.50	562	35%

13. Fred Winterling rented a car on a weekend special. He paid $17.95 per day for an economy car with unlimited mileage. He kept the car from noon Thursday to noon Monday. What was the total cost? $71.80

14. Velma Walker arranged for a one-way rental. She paid $48.75 per day. The first 700 miles were free and she drove 825 miles in three days. The mileage charge was $0.43 per mile. Find the total cost. $200.00

DECISION

15. Call a local car rental agency. Decide whether it is better to rent on a weekend special rate or a by-the-day rate over a weekend.

MENTAL CALCULATION

QUICK MULTIPLICATION BY SOME DECIMALS

To multiply by decimals, you can multiply by a whole number and divide by 10.

EXAMPLE 1.   Multiply 23 × 1.6.

PLAN: **Step 1.**   First multiply by 16. Double 4 times.

$$23 \times 2 = 46$$
$$46 \times 2 = 92$$
$$92 \times 2 = 184$$
$$184 \times 2 = 368$$
$$23 \times 16 = 368$$

Step 2.   Divide by 10.

$$368 \div 10 = 36.8$$

EXAMPLE 2.   Multiply 83 × 0.8.

PLAN: **Step 1.**   Multiply 83 by 8. Double 3 times.

$$83 \times 8 = 664$$

Step 2.   Divide by 10.

$$664 \div 10 = 66.4$$

PRACTICE

Multiply mentally.

1. 26 × 1.6 41.6   **2.** 22 × 1.6 35.2   **3.** 31 × 1.6 49.6   **4.** 42 × 1.6 67.2

5. 15 × 0.8 12   **6.** 17 × 0.8 13.6   **7.** 83 × 0.8 66.4   **8.** 75 × 0.8 60

9. 23 × 0.4 9.2   **10.** 19 × 0.4 7.6   **11.** 52 × 3.2 166.4   **12.** 64 × 3.2 204.8

RECREATIONAL VEHICLES

With a recreational vehicle, vacationers can drive to visit national
parks and can stay in special camping areas.

Mitsa and Ellen Nagatomi and their children enjoy camping. They
rented a recreational vehicle (RV) for a two-week camping trip.

EXAMPLE 1.   The Nagatomis rent an RV for $325 per week plus $.10 per
mile. Estimate the cost of the RV for a 1200 mile round trip.

PLAN: **Step 1.**   Multiply to find the RV cost.
$$2 \times \$325 = \$650$$

Step 2.   Multiply to find the mileage cost.
$$\$0.10 \times 1200 = \$120$$

Step 3.   Add to find the total.
$$\$650 + \$120 = \$770$$

TRY THIS

1. The Bender family rents an RV for $380 per week plus $.11 per mile. Estimate the cost of the RV for a one-week round trip of about 800 miles from Amarillo, Texas to Denver, Colorado. $468

EXAMPLE 2. Chester and Ida Fritz rent an RV for $69 per day plus $.12 per mile. Estimate the cost of the RV for a four day round trip of about 650 miles from Little Rock, Arkansas to Nashville, Tennessee.

PLAN:

Step 1. Multiply to find the base cost.

4 days × $69 = $276

Step 2. Multiply to find the mileage cost.

$.12 × 650 = $78

Step 3. Add to find the total.

$276 + $78 = $354

The rental for the RV will be $354.

TRY THIS

2. The Nelson family rents a camper for $72 per day plus $.13 per mile. Estimate the cost of the camper for a five day round trip of about 820 miles from Pocatello, Idaho to the Black Hills of South Dakota. $450

EXAMPLE 3. The O'Briens own a pop-up tent camping trailer. They estimate that to tow the trailer 100 miles they use an extra gallon of gasoline. About how many extra gallons can they expect to use on a 1228 mile trip from Muncie, Indiana to Sioux City, Iowa?

1228 ÷ 100 = 12.28

They can expect to use about 12 extra gallons of gasoline.

TRY THIS

3. Jack and Phyllis Mitchell own a small travel trailer. They estimate that to tow the trailer 100 miles they use about 2 extra gallons of gasoline. About how many extra gallons can they expect to use on a 1650 mile round trip from Walla Walla, Washington to the Grand Canyon? 33 gal

EXAMPLE 4. The Silvas own a van camper. They know that they get about 11 miles per gallon. They plan to tow their boat. They estimate that to tow the boat and trailer 100 miles, they use an extra gallon of gasoline. About how many gallons of gasoline can they expect to use on a 1280 mile trip?

PLAN: **Step 1.** Find the amount of gasoline with the boat.

$$1280 \div 11 = 116$$

Step 2. Find the extra gallons for the boat.

$$1280 \div 100 = 12.8 \approx 13$$

Step 3. Add to find the total.

$$116 + 13 = 129 \approx 130 \qquad \textit{Round to the nearest 10 gallons.}$$

They estimate they will use about 130 gallons.

TRY THIS

4. Roger and Linda Ng own a Class A Motor Home. They know that they get about 7 miles per gallon. If they tow their boat and trailer, they estimate they use an extra 2 gallons of gasoline for every 100 miles. About how much gas can they expect to use on a 1550-mile trip? **250 gal**

EXAMPLE 5. Shady Springs costs $6 per night. The O'Briens plan to stay seven days and nights. They estimate that food will cost them $9 per meal for two meals a day. Not including gasoline costs, how much will the camping trip cost?

PLAN: **Step 1.** Multiply to find the campground costs.

$$\$6 \text{ per night} \times 7 \text{ nights} = \$42$$

Step 2. Multiply to find the cost for food.

$$\$18 \text{ per day} \times 7 \text{ days} = \$126$$

Step 3. Add to find the total cost.

$$\$42 + \$126 = \$168$$

TRY THIS

5. Jack and Phyllis Mitchell are experienced campers. They went on a two-week camping trip. They stayed at several campgrounds, with an average cost of $8 per night. They estimate their food costs at $15 per day. They spent $160 on gasoline. Estimate the total cost of their trip. **$480**

EXERCISES

1. The Bianco family rents an RV for $335 per week plus $0.12 per mile. Estimate the cost of the RV for a 3 week, 2000 mile round trip from Akron, Ohio to Halifax, Nova Scotia. **$1245**

2. Dick and Marie Feinburg rent an RV for $348 per week plus $0.10 per mile. Estimate the cost of the RV for a 2 week, 1700 mile round trip from Tulsa, Oklahoma to Gainesville, Florida. **$866**

3. Lester and Rose Evans rent an RV for $73 per day plus $0.11 per mile. Estimate the cost of the RV for a three day 800 mile round trip from Saginaw, Michigan to Springfield, Illinois. **$307**

4. The Mushnick family rents an RV for $68 per day plus $0.13 per mile. Estimate the cost of the RV for a five day 475 mile round trip from Charleston, West Virginia to Gettysburg, PA. **$401.75**

5. The Sullivan family owns a Class C Mini-Motor Home. They know that they get about 9 miles per gallon. About how many gallons of gasoline can they expect to use on a 1040 mile round trip from Jackson, Mississippi to Augusta, Georgia? **120 gal**

6. Bill and Cherie Zachmeyer own a van camper. They know that they get about 12 miles per gallon. About how many gallons of gasoline can they expect to use on an 850 mile round trip from Santa Cruz, California to Crater Lake, Oregon? **70 gal**

7. The Silvas visit Morrison Meadows Campground. The cost is $8 per night. They plan to stay eight days and nights. They estimate that food will cost them $11 per meal, two meals per day. Not including gasoline, how much will the trip cost? **$240**

8. Roger and Linda Ng and their two children camp at River Valley Ranch. The cost is $9 per day. They plan to stay seven days. Food costs are estimated at $20 per day. Not including gasoline, how much will the trip cost? **$203**

ON YOUR OWN

9. Visit a local RV dealer. Find out about the cost of various types of RVs.

10. Find out where campgrounds are located in your area. Phone and ask about facilities and fees.

AIR TRAVEL

Current airline ticket prices can be obtained from airline ticket counters as an illustrative aid.

Airlines pay travel agents a commission for their work in planning
air travel and writing tickets for travelers.

Steve Baxton is a travel agent. Steve took classes at a junior college
after high school graduation. He answered a newspaper ad and was
hired by a travel agency.

Steve can help you plan a trip. He can make hotel and plane reser-
vations. He can also give you maps and lists of attractions.

Travel agents receive a commission from the airlines and hotels.
They also can take advantage of reduced rates for personal travel.

When Steve writes an airline ticket for you, he must show both the
base fare and the tax. Steve uses a chart like the one on page 295.

EXAMPLE 1.   Steve writes a ticket with a total cost of $282. What is the
base fare and the tax?

Find $282 in the total column.

Read across to find the base fare and the tax.
The base fare is $261.11.
The tax is $20.89.

	8% Tax	Base Fare	Excess Baggage 0.7% of Total Fare	Percent of Base Fare and 8% Tax					
Total				50%	8% Tax	66 2/3%	8% Tax	83%	8% Tax
281.00	20.81	260.19	1.97	130.10	10.41	173.48	13.88	215.96	17.28
282.00	20.89	261.11	1.98	130.56	10.44	174.12	13.93	216.74	17.34
283.00	20.96	262.04	1.99	131.02	10.48	174.73	13.98	217.53	17.40
284.00	21.04	262.96	1.99	131.48	10.52	175.34	14.03	218.30	17.46
285.00	21.11	263.89	2.00	131.95	10.56	175.94	14.08	219.04	17.52
286.00	21.19	264.81	2.01	132.41	10.59	176.59	14.13	219.82	17.59
287.00	21.26	265.74	2.01	132.87	10.63	177.19	14.18	220.56	17.64
288.00	21.33	266.67	2.02	133.34	10.67	177.80	14.22	221.36	17.71
289.00	21.41	267.59	2.03	133.80	10.70	178.44	14.28	222.14	17.77
290.00	21.48	268.52	2.03	134.26	10.74	179.05	14.32	222.88	17.83
291.00	21.56	269.44	2.04	134.72	10.78	179.64	14.37	223.67	17.89
292.00	21.63	270.37	2.05	135.19	10.82	180.30	14.42	224.41	17.95
293.00	21.70	271.30	2.06	135.65	10.85	180.90	14.47	225.20	18.02
294.00	21.78	272.22	2.06	136.11	10.89	181.50	14.52	225.98	18.08
295.00	21.85	273.15	2.07	136.58	10.93	182.15	14.57	226.72	18.14
296.00	21.93	274.07	2.08	137.04	10.96	182.75	14.62	227.51	18.20
297.00	22.00	275.00	2.08	137.50	11.00	183.35	14.67	228.25	18.26
298.00	22.07	275.93	2.09	137.97	11.04	183.97	14.72	229.02	18.32
299.00	22.15	276.85	2.10	138.43	11.07	184.62	14.77	229.81	18.38
300.00	22.22	277.78	2.10	138.89	11.11	185.22	14.82	230.60	18.45
301.00	22.30	278.70	2.11	139.35	11.15	185.82	14.87	231.33	18.51
302.00	22.37	279.63	2.12	139.82	11.19	186.47	14.92	232.12	18.57
303.00	22.44	280.56	2.13	140.28	11.22	187.07	14.97	232.86	18.63
304.00	22.52	281.48	2.13	140.74	11.26	187.67	15.01	233.65	18.69
305.00	22.59	282.41	2.14	141.21	11.30	188.32	15.07	234.44	18.76
306.00	22.67	283.33	2.15	141.67	11.33	188.92	15.11	235.17	18.81
307.00	22.74	284.26	2.15	142.13	11.37	189.52	15.16	235.97	18.88
308.00	22.81	285.19	2.16	142.60	11.41	190.18	15.21	236.71	18.94
309.00	22.89	286.11	2.17	143.06	11.44	190.77	15.26	237.49	19.00
310.00	22.96	287.04	2.17	143.52	11.48	191.38	15.31	238.28	19.06

TRY THIS

Find the base fare and tax on the following tickets:

1. $ 287   **2.** $ 284   **3.** $ 293   **4.** $ 304

1. $265.74, $21.26   2. $262.96, $21.04   3. $271.30, $21.70   4. $281.48, $22.52

Steve says that sometimes there are special rates. For example, children can often travel at two thirds of the regular rate. Steve uses the same type of chart for these tickets.

EXAMPLE 2. Steve writes tickets for Dick and Candi Braun and their daughter Kelly. The total fare per ticket is $ 297. Kelly can travel at the $66\frac{2}{3}\%$ rate. How much is Kelly's ticket?

Look in the $66\frac{2}{3}\%$ column and the $ 297 row.
The base fare is $ 183.35. The tax is $ 14.67.
The total fare is $ 198.02.

Find the base fare and tax for these special-rate tickets with the indicated total amounts.

	Total	Special Rate	Base Fare	Tax		
5.	$305	Child's	?	?	$188.32	$15.07
6.	$285	50%	?	?	$131.95	$10.56
7.	$301	83%	?	?	$231.33	$18.51
8.	$289	Child's	?	?	$178.44	$14.28

Travel agents usually get 8% of the base fare as commission. The rate of commission can vary because of distance, time of year, and the age of the person traveling.

EXAMPLE 3. Find Steve's commission of the Brauns' trip (Example 2). He gets 8% commission on an adult's ticket and 5% on a child's.

PLAN:

Step 1. Use the table to find the base fare of an adult's ticket.

The base fare is $275.

Step 2. Multiply to find the commission on one adult ticket.

$0.08 \times \$275 = \$22$

Step 3. Use the table to find the base fare of a child's ticket.

The base fare is $183.35.

Step 4. Multiply to find the commission on one child's ticket.

$0.05 \times \$183.35 \approx \$9.17$

Step 5. Add to find his total commission.

$\$22 + \$22 + \$9.17 = \$53.17$

Find the indicated commission on tickets with these total costs. Use the table on page 295 to find the base fare.

9. 8% on $292 $21.63   **10.** 8% on $285 $21.11
11. 10% on $288 $26.67   **12.** 6% on $303 $16.83

EXERCISES

Use the table on page 295.

Find the base fare and tax on airline tickets with the costs listed below.

1. $ 281 $260.19, $20.81   **2.** $ 291 $269.44, $21.56

3. $ 282 $261.11, $20.89   **4.** $ 302 $279.63, $22.37

5. $ 307 $284.26, $22.74   **6.** $ 300 $277.78, $22.22

Find the base fare and tax on these special-rate tickets.

	Total	Special Rate	Base Fare	Tax
7.	$ 284	Child's	$175.34	$14.03
8.	$ 308	50%	$142.60	$11.41
9.	$ 298	83%	$229.02	$16.32
10.	$ 281	83%	$215.96	$17.28
11.	$ 309	Child's	$190.77	$15.26
12.	$ 300	50%	$138.89	$11.11

Find the base fare and commission on the base fare of these tickets.

	Rate	Total Ticket Cost	Base Fare	Commission
13.	8%	$ 297	$275.00	$22.00
14.	$8\frac{1}{2}\%$	$ 290	$269.52	$22.92
15.	$9\frac{1}{2}\%$	$ 286	$261.41	$25.18
16.	9%	$ 310	$282.02	$25.38
17.	8%	$ 303	$280.56	$22.44

ON YOUR OWN

Call a local travel agent.

Select a trip and compare the costs of traveling by car, bus, or train.

Discuss the advantages and disadvantages of each type of travel.

CHAPTER REVIEW

1. Use the table below.
   Find the sticker price: $8746
   Sedan
   Air conditioning
   Tinted glass
   CB radio

2. Use the table below.
   Find the total cost: $5891.58
   Coupe
   AM–FM radio
   Power steering
   Rear window defogger
   Sales tax 6%
   Dealer preparation $150
   License fee $25

	Hatchback Coupe	Coupe	Sedan	Sports Model
Base price	$4700	$4999	$7759	$14,959
Custom interior	161	standard	standard	standard
Deluxe exterior	112	137	standard	standard
Air conditioning	531	564	647	standard
Tinted glass	64	70	90	standard
AM radio	81	81	92	standard
AM-FM radio	94	143	156	standard
CB radio	195	210	250	279
Power brakes	76	76	standard	standard
Power steering	148	148	standard	standard
Wheel covers	56	63	75	standard
Rear window defogger	95	103	109	109
Automatic transmission	275	300	300	325
Sun roof	375	400	425	425

3. Find the total cost. $2346.08

Street bike	$1925
CB radio	$210
Sales tax	$4\frac{1}{2}\%$
Dealer preparation	$75
License fee	$40

4. Find the total cost. $514.75

Moped	$425
Sales tax	7%
Dealer preparation	$35
License fee	$25

5. John Dornbusch is buying a pickup truck for $9150. A 20% down payment is expected. How much down payment is required? $1830

6. Ann Dyslecki is buying a sports car. She financed $ 5590 at her bank and agreed to repay it in four years. Her monthly payment was $ 149.60. Find the total amount to be repaid and the finance charge. $7180.80, $1590.80

7. Jack Fenwick bought a new van which costs $ 9360. He financed $ 4300 at his credit union at a rate of 13.5%. If he agrees to repay the loan in two years, the monthly payments will be $ 205.44. If he agrees to repay the loan in three years, the monthly payments will be $ 145.92. Find the difference in the total amounts to be repaid. $322.56

8. Find the total repair bill for Mr. Dwyer's car. The taxable charges are $ 84.30, the sales tax is 6%. The labor costs are $ 162. $251.36

9. Find the stopping distance for a car going 45 mph on a dry concrete road. 84.4 ft
Use the formula $D = \dfrac{S^2}{30f}$ and the chart on page 279.

10. Use the nomogram on page 279. Estimate the speed of a car which left a skid mark 190 feet long. The road surface was wet concrete. 50 mph

11. Use the map on page 282. Find the distance between York, Pennsylvania and Washington, D.C. 95 mi

12. Juana Medina estimates that she will average 40 miles per hour on a trip from Cumberland, Maryland to Baltimore. About how long will the trip take? 3.475 hr

13. Juana knows that her car averages about 28 miles per gallon. About how many gallons of gasoline will she use on the trip described in exercise 12? 5 gal

14. Find the rental cost for a car which costs $ 48.85 per day. The cost per mile is $ 0.51. The car is kept six days and driven 623 miles. $610.83

15. Homer and Bernice Alexander are planning a camping trip. The cost at their favorite campground is $ 3 per night. They plan on staying two nights and two days. Food costs are $ 5 per day. Not including gasoline, how much will the trip cost? $16

16. Find the base fare and tax on an airline ticket which costs $ 309. Use the table on page 295. $286.11, $22.89

SKILLS REVIEW

SKILL 12 Rounding decimals and money

Round to the underlined place.

1. 1<u>5</u>.6 16   **2.** 2<u>3</u>.4 23   **3.** 1<u>9</u>.5 20   **4.** 26<u>4</u>.09 264

5. $11<u>4</u>.96 $115   **6.** $1<u>3</u>0.85 $130   **7.** $189.<u>9</u>5 $190.00   **8.** 476.5<u>1</u>8 476.52

SKILL 34 Writing fractions as decimals

Convert to a decimal. Round to the nearest hundredth.

9. $\frac{2}{5}$ 0.4   **10.** $\frac{3}{4}$ 0.75   **11.** $\frac{3}{8}$ 0.38   **12.** $\frac{5}{16}$ 0.31

13. $\frac{2}{7}$ 0.29   **14.** $\frac{7}{9}$ 0.78   **15.** $\frac{6}{11}$ 0.55   **16.** $\frac{5}{12}$ 0.42

SKILL 36 Writing fractions as mixed numbers

Convert to a mixed number.

17. $\frac{11}{3}$ $3\frac{2}{3}$ **18.** $\frac{9}{4}$ $2\frac{1}{4}$ **19.** $\frac{29}{5}$ $5\frac{4}{5}$ **20.** $\frac{557}{12}$ $46\frac{5}{12}$

SKILL 42 Least common denominator

Find the least common denominator (LCD).

21. $\frac{1}{3}, \frac{1}{5}$ 15   **22.** $\frac{3}{4}, \frac{2}{5}$ 20   **23.** $\frac{1}{2}, \frac{3}{4}$ 4   **24.** $\frac{5}{6}, \frac{1}{3}$ 6

25. $\frac{5}{6}, \frac{8}{9}$ 18   **26.** $\frac{5}{6}, \frac{3}{4}$ 12   **27.** $\frac{3}{4}, \frac{1}{6}, \frac{2}{3}$ 12   **28.** $\frac{7}{8}, \frac{5}{6}, \frac{1}{2}$ 24

SKILL 44 Converting percents to decimals

Convert to a decimal.

29. 16% 0.16   **30.** 25% 0.25   **31.** 8% 0.08   **32.** 3% 0.03

SKILL 16 Adding decimals

Add.

33.
$$\begin{array}{r} 4.98 \\ 3.7 \\ + 5.876 \\ \hline 14.556 \end{array}$$
34.
$$\begin{array}{r} 9.72 \\ 8.746 \\ + 8.9 \\ \hline 27.366 \end{array}$$
35.
$$\begin{array}{r} 12.4 \\ 6.78 \\ 0.39 \\ + 0.668 \\ \hline 20.238 \end{array}$$
36.
$$\begin{array}{r} 7.328 \\ 0.09 \\ 1.4268 \\ + 0.6 \\ \hline 9.4448 \end{array}$$

SKILL 18 Subtracting whole numbers

Subtract.

37.   6287
         − 1938
         ‾‾‾‾‾
          4349

38.   62,486
        − 19,197
        ‾‾‾‾‾‾‾
         43,289

39.   427,685
        − 388,747
        ‾‾‾‾‾‾‾‾
          38,938

40.   75,003
        − 19,437
        ‾‾‾‾‾‾‾
         55,566

SKILL 20 Subtracting decimals

Subtract.

41.   7.43
        − 4.68
        ‾‾‾‾‾
         2.75

42.   3.786
        − 1.9
        ‾‾‾‾‾
         1.886

43.   6.3
        − 1.428
        ‾‾‾‾‾
         4.872

44.   8
        − 7.34
        ‾‾‾‾‾
         0.66

SKILL 51 Division: 2- and 3-digit divisors

Divide. Round to the nearest tenth.

45. $16\overline{)432}$ → 27

46. $526\overline{)42{,}606}$ → 81

47. $32\overline{)200}$ → 6.3

48. $50\overline{)75}$ → 1.5

49. $625\overline{)1500}$ → 2.4

50. $63\overline{)9487}$ → 150.6

51. $497\overline{)23{,}860}$ → 48.0

52. $429\overline{)34{,}420}$ → 80.2

SKILL 61 Subtracting fractions

Subtract. Simplify when possible.

53. $\frac{7}{8} - \frac{1}{8}$ $\frac{3}{4}$

54. $\frac{11}{12} - \frac{1}{12}$ $\frac{5}{6}$

55. $\frac{3}{5} - \frac{1}{2}$ $\frac{1}{10}$

56. $\frac{7}{10} - \frac{3}{5}$ $\frac{1}{10}$

57. $\frac{2}{3} - \frac{1}{4}$ $\frac{5}{12}$

58. $\frac{3}{4} - \frac{1}{6}$ $\frac{7}{12}$

59. $\frac{7}{12} - \frac{1}{10}$ $\frac{29}{60}$

60. $\frac{5}{16} - \frac{1}{12}$ $\frac{11}{48}$

SKILL 68 Finding what percent a number is of another

61. What percent of 20 is 12? 60%   **62.** 75 is what percent of 150? 50%

63. 20 is what percent of 30? $66\frac{2}{3}\%$ **64.** 21 is what percent of 24? $87\frac{1}{2}\%$

SKILL 73 Changing customary units

Make these changes.

65. 6 ft = ___72___ in.   **66.** 8 pt = ___16___ cups

67. 48 in. = ___4___ ft   **68.** 60 min = ___3600___ sec

SKILL 75 Subtracting measurements

69.   4 ft 8 in.
        − 2 ft 6 in.
        ‾‾‾‾‾‾‾‾
         2 ft 2 in.

70.   9 ft 1 in.
        − 3 ft 7 in.
        ‾‾‾‾‾‾‾‾
         5 ft 6 in.

71.   11 ft
        − 4 ft 5 in.
        ‾‾‾‾‾‾‾‾
         6 ft 7 in.

72.   10 min 48 sec
        − 8 min 32 sec
        ‾‾‾‾‾‾‾‾‾‾
          2 min 16 sec

9
SPORTS,
HOBBIES,
AND RECREATIONS

SPORTS RECORDS

The first Indianapolis Speedway Race in 1911 was won by Ray Harroun with an average speed of 74.59 mph. Race cars today are built to go two or three times that speed.

Dale Jarvis has a hobby of collecting and comparing sports records. He began his hobby by comparing baseball records. Later his interests expanded to other sports events including the Olympic Games.

EXAMPLE 1.   Who is faster?

Winning speed at the Indianapolis 500 race:
1911 . . . Ray Harroun . . . . . 74.590 miles per hour
1972 . . . Mark Donohue . . . . 163.465 miles per hour

Compare by subtracting.

$163.465 - 74.590 = 88.875$

Donohue was faster by 88.875 miles per hour.

Find the difference in these Major League baseball records.

1. Home run champions:
1918 . . . Cliff Cravath, Philadelphia . . . 8 home runs
1961 . . . Roger Maris, New York . . . . . 61 home runs
Maris, 53

2. Consecutive games played:
1923–39 . . . Lou Gehrig. . . . 2130
1914–26 . . . Everett Scott . . . 1307 Gehrig, 823

In swimming, speed skating, and many other sports, the times are reported in minutes, seconds, and hundredths of a second.

minutes   seconds

2:12.37

EXAMPLE 2.   Who is faster? Find the difference.

Women's 100-meter freestyle swimming:
1912 . . . Fanny Durack, Australia. 1:22.20
1980 . . . Barbara Krause, East Germany . . . 0:54.79

PLAN: **Step 1.**   Compare by subtracting.

1 minute 22.20 seconds
−0 minute 54.79 seconds

Step 2.   Seconds cannot be subtracted. Rename 1 minute as 60 seconds.

0   82.20
1 minute 22.20 seconds
−0 minute 54.79 seconds
27.41 seconds

Barbara Krause's time is faster by 27.41 seconds.

Who is faster? Find the difference.

3. Men's 100-meter freestyle swimming:
1912 . . . Duke P. Kahanamaku, United States . . 1:03.40
1976 . . . Jim Montgomery, United States. 0:49.99
Montgomery, 0:13.41

4. Women's 1500-meter speed skating:
1960 . . . Lydia Skobikova, USSR 2:52.20
1980 . . . Anne Borckink, Netherlands . . . 2:10.95
Borckink, 0:41.25

To compare track and field results we often need to change units to make the subtraction possible.

EXAMPLE 3. Whose distance is better? Find the difference.

Men's shotput:
1896 . . . Robert Garret, United States . . . 36 ft $9\frac{3}{4}$ in.
1980 . . . Vladimir Kiselyov, USSR . . . . . 70 ft $\frac{1}{2}$ in.

PLAN: **Step 1.** Compare by subtracting.

$$70 \text{ ft } \tfrac{1}{2} \text{ in.}$$
$$-36 \text{ ft } 9\tfrac{3}{4} \text{ in.}$$

Step 2. Inches cannot be subtracted. Rename 1 foot as 12 inches.

$$69 \text{ ft } 12\tfrac{1}{2} \text{ in.} \qquad \textit{Rename 70 ft as 69 ft 12 in.}$$
$$-36 \text{ ft } 9\tfrac{3}{4} \text{ in.}$$
$$\overline{33 \text{ ft } 2\tfrac{3}{4} \text{ in.}}$$

Kiselyov's distance is better by 33 ft $2\frac{3}{4}$ in.

Whose distances are better? Find the difference.

TRY THIS

5. Women's discus throw:
1928 . . . Helena Konopacka, Poland . . . . 129 ft 11 in.
1976 . . . Evelin Schlaak, East Germany . . 226 ft 4 in.
Schlaak, 96 ft 5 in.
6. Men's running high jump:
1896 . . . Ellery Clark, United States . . . . 5 ft $11\frac{1}{4}$ in.
1968 . . . Dick Fosbury, United States . . . 7 ft $4\frac{1}{4}$ in.
Fosbury, 1 ft 5 in.

EXERCISES

Subtract the following times.

1. $1{:}16.14$	**2.** $4{:}37.12$	**3.** $2{:}18.06$	**4.** $3{:}14.28$
$-1{:}09.10$	$-3{:}18.42$	$-1{:}37.01$	$-1{:}26.52$
7.04	18.70	41.05	1:47.76

Subtract the following distances.

5. 130 ft 8 in.
      − 111 ft 4 in.
      ‾‾‾‾‾‾‾‾‾‾
        19 ft 4 in.

6. 87 ft 9 in.
      − 32 ft 11 in.
      ‾‾‾‾‾‾‾‾‾‾
        54 ft 10 in.

7. 13 ft 2 in.
      − 6 ft 11 in.
      ‾‾‾‾‾‾‾‾‾‾
        6 ft 3 in.

8. 8 ft $3\frac{1}{2}$ in.
      − 5 ft $9\frac{1}{4}$ in.
      ‾‾‾‾‾‾‾‾‾‾
        2 ft $6\frac{1}{4}$ in.

Whose record is better? Find the difference.

9. World 1-mile land speed driving record:
1904 . . . Henry Ford, Ford 999 . . . . 91.370 mph
1970 . . . Gary Gabelich, Blue Flame . . . . 622.407 mph **Gabelich, 531.037 mph**

10. Men's 100-meter backstroke:
1924 . . . Warren Kealoha, United States 1:13.2
1976 . . . John Naber, United States . . . . 0:55.49 **Naber, 0:17.71**

11. Women's downhill Alpine skiing:
1948 . . . Heidi Schlunegger, Switzerland 2:28.3
1976 . . . Rosi Mittermeier, West Germany . . . . . 1:46.16 **Mittermeier, 0:42.14**

12. Men's running high jump:
1896 . . . Ellery Clark, United States . . . . 5 ft $11\frac{1}{4}$ in.
1980 . . . Gerd Wessig, East Germany . . . . 7 ft 9 in. **Wessig, 1 ft $9\frac{3}{4}$ in.**

13. Women's long jump:
1948 . . . Olga Gyarmati, Hungary . . . . 18 ft $8\frac{1}{4}$ in.
1972 . . . Heidemarie Rosendahl, West Germany . . . 22 ft 3 in. **Rosendahl, 3 ft $6\frac{3}{4}$ in.**

14. Men's 1500-meter run:
1896 . . . Edwin Flack, Australia 4:34.2
1968 . . . Kipchoge Keino, Kenya. . . . . 3:34.9 **Keino, 0:59.3**

15. Women's 100-meter butterfly:
1956 . . . Shelley Mann, United States 1:11.0
1980 . . . Mary T. Meagher, United States . . . . . . 0:59.26 **Meagher, 0:11.74**

ON YOUR OWN

16. Obtain a current sports records book or almanac. Look up the most recent records in each event listed in the Examples, Try This, and Exercises above. Calculate the differences from older records.

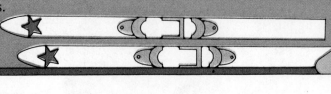

PROBLEM SOLVING HINTS

Bruce Peck was elected president of the county baseball league.
He has to schedule a single elimination tournament for seven teams.
Bruce has never made a schedule for an odd number of teams.
To find a plan, he tries a schedule for three and five teams.

Three Teams

BYE
Team A
Team B   WINNER
Team C

Five Teams

BYE
Team A
Team B
Team C
Team D   WINNER
BYE
Team E
BYE

In the first round Bruce does not schedule games for some teams.
This is called a BYE. This causes the second round to have an even
matching of teams. He observes the pattern 8, 4, 2, 1. Bruce then
applies this idea to seven teams.

BYE
Team A
Team B
Team C
Team D   WINNER
Team E
Team F
Team G

HINT   Some problems can be solved by trying simpler cases.

BOWLING

Many players can knock down all ten pins in a single roll, but to do it twelve times in a row is a perfect game and very rare.

Pat Cook is the secretary of the Star Rollers Bowling League. She collects dues and pays the bowling lane fees. She computes member's averages and handicaps. She also keeps records of team standings and assigns lanes for each game.

The score sheet for a bowling game has ten *frames*. On each turn a player's score is recorded in a frame. On each turn a player gets two tries to knock down all ten pins. The number knocked down in two tries is written in the frame.

six pins on first ball
two pins on second ball

A frame that does not include a spare or a strike is is called an open frame.

Score for the frame is 8.

EXAMPLE 1.   Record these results and find the score.

The common term for total score is total pins.

Frame 1: Six pins on ball 1   **Frame 2:** Seven pins on ball 1

Three pins on ball 2   Two pins on ball 2

PLAN: **Step 1.**   Record the results.

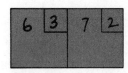

Step 2.   Find totals for each frame and add.

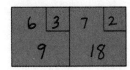

1. Record these results and find the score.

 TRY THIS

Frame 1:   Six pins on ball 1
No pins on ball 2 6

Frame 2:   Four pins on ball 1
Five pins on ball 2 15

If a player gets all ten pins on the first ball of a frame, this is a *strike*. Mark an X, like this:

The score for this frame is 10 plus the number of pins scored by the next *two* balls.

If a player gets all ten pins using two balls, this is a *spare.* Mark a slash, like this:

The score for this frame is 10 plus the number of pins scored by the *first* ball in the next frame.

EXAMPLE 2.   Find the score in each frame.

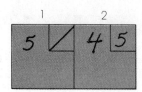

Make sure students understand that in the case of a spare, the score of the frame cannot be found until the next ball is thrown.

The slash mark indicates a spare. The score for the first frame is 10 plus 4 from the next ball—a total of 14. Nine points in the next frame makes the total 23.

EXAMPLE 3.   Find the score in each frame.

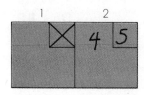

In the case of a strike, the score of the frame cannot be found until the next two balls are thrown.

PLAN: **Step 1.**   The X-mark indicates a strike.

The score for the first frame is 10 plus the number of pins knocked down in the next two throws.

$10 + 4 + 5 = 19$ pins

Step 2.   Add the pins knocked down in the second frame to the score in the first frame.

$19 + 4 + 5 = 28$ pins

You get two throws in the last frame. If you score a spare, you get one extra throw; if you score a strike, you get two extra throws.

EXAMPLE 4.   Find the final game score.

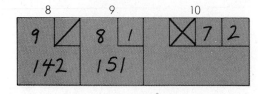

The score in frame 10 is 10 plus 7 plus 2, or 19. So the game score is $151 + 19$ or 170.

2. Find the score for each frame and the total score.

7	8	9	10
	7 /	2 5	☒ 6 1
124	136	143	160

Each week Pat computes each bowler's average.

EXAMPLES.

5. Find the average. Round to the nearest whole number.

Carla's game scores are 170, 182, 147.

PLAN:

Step 1. Add the game scores.

$170 + 182 + 147 = 499$

Step 2. Divide by the number of games.

$499 \div 3 \approx 166$

Carla's average is 166.

6. In 54 games Max's total score is 8692.

$8692 \div 54 \approx 161$ Max's average is 161.

Find the average. Round to the nearest whole number.

3. Tom's game scores are 192, 212, 178. **194**

4. In 45 games Donna's total score is 6207. **138**

To balance teams and make games closer, handicaps are added to some of the players' scores. In Pat's league the handicap is computed on a basic score of 180. The formula is **The base score, 180 in this case, varies from one league to another.**

$H = 80\% \times (180 - A)$

H stands for the player's handicap. A stands for the player's average.

If a bowler's average is over 180, the handicap is 0.

EXAMPLE 7.

Find the handicap for Bert whose average is 151.

$H = 80\% \times (180 - A)$

$\quad = 0.80 \times (180 - 151)$ *Substitute.*

$\quad = 0.80 \times 29$ *Work inside the parenthesis first.*

$\quad \approx 23$ *Round to nearest whole number.*

Bert's handicap is 23.

Find the handicap.

5. Lora's average is 140. 32
6. John's average is 170. 8
7. Fred's average is 181. 0

To find which team won a game, add each player's handicap to the *scratch score* (score without handicap).

EXAMPLE 8.　　Find which team won.

Spare Parts	Scratch	Handicap	Scattered Pins	Scratch	Handicap
J. Spaulding	142	51	M. Hendricks	107	63
L. Smith	120	50	P. Tafaya	132	38
J. Walker	124	42	B. Demick	170	18
B. Branch	170	21	A. McKinlay	162	22

PLAN:　**Step 1.**　Add to find the total scratch scores.

Spare Parts: $142 + 120 + 124 + 170 = 556$
Scattered Pins: $107 + 132 + 170 + 162 = 571$

Step 2.　Add to find the total handicaps.

Spare Parts: $51 + 50 + 42 + 21 = 164$
Scattered Pins: $63 + 38 + 18 + 22 = 141$

Step 3.　Add the total scratch scores and the total handicaps.

Spare Parts: $556 + 164 = 720$
Scattered Pins: $571 + 141 = 712$

The Spare Parts won by a score of 720 to 712.

8. Find which team won. The Duck Pins won by a score of 567 to 566.

Duck Pins	Scratch	Handicap	Strikers	Scratch	Handicap
E. Anderson	123	66	J. Gatzke	98	74
A. Alexander	170	13	P. Hoffman	161	32
J. Dyer	185	10	G. Fox	175	26

EXERCISES

Find the score in each frame and the total.

1.

7	1	6	2	9	0	4	4	8	/	7	1	✕	6	2	6	/	7	2
8		16		25		33		50		58		76		84		101		110

2.

9	/	8	/	7	/	9	/	8	/	8	/	✕	7	✕	✕	7	/	9
18		35		54		72		90		110		130		150		170		189

Find the average.

3. Game scores: 142, 156, and 174 157   **4.** Game scores: 145, 162, 201 169

5. Total pins: 487 Games: 3 162   **6.** Total pins: 7020 Games: 45 156

Find the handicap. Use the formula on page 311.

7. Bowler's average 146 27   **8.** Bowler's average 172 6

9. Bowler's average 150 24   **10.** Bowler's average 118 50

11. Find which team won. Thursday Nighters won by a score of 564 to 547.

Thursday Nighters	Scratch	Handicap	Never Splitters	Scratch	Handicap
R. Lee	122	51	S. Clark	140	31
S. Kotoff	117	75	B. Willett	128	64
R. Lehnert	163	36	C. Dennis	144	40

12. A perfect score in bowling is 12 strikes. Make a score sheet like the one in Exercise 1. What is the score? 300

13. If a player gets a spare in every frame, what would the score be? Not enough information.

ON YOUR OWN

14. Find the cost of each of the following:

   a. One game at a bowling alley   **b.** Bowling ball   **c.** Bowling bag

SCUBA DIVING
SCUBA stands for Self-Contained Underwater Breathing Apparatus.

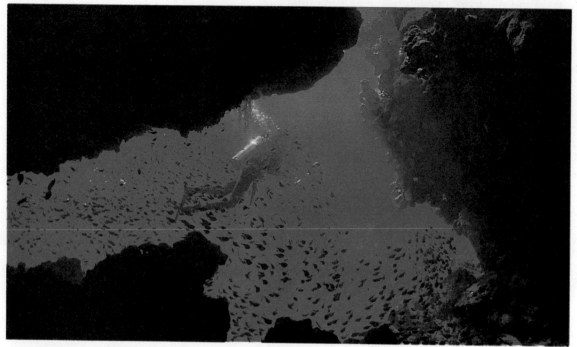

The blue-green beauty and complete quiet of the underwater world
can be experienced first-hand by SCUBA divers.

Len and Arlene Orsini enjoy scuba diving. They learned that air
exerts a pressure of 14.7 pounds per square inch at sea level. This is
called one atmosphere (1 atm). Underwater pressure is calculated
using these formulas:

For salt water, $P = 1 + \dfrac{d}{33}$; for fresh water, $P = 1 + \dfrac{d}{34}$.

P stands for the pressure measured in atmospheres.
d stands for the depth of water measured in feet.

In the formula, 1 stands for one
atmosphere of air pressure at sea level.

EXAMPLE

1. Use the correct formula to find the pressure.

Depth of 15 feet in salt water.

$$P = 1 + \frac{d}{33}$$

$$= 1 + \frac{15}{33} \qquad \textit{Substitute.}$$

$$= 1 + 0.455, \text{ or } 1.455 \text{ atmospheres.}$$

Find the pressure at these depths.

1. 10 feet in salt water
1.303 atm

2. 40 feet in fresh water
2.176 atm

The Orsinis calculate the *maximum time* for a dive with this formula:

$$T = \frac{v}{kP}$$

T stands for the maximum time for a dive in minutes.
v stands for the volume of air in the air tanks in cubic feet.
k stands for the volume of air the diver uses per minute (air-use rate). This amount is in cubic feet per minute.
P stands for the pressure in atmospheres.

EXAMPLE 2.   Find the maximum time for this dive.

There are 37 cubic feet of air in the tank, $v = 37$.
The air-use rate is 0.80 cubic feet per minute, $k = 0.80$.
The dive will be in fresh water to a depth of 20 feet, $d = 20$.

PLAN: **Step 1.**   Use the fresh-water formula to find the pressure.

$$P = 1 + \frac{d}{34} \approx 1.588 \text{ atm}$$ *Substitute 20 for d.*

Step 2.   Use the formula to find the maximum time for the dive. **When calculating the length of a dive, always round down. Otherwise, the diver may stay down longer than is safe.**

$$T = \frac{v}{kP}$$

$$= \frac{37}{0.8 \times 1.588}$$ *Substitute.*
Round to the nearest

$$\approx \frac{37}{1.270}$$ *thousandth.*

$$= 29.1 \approx 29 \text{ minutes}$$ *Round down to the nearest minute.*

The dive should last no more than 29 minutes.

Find the maximum time for each dive.

	Air in tank v (ft³)	Air-use rate k (ft³ per min)	Depth of dive d (ft)	Type of water
3.	40	0.9	15	salt 30 min
4.	25	1.0	25	fresh 14 min

EXERCISES

Find the value of P or T.

1. $P = 1 + \dfrac{10}{33}$ 1.303 **2.** $P = 1 + \dfrac{100}{34}$ 3.941 **3.** $P = 1 + \dfrac{250}{33}$ 8.576

4. $T = \dfrac{50}{(.75)(1.6)}$ 41.667 **5.** $T = \dfrac{25}{(.50)(2.1)}$ 23.810 **6.** $T = \dfrac{35}{(.6)(1.88)}$ 31.028

Find the pressure.

7. Depth of 35 feet in salt water
2.061 atm

8. Depth of 50 feet in salt water 2.515 atm

9. Depth of 20 feet in fresh water
1.588 atm

10. Depth of 34 feet in fresh water 2.000 atm

Find the maximum time for the dive.

	Air in tank, v (ft³)	Air-use rate, k (ft³ per min)	Depth of dive, d (ft)	Type of water
11.	50 41 min	0.75	20	salt
12.	45 15 min	1.50	30	fresh
13.	52 28 min	0.85	40	fresh
14.	60 26 min	0.95	45	salt
15.	25 20 min	0.60	35	fresh
16.	80 55 min	1.00	15	fresh
17.	40 34 min	0.70	22	salt
18.	35 30 min	0.65	25	salt
19.	75 59 min	0.80	20	salt
20.	27 10 min	1.05	50	fresh
21.	55 44 min	0.90	25	salt
22.	85 27 min	1.55	35	fresh
23.	20 9 min	1.00	40	fresh
24.	30 24 min	0.85	15	fresh
25.	65 67 min	0.60	20	salt
26.	70 31 min	0.95	45	salt

ON YOUR OWN

27. Find the meaning of nitrogen narcosis (rapture of the depths).

28. List some equipment used in SCUBA diving.

MENTAL CALCULATION

SPECIAL MULTIPLICATION

If your multiplier is near 10 or 100, you can sometimes find the answer quickly. Simply multiply by 10 or 100 and adjust your answer by adding or subtracting.

EXAMPLE 1.   Multiply 9×23.

Multiply by 10. $10 \times 23 = 230$
Subtract 23. $230 - 20 = 210$ $210 - 3 = 207$

So, $9 \times 23 = 207$.

EXAMPLE 2.   Multiply 8×48.

Multiply by 10. $10 \times 48 = 480$
Subtract 48 twice or subtract 96.
This can be done by subtracting 100 and adding 4.

$480 - 100 = 380$ and $380 + 4 = 384$

So, $8 \times 48 = 384$.

EXAMPLE 3.   Multiply 99×13.

Multiply by 100. $100 \times 13 = 1300$
Subtract 13. $1300 - 13 = 1287$

So, $99 \times 13 = 1287$.

PRACTICE

Multiply mentally.

1. 9×32 288   **2.** 9×52 468   **3.** 9×81 729   **4.** 8×46 368

5. 8×53 424   **6.** 99×15 1485   **7.** 99×18 1782   **8.** 98×32 3136

9. 101×56 5656   **10.** 102×83 8466   **11.** 97×16 1552   **12.** 102×49 4998

FOOTBALL

All the players do their part in trying to control the ball as the team nears the goal line and touchdown.

Joe McKay keeps the official records at football, baseball, and basketball games. He can also referee or umpire games. Joe attended clinics in each sport to qualify for these jobs. To keep up-to-date on rule changes, he takes refresher courses each year. He is paid for each game he works. He also makes extra money by reporting scores to the local newspapers.

The 100-yard football field is shown in Example 1. Starting at each end, a line is drawn across the field every ten yards. The 50-yard line is at the center and divides one team's side from the other.

Markers set along the sidelines help you calculate the distance the ball moves on a play. When the ball crosses the 50-yard line, you can calculate as shown in Example 1.

EXAMPLE 1.   The football was kicked from the Raiders' 35-yard line to the Rams' 20-yard line. How long was the kick?

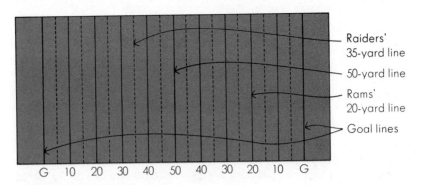

Raiders'
35-yard line

50-yard line

Rams'
20-yard line

Goal lines

G 10 20 30 40 50 40 30 20 10 G

PLAN: **Step 1.**   Find the distance from the Raiders' 35-yard line to the 50-yard line.

$50 - 35 = 15$

Step 2.   Find the distance from the 50-yard line to the Rams' 20-yard line.

$50 - 20 = 30$

Step 3.   Add to find the total distance.

$15 + 30 = 45$ It was a 45-yard kick.

Find the total distance.

TRY THIS

1. A run from the Rams' 27-yard line to the Raiders' 32-yard line 41 yd

2. A pass from the Raiders' 41-yard line to the Rams' 19-yard line 40 yd

3. A run from your 8-yard line to your 24-yard line 16 yd

A statistic often included in football is a player's rushing average. It indicates how far a player can be expected to carry the ball on one play. The rushing average can be found by the formula:

$R = \dfrac{y}{n}.$

R stands for the player's rushing average.
y stands for the total number of yards rushed.
n stands for the number of times the player carried the ball.

EXAMPLE 2.   Find the rushing average for Mike Adams. He ran 92 yards in 12 carries.

$$R = \frac{y}{n}$$

$$= \frac{92}{12}$$

$$\approx 7.7 \qquad \textit{Round to the nearest tenth.}$$

Mike's rushing average is 7.7 yards per carry.

TRY THIS

Find the rushing average.

4. George Jones carries 8 times for 30 yards. 3.8 yd
5. Larry Burns carries 16 times for 85 yards. 5.3 yd
6. Total team carries 36 times for 207 yards. 5.8 yd

Another statistic often calculated in football is the pass completion percent. Use this formula:

$$P = \frac{c}{a}$$

P stands for the pass completion percent.
c stands for the number of passes completed.
a stands for the number of passes attempted.

EXAMPLE 3.   Use the formula to find Jeff Harris' pass completion percent. He completed 8 passes in 15 attempts.

$$P = \frac{c}{a}$$

$$= \frac{8}{15}$$

$$= 0.533$$

$$= 53.3\%$$

Jeff's pass completion percent is 53.3%.

TRY THIS

Find the pass completion percents.

7. Dana Washington: 6 completions for 10 attempts. 60%
8. Jerome Zarndt: 7 completions for 12 attempts. 58.3%
9. The Jets: 21 completions for 37 attempts. 56.8%

EXERCISES

Find the total distance.

1. A kick from your 38-yard line to the opponents' 27-yard line 35 yd

2. A run from your 27-yard line to the opponents' 31-yard line 42 yd

3. A pass from your 46-yard line to the opponents' 46-yard line 8 yd

4. A run from your 23-yard line to your 36-yard line 13 yd

5. A pass from your opponents' 43-yard line to your opponents' 17-yard line 26 yd

Find the rushing average.

6. 9 carries for 40 yards 4.4 yd

7. 12 carries for 70 yards 5.8 yd

8. 18 carries for 109 yards 6.1 yd

9. 37 carries for 192 yards 5.2 yd

10. 54 carries for 222 yards 4.1 yd

Find the pass completion percent.

11. 5 completions out of 11 attempts 45.5%

12. 7 completions out of 15 attempts 46.7%

13. 12 completions out of 24 attempts 50.0%

14. 31 completions out of 42 attempts 73.8%

15. 12 completions out of 32 attempts 37.5%

ON YOUR OWN

16. Find out what these football terms mean:

PAT, turnover, offsetting penalties, delay-of-game penalty

17. Look in the sports page of a newspaper or sports magazine. Find some rushing averages and pass completion records.

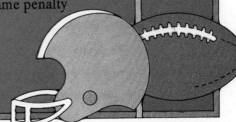

BASEBALL

Facts about every play in this major league game are recorded so that sports statistics can be immediately brought up to date.

Jerri Hawk is a sportswriter for a newspaper. Jerri liked journalism, English, and sports during high school. This background helped her get a job with the newspaper.

Jerri's favorite sport is baseball. One statistic she often reports is a player's batting average. It can be found by the formula:

$$B = \frac{h}{a}$$

B stands for the batting average.
h stands for the number of hits.
a stands for the number of times at bat.

Walks, hit batters, sacrifice flies or bunts, and interference calls are not counted in times at bat.

The average is rounded to the nearest thousandth.

EXAMPLE 1.   Find the batting average for Craig Green. In 75 times at bat he had 22 hits.

$$B = \frac{h}{a} = \frac{22}{75} \approx 0.293 \qquad \textit{Round to the nearest thousandth.}$$

Craig's average is .293. This means he got hits in 29.3% of his times at bat.

Jerri sometimes calculates the number of hits a player needs to get a certain batting average. The formula is

$$n = [a \times (b + e)] - h$$

n stands for the number of hits needed to get a certain average.
a stands for the wanted batting average.
b stands for the present number of times at bat.
e stands for the number of times at bat to come.
h stands for the present number of hits.

EXAMPLE 2. Nancy has 23 hits in 85 times at bat for a .271 batting average. She expects to get 32 more times at bat this season. How many hits does she need to get a .300 batting average?

Use the formula:

$$n = [a \times (b + e)] - h$$
$\quad = [0.300 \times (85 + 32)] - 23$ *Substitute the correct numbers.*
$\quad = [0.300 \times 117] - 23$ *Do the work in the parentheses first.*
$\quad = 35.1 - 23$ *Do the work in the brackets next.*
$\quad = 12.1$
$\quad \approx 13$ hits   *Round up to the next hit.*

We round up because 12 hits would give Nancy 35 hits for only a .299 average; 13 hits will give her an average of .308.

Another statistic is the earned run average. The ERA is based on 9 innings of play. An earned run is a run charged to the pitcher. The formula used to calculate an ERA is

$$\text{ERA} = \frac{9r}{I}$$ An unearned run is a run due to an error. It is not charged to the pitcher.

r stands for the number of earned runs.
I stands for the number of innings pitched.

EXAMPLE 3.   Marty Banda pitched 29 innings and gave up 8 earned runs. What is his ERA?

$$ERA = \frac{9r}{I} = \frac{9 \times 8}{29} = 2.48 \approx 2.5$$

Marty's ERA is 2.5.

TRY THIS

Find the ERA.

5. Sherri Gonzales pitched 50 innings and gave up 20 earned runs. 3.6

6. Mike Walker pitched 63 innings and gave up 32 earned runs. 4.6

A statistic often reported in newspapers is *Games Back*. Games Back shows a team's position compared to the leading team. It is the number of games the leading team must lose and the trailing team must win to tie for the lead.

Jerri shows how Games Back is calculated. The formula used is

$G = \dfrac{W + L}{2}$ When the leading team's number of games ahead becomes greater than the number of games left to play in a season, that team has clinched first place in the league.

G stands for Games Back.

W stands for the *difference* between the two teams in the number of wins.

L stands for the *difference* between the two teams in the number of losses.

EXAMPLE 4.   Find the Games Back for the Angels.

	Wins	Losses
Leader	72	64
Angels	65	74

$$G = \frac{W + L}{2}$$
$$= \frac{(72 - 65) + (74 - 64)}{2}$$
$$= \frac{7 + 10}{2} = \frac{17}{2} = 8\frac{1}{2}$$

The Angels are $8\frac{1}{2}$ games back of the leader.

Find the Games Back.

7.

	Wins	Losses	
Leader	42	20	
Tigers	36	26	6 games back

EXERCISES

Find the batting average.

1. 9 hits in 36 times at bat .250   **2.** 20 hits in 84 times at bat .238

3. 42 hits in 126 times at bat .333   **4.** 102 hits in 396 times at bat .258

5. 120 hits in 300 times at bat .400   **6.** 120 hits in 310 times at bat .387

7. A batter now has 30 hits in 70 times at bat for a .429 batting average. There will be 38 more times at bat. How many more hits are needed to get a .450 average? 19 hits

8. A batter now has 64 hits in 250 times at bat for a .256 batting average. There will be 100 more times at bat. How many more hits are needed to get a .300 average? 41 hits

Find the ERA.

9. 10 earned runs in 40 innings pitched 2.3   **10.** 8 earned runs in 73 innings pitched 1.0

11. 25 earned runs in 120 innings pitched 1.9   **12.** 12 earned runs in 55 innings pitched 2.0

Find the Games Back.

13.

	Wins	Losses
Leader	27	14
Yankees	21	20

6 games back

14.

	Wins	Losses	
Leader	76	50	
Giants	60	67	$16\frac{1}{2}$ games back

ON YOUR OWN

15. Find what is considered a very good batting average in

a. Major League baseball   **b.** High school softball (slow pitch)

BASKETBALL

Another field goal adds two points to the scores, as these
professional teams vie in a typical high-scoring game.

Roberto Taylor earns extra money as the official scorer at basketball
games. He took a course given by the local Officials Association to
learn the rules and procedures.

Here is how Roberto records individual scoring:
2 (field goals made, 2 points)   / (field goal missed, 0 points)
Ø (free throw made, 1 point)   0 (free throw missed, 0 points)

		Official Score Sheet				
Number	Name	1st quarter	2nd quarter	3rd quarter	4th quarter	Total Points
12	L. TURNER	// 2 0	/ ⊠ ⊠ 2 /	// ⊠ 2	0 ⊠ ⊠ 0	
15	P. JACKSON	2 2 2 // ⊠	2 2 // ⊠ ⊠ /	⊠ ⊠ 0 2	/ 2 / 2 2	
23	J. RUIS	/ 2 0 0 / 2	⊠ ⊠ ⊠ 2 2 /	/// ⊠ ⊠	2 ⊠ ⊠	

At the end of the game Roberto calculates each player's total
number of points. His calculations are the official scores.

EXAMPLE 1. Find the number of points scored by L. Turner.

PLAN: **Step 1.** Count the number of field goals made and multiply by 2.

There are 3. So, $3 \times 2 = 6$ points.

Step 2. Count the number of free throws made.

There are 5, for 5 points.

Step 3. Add to find the total points.

$6 + 5 = 11$ total points

TRY THIS

Find the number of points scored.

1. P. Jackson **23 points** **2.** J. Ruis **17 points**

At the end of the game Roberto also calculates each player's and the team's field goal and free throw percents. The formula for both is

$P = \dfrac{m}{a}.$

P stands for the percent made.
m stands for the number made.
a stands for the number of attempts.

EXAMPLE 2. Find the percent of field goals made.

B. Tully made 5 field goals out of 13 attempts.
Substitute the correct numbers in the formula.

$P = \dfrac{m}{a}.$

$= \dfrac{5}{13} \approx 0.38$ *Round to the nearest hundredth.*

$= 38\%$

B. Tully made 38% of his field goal attempts.

TRY THIS

Find the percent made.

3. C. Black made 8 out of 11 free throw attempts. **73%**
4. S. Alan made 9 out of 16 field goal attempts. **56%**
5. The team made 34 out of 75 field goal attempts. **45%**

EXERCISES

Find the total points.

		Official Score Sheet				
Number	Name	1st quarter	2nd quarter	3rd quarter	4th quarter	Total Points
10	L. HAAS	⊗⊗///	2220	/2/22/	⊗000	
13	P. JONES	222///	/22⊗⊗	0⊗⊗⊗2	2//2	
24	A. JONES	//22⊗	⊗⊗//20	0⊗2/22	2//⊗⊗	
33	M. PERRY	2//2⊗	2///⊗2	2//2	⊗⊗2//	

1. L. Haas **14 points**   **2.** P. Jones **21 points**

3. A. Jones **20 points**   **4.** M. Perry **18 points**

Find the percent made.

5. D. Red Eagle made 3 out of 7 field goal attempts. **43%**

6. L. Abrams made 7 out of 13 field goal attempts. **54%**

7. C. Aaron made 39 out of 68 field goal attempts. **57%**

8. K. Martin made 6 out of 12 free throw attempts. **50%**

9. J. Marquez made 8 out of 8 free throw attempts. **100%**

10. B. Lindsay made 28 out of 36 free throw attempts. **78%**

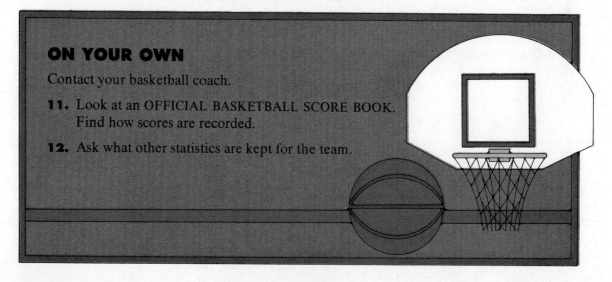

ON YOUR OWN

Contact your basketball coach.

11. Look at an OFFICIAL BASKETBALL SCORE BOOK. Find how scores are recorded.

12. Ask what other statistics are kept for the team.

ESTIMATING

We use calculators frequently in everyday life. It is important to be able to estimate to make sure that the calculator answer is reasonable. Estimate the following.

1. 821 + 54 + 639

2. 916 + 428 + 185

3. $14.56 + $29.05 + $6.46

4. $27.95 × $64.87 + $7.26

5. 654 − 283

6. 921 − 309

7. $26.42 − $9.81

8. $53.29 − $17.84

9. 53 × 26

10. 86 × 17

11. 216 × 32

12. 394 × 41

13. 863 ÷ 41

14. 916 ÷ 33

15. 1436 ÷ 229

16. 2639 ÷ 886

17. 23% × $188.16

18. 35% × $274.91

19. 12% × $64.75

20. 73% × $87.15

21. How many boxes of 12″ by 12″ floor tiles are needed to cover a 9′ by 12′ floor?

22. What will it cost to rent a car for a week at $29 a day, with no mileage costs?

23. It takes five yards of material to make a dress. The pattern is $1.95 and the thread is 99¢. How much will it cost if the material is $2.96 a yard?

24. How much will four new tires cost if each tire costs $29.95 each plus 5% sales tax?

GOLF

Golf courses can be found in the mountains, the desert, at the
beach, or in city-owned parks and recreation centers.

Jan Pine is an assistant manager at the Rolling Hills Golf Course.
Jan started working part time at the golf course while in high school.
After graduation she worked there full time doing several different
jobs. She now supervises the workers on the grounds crew and in the
concession shops.

In golf the player with the lowest score (number of strokes) wins the
game. In most games 18 holes are played.

These terms are used in golf.

Par, the number of strokes typical of an expert player
birdie, 1 stroke less than par on a hole
eagle, 2 strokes less than par on a hole
bogie, 1 stroke more than par on a hole
double bogie, 2 strokes more than par on a hole
triple bogie, 3 strokes more than par on a hole

EXAMPLES.   Find the number of strokes.

1. A player shoots a bogie on a par 4 hole.

$$4 + 1 = 5$$

A bogie means par plus 1. The hole took 5 strokes.

2. On a par 73 course a player shoots 4 birdies, 2 eagles, 3 bogies, and 3 double bogies.

PLAN: **Step 1.**   Subtract the strokes in birdies and eagles from 73.

$$(4 \times 1) + (2 \times 2) = 4 + 4 = 8$$
$$73 - 8 = 65$$

There is no need to add or subtract for those holes made in par.

Step 2.   Add the strokes for bogies to that score.

$$(3 \times 1) + (3 \times 2) = 3 + 6 = 9$$
$$65 + 9 = 74$$

The player used 74 strokes.

TRY THIS

Find the number of strokes.

1. The 7th hole is par 3. Juana shoots a double bogie. 5 strokes

2. The 11th hole is par 5. Danny shoots an eagle. 3 strokes

3. The 13th hole is par 4. Earl shoots a triple bogie. 7 strokes

4. On a par 72 course, Peggy shoots 5 birdies, 1 eagle, 4 bogies, and 2 double bogies. 73 strokes

---

Total scores can also be compared to par. These are shown by positive and negative numbers. The score $+12$ means 12 strokes over par, and -5 means 5 strokes under par.

EXAMPLES.   Find the number of strokes.

3. On a par 72 course a player finishes at $+15$.

$$72 + 15 = 87$$

The player had 87 total strokes

4. On a par 75 course a player finishes at -6.

$$75 - 6 = 69$$

The player had 69 total strokes.

5. On a par 71 course Bert finishes at $+25$. 96 strokes

6. On a par 70 course Sandy finishes at -3. 67 strokes

7. On a par 75 course Ling finishes at par. 75 strokes

Golf courses get the *par rating* by using a formula. This allows golfers to compare different courses. The formula is

$P = \dfrac{l}{200} + 38.25$. Golf course par ratings can also be affected by other difficulty factors, such as the terrain and obstacles.

P stands for the par rating.
l stands for the length of the course in yards.

EXAMPLE 5. Use the formula to find the course rating for a 6057-yard course.

$$P = \frac{l}{200} + 38.25$$

$$= \frac{6057}{200} + 38.25$$

$$= 30.285 + 38.25$$

$$= 68.535 \approx 69$$

It is a par 69 course.

Find the course par rating.

8. 7200-yard course 74 par course **9.** 5856-yard course 68 par course

Find the number of strokes.

1. The 6th hole is par 4. A player shoots a bogie. 5 strokes

2. The 15th hole is par 3. A player shoots par. 3 strokes

3. The 8th hole is par 5. A player shoots an eagle. 3 strokes

4. On a par 70 course a player shoots 3 birdies, 4 bogies, and 2 double bogies. 75 strokes

5. On a par 73 course a player shoots 4 birdies, 1 eagle, 3 bogies, and 2 double bogies. **74 strokes**

6. On a par 68 course a player finishes at + 10. **78 strokes**

7. On a par 70 course a player finishes 37 over par. **107 strokes**

8. On a par 71 course a player finishes 3 under par. **68 strokes**

9. On a par 74 course a player finishes with a −5. **69 strokes**.

10. On a par 72 course a player finishes 8 under. **64 strokes**

Find the course par rating.

11. 7065-yard course **74 par course**

12. 6285-yard course **70 par course**

13. 7247-yard course **74 par course**

14. 6840-yard course **72 par course**

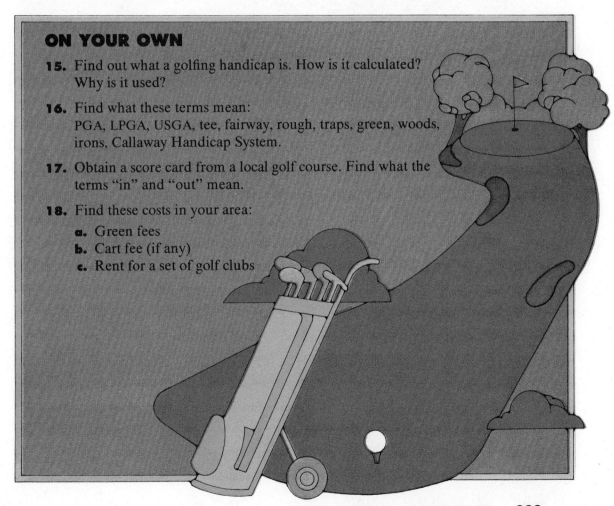

ON YOUR OWN

15. Find out what a golfing handicap is. How is it calculated? Why is it used?

16. Find what these terms mean:
PGA, LPGA, USGA, tee, fairway, rough, traps, green, woods, irons, Callaway Handicap System.

17. Obtain a score card from a local golf course. Find what the terms "in" and "out" mean.

18. Find these costs in your area:
   a. Green fees
   b. Cart fee (if any)
   c. Rent for a set of golf clubs

SAILING

Sailing ships participate in annual races that create a memorable
sight for viewers near the Atlantic Ocean.

Ian Johnson's hobby is sailing. He first learned some techniques and
skills from friends who sail. He since has taken courses offered by
the District Coast Guard Auxiliary in sailing and basic seamanship.

Two terms often used in sailing are
nautical mile, about 6076 feet (compared to 5280 feet in a statute
mile), and *knot,* a speed of 1 nautical mile per hour.

One nautical mile is the
length of one minute of
longitude at the equator. One
minute of longitude is $\frac{1}{60}$ of
a degree of longitude.

The horizon is the top of the earth's curve. At sea, objects beyond
the horizon are hidden from view. Taller objects can be seen from
greater distances. Ian learned to use this chart to find distances for
objects of various heights.

VISUAL DISTANCES AT SEA											The distances on the chart are rounded to the nearest 0.1 mile.
Height in Feet	1	2	3	4	5	10	15	20	25	30	
Distance to Horizon in Nautical Miles	1.1	1.7	2.0	2.3	2.5	3.6	4.4	5.1	5.7	6.3	

EXAMPLE 1. John is sitting in a small boat. At his present position his line of sight is 4 feet above the water. How far is it to a point on the horizon?

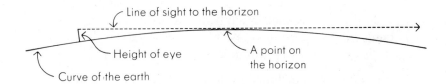

The chart shows that it is 2.3 nautical miles to the horizon.

EXAMPLE 2. You are in a rowboat. Your eyes are about 3 feet above the water. You see the top of a lighthouse just on the horizon. You know that the lighthouse is 25 feet high. How far away is the lighthouse?

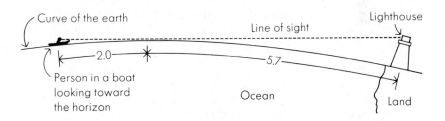

PLAN: **Step 1.** Use the chart to find your distance to the horizon.
3 feet is 2.0 nautical miles

Step 2. Find the distance from the lighthouse to the horizon.
25 feet is 5.7 nautical miles

Step 3. Add to find the total distance.
2.0 + 5.7 = 7.7 nautical miles

The lighthouse is 7.7 nautical miles away.

TRY THIS

Find the distance.

1. Your eyes are 5 feet above the water. How far are you from a point on the horizon? 2.5 nautical miles

2. Your eyes are 2 feet above the water. You see the top of the mast of another boat you know is 20 feet high. How far are you from the other boat? 6.8 nautical miles

---

Ian also learned to use forms of the distance formula $d = rt$. These are the formulas he learned:

$$d = \frac{rt}{60} \qquad r = \frac{60d}{t} \qquad t = \frac{60d}{r}$$

Time is usually considered in hours when using the distance formula. In sailing, however, time is always considered in minutes.

d stands for the distance in nautical miles.
r stands for the speed in knots.   1 nautical mile per hour
t stands for the time in minutes.

The number 60 is included in these formulas because time is measured in minutes rather than hours.

EXAMPLE 3. You sail at an average speed of 6.3 knots for 1 hour and 45 minutes. How far have you traveled to the nearest tenth of a nautical mile?

PLAN: **Step 1.** Change the time to minutes
$t = 1 \text{ hr } 45 \text{ min} = 105 \text{ min}$

Step 2. To find the distance traveled,

$$d = \frac{rt}{60}$$
$$= \frac{6.3 \times 105}{60} \qquad \textit{Substitute.}$$
$$= \frac{661.5}{60}$$
$$= 11.025 \approx 11.0 \text{ miles}$$

To the nearest tenth, you have traveled 11.0 nautical miles.

EXAMPLE 4. It takes you 1 hour and 52 minutes to sail 15.4 nautical miles. What is your average speed to the nearest tenth?

PLAN: **Step 1.** Change the time to minutes.
$t = 1 \text{ hr } 52 \text{ min} = 112 \text{ min}$

Step 2. To find the speed use the formula:

$$r = \frac{60d}{t}$$
$$= \frac{60 \times 15.4}{112} \qquad \textit{Substitute.}$$
$$= \frac{924.0}{112}$$
$$= 8.25 \approx 8.3 \text{ knots}$$

Your average speed to the nearest tenth is 8.3 knots.

3. It took 34 minutes to sail 4.3 nautical miles. What was the speed? **7.6 knots**

4. You sail at a speed of 4.9 knots for 17.8 nautical miles. How much time did it take? **218 minutes or 3.6 hr**

EXERCISES

Use the chart on page 334 for exercises 1–3 to find the distance.

1. Your eyes are 5 feet above the water. How far is the horizon? **2.5 nautical miles**

2. Your eyes are 3 feet above the water. You see the top of another boat that is 5 feet tall. How far away is that boat? **4.5 nautical miles**

3. Your eyes are 10 feet above the water. You see the top of a building that you know is 25 feet tall. How far away is the building? **9.3 nautical miles**

4. You sail at a speed of 6.8 knots for 1 hour and 30 minutes. What distance did you travel? **10.2 nautical miles**

5. It took 2 hours and 10 minutes to sail 17.3 nautical miles. What was the speed? **8.0 knots**

6. You sail at a speed of 3.9 knots for 7.1 nautical miles. How much time did it take? **109 minutes or 1.8 hr**

7. It took 37 minutes to sail 1.9 nautical miles. What was the speed? **3.1 knots**

8. You sail at a speed of 4.8 knots for 1 hour and 6 minutes. What distance was traveled? **5.3 nautical miles**

9. You sail at a speed of 10.2 knots for 19 nautical miles. How much time did it take? **112 minutes or 1.9 hr**

ON YOUR OWN

10. Find what these terms mean: forward, aft, starboard, port, bow, stern, catboat, catamaran, sloop, ketch, yawl, schooner.

HEALTH CLUB

Sue Moore is a physical fitness director at the Athenian West Club. She took courses in physical fitness and nutrition to qualify for her job.

Sue recommends that the pulse rate be checked regularly. Your pulse rate tells how many times your heart beats per minute. During exercise, your pulse rate will increase, but it should not exceed a number that depends on your age. She uses this formula:

$p = 80\% \times (220 - a)$

p stands for the maximum pulse rate.
a stands for the person's age.

EXAMPLE 1. Use the formula to find the recommended maximum pulse rate during exercises for Anne who is 17 years old.

$$
\begin{aligned}
p &= 80\% \times (220 - a) \\
&= 80\% \times (220 - 17) && \textit{Substitute.} \\
&= 0.80 \times 203 && \textit{Do the work in the parentheses first.} \\
&= 162.40 \approx 162 \text{ beats per minute} && \textit{Use 0.80 for 80\%.}
\end{aligned}
$$

Anne's maximum pulse rate should be 162 beats per minute.

TRY THIS   **1.** Find the recommended maximum pulse rate during exercise for Grace who is 42 years old. **142 beats per min**

Sue also helps men and women plan weight-lifting programs. A *toning* program maintains fitness. A *training* program is aimed at athletic competition.

The amount of weight to be lifted is found using these formulas:

Toning program: $w = 50\% \times m$ Training program: $w = 80\% \times m$

w stands for the amount of weight you should use.
m stands for the maximum (heaviest) weight you can lift.

EXAMPLE 2. Use the correct formula to find the correct weight for leg lifts in a toning program. The maximum weight you can lift is 180 lbs.

$w = 50\% \times m = 0.50 \times 180 = 90$

90 pounds is the weight to be used.

Find the weight to be used.

2. Toning program: bench press
The maximum weight Ben can lift is 135 pounds. 67.5 lb

3. Training program: bicep curl
The maximum weight Martha can lift is 140 pounds. 112 lb

EXERCISES

Find the recommended maximum pulse rate during exercise for:

1. Leta who is 15 years old. 164 beats per min

2. David who is 18 years old. 162 beats per min

3. Cyndi who is 25 years old. 156 beats per min

4. Leon who is 40 years old. 144 beats per min

5. Paula who is 60 years old. 128 beats per min

Find the weight to be used.

	Program	Event	Maximum Weight (lb)	
6.	Toning	shoulder press	60	30 lb
7.	Training	tricep press	50	40 lb
8.	Toning	upright row	70	35 lb
9.	Training	sitting chest press	100	80 lb
10.	Toning	standing calf press	95	$47\frac{1}{2}$ lb

ON YOUR OWN

11. Talk with your physical education teacher. Find what these terms mean: repetitions and sets.

12. Call a local health club, YMCA, or YWCA. Ask what physical fitness programs they offer. Find out what they charge.

CHAPTER REVIEW

Find the difference.

1. 100-meter run for women:
1928 . . . Elizabeth Robinson, United States 0:12.2
1968 . . . Wyomia Tyus, United States 0:11.0 0:01.2

2. Decathlon:
1972 . . . Nikola Avilov . . . . 8454 pts
1976 . . . Bruce Jenner, United States . . . 8618 pts 164 pts

3. Running high jump:
1964 . . . Valery Brumel, USSR . . . . . . 7 ft $1\frac{3}{4}$ in.

1968 . . . Dick Fosburg, United States . . . 7 ft $4\frac{1}{4}$ in. $2\frac{1}{2}$ in.

Find the bowling score in each frame and the total.

4.

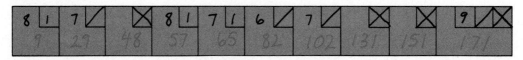

5. Find the average.
Game scores: 162, 156, 204 174

6. Find the maximum time for this scuba dive.

Air in tank is 17 cubic feet.
Air-use rate is 0.80 cubic feet per minute.
Depth of 15 feet in fresh water.

(Fresh-water formula is $P = 1 + \dfrac{d}{34}$.) 14 min

7. Find the maximum time for the dive in #6 if it is in salt water.

(Salt-water formula is $P = 1 + \dfrac{d}{33}$.) 14 min

8. Find the football rushing average.
16 carries for 107 yards. 6.7 yd per carry

9. Find the pass completion percent.
9 completions for 12 attempts. 75%

10. Find the baseball batting average.
11 hits for 41 times at bat. **.268**

11. Find the earned run average.
13 earned runs in 32 innings pitched. **3.7**

12. Find the Games Back. **2½ games back**

	Wins	Losses
Leader	26	20
Sox	21	20

Find the percent made.

13. 9 field goals in 15 attempts. **60%**

14. 17 free throws in 21 attempts. **81%**

Find the golf strokes. (Exercises 15–16)

15. The 12th hole is par 5. A player shoots a bogie. **6 strokes**

16. The course is par 72. A player shoots +9. **81 strokes**

17. Find the course par rating.
7047-yard course **73 par course**

18. You sail at a speed of 9.4 knots for 2 hours and 40 minutes.
What distance did you travel? **25 nautical miles**

19. It took 1 hour and 20 minutes to sail 12.2 nautical miles. What
was the speed? **9.2 knots**

20. Find the recommended maximum pulse rate for exercising for
a person who is 19 years old. **161 beats per min**

SKILLS REVIEW

SKILL 12 Rounding decimals and money

Round to the underlined place.

1. $<u>4</u>.68 $5
2. $27.<u>0</u>9 $27
3. $13<u>8</u>.72 $139
4. $25<u>9</u>.65 $260

5. 1.5<u>6</u> 1.6
6. 13.<u>0</u>1 13.0
7. 318.0<u>9</u>7 318.10
8. 47.239<u>5</u> 47.240

SKILL 15 Adding money

Add.

9.
```
  $ 8.94
    0.75
  + 9.27
  $18.96
```

10.
```
  $ 9.87
    6.54
  + 0.46
  $16.87
```

11.
```
  $ 7486
  + 9281
  $16,767
```

12.
```
  $ 46,287
  + 94,789
  $141,076
```

SKILL 16 Adding decimals

Add.

13.
```
  13.767
   4.382
 + 7.689
  25.838
```

14.
```
  0.78
  6.94
+ 4.81
 12.53
```

15.
```
     9
  19.4
  0.98
 +  6
 35.38
```

16.
```
  27.93
  672
    4.2
 + 18
 722.13
```

SKILL 19 Subtracting money

Subtract.

17.
```
  $ 79.48
  − 27.39
  $52.09
```

18.
```
  $ 68.14
  − 39.25
  $28.89
```

19.
```
  $ 432.87
  −  76.98
  $355.89
```

20.
```
  $ 153.82
  −  77.77
  $76.05
```

SKILL 20 Subtracting decimals

Subtract.

21. 5 − 1.25 − 2.1 1.65
22. 6.98 − 5 − 1.7 0.28

23. 6.7 − 4.381 − 1.72 0.599
24. 557.62 − 68.25 − 295.00 194.37

25. 8.76 − 3.8 − 2.99 1.97
26. 465.23 − 187.912 − 88.74 188.578

SKILL 22 Multiplying whole numbers

Multiply.

27.
```
    89
 ×   7
   623
```

28.
```
    927
 ×   42
 38,934
```

29.
```
    4281
 ×    81
 346,761
```

30.
```
    928
 ×  480
 445,440
```

342

SKILL 24 Special products: Whole numbers

Multiply.

31. $\begin{array}{r} 85 \\ \times\ 100 \\ \hline 8500 \end{array}$ **32.** $\begin{array}{r} 73 \\ \times\ 1000 \\ \hline 73,000 \end{array}$ **33.** $\begin{array}{r} 946 \\ \times\ 10,000 \\ \hline 9,460,000 \end{array}$ **34.** $\begin{array}{r} 852 \\ \times\ 100,000 \\ \hline 85,200,000 \end{array}$

SKILL 27 Multiplying decimals

Multiply.

35. $\begin{array}{r} 73.07 \\ \times\ 8 \\ \hline 584.56 \end{array}$ **36.** $\begin{array}{r} 9.82 \\ \times\ 33 \\ \hline 324.06 \end{array}$ **37.** $\begin{array}{r} 8.71 \\ \times\ 0.32 \\ \hline 2.7872 \end{array}$ **38.** $\begin{array}{r} 47.84 \\ \times\ 36 \\ \hline 1722.24 \end{array}$

SKILL 50 Dividing whole numbers: 1-digit divisor, remainders

Divide.

39. $36 \div 7$ 5r1 **40.** $71 \div 3$ 23r2 **41.** $92 \div 4$ 23 **42.** $186 \div 7$ 26r4

43. $8\overline{)4012}$ 501r4 **44.** $6\overline{)3685}$ 614r1 **45.** $7\overline{)42,017}$ 6002r3 **46.** $9\overline{)87,319}$ 9702r1

SKILL 51 Division: 2- and 3-digit divisors

Divide. Round to the nearest hundredth.

47. $10\overline{)897}$ 89.7 **48.** $10\overline{)11,294}$ 1129.4 **49.** $610\overline{)24,626}$ 40.37 **50.** $187\overline{)17,000}$ 90.91

SKILL 52 Dividing a decimal by a decimal

Divide. Round to the nearest hundredth.

51. $4.8\overline{)12}$ 2.5 **52.** $3.2\overline{)144}$ 45 **53.** $4.16\overline{)489}$ 117.55 **54.** $2.08\overline{)900}$ 432.69

SKILL 67 Finding a percent of a number

Solve.

55. 18% of $396 is what number? $71.28 **56.** 25% of 46.2 is what number? 11.55

57. What is 8% of $27.50? $2.20 **58.** Find 10% more than $360. $396

59. What is 29% more than 472? 608.88 **60.** Find 1% more than 10.9. 11.009

SKILL 69 Finding a number given a percent

Solve.

61. $6 is 10% of what number? $60 **62.** $7 is 20% of what number? $35

63. $8 is $33\frac{1}{3}$% of what number? $24 **64.** $12 is $12\frac{1}{2}$% of what number? $96

65. $26.40 is 40% of what number? $66 **66.** $10.01 is 26% of what number? $38.50

10
OTHER
OCCUPATIONS

PHYSICAL FITNESS

Running has become a popular way to stay fit, and running in races lets people share their enthusiasm for being fit.

Mitch Jensen is an exercise technician. He received special training and then passed an exam to become certified as a technician. Mitch says that one measure of physical fitness is the ratio of body fat to total body weight. He uses this formula for men.

$$F = 0.49W + 0.45P - 6.36R + 8.71$$

F stands for percent of body fat.
W stands for the waist circumference in centimeters.
P stands for the skin fold above the pectoral muscle in millimeters.
R stands for the wrist diameter in centimeters.

EXAMPLE 1.   Find the percent of body fat for Jon Capin.

$W = 80.8$ cm, $P = 6.0$ mm, $R = 6.0$ cm
$$\begin{aligned} F &= 0.49W + 0.45P - 6.36R + 8.71 \\ &= 0.49(80.8) + 0.45(6.0) - 6.36(6.0) + 8.71 \qquad \textit{Substitute.} \\ &\approx 39.59 + 2.7 - 38.16 + 8.71 \qquad\qquad\quad \textit{Calculate.} \\ &\approx 12.84 \end{aligned}$$

The percent of body fat is about 12.8%.

Here is a table that groups men by the percent of body fat.

Percent	Group
Below 10.0%	Very lean
10.0–14.0	Lean
14.1–19.0	Average
19.1–24.0	Overweight
Over 24.0	Very overweight

Jon Capin (Example 1), with 12.8% body fat, would be considered lean.

TRY THIS

1. Find the percent of body fat for Gordon Thomas. His measurements are

$W = 81.3$ cm, $P = 2$ mm, $R = 5.4$ cm

Into what group does Gordon fall? 15.1%   Average

Mitch also finds the *vital capacity.* This is the amount of air you can exhale after one deep breath. This formula gives an estimate of the vital capacity for women.

$V = 0.041h - 0.018A - 2.69$

V stands for vital capacity in liters.
h stands for height in centimeters.
A stands for age in years.

Mention that there are machines that can accurately measure a person's vital capacity. This formula gives only an estimate. Athletes may develop vital capacities of up to 7 L. An average for women is around 3 L.

EXAMPLE 2.   Find the vital capacity for Cherie Meyer.

$h = 144.7$ cm
$A = 31$ years
$V = 0.041h - 0.018A - 2.69$
$\quad = 0.041(144.7) - 0.018(31) - 2.69 \qquad$ *Substitute.*
$\quad = 5.9327 - 0.558 - 2.69 \approx 2.7$

Cherie's vital capacity should be about 2.7 liters.

TRY THIS

2. Find the vital capacity for Diane Wiley.

$h = 149$ cm
$A = 44$ years 2.6 L

EXERCISES

Use the formula $F = 0.49W + 0.45P - 6.36R + 8.71$ to find the percent of body fat.

1. $W = 81, P = 5.4, R = 6.2$ 11.4

2. $W = 105, P = 6.0, R = 7.1$ 17.7

Use the formula $V = 0.041h - 0.018A - 2.69$ to find the vital capacity.

3. $h = 152, A = 13$ 3.3

4. $h = 160, A = 67$ 2.7

5. $h = 176, A = 15$ 4.3

Find the percent of body fat for these men. Name the group to which each man belongs. Use the chart on page 346.

	Man	Waist, W (cm)	Pectoral muscle, P (mm)	Wrist, R (cm)	Percent of body fat	
6.	Terry Kaufman	86.4	3	6.4	?	11.7 lean
7.	Harry Kipp	111.8	24	8	?	23.4 overweight
8.	Danny Martinez	88.9	5.5	7.0	?	10.2 lean
9.	J. P. Meyer	90.5	7	6.2	?	16.8 average
10.	Charles Chiaparelli	81.3	3	7	?	5.4 very lean
11.	Bruce Berger	94.2	6	6.3	?	17.5 average

Find the vital capacity for these women.

	Woman	Height, h (cm)	Age, A (yr)	Vital capacity (liters)	
12.	Nancy Parkins	148	27	?	2.9
13.	Addie Brown	154	42	?	2.9
14.	Elaine Koppelman	146	50	?	2.4
15.	Betty Rubin	162	18	?	3.6
16.	Anna Zambouris	156	46	?	2.9
17.	Milly Duncan	161	61	?	2.8

PHYSICAL THERAPY

Only skiers who have followed a carefully planned program for muscle development can show off their ability with safety.

Mary Harvey is a physical therapist. She graduated from a four-year training program at a local college. She specializes in sports medicine. She helps people injured in sport activities.

Mary says muscle strength can be measured by a machine in foot-pounds. The strength of an injured muscle is compared to the strength of the similar normal muscle.

A foot-pound is a unit of measure of work.

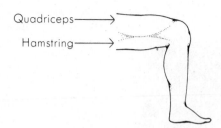

The quadriceps and hamstring are important muscles. Generally, the hamstring should be from 40–60% as strong as the quadriceps. Also, there should be no more than a 10% difference between the similar muscles of the legs.

Typical Quadriceps Strength	
Average Person	40 foot–pounds
High School Football Player	60 foot–pounds
College Football Player	90 foot–pounds

A person with a damaged knee has the following readings:

	Bad Leg	Good Leg
Quadriceps	25 ft–lb	70 ft–lb
Hamstring	15 ft–lb	40 ft–lb

EXAMPLE 1. Is the hamstring of the good leg within acceptable limits?

40% of 70 = 0.4 × 70 = 28
60% of 70 = 0.6 × 70 = 42

The hamstring strength of 40 ft–lb is acceptable.

EXAMPLE 2. To what strength should they try to increase the bad leg?

PLAN:

Step 1. Find 10% above and below the strength of the quadriceps.

10% of 70 = 7
70 + 7 = 77, 70 − 7 = 63

The quadriceps should be between 63 and 77 ft–lb.

Step 2. Find 10% above and below the strength of the hamstrings.

10% of 40 = 4
40 + 4 = 44, 40 − 4 = 36

The hamstring should be between 36 and 44 ft–lb.

A person with a damaged knee has the following readings:

	Bad Leg	Good Leg
Quadriceps	30 ft–lb	75 ft–lb
Hamstring	22 ft–lb	42 ft–lb

TRY THIS

1. Is the hamstring of a good leg within acceptable limits? Yes
2. To what strength should the weak leg be increased?
   quadriceps: 67.5–82.5 ft–lb, hamstring: 37.8–46.2 ft–lb

Mary says that to increase muscle size and strength, you should exercise with weights that are at least 75% of your maximum strength.

EXAMPLE 3.   Thelma Martin can lift 40 lb. What is the minimum weight she should lift when exercising to increase strength?

$$75\% \times 40 = 30$$

She should lift at least 30 lb of weight.

TRY THIS

3. Mimi Chang can lift a maximum of 50 lb. What is the minimum weight she should lift when exercising to increase strength? **37.5 lb**

Each day of exercises should include three sets of ten lifts for each muscle group. If you exercise three to five times per week using 75% of your maximum weight, your strength should increase 3% each week.

EXAMPLE 4.   Fred Reinhardt can press (lift) a maximum of 42 kg with his legs. He exercises three to five times per week at the 75% level. What will be his expected maximum strengths at the end of the first and second weeks?

PLAN: **Step 1.**   Find the increase after 1 week.
Take 3% of 42.
Add this amount to 42.

$$3\% \times 42 = 1.26$$
$$42 + 1.26 = 43.26$$

Step 2.   Find the increase after 2 weeks.
Take 3% of 43.26.
Add this amount to 43.26.

$$3\% \times 43.26 = 1.2978 \approx 1.30$$
$$43.26 + 1.30 = 44.56$$

Fred will be able to press about 44.56 kg.

TRY THIS

4. Tom Bellis can press a maximum of 52 kg with his legs. He exercises 4 times per week at the 75% level. What are the expected maximum strengths at the end of the first and second weeks? **53.56 kg; 55.17 kg**

EXERCISES

Here are muscle strength readings for three people with damaged legs. Tell whether the hamstring of the good leg is within acceptable limits. To what strength should the therapist try to increase the bad leg?

	Person	Muscle	Bad Leg	Good Leg
1.	Charlene Moore	Quadriceps	27 ft–lb	49 ft–lb
		Hamstring	19 ft–lb	27 ft–lb
2.	Dave Young	Quadriceps	31 ft–lb	72 ft–lb
		Hamstring	21 ft–lb	30 ft–lb
3.	Bobbi Vance	Quadriceps	32 ft–lb	68 ft–lb
		Hamstring	19 ft–lb	27 ft–lb

For each of the following persons, the maximum weight which can be lifted is given. Tell the minimum weight to be lifted when exercising to increase strength.

	Person	Maximum weight which can be lifted
4.	Frank Vella	120 lb 90 lb
5.	Angela Salinos	68 lb 51 lb
6.	Mike Mason	63 kg 47 kg
7.	Sally Smithson	34 kg 26 kg

8. Rick Fields can lift a maximum of 56 kg with his legs. He exercises 5 times per week at the 75% level. What are the expected maximum strengths at the end of the first and second weeks? **57.68 kg; 59.4 kg**

ON YOUR OWN

9. Contact a physical therapist. Find out what machine is used to measure strength. Report to the class on other types of therapy.

LAB TECHNOLOGY

Hemoglobin is a chemical in red blood cells that joins with oxygen and gives red blood cells their color. When a blood sample is whirled rapidly in a circle, or centrifuged, the cells are separated from a clear yellowish liquid called plasma. 55% of blood is plasma; 91% of plasma is water.

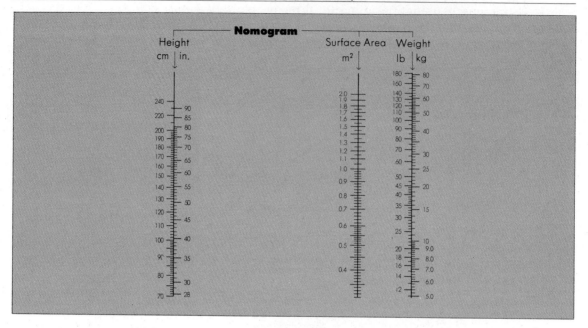

Dale Kief is a lab technician. She runs many tests for doctors and patients. Dale needed special college training for her job.

In some tests, Dale must estimate the surface area of the body. One way to do this is by using a chart called a *nomogram*.

Body surface area is needed in some kidney function tests.

EXAMPLE 1. Estimate the body surface area of a patient who weighs 40 kg and is 140 cm tall.

PLAN: **Step 1.** Find 40 kg in the weight column of the nomogram.

Step 2. Find 140 cm in the height column.

Step 3. Join these two points with a straight line.

Step 4. Read the surface area where the line crosses the column headed Surface Area.

The surface area is 1.25 m².

TRY THIS **1.** Estimate the body surface area of a patient who is 170 cm tall and weighs 60 kg. 1.7 m²

Another of Dale's jobs is to find the amount of oxygen in the blood.
To do this, she analyzes the blood *plasma* and the *hemoglobin*.
First, Dale uses a machine to find the oxygen pressure in the plasma.
To calculate the amount of oxygen dissolved in the plasma, Dale uses
the formula: This test is needed in respiratory therapy and in the
treatment of lung disorders such as emphysema,
$W = 0.003P$ asthma, and chronic bronchitis.

W stands for the number of milliliters of oxygen dissolved in 100
  mL of whole blood plasma.
P stands for the oxygen pressure measured in millimeters of
  mercury (mm Hg). This pressure is a machine reading.

EXAMPLE 2.   Find the number of mL of oxygen dissolved in the blood
plasma of Jean Bowman with a *P* reading of 85.

$$W = 0.003P$$
$$= 0.003(85) \quad \text{Substitute.}$$
$$= 0.255$$

There are about 0.26 mL of oxygen in the plasma.

TRY THIS   **2.** Find the number of mL of oxygen dissolved in the blood
plasma of Dick Faulk with a *P* reading of 91. 0.27 mL

Next, Dale finds the amount of oxygen in the hemoglobin of the red
blood cells. A machine reading tells Dale the amount of hemoglobin
in 100 mL of blood. It also tells the percent of oxygen in the
hemoglobin. Dale then uses this formula:

$H = 1.36gs$

H stands for the mL of oxygen in the hemoglobin of 100 mL of
  whole blood.
g stands for the number of grams of hemoglobin in 100 mL of
  whole blood.
s stands for the percent of oxygen in the hemoglobin.

EXAMPLE 3.   Find the amount of oxygen in the hemoglobin of the 100-mL
blood sample of Jean Bowman.

$$g = 12$$
$$s = 91\%$$
$$H = 1.36gs$$
$$= 1.36 \times 12 \times 0.91 \quad \text{Substitute.}$$
$$= 14.8512$$

There are about 14.85 mL of oxygen in the hemoglobin.

TRY THIS

3. Find the amount of oxygen in the hemoglobin of the 100-mL blood sample of Dick Faulk. 18.28 mL

$$g = 14 \qquad s = 96\%$$

To find the total amount of oxygen in the blood, Dale adds the amount of oxygen in the plasma to the amount in hemoglobin $(W + H)$.

EXAMPLE 4. Find the total amount of oxygen in the 100–mL blood sample of Jean Bowman. This example requires the formulas discussed in Examples 2 and 3.

There are 0.26 mL of oxygen in the plasma (Example 2). There are 14.8512 mL of oxygen in the hemoglobin (Example 3). Add to find the total amount in the blood.
0.26 + 14.85 = 15.11 mL of oxygen in the blood sample.

EXAMPLE 5. Find the total amount of oxygen in a 100-mL blood sample of Ben Poscover. The following machine readings are given: $P = 92$, $g = 13$, and $s = 93\%$.

PLAN: **Step 1.** First, find the amount of oxygen dissolved in the plasma.

$$W = 0.003P$$
$$= 0.003 \times 92$$
$$= 0.276$$

There are about 0.28 mL of oxygen dissolved in the plasma.

Step 2. Find the amount of oxygen in the hemoglobin.

$$H = 1.36gs$$
$$= 1.36 \times 13 \times 0.93$$
$$= 16.4424$$

There are about 16.44 mL of oxygen in the hemoglobin.

Step 3. Add to find the total.

$$0.28 + 16.44 = 16.72$$

There are about 16.72 mL of oxygen in the blood.

TRY THIS

4. Find the total amount of oxygen in a 100–mL blood sample of Millie Drier. The following machine readings are given: $P = 96$, $g = 15$, and $s = 96\%$. 19.87 mL

EXERCISES

Estimate the body surface area for patients with the following
weights and heights. Use the nomogram on page 352.

	Patient	Weight (kg)	Height (cm)	Body Surface Area
1.	Don Moore	78	180	? 2.0 m²
2.	Nancy Parkins	54	155	? 1.55 m²
3.	Carol Weimer	45	145	? 1.36 m²
4.	Pietr Hitzig	34	188	? 1.26 m²
5.	Manny Hernandez	79	168	? 1.9 m²
6.	Leroy Johnson	67	162	? 1.75 m²

For each of the following patients, find the total amount of oxygen
in a 100–mL blood sample.

	Patient	Oxygen Pressure, P (mm Hg)	Grams of Hemoglobin, g	Percent of Oxygen, s	
7.	Dave Gamble	88	15	89	18.42 mL
8.	Bonnie Post	96	14	92	17.80 mL
9.	Jim Plumhoff	92	13	96	17.25 mL
10.	Jennifer Weible	84	16	88	19.40 mL
11.	Fred Weiss	95	14	91	17.61 mL
12.	Lou Sabatino	97	12	98	16.28 mL
13.	Debbie Levine	79	11	91	13.85 mL
14.	William Ruiz	83	15	90	18.61 mL
15.	Carol Coffeen	90	14	96	18.55 mL

ON YOUR OWN

16. Locate and interview a lab technician in your community.
Report to the class on some of the other activities of a lab
technician.

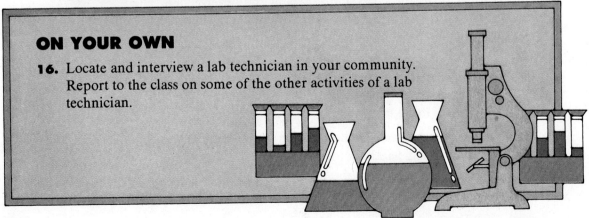

TRAFFIC ENGINEERING

Traffic engineers know that proper controls and careful planning are needed to keep traffic moving smoothly.

Greg Jones is a traffic engineer. Greg went to college where he studied civil engineering. He then took a job with the city highway department. Traffic engineers like Greg study the flow of traffic. They may decide to put a stop sign at a dangerous intersection. They may decide to put in a traffic signal at an intersection where a cross street meets a busy highway.

One part of Greg's job is to set the green time for each direction on a traffic signal. Green time is usually longer on the busier street. But it cannot be so long that drivers on the cross street become angry for having to wait the extra time.

A *light cycle* is the time needed for a traffic signal to change from green to yellow to red, and back to green again.

Light timings are based on the number of cars traveling in each lane of the road. Light timings are measured in vehicles per light cycle.

EXAMPLE 1. The average number of vehicles traveling River Road is 85 vehicles every 10 minutes. The light cycle is 75 seconds. Find the number of vehicles per light cycle.

PLAN: **Step 1.** Find the number of light cycles in 10 minutes. First, change the minutes to seconds.

$$10 \times 60 = 600$$

Then, divide by the number of seconds per cycle.
$$600 \div 75 = 8$$

There are 8 light cycles in 10 minutes.

Step 2. Divide to find the number of vehicles per cycle.

$$85 \div 8 \approx 10.6$$

The average number of vehicles per light cycle is 10.6.

TRY THIS

1. Find the average number of vehicles per light cycle on a street that averages 115 vehicles every 20 minutes. The light cycle is 80 seconds. 7.7

To find the green time for traffic lights, Greg uses Greenshield's Formula.

$$G = 2.1n + 3.7$$

G stands for the green time in seconds.
n stands for the average number of vehicles traveling in each lane per light cycle.

This formula is based on the fact that on the average it takes 3.7 seconds for the first car to go through the intersection and then 2.1 seconds for each car thereafter.

EXAMPLE 2. Find the green time for a traffic signal on a street that averages 20 vehicles in each lane per cycle.

$$G = 2.1n + 3.7$$
$$= 2.1(20) + 3.7 \qquad \textit{Substitute.}$$
$$= 42 + 3.7 \qquad \textit{Calculate.}$$
$$= 45.7 \quad \text{The green time is about 46 seconds.}$$

TRY THIS

2. Find the green time for a traffic signal on a street that averages 16 vehicles in each lane per cycle. 37 sec

---

EXAMPLE 3.   At a certain intersection the light cycle is 90 seconds. The cross street averages 125 vehicles in each lane every 15 minutes. Find the green time for this cross street.

PLAN: **Step 1.**   Find the number of cycles in 15 minutes. Change the minutes to seconds.

$$15 \times 60 = 900$$

Divide by the number of seconds per cycle.

$$900 \div 90 = 10$$

Step 2.   Divide to find the number of vehicles per cycle.

$$125 \div 10 = 12.5$$

Step 3.   Use Greenshield's Formula to find the green time. Substitute 12.5 for n from Step 2.

$$
\begin{aligned}
G &= 2.1n + 3.7 \\
&= 2.1(12.5) + 3.7 \\
&= 26.25 + 3.7 \\
&= 29.95 \quad \text{The green time is about 30 seconds.}
\end{aligned}
$$

TRY THIS

3. An intersection has a light cycle of 120 seconds. A cross street averages 140 vehicles per lane during a 22-minute period. Find the green time for the cross street. **30 sec**

The yellow time depends on the speed limits. Greg finds that time by the formula:

$$Y = 0.05v + 1$$

Y stands for the yellow time.
v stands for the speed limit in miles per hour.

Point out that it makes sense to have longer yellow times at intersections where cars travel at higher rates of speed.

EXAMPLE 4.   Find the yellow time for a traffic light on a street with a speed limit of 30 mph.

$$
\begin{aligned}
Y &= 0.05v + 1 \\
&= 0.05(30) + 1 \\
&= 1.5 + 1 \\
&= 2.5 \quad \text{The yellow time is 2.5 seconds.}
\end{aligned}
$$

TRY THIS

4. Find the yellow time for a traffic light on a street with a speed limit of 25 miles per hour. **2.3 sec**

EXERCISES

Substitute and evaluate.

1. $Y = 0.05(v) + 1, v = 50$ **3.5**

2. $Y = 0.05(a) + 1, a = 55$ **3.75**

3. $G = 2.1(x) + 3.7, x = 25$ **56.2**

4. $G = 2.1(b) + 3.7, b = 18$ **41.5**

Find the number of vehicles per cycle.

5. 100 vehicles every 10 minutes with a light cycle of 90 seconds **15**

6. 165 vehicles per 15 minutes with a light cycle of 80 seconds **14.7**

7. 120 vehicles per 5 minutes with a light cycle of 100 seconds **40**

8. 180 vehicles per 15 minutes with a light cycle of 120 seconds **24**

9. 95 vehicles per 10 minutes with a light cycle of 85 seconds **13.5**

10. 160 vehicles per 20 minutes with a light cycle of 90 seconds **12**

Find the green time for a signal light that averages the following number of vehicles per lane in a given cycle. Use $G = 2.1v + 3.7$.

11. 15 vehicles **35.2 sec** **12.** 42 vehicles **91.9 sec** **13.** 21 vehicles **47.8 sec** **14.** 34 vehicles **75.1 sec**

Use the formula $Y = 0.05v + 1$ to find the yellow time for traffic lights on roads with the following speed limits:

15. 40 mph **3 sec** **16.** 35 mph **2.75 sec** **17.** 20 mph **2 sec** **18.** 45 mph **3.25 sec**

19. An intersection has a 100-second signal light cycle. A cross street averages 250 vehicles in each lane every 20 minutes. Find the green time for the cross street. **47.5 sec**

20. An intersection has a 150-second signal light cycle. The cross street averages 280 vehicles in each lane during a 27-minute period. Find the green time for the cross street. **58.1 sec**

ON YOUR OWN

21. Time a traffic light in your community during a busy period. Find the average number of vehicles per lane in each cycle. Apply Greenshield's Formula. Compare your result to the actual length of the green time.

INSTALLING SOLAR HEAT

Besides solar collectors, the energy-saving house has adequate insulation, double-glazed windows, and few north-facing windows.

George Hurst installs solar heating systems. George was a plumber before he began solar energy work. He says that older houses sometimes use solar energy for heating water. New houses can be planned so that space heating can be done with solar energy.

Solar panels are used to collect sunlight. The number of panels needed depends on the living area and the type of climate. George takes 35% of the living area (for mild climates) to find the total surface area of solar panels needed. He then divides that number by the area of one panel (21 ft²) to find the total number of panels needed.

The 35% figure is based on experience in temperate climates.

EXAMPLE 1. Find the number of 3 ft × 7 ft solar panels needed to heat a two-story house with this floor plan.

40 ft

30 ft

PLAN: **Step 1.** Find the living area.

$$A = l \times w$$
$$= 40 \times 30$$
$$= 1200 \text{ ft}^2$$

There are two floors, so the total area is
$2 \times 1200 = 2400 \text{ ft}^2$.

Step 2. Take 35% of the total living area.

$$35\% \times 2400 = 0.35 \times 2400 = 840 \text{ ft}^2$$

Step 3. Divide by the area of one panel to find the number of panels needed.

$$840 \div 21 = 40$$

About 40 panels are needed.

TRY THIS

1. Find the number of solar panels needed to heat a two-story house with this floor plan. **31 panels**

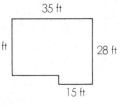

The National Energy Act of 1978 allows a tax credit for a solar water-heating system. The tax credit is 30% of the first $2000 spent, plus 20% for other costs up to $10,000.

EXAMPLE 2. Find the tax credit for a solar water system costing $2700.

PLAN: **Step 1.** Find the credit on the first $2000.

$$30\% \text{ of } \$2000 = 0.30 \times 2000 = \$600$$

Step 2. Find the credit on the amount over $2000.

$$\$2700 - \$2000 = \$700$$
$$20\% \text{ of } \$700 = 0.20 \times 700 = \$140$$

Step 3. Add to find the total credit.

$$\$600 + \$140 = \$740 \quad \text{The total tax credit is } \$740.$$

TRY THIS **2.** Find the tax credit on a solar water system costing $3200. **$840**

EXERCISES

Use the method of Example 1. Find the number of solar panels
needed for houses with these floor plans.

1. One-story house 23 panels   **2.** Two-story house 33 panels   **3.** Two-story house 38 panels

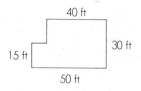

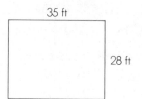

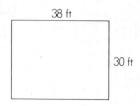

4. One-story house 27 panels   **5.** One-story house 26 panels   **6.** Two-story house 30 panels

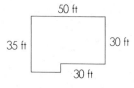

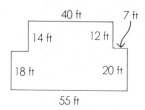

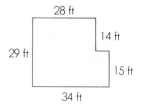

Find the tax credit for a solar water system with these costs.

7. $ 3400.00 $880   **8.** $ 2900.00 $780

9. $ 4185.00 $1037   **10.** $ 3925.00 $985

11. $ 5225.75 $1245.15   **12.** $ 7056.00 $1611.20

13. $ 10,900.00 $2200   **14.** $ 1652.00 $495.60

DECISION

Call a local electric or solar energy company.

15. Find out about how much can be saved per year by installing
a solar water-heating system.

16. Find how many years it will take until the total savings equals
the installation costs.

17. Decide if you think it is worth converting to a solar water-
heating system.

PRACTICE ESTIMATING

You have already seen how to estimate different quantities. See how well you do on these.

PRACTICE

Estimate.

1. The area of a floor 12 ft by $23\frac{1}{2}$ ft 200 ft²

2. The volume of a room 11 ft by 16 ft by 9 ft 1600 ft³

3. The cost of 51 meters of rope at 73¢ per meter $40

4. The number of automobiles in a shopping-center parking lot Answers will vary.

5. 18% of $ 37.20 $8

6. 14 is what percent of 32? 50%

7. The cost of one student's school supplies for one year Answers will vary.

8. The distance you walk in one day Answers will vary.

9. The cost of a rug 9 ft by 12 ft at $ 11.55 per square yard $120

10. The number of basketballs it takes to fill a phone booth About 80.

11. The number of seats in your school's stadium Answers will vary.

12. The area of a triangular roof which is 31 ft wide and $12\frac{1}{2}$ ft high 180 ft²

13. The width of your desk in centimeters Answers will vary.

14. 15% of $ 18.35 $2.70

15. The cost of this dinner: soup $ 1.25, salad $ 2.15, roast beef $ 9.65, dessert $ 1.10, coffee $ 0.45 $14.60

16. 235 + 56 + 974 1300

17. $ 62.50 − $ 16.82 $40

18. 629 × 54 30,000

ELECTRONICS TECHNOLOGY

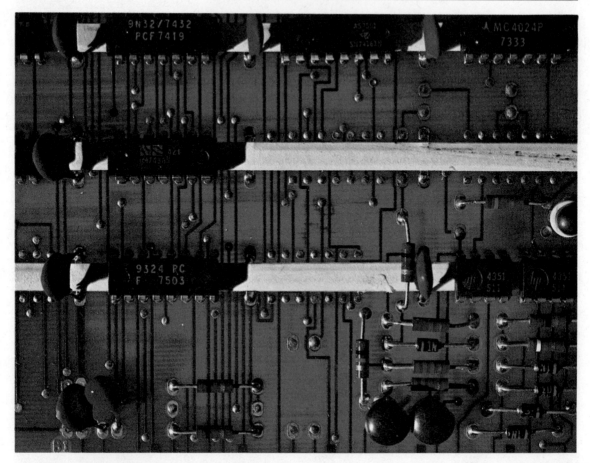

Resistors are an important part of this circuit board.

Ted Krantski is an electronics technician. Ted received special training at an electronics school. He is self-employed. Ted repairs citizens' band radios (CB's), car radios, television sets, and home computers. Ted uses electrical *resistors* in his repair work.

Each resistor has four colored bands. The colors of the first three bands stand for numbers, as shown in this chart.

Color	Brown	Black	Red	Orange	Yellow	Green	Blue	Violet	Gray	Silver
Number	0	1	2	3	4	5	6	7	8	9

EXAMPLE 1.   What numbers are shown on the resistor?

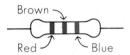

The numbers 2, 0, and 6 are shown.

TRY THIS

1. What numbers are shown on this resistor? 5, 4, and 3

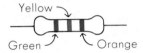

When electricity flows through a wire, there is always some resistance. Resistance is measured in *ohms*. The number of ohms of electrical resistance for a resistor is given by the color code.

This coding system can show any number from 1 to 99 $\times$ 10^9.

The resistor in Example 1 shows the numbers 2, 0, and 6. The first two numbers give the two-digit number 20. The third number, 6, is the exponent in the expression 10^6. Thus, the resistance in Example 1 is 20×10^6 ohms. We know that 10^6 means $10 \times 10 \times 10 \times 10 \times 10 \times 10$ or 1,000,000 (one million). So, the resistance is 20,000,000 ohms.

EXAMPLE 2.   Find the resistance.

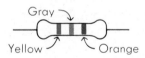

The numbers are 4, 8, and 3.
This means 48×10^3.
$10^3 = 10 \times 10 \times 10 = 1000$
$48 \times 1000 = 48,000$ The resistance is 48,000 ohms.

TRY THIS

2. Find the resistance. 250,000 ohms

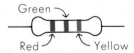

The fourth color band tells the tolerance or error allowed in the manufacturing of resistors.

Code	
No fourth band	20% Tolerance
Silver	10% Tolerance
Gold	5% Tolerance

In Example 2 there is no fourth band. So, the resistance can be either 20% higher or 20% lower than that given by the color.

EXAMPLE 3.   Find the tolerance for the resistor in Example 2.

The calculated resistance is 48,000 ohms.
20% of 48,000 = 9600 ohms

The resistance could be as low as 48,000 − 9600 = 38,400 ohms.
The resistance could be as high as 48,000 + 9600 = 57,600 ohms.

TRY THIS

3. Find the resistance and tolerance for this resistor. **6100 ± 610 ohms**

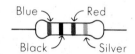

Blue   Red
Black   Silver

Electricity flows with a force measured in *volts*. The *rate* of flow is measured in *amperes*. We already know that resistance is measured in ohms.

The amperage can be found by using an ammeter.

To calculate electrical resistance, Ted uses this formula:

$$R = \frac{E}{I}$$

R stands for resistance in ohms.
E stands for voltage in volts.
I stands for electric current in amperes.

In actual practice, the wattage rating of a resistor is also important.

EXAMPLE 4.   Ted wants to install a radio in his truck. He needs to use a resistor to lower the voltage 24 volts. The radio will draw 0.32 amps. What resistance is needed?

$$R = \frac{E}{I}$$

$$= \frac{24}{0.32}$$

$$= 75 \quad \text{A 75-ohm resistor should be used.}$$

4. Calculate the electrical resistance when the voltage is 12 volts and the current drawn is 0.38 amps. 31.6 ohms

EXERCISES

Find the resistance and tolerance for these resistors.

1. Red / Black / Yellow   120,000 ± 24,000 ohms

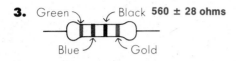

2. Brown / Red / Green   2,000,000 ± 400,000 ohms

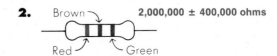

3. Green / Black / Blue / Gold   560 ± 28 ohms

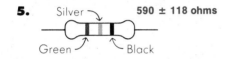

4. Violet / Orange / Gray / Gold   78,000 ± 3900 ohms

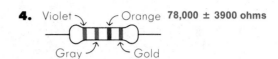

5. Silver / Green / Black   590 ± 118 ohms

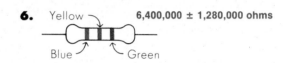

6. Yellow / Blue / Green   6,400,000 ± 1,280,000 ohms

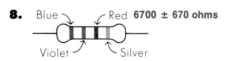

7. Blue / Green / Black / Gold   6,100,000 ± 305,000 ohms

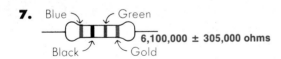

8. Blue / Red / Violet / Silver   6700 ± 670 ohms

9. Black / Yellow / Blue / Silver   160,000 ± 16,000 ohms

10. Red / Yellow / Green / Gold   250,000 ± 12,500 ohms

Use the formula $R = \dfrac{E}{I}$. Calculate the resistance for each case.

	Voltage, E (Volts)	Current, I (Amperes)	
11.	12	0.36	33.3 ohms
12.	12	0.42	28.6 ohms
13.	24	0.62	38.7 ohms
14.	24	0.58	41.4 ohms
15.	110	0.5	220 ohms
16.	220	0.5	440 ohms

ART

Every painter and sculptor hopes for the recognition that comes
with having works displayed in a famous art gallery.

Elva O'Connell is an artist. She has a natural talent for art and has
taken many courses in painting and sculpture to learn special
techniques and skills.

Sometimes Elva sells her work in an art gallery. The gallery keeps
35% of each sale as its commission. Elva gets 65% of the sales price.
She must set the sales price based on how much she wants to receive
from the gallery.

EXAMPLE 1. Find the gallery price.
An artist wants $ 50 and gets 65% of the gallery price.

PLAN: **Step 1.** State the problem.
$ 50 is 65% of what price?

Step 2. Translate. Change the percent to a decimal.
$50 = 0.65 \times n$

Step 3. To solve for *n*, divide each side by 0.65.

$$\frac{50}{0.65} = \frac{0.65 \times n}{0.65}$$

$$\frac{50}{0.65} = n$$

Step 4. Divide to find *n*. Round to the nearest dollar.

$$n = \frac{50}{0.65} \approx \$\,77$$

The gallery price is about $ 77.

TRY THIS

Find the gallery price.

1. An artist wants $ 60 and gets 60% of the gallery price. $100

2. An artist wants $ 100 and gets 75% of the gallery price. $134

Some galleries or shops buy an artist's work outright. They then *keystone* to set the gallery or shop price to customers. The keystone price covers the gallery's expenses, such as cost of the work and overhead, and allows for a profit. A typical keystone is 3 times the artist's price plus 10%.

EXAMPLE 2. Find the keystone price.
The artist was paid $ 45.

PLAN: **Step 1.** Multiply the artist's price by 3.
$ 45 × 3 = $ 135

Step 2. Find 10% of this amount.
0.10 × $ 135 = $ 13.50

Step 3. Add to find the keystone price.
$ 135.00 + $ 13.50 = $ 148.50

The keystone price is $ 148.50.

TRY THIS

Find the keystone price.

3. An artist was paid $ 50. $165

4. An artist was paid $ 100. $330

EXERCISES

Find the gallery price.

1. Anne O'Donnell displays her sculpture at the New Art Gallery. She asks $ 75 for each sculpture piece and receives 70% of the gallery price. $107

2. Andy Riggs makes large ceramic pots by hand. For his pieces he wants $ 60 and gets 75% of the gallery price. $80

3. Rudolph Zepeda shows oil paintings. He asks $ 125 for each painting and receives 65% of the gallery price. $192

4. Mary Herrmann is a design artist. For each mural she displays at the Seashore Gallery she asks $ 250 and receives 80% of the gallery price. $313

Find the keystone price. Use the rate in Example 2.

5. Tye Hansen was paid $ 60 for a watercolor painting. $198

6. Trina Ording received $ 75 for a ceramic pot. $247.50

7. Carla Norman was paid $ 100 for an oil painting. $330

8. Jeffrey Hernandez received $ 35 for a sculpture piece. $115.50

9. Paul Sanna received $ 55 for a painting. $181.50

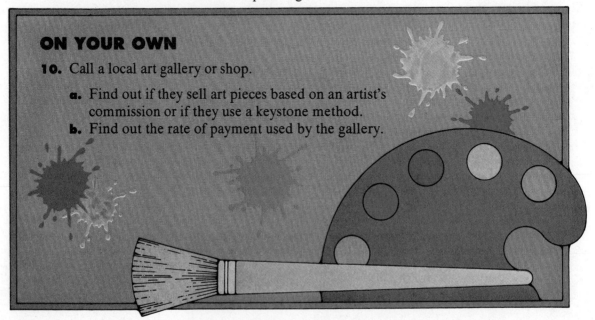

ON YOUR OWN

10. Call a local art gallery or shop.

a. Find out if they sell art pieces based on an artist's commission or if they use a keystone method.

b. Find out the rate of payment used by the gallery.

MENTAL CALCULATION

QUICK DIVISION BY 10, 100, 1000; 5, 50, 500

To divide by 10, 100, 1000, etc., count the number of zeros. Then move the decimal point that number of places to the left.

EXAMPLE 1.   Divide 4.54 by 10.

10 has one zero. Move the decimal one place to the left.

$4.54 \div 10 = 0.454$

EXAMPLE 2.   Divide 42.95 by 1000.

1000 has three zeros. Move the decimal point three places to the left.

$42.95 \div 1000 = 0.04295$

To divide by 5, 50, or 500, divide by 10, 100, or 1000, respectively, and then double the result.

EXAMPLE 3.   Divide 160 by 50.

Divide by 100. $160 \div 100 = 1.60$
Double the result. $2 \times 1.60 = 3.20$

$160 \div 50 = 3.20$

PRACTICE

Divide mentally.

1. $48 \div 10$ 4.8

2. $6.23 \div 10$ 0.623

3. $56.9 \div 10$ 5.69

4. $4329 \div 10$ 432.9

5. $682 \div 100$ 6.82

6. $1429 \div 100$ 14.29

7. $8.639 \div 1000$ 0.008639

8. $23.56 \div 1000$ 0.02356

9. $8436 \div 1000$ 8.436

10. $18 \div 5$ 3.6

11. $26 \div 5$ 5.2

12. $4.6 \div 5$ 0.92

13. $290 \div 50$ 5.8

14. $583 \div 50$ 11.66

15. $97 \div 50$ 1.94

16. $122 \div 500$ 0.244

SOLVING FORMULAS

It is often important to be able to solve a formula for an unknown quantity. Formulas are equations, so we can use equation-solving principles.

THE ADDITION PRINCIPLE

If an equation $a = b$ is true, then $a + c = b + c$ is true. (You can add the same number on both sides of the equation.)

EXAMPLE 1.   Solve $K = R + 23$ for R.

$$K = R + 23$$
$$K - 23 = R + 23 - 23 \qquad \textit{Use the addition principle.}$$
$$K - 23 = R + 0 \qquad \textit{Add } -23 \textit{ to both sides.}$$
$$K - 23 = R \qquad \textit{Simplify.}$$

> **TRY THIS**
> 1. Solve $M = H + 97$ for H. **H = M − 97**
> 2. Solve $Q = X - 32$ for X. **X = Q + 32**

THE MULTIPLICATION PRINCIPLE

If an equation $a = b$ is true, then $a \times c = b \times c$ is true. (You can multiply on both sides of the equation by the same number.)

EXAMPLE 2.   Solve $F = M \times A$ for M.

$$F = M \times A$$
$$F \times \frac{1}{A} = M \times A \times \frac{1}{A} \qquad \textit{Use the multiplication principle.}$$
$$F \times \frac{1}{A} = M \times \frac{A}{A} \qquad \textit{Multiply on both sides by } \frac{1}{A}.$$
$$\frac{F}{A} = M \times 1 \qquad \textit{Simplify.}$$
$$\frac{F}{A} = M$$

> **TRY THIS**
> 3. Solve $A = G \times T$ for G. **G = $\frac{A}{T}$**
> 4. Solve $T = P \times R$ for R. **R = $\frac{T}{P}$**

Sometimes you may need to use both principles.

EXAMPLE 3. Solve $P = 2W + L$ for W.

$$P = 2W + L$$

$$P - L = 2W + L - L$$ *Use the addition principle;*
$$P - L = 2W + 0$$ *add $-L$.*

$$P - L = 2W$$ *Simplify.*

$$\frac{1}{2}(P - L) = \frac{1}{2}(2W)$$ *Use the multiplication principle;*
multiply by $\frac{1}{2}$.

$$\frac{P - L}{2} = W$$ *Simplify.*

TRY THIS   **5.** Solve $Q = \frac{1}{2}M + G$ for M. $M = 2(Q - G)$

Ted Krantski, an electronics technician, uses the formula $W = E \times I$ to calculate electrical power.

W stands for power in watts, E stands for the number of volts, I stands for the current in amps.

EXAMPLE 4. Find the current used by a toaster with a wattage of 800W in a 120-volt circuit.

PLAN: **Step 1.** Solve the formula $W = E \times I$ for I.

$$W = E \times I$$

$$\frac{1}{E} \times W = \frac{1}{E}(E \times I)$$ *Multiply on both sides by $\frac{1}{E}$.*

$$\frac{1}{E} \times W = \frac{E}{E} \times I$$

$$\frac{W}{E} = 1 \times I$$

$$\frac{W}{E} = I$$

Step 2. Substitute.

$$I = \frac{W}{E}$$

$$= \frac{800}{120}$$

$$= 6.7 \quad \text{The toaster uses about 6.7 amps.}$$

6. An electric fry pan uses 110 amps of current and has a resistance of 12 ohms. Find the voltage required. Use the formula $R = \frac{E}{I}$, where R is resistance, E is the number of volts, and I is the number of amps. **1320 volts**

EXAMPLE 5. Find the approximate length in yards of a golf course with a par of 72. Use the formula $P = \frac{L}{200} + 38.25$, where P is par and L is the length in yards.

PLAN: **Step 1.** Solve the formula for L.

$$P = \frac{L}{200} + 38.25$$

$$P - 38.25 = \frac{L}{200} + 38.25 - 38.25 \qquad \text{Subtract 38.25 on both sides.}$$

$$P - 38.25 = \frac{L}{200} \qquad \text{Multiply on both sides by 200.}$$

$$200(P - 38.25) = L \times \frac{200}{200}$$

$$200(P - 38.25) = L$$

Step 2. Substitute.

$$200(P - 38.25) = L$$
$$200(72 - 38.25) = L$$

Step 3. Calculate.

$$200(33.75) = L$$
$$6750 = L$$

The length of the course is about 6750 yards.

7. The yellow time for a traffic light is 4 seconds. Find the speed limit for the road in miles per hour. Use the formula $Y = 0.05V + 1$, where Y is the yellow time in seconds and V is the speed limit in miles per hour. **60 miles per hour**

8. How many more hits does a batter need to get a .500 average? She has 75 hits in 170 times at bat for a .441 average and expects to be at bat 40 more times. Use the formula, $n = [a \times (b + e)] - h$, where n is the number of hits needed, a is the wanted average, b is the times at bat, e is the times at bat to come, and h is the present number of hits. **30 hits**

EXERCISES

Solve for the indicated letter.

1. $X = Y + 19$ for Y

3. $M = S + 1.6$ for S

5. $Z = W - 3$ for W

7. $W = G \times S$ for S

9. $A = B \times R$ for B

11. $S = \frac{X}{V}$ for X

13. $R = 2S + H$ for S

15. $A = 1.5G + M$ for G

17. $S = 3.5H - A$ for H

2. $G = F + 32$ for F

4. $B = E + 5.8$ for E

6. $N = C - 8$ for C

8. $H = P \times R$ for R

10. $T = V \times W$ for V

12. $G = \frac{H}{T}$ for H

14. $M = 3Q + F$ for Q

16. $Z = 2.6F + R$ for F

18. $V = 1.2 \times R - M$ for R

1. $Y = X - 19$

3. $S = M - 1.6$

5. $W = Z + 3$

7. $S = \frac{W}{G}$

9. $B = \frac{A}{R}$

11. $X = S \times V$

13. $S = \frac{R-H}{2}$

15. $G = \frac{A-M}{1.5}$

17. $H = \frac{S+A}{3.5}$

2. $F = G - 32$

4. $E = B - 5.8$

6. $C = N + 8$

8. $R = \frac{H}{P}$

10. $V = \frac{T}{W}$

12. $H = G \times T$

14. $Q = \frac{M-F}{3}$

16. $F = \frac{Z-R}{2.6}$

18. $R = \frac{V+M}{1.2}$

19. Find the speed in knots of a sailboat that took 2 hours and 18 minutes to sail 19.4 nautical miles. Use the formula $d = \frac{rt}{60}$, where d is the distance in nautical miles, r is the speed in knots, and t is the time in minutes. **8.4 knots**

20. Find the time in minutes it takes a sailboat to sail 21.5 nautical miles at a rate of 4.6 knots. Use the formula of Exercise 19. **280.4 min**

21. Find the depth of a scuba diver in seawater when the pressure is 1.825 atmospheres. Use the formula $P = 1 + \frac{D}{33}$ where P is the pressure in atmospheres and D is the depth in feet. **27.2 ft**

22. A baseball pitcher has an earned run average (ERA) of 4.25. He has given up 22 earned runs (r). Find the number of innings (I) he has pitched. Use the formula $\text{ERA} = \frac{9r}{I}$. **46.6 innings**

23. Don Webb's recommended maximum pulse rate for exercising is 128. Find Don's age. Use the formula $P = 80\% \times (220 - A)$, where P is the recommended pulse rate and A is the age. **60**

24. The green time (G) for a traffic signal is 50 seconds. Estimate the number of vehicles (n) passing through during that time. Use Greenshield's Formula, $G = 2.1n + 3.7$. **22**

25. Eric Van Doren pitched 125 innings and gave up 58 earned runs. Use the formula $\text{ERA} = \frac{9r}{I}$ to find his earned run average. **4.2**

26. Find the approximate length in yards of a golf course with a par of 80. Use the formula $P = \frac{L}{200} + 38.25$. **8350**

CHAPTER REVIEW

1. Use the formula $F = 0.49W + 0.45P - 6.36R + 8.71$ to find the percent of body fat for Matt Brauer.
   $W = 83.5$ cm,
   $P = 4$ mm, and
   $R = 7.4$ cm. **4.4%**

2. Use the formula $V = 0.041h - 0.018A - 2.69$ to find the vital capacity for Ivy Fraden. Her height (h) is 160 cm and age (A) is 24 years. **3.4L**

3. A person with a damaged knee has the following muscle machine readings.

	Bad Leg	Good Leg
Quadriceps	32	73
Hamstring	24	43

   Is the hamstring of the good leg within acceptable limits? To what strength should the bad leg be increased? **Yes; quadriceps, 65.7–80.3 ft–lb; hamstring, 38.7–47.3 ft–lb**

4. Ike Ayers can lift a maximum of 53 kg with his legs. He exercises 5 times per week at the 75% level. What are the expected maximum strengths at the end of the first and second weeks? **54.59 kg; 56.23 kg**

5. Estimate the body surface area of Carrie Fiskgaw. She weighs 55 kg and is 73 in. tall. Use the nomogram on page 352. **1.7 m²**

6. Find the amount of oxygen in the hemoglobin of a 100-mL blood sample with $g = 18$ and $s = 93\%$. Use $H = 1.36gs$. **22.77 mL**

7. Find the total amount of oxygen in a 100-mL blood sample of Nancy Spinnato. $P = 83$; $g = 14$ and $s = 85\%$. Use the formula $W = 0.003P$ to find the amount in the plasma and $H = 1.36gs$ to find the amount in the hemoglobin. **16.43 mL**

8. An intersection has a 95-second signal light cycle. Two cross streets average 200 vehicles in a 10-minute period. Use the formula $G = 2.1n + 3.7$ to find the green time for a side street. **70.2 sec**

9. Use the formula $Y = 0.05v + 1$ to find the yellow time on a road with a speed limit of 35 mph. **2.75 sec**

10. Find the number of solar panels needed to heat a two-story house with this floor plan. Each panel is 3 ft × 7 ft. **60 panels**

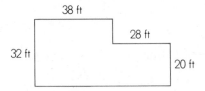

11. Find the tax credit for a solar hot water system costing $2950. **$790**

12. What is the resistance for this resistor. **8600 ± 860 ohms**

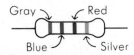

13. Use the formula $R = \frac{E}{I}$ to calculate the resistance, when the voltage is 110 and the amperage is 6.5. **16.9 ohms**

14. Find the gallery price for an art piece where the artist asks $150 and receives 65% of the gallery price. **$231**

15. An artist was paid $65. The keystone price is 3 times the artist's price plus 10%. Find the keystone price. **$201.50**

Solve each formula for the indicated letter.

16. $W = fd$, for d $\ d = \frac{W}{f}$

17. $C = 0.05M + 1.25$, for M $\ M = \frac{C - 1.25}{0.05}$

SKILLS REVIEW

SKILL 49 Translating to number sentences

Translate. Convert each percent to a decimal or fraction.

1. What is 18% of 63? n = 0.18 × 63
2. 8% of what number is 12? 0.08 × n = 12

3. What percent of 10 is 8?
   n × 10 = 8
4. What is 50% of 72.5? n = 0.50 × 72.5

5. What percent of 16 is 12?
   n × 16 = 12
6. $27\frac{1}{2}$% of what number is 55? 0.27$\frac{1}{2}$ × n = 55

SKILL 14 Adding whole numbers

Add.

7.   7284
   +   6985
      14,269

8.   37,487
   + 28,643
      66,130

9.   328,412
   + 149,386
     477,798

10.   329,421
      658,187
   + 86,294
    1,073,902

SKILL 16 Adding decimals

Add.

11.   7.398
   + 0.475
      7.873

12.   63.284
   + 19.986
      83.270

13.   16.284
       9.786
       4.395
   +   5.007
      35.472

14.   126.842
      1387
         2.94
   + 117.062
     1633.844

SKILL 18 Subtracting whole numbers

Subtract.

15.   477
   −   269
       208

16.   1525
   −   776
       749

17.   34,937
   − 17,679
     17,258

18.   315,264
   − 276,581
      38,683

SKILL 20 Subtracting decimals

Subtract.

19.   4.26
   − 3.9
      0.36

20.   4.27
   − 1.835
      2.435

21.   8.764
   − 5
      3.764

22.   7
   − 3.843
      3.157

SKILL 22 Multiplying whole numbers

Multiply.

23.   249
   ×   30
      7470

24.   806
   ×   44
     35,464

25.   9040
   ×   87
     786,480

26.   761
   × 427
     324,947

378

SKILL 25 Estimating products — whole numbers

Estimate the products.

27. $\begin{array}{r} 420 \\ \times\ \ 9 \\ \hline 3600 \end{array}$ **28.** $\begin{array}{r} 590 \\ \times\ \ 38 \\ \hline 24{,}000 \end{array}$ **29.** $\begin{array}{r} 421 \\ \times\ 395 \\ \hline 160{,}000 \end{array}$ **30.** $\begin{array}{r} 7284 \\ \times\ 387 \\ \hline 2{,}800{,}000 \end{array}$

SKILL 27 Multiplying decimals

Multiply.

31. $\begin{array}{r} 0.84 \\ \times\ \ \ 7 \\ \hline 5.88 \end{array}$ **32.** $\begin{array}{r} 87 \\ \times\ 0.006 \\ \hline 0.522 \end{array}$ **33.** $\begin{array}{r} 569 \\ \times\ 0.05 \\ \hline 28.45 \end{array}$ **34.** $\begin{array}{r} 437 \\ \times\ 0.08 \\ \hline 34.96 \end{array}$

SKILL 50 Dividing whole numbers: 1-digit divisors, remainders

Divide.

35. $8\overline{)30}$ — 3r6
36. $7\overline{)84}$ — 12
37. $6\overline{)407}$ — 67r5

38. $9\overline{)184}$ — 20r4
39. $7\overline{)45{,}721}$ — 6531r4
40. $5\overline{)40{,}198}$ — 8039r3

SKILL 51 Division: 2- and 3-digit divisors

Divide. Round to the nearest hundredth.

41. $42\overline{)1764}$ — 42
42. $68\overline{)3604}$ — 53
43. $858\overline{)51{,}480}$ — 60

44. $76\overline{)30{,}786}$ — 405.08
45. $623\overline{)4463}$ — 7.16
46. $369\overline{)35{,}893}$ — 97.27

SKILL 52 Dividing a decimal by a decimal

Divide. Round to the nearest hundredth.

47. $0.4\overline{)0.08}$ — 0.2
48. $0.7\overline{)2.688}$ — 3.84
49. $0.31\overline{)1.0788}$ — 3.48

50. $0.06\overline{)34.681}$ — 578.02
51. $9.6\overline{)20.15}$ — 2.10
52. $0.83\overline{)3.467}$ — 4.18

SKILL 72 Changing metric units

Make these changes.

53. 4 L = __4000__ mL   **54.** 438 mL = __0.438__ L

55. 8605 g = __8.605__ kg   **56.** 814 mg = __0.814__ g

SKILL 87 Evaluating formulas

Evaluate each formula.

57. $C = \pi d$, $d = 10$, $\pi = 3.14$ 31.4 **58.** $F = \dfrac{9}{5}C + 32$, $C = 35°$ 95°

11
COMPUTERS

COMPUTER PROGRAMMER

The personal computer, together with the easy BASIC language, has changed the ways we find information and solve problems.

Bob Cox is a computer programmer. He took computer courses in high school. He also had additional training in junior college. Bob says that there are many computer languages. One of the simplest is called BASIC. Here are some symbols from the BASIC language.

BASIC means Beginner's All-Purpose Symbolic Instruction Code.

Symbol	Meaning	Example
*	multiply	$3 * 2$ means 3×2 or 6
/	divide	$8/4$ means $8 \div 4$ or 2
+	add	$8 + 3 = 11$
—	subtract	$19 - 11 = 8$
↑	raise to a power	$4 \uparrow 3$ means 4^3 or $4 \times 4 \times 4$ or 64

EXAMPLES. In BASIC, how would you tell a computer to do the following?

1. Multiply 3 by 4. $3 * 4$

2. Divide 10 by 0.05. $10/0.05$

3. Raise 2 to the 3rd power. $2 \uparrow 3$

4. Subtract 6 from 12. $12 - 6$

A computer performs operations in this order:

1. Do operations within parentheses first.
2. Next, evaluate exponential expressions.
3. Then multiply and divide from left to right.
4. Finally, add and subtract from left to right.

Simplify. Use the four rules of order.

5. $7 + 3 * 5$

Check the order list. There are no parentheses and no exponents. So, do $3 * 5$ first. $3 * 5 = 15$

$7 + 15 = 22$

6. $(7 + 3) * 5$

Do the operation within parentheses first. $7 + 3 = 10$
$10 * 5 = 50$

7. $12/3 + 6 * 2 - 1$

There are no parentheses or exponents.
Multiply and divide from left to right.
$12/3 = 4$ and $6 * 2 = 12$
$4 + 12 - 1$

Then add and subtract from left to right. $4 + 12 = 16$
$16 - 1 = 15$

TRY THIS

Simplify. Use the four rules of order.

1. $30 - 15/3 * 5$ 5
2. $36 - 2 * 2 \uparrow 3$ 20
3. $(36 - 2) * 2 \uparrow 3$ 272
4. $6/12 + 3 \uparrow 2 * 2 - 10$ 8.5

Suppose $A = 25$, $B = 4$, $C = 8$ and $D = 6$. Evaluate the following as a computer would.

8. $A * B \uparrow 2$

Evaluate powers first. $B \uparrow 2$ means B^2, so
$A * B \uparrow 2$ means $A \times B^2$.
$A \times B^2 = 25 \times 4^2$ *Substitute.*
$\quad\quad = 25 \times 16$
$\quad\quad = 400$

9. (B + C)/D

Work within parentheses first.
(B + C)/D means (B + C) ÷ D.
(B + C) ÷ D = (4 + 8) ÷ 6   *Substitute.*
= 12 ÷ 6
= 2

TRY THIS

Suppose A = 30, B = 10, C = 4, and D = 3. Evaluate the following as a computer would.

5. A * D − B 80   **6.** B ↑ 2 * C 400
7. D * C ↑ 3 192   **8.** (A + C) * B 340

EXERCISES

Tell a computer to do the following in BASIC.

1. Multiply 18.3 by 9.6 and then subtract 5.8. 18.3 * 9.6 − 5.8

2. Find 6 to the 3rd power. 6 ↑ 3

3. Divide 73 by 19.45 and then add 53. 73/19.45 + 53

4. Subtract 34 from 68 and then multiply by 2. (68 − 34) * 2

Simplify. Use the four rules of order.

5. 25/10 + 5 * 2.5 15   **6.** 16 + 2 ↑ 3 * 4 48

7. (10 − 3 ↑ 2) * 2001 2001   **8.** 1/(121 − 71) * 100 − 2 0

9. (1/2 + 1/8) * 2 1.25   **10.** (6 + 4) ↑ 2 − 50 50

11. 3/(6 + 9) * 15 3   **12.** 42 − 40/4 + 6 ↑ 2 68

13. (42 − 40)/4 + 6 ↑ 2 36.5   **14.** 42 − 40/(4 + 6 ↑ 2) 41

Suppose A = 13, B = 4, C = 6, and D = 8. Evaluate the following as a computer would.

15. A * B − C 46   **16.** D + B ↑ 2 24

17. (C + D) * 2 28   **18.** D/B + A * C 80

19. B ↑ 3 − A 51   **20.** A + B * 6 37

COMPUTER PROGRAMS

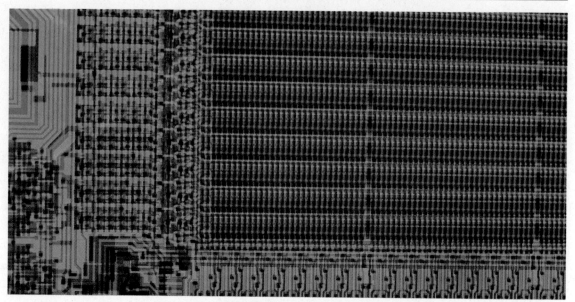

The key to the computer's speed and smallness is the silicon chip, replacing wires and tubes of the original computers.

Bob Cox says that computers are powerful because they can do many calculations very rapidly. The program stored in the computer memory is the key to this speed. A BASIC program has numbered statements and uses all capital letters.

EXAMPLE 1.   Here is a BASIC program. It tells the computer to find the average of two numbers, P and Q. Explain what each statement tells the computer. What is the printout for this program?

LINE NUMBER	STATEMENT
10	READ P, Q
20	LET A = (P + Q)/2
30	PRINT A
40	DATA 4, 9
50	END

Tells the computer to read the numbers P and Q from DATA.

Tells the computer to add P and Q, divide by 2, and call this number A.

Tells the computer to print the average, the value of A.

Tells the computer to accept 4 for P and 9 for Q.

Tells the computer the program is finished.

The printout for this program would be **6.5**.

In a LET statement such as Statement 20 above, all values to the right of the equal sign must be known. If you have a computer that understands BASIC, enter this program.

NEW, RUN, and LIST are system commands. They do not use a numbered statement. Type LIST and see if your program has been stored in the computer memory. Now type RUN and see if you get the correct printout.

This program tells the computer to find C, the total number of cents in D dimes and N nickels.

TRY THIS

```
10  READ D , N
20  LET C = 10 * D + 5 * N
30  PRINT C
40  DATA 6 , 11
50  END
```

1. Explain what each line tells the computer. See answer section.

2. What is the printout for this program? 115

COMPUTER HINTS

1. The mark on the screen showing that the computer is ready for your program is called the cursor. You must always have a cursor before you begin to type.

2. First, type NEW so that your program will not be mixed into other statements already stored in the computer.

3. Read each line carefully and make corrections before you press the return key. Use the back arrow to backspace.

4. Each statement line must be numbered. The computer reads each line in numerical order even if you type them out of order.

5. Punctuation, spelling, and parentheses must be exact or they will not be understood by the computer.

If you have a computer that understands BASIC, enter the program shown in the Try This above. Run the program to be sure it gives the correct answer. Then change the two data values in line 40 and run the program again.

Run the programs on the next page with similar changes in the data line.

EXAMPLE 2. Here is a BASIC program. It tells the computer to find the perimeter of a rectangle. Explain what each statement tells the computer. What is the printout for this program?

Tells the computer to read the numbers L and W from a DATA statement.

Tells the computer to multiply L and W each by 2, then add these products and call the sum P.

```
10    READ L , W
20    LET P = 2 * L + 2 * W
30    PRINT "THE PERIMETER IS"; P
40    DATA 10, 7
50    END
```

Tells the computer to print THE PERIMETER IS and then the value of P.

Tells the computer to accept 10 for L and 7 for W.

The printout for this program is THE PERIMETER IS 34.

TRY THIS

This program tells the computer to find the perimeter of a square.

```
10    READ S
20    LET P = 4 * S
30    PRINT "THE PERIMETER IS"; P
40    DATA 26
50    END
```

3. Explain what each line tells the computer. See answer section.

4. What is the printout for this program? PERIMETER IS 104

EXERCISES

Here is a BASIC program. It tells the computer to find the average of three numbers.

```
10    READ X , Y , Z
20    LET A = (X + Y + Z)/3
30    PRINT A
40    DATA 16 , 8 , 18
50    END
```

1. Explain what each line of the program means. See answer section.

2. What is the printout for this program? 14

This BASIC program tells the computer to find A, the area of a rectangle with length L and width W.

```
10   READ L , W
20   LET A = L * W
30   PRINT "THE AREA IS"; A
40   DATA 60 , 25
50   END
```

3. Explain what each line of the program means. See answer section.

4. What is the printout for this program? THE AREA IS 1500

This BASIC program tells the computer to find C, the Celsius temperature, given F, the Fahrenheit temperature.

```
10   READ F
20   LET C = 5/9 * (F — 32)
30   PRINT "THE CELSIUS TEMPERATURE IS"; C
35   GO TO 10
40   DATA 32 , 100 , 78
50   END
```

The first number in the DATA line is used the first time as a value for F. The second number in the DATA line is used the second time, etc.

5. Explain what each line of the program means. See answer section.

6. What is the printout? Note that the DATA line gives the computer three values for F. The computer will find C for each.
THE CELSIUS TEMPERATURE IS 0   THE CELSIUS TEMPERATURE IS 25.5556
THE CELSIUS TEMPERATURE IS 37.7778

ON YOUR OWN

If you have a computer available, enter each of the programs above.

7. Run the first program. Use it to find the average of groups of three numbers. Remember to change the DATA line.

8. Run the second program. Use it to find the area for various rectangles. Be sure to change the DATA line.

9. Run the third program. Use it to find the Celsius temperature for various Fahrenheit temperatures. Be sure to change the DATA line.

COMPUTERS AND FORMULAS

Computers can be used to evaluate formulas. To do so, first translate the formula into computer language.

EXAMPLES. Translate these formulas into BASIC.

FORMULA	BASIC TRANSLATION
1. $r = \dfrac{d}{t}$	R = D/T
2. $D = \dfrac{1}{5}S$	D = 1/5 * S
3. $G = 0.014\, r^2 h$	G = 0.014 * R ↑ 2 * H

TRY THIS

Translate these formulas from earlier chapters into BASIC.

1. $I = Prt$ I = P * R * T   **2.** $d = \dfrac{S^2}{30f}$ D = S ↑ 2/(30 * F)

3. $d = rt$ D = R * T   **4.** $A = \dfrac{h \times (B + b)}{2}$ A = H * (B + SB)/2

Mitch Jensen, exercise technician, was introduced in Chapter 10. He uses a microcomputer in his work. Recall the formula for finding F, the percent of body fat.

$$F = 0.49\, W + 0.45\, P - 6.36\, R + 8.71$$

One of the advantages of using a computer is that Mitch can use the formula over and over for different clients.

EXAMPLE 4. Write a program in BASIC which evaluates the formula for percent of body fat.

PLAN: **Step 1.** Translate the formula into BASIC.

$$F = 0.49 * W + 0.45 * P - 6.36 * R + 8.71$$

Step 2. Write the program.

```
10   READ W , P , R
20   LET F = 0.49 * W + 0.45
     * P - 6.36 * R + 8.71
30   PRINT F
40   DATA 80.8, 6, 6
50   END
```

Tell the computer what information you will give it.

Tell the computer what the formula is.

Tell the computer to print the value of F.

If you have a computer, enter this program and run it for several values of W, P, and R. (See Chapter 10, page 347 for other data.)

EXERCISES

Translate these formulas from earlier chapters into BASIC.

1. $A = Prt + P$
A = P * R * T + P

2. $S = R - \dfrac{W}{N - 1}$
S = R − W/(N − 1)

3. $f = \dfrac{ab}{ab - d}$
F = A * B/(A * B − D)

4. $A = l \times w$
A = L * W

5. $p = \dfrac{L}{200} + 38.25$
P = L/200 + 38.25

6. $p = 2w + 2l$
P = 2 * W + 2 * L

7. $A = \dfrac{B \times h}{2}$
A = B * H/2

8. $C = \pi \times d$
C = 3.14 * D

9. $h = 0.8 \times (180 - A)$
H = 0.8 * (180 − A)

10. $R = \dfrac{E}{I}$
R = E/I

11. $W = E \times I$
W = E * I

12. $I = Prt$
I = P * R * T

13. Dale Kief, lab technician, was introduced in Chapter 10. Dale has programmed the formulas $W = 0.003P$ and $H = 1.36gs$ into a microcomputer. Write programs in BASIC for these formulas. See answer section.

14. Choose any formula from exercises 1–12. Write a program in BASIC for that formula. Answers will vary.

ON YOUR OWN

15. If you have a computer enter the programs that you wrote. Run the programs for several values of the variable. See Chapter 10 for data.

NUMERICAL CONTROL PROGRAMMER

Computer-controlled machines are especially useful in manufacturing plants where heat, radioactivity, or complex machinery may be dangerous for human workers.

Diane Ng is a numerical control programmer. She writes programs which tell computer-controlled machines what to do. Diane worked first as a machinist. She received on-the-job training as a programmer.

Each instruction that Diane writes for a drill press tells it where to drill a hole. The point where the *x*-axis and *y*-axis cross is called the *origin*. A hole is located by two numbers measured from the origin.

If a hole is to the right of the origin its *x*-value is positive. If a hole is to the left of the origin its *x*-value is negative. If a hole is above the origin its *y*-value is positive. If a hole is below the origin its *y*-value is negative.

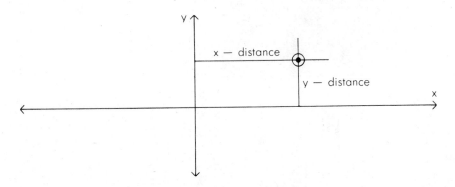

EXAMPLE 1.   Four holes are to be drilled in the metal plate shown below. What instructions should be given to drill hole A? The instruction for hole A would be $x + 1.5, y + 0.75$.

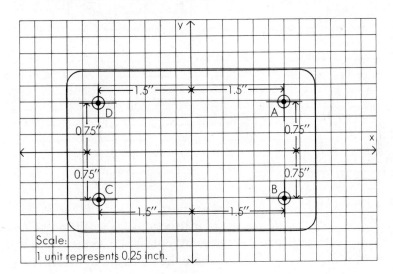

Use the diagram for Example 1.

1. $x + 1.5, y - 0.75$
2. $x - 1.5, y - 0.75$
3. $x - 1.5, y + 0.75$

TRY THIS

1. What instruction should be given to drill hole B?
2. What instruction should be given to drill hole C?
3. What instruction should be given to drill hole D?

EXAMPLE 2. Here is a list of instructions for a drill press. Use graph paper. Let one unit represent 0.25 inch. Draw an x-axis and a y-axis. Show where the holes are to be drilled.

HOLE	x-DATA	y-DATA
A	$x + 1.0$	$y - 2.25$
B	$x - 0.5$	$y - 1.5$
C	$x + 2.5$	$y + 0.0$
D	$x - 0.75$	$y + 1.25$

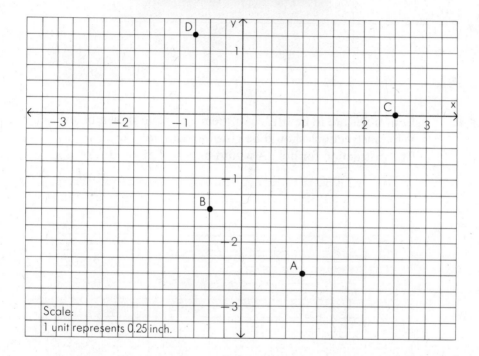

Scale:
1 unit represents 0.25 inch.

Here is a list of instructions for a drill press. Use graph paper. Let one unit represent 0.25 inch. Draw an x-axis and y axis. Show where the holes are to be drilled. See answer section.

TRY THIS

	HOLE	x-DATA	y-DATA
4.	A	$x + 0.75$	$y + 1.25$
5.	B	$x - 1.25$	$y - 0.25$
6.	C	$x + 2.5$	$y + 1.5$
7.	D	$x + 0.0$	$y - 1.75$

1-8. What instructions should be given to drill the holes A to H?

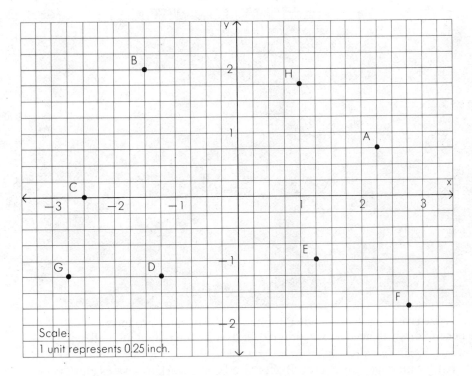

Here is a list of instructions for a drill press. Use graph paper.
Let one unit represent 0.25 inch. Draw an x-axis and y-axis. Show
where the holes are to be drilled.

	HOLE	x-DATA	y-DATA
9.	A	x + 1.5	y + 0.25
10.	B	x − 0.75	y + 2.5
11.	C	x + 2.25	y − 1.75
12.	D	x − 0.25	y + 2.25

	HOLE	x-DATA	y-DATA
13.	E	x − 1.25	y − 0.75
14.	F	x + 2.75	y + 1.5
15.	G	x + 0.0	y − 2.25
16.	H	x + 1.75	y − 0.0

ON YOUR OWN

17. Call several local manufacturing plants. Ask if they use any
numerical-controlled machinery. If possible, obtain copies of
programs used.

STORE MANAGER

Computerized cash registers provide information about which products
have been sold, which need to be reordered, and which are not selling well.

Laura Rittler manages the Stereo Place. She began work as a sales clerk.
Laura took business courses in night school and later became manager.

One of Laura's jobs is to keep an accurate inventory and sales
record. To do so she needs to know the number of items in stock,
the number sold, and the price of each item. Here is a partial list
of items from the Stereo Place.

```
INVENTORY REPORT FOR JANUARY:   THE STEREO PLACE
ITEM NO.    ITEM               IN STOCK, JAN 1    NO. SOLD IN JAN    SELLING PRICE
1           SPEAKER CONTROL     50                 22                 13.50
2           AUDIO CABLE         80                 12                  9.20
3           VIDEO CASSETTE      300                160                17.80
4           STEREO HEADPHONE    90                 60                 37.50
5           AM/FM SYSTEM        20                 6                 359.00
```

Quick access to current information is a main feature of a computer.
The Stereo Place uses computerized cash registers. Each time an
item is purchased the clerk enters the item number. The computer
keeps a record of sales and provides an up-to-date inventory.

To find the number in stock at the beginning of a month, the computer subtracts the number sold from the number in stock. To find gross sales, the computer multiplies the selling price by the number sold.

EXAMPLE 1. For Item 1, find the number in stock at the beginning of February and the gross sales. Assume no stock was added in January.

In Stock, Feb 1 = In Stock, Jan 1 − no. sold
$$= 50 - 22$$
$$= 28$$

Gross sales = selling price × no. sold
$$= \$13.50 \times 22$$
$$= \$297.00$$

TRY THIS

1. For Items 2 and 3 find the number of items in stock on February 1 and the gross sales for January. Assume no stock was added in January. 68, $110.40 140, $2848

The computer uses a program such as this to keep an inventory:

```
10  PRINT "IN STOCK JAN 1" , "SOLD" ,
    "SELLING PRICE" , "IN STOCK FEB 1" ,
    "GROSS SALES"
20  FOR I = 1 TO 5
30  READ N , S , P
40  LET L = N - S
50  LET G = S *P
60  PRINT I " . " N , S , P , L , G
70  NEXT I
80  DATA 50 , 22 , 13.50 , 80 , 12 ,
    9.20 , 300 , 160 , 17.80 , 90 , 60 ,
    37.50 , 20 , 6 , 359
90  END
```

The computer reads line 20 and lets I = 1. It then does lines 30 to 60 in order. At line 70, a NEXT statement, it adds 1 to I and goes back to line 20. It repeats this process until I is six. Then the program ends. This is called a FOR-NEXT loop.

In line 80, the computer reads data in groups of three for N , S and P.

The printout should look like this.

IN STOCK JAN 1.	SOLD	SELLING PRICE	IN STOCK FEB 1	GROSS SALES
1. 50	22	13.50	28	297
2. 80	12	9.20	68	110.40
3. 300	160	17.80	140	2848
4. 90	60	37.50	30	2250
5. 20	6	359.00	14	2154

If you have a computer, enter and run this program. Make up and enter data for other items. Find the number IN STOCK, FEB 1 and the gross sales. Explain each step of the program.

Here is another partial listing of items from The Stereo Place.

```
MONTH: JANUARY

ITEM NO.        ITEM            COST        SOLD IN JAN        SELLING PRICE
6               90-MIN TAPES    1.86        128                3.38
7               AM/FM STEREO    82.00       14                 150.00
8               CLOCK RADIO     22.00       11                 39.95
9               MICROPHONE      4.00        20                 7.40
10              EARPHONE        1.13        23                 2.05
```

The computer also computes the total profit per item. To find the profit per item, the computer subtracts the cost from the selling price. Then it multiplies the profit per item by the number sold to find the total profit for each item.

EXAMPLE 2.   For Item 6, find the profit for January.

Profit per Item = selling price − cost
$$= \$3.38 - \$1.86$$
$$= \$1.52$$

Profit = profit per item × number sold
$$= \$1.52 \times 128$$
$$= \$194.56$$

TRY THIS   **2.** For Items 7 and 8 above, find the profit for January.
$952, $197.45

This BASIC program will find profit for each item in much the same way as a computerized cash register. See answer section.

```
10    PRINT "ITEM", "COST", "SOLD",
      "SELLING PRICE", "PROFIT"
20    FOR I = 6 TO 10
30    READ C , N , S
40    LET P = (S − C) * N
50    PRINT I , C , N , S , P
60    NEXT I
70    DATA 1.86, 128, 3.38, 82, 14, 150,
      22, 11, 39.95, 4, 20, 7.40, 1.13,
      23, 2.05
80    END
```

Line 20 is the beginning of a FOR-NEXT loop where I takes on the values of 6, 7, 8, 9, and 10.

See answer section.

Here is a partial list of items from The Stereo Place.

```
MONTH:  FEBRUARY

ITEM NO.   ITEM              IN STOCK, FEB 1   COST      SOLD IN FEB   SELLING PRICE
1          FUSE HOLDER       24                 0.58      8             1.05
2          VIDEO CASSETTE    120                7.08      63            12.88
3          TURNTABLE         25                 110.00    18            200.00
4          STEREO WALL JACK  40                 1.62      18            2.95
5          CAR SPEAKERS      28                 24.72     20            44.95
6          AM/FM CAR STEREO  25                 143.00    17            260.00
7          TAPE DECK         30                 192.50    14            350.00
8          TEST TAPE         100                3.36      36            6.10
```

1–8. For Items 1–8 find the number of items remaining in stock on Feb 28. Assume no stock was added in February.

9–16. For Items 1–8 find the profit for February.

17. The following program will find the total sales and total profit. Explain each step of the program. If you have a computer, enter and run the program for the items in Ex. 1.

```
10    PRINT "ITEM", "SOLD", "SELLING PRICE",
      "GROSS SALES", "PROFIT"
11    LET T = 0
12    LET M = 0
20    FOR I = 1 TO 8
30    READ C , N , S
40    LET G = N * S
50    LET P = (S - C) * N
60    PRINT I, N, S, G, P
70    LET T = T + G
80    LET M = M + P
90    NEXT I
100   PRINT "TOTAL PROFIT IS"; M
110   PRINT "TOTAL SALES IS"; T
120   DATA .58, 8, 1.05, 7.08, 63, 12.88, 110,
      18, 200, 1.62, 18, 2.95
130   DATA 24.72, 20, 44.95, 143, 17, 260,
      192.50, 14, 350, 3.36, 36, 6.10
140   END
```

In line 70, the equal sign is used in a different way. It means replace T with the value of T + G. In line 80 we have a similar situation.

THE HOME COMPUTER

Today's computers can work much more efficiently than these early computers, which represented great breakthroughs in technology.

Bill Denning is a book salesman. He must keep accurate records of his travel expenses. Here are Bill's expenses for one month when he made twelve sales trips.

Trip	Food	Lodging	Auto (Miles)
1	$19.45	$26.00	50
2	$45.78	$72.00	150
3	$35.60	$84.60	300
4	$50.00	$0.00	75
5	$39.62	$45.80	220
6	$24.56	$29.80	180
7	$97.98	$250.80	450
8	$65.90	$75.00	306
9	$34.67	$41.80	263
10	$19.00	$0.00	27
11	$84.50	$129.80	320
12	$63.85	$92.00	408

Bill uses his home computer to record his monthly expenses. The computer first finds a subtotal for each trip.

EXAMPLE.   Find the subtotal for the first trip.
                 The auto allowance is $0.21 per mile.

PLAN: **Step 1.**   Find the auto cost.

$$\$0.21 \times 50 = \$10.50$$

Step 2.   Add to find the subtotal.

$$\$19.45$$
$$26.00$$
$$\underline{10.50}$$
$$\$55.95$$

TRY THIS

1. Find the subtotal for Trip 2. $149.28
2. Find the subtotal for Trip 7. $443.28
3. Find the subtotal for Trip 10. $24.67

This computer program will find the subtotal for each trip and the monthly total.

```
10   PRINT "TRIP" , "FOOD" , "LODGING" , "AUTO(MILES)" , "SUBTOTAL"
20   PRINT
30   LET G = 0
40   FOR I = 1 TO 12
50   READ F , L , A
60   LET T = F + L + .21 * A
70   PRINT I , F , L , A , T
80   LET G = G + T
90   NEXT I
100  PRINT
110  PRINT "THE MONTHLY TOTAL IS $" ; G
120  DATA 19.45 , 26 , 50 , 45.78 , 72 , 150 , 35.6 , 84.6 , 300 , 50 , 0 , 75 ,
     39.62 , 45.8 , 220
130  DATA 24.56 , 29.8 , 180 , 97.98 , 250.8 , 450 , 65.9 , 75 , 306 , 34.67 ,
     41.8 , 263 , 19 , 0 , 27
140  DATA 84.5 , 129.8 , 320 , 63.85 , 92 , 408
150  END
```

If you have a computer, run this program and find the monthly total. Make up data for other sales trips and use this program to find the subtotals and monthly total. Be sure to change line 40 for the number of trips. Lines 120, 130, and 140 will contain your new data.

Bill Denning also uses his home computer to keep his checkbook balanced. Here is a list of Bill's checks and deposits for a month.

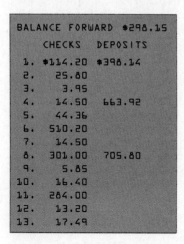

```
BALANCE FORWARD $298.15
     CHECKS    DEPOSITS
 1.  $114.20  $398.14
 2.    25.80
 3.     3.95
 4.    14.50   663.92
 5.    44.36
 6.   510.20
 7.    14.50
 8.   301.00   705.80
 9.     5.85
10.    16.40
11.   284.00
12.    13.20
13.    17.49
```

This computer program produces the information found on a check stub. B stands for Balance Forward, D stands for Amount of Deposit, and C stands for Amount This Check.

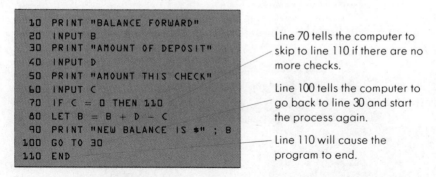

```
 10  PRINT "BALANCE FORWARD"
 20  INPUT B
 30  PRINT "AMOUNT OF DEPOSIT"
 40  INPUT D
 50  PRINT "AMOUNT THIS CHECK"
 60  INPUT C
 70  IF C = 0 THEN 110
 80  LET B = B + D - C
 90  PRINT "NEW BALANCE IS $" ; B
100  GO TO 30
110  END
```

Line 70 tells the computer to skip to line 110 if there are no more checks.

Line 100 tells the computer to go back to line 30 and start the process again.

Line 110 will cause the program to end.

If you have a computer, run the above program. Use the data for Bill Denning's checking account. Here is part of a printout.

```
BALANCE FORWARD?  298.15
AMOUNT OF DEPOSIT?  398.14
AMOUNT THIS CHECK?  114.20
NEW BALANCE IS $  582.09

AMOUNT OF DEPOSIT?  0
AMOUNT THIS CHECK?  25.80
NEW BALANCE IS $  556.29

AMOUNT OF DEPOSIT?  0
AMOUNT THIS CHECK?  3.95
NEW BALANCE IS $  552.34
```

EXERCISES

Here are Bill Denning's expenses for a month when he made ten sales trips.

```
TRIP   FOOD      LODGING    AUTO (MILES)
 1    $38.29    $72.00     120 $135.49
 2    $46.83    $110.25    210 $201.18
 3    $53.29    $83.75     186 $176.10
 4    $27.53    $0.00      82  $44.75
 5    $62.38    $95.00     260 $211.98
 6    $187.62   $263.85    510 $558.57
 7    $93.65    $142.69    320 $303.54
 8    $23.18    $0.00      80  $39.98
 9    $65.29    $35.86     62  $114.17
10    $73.86    $51.90     87  $144.03
```

1. If you have a computer, use the program on page 399 to find the subtotal for each trip and the monthly total. Be sure to change line 40 to FOR I = 1 TO 10 and enter the new data for lines 120, 130, and 140. See answer section.

2-11. If you do not have a computer, find the subtotal for each trip. Recall that Bill is paid $ 0.21 per mile auto allowance.

12. Find the total expenses for the month. $1929.79

Here is a list of Bill's checks and deposits for another month.

```
BALANCE FORWARD $386.29
          CHECKS      DEPOSITS
 1.      $28.53      $216.52      $574.28
 2.      $62.55                   $511.73
 3.      $87.00                   $424.73
 4.      $10.80      $722.92      $1136.85
 5.      $8.16                    $1128.69
 6.      $125.83                  $1002.86
 7.      $68.42      $462.00      $1396.44
 8.      $78.03                   $1318.41
 9.      $228.97                  $1089.44
10.      $18.32      $216.38      $1287.50
11.      $2.65                    $1284.85
12.      $109.38                  $1175.47
```

13. If you have a computer, use the program on page 400 to find his new balance after each transaction.

CHAPTER REVIEW

In BASIC, how would you tell a computer to do the following?

1. Subtract 23 from 75 and then multiply by 6. (75 − 23) * 6

2. Find 3 to the 5th power. 3 ↑ 5

Simplify. Use the four rules of order.

3. 28 + 5/5 * 2 30   **4.** (40 − 5)/7 + 2 ↑ 2 9

5. 5/(15 − 5) * 2 − 1 0   **6.** 20 − 8/4 * (2 + 5) 6

Suppose A = 12, B = 3, C = 5, and D = 10. Evaluate the following.

7. A * B − C 31   **8.** A + C ↑ 2 37   **9.** (B + C) * D 80   **10.** D/C + A * B 38

The following program tells the computer to find A, the area of a triangle with height H, and base B.

```
10   READ H, B
20   LET A = H * B/2
30   PRINT "THE AREA IS"; A
40   DATA 78, 30
50   END
```

11. What is the printout for this program? The area is 1170.

12. Change line 30 so the height and base are also printed. 30   PRINT "A TRIANGLE WITH HEIGHT"; H "AND BASE"; B "HAS AN AREA OF"; A

13. What is the printout for this program? 1   4   9   16   25
(other answers possible)

```
10   FOR I = 1 TO 5
20   PRINT I↑2,
30   NEXT I
40   END
```

14. Change line 20 so that the program will find I³. Give the printout.
20   PRINT I ↑ 3,   1   8   27   64   125

Translate these formulas into BASIC.

A = 1/2 * H * (X + Y)   G = 2.1 * N + 3.7

15. $A = \frac{1}{2}h(x + y)$ **16.** $G = 2.1n + 3.7$

17–20. What instructions should be given to drill holes A, B, C, and D?

17. X + 0.75, Y + 0.25
18. X − 0.25, Y − 0.25
19. X − 0.75, Y + 0
20. X + 1.75, Y − 0.50

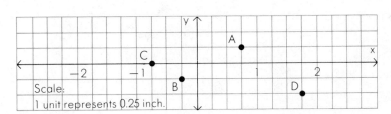

Scale:
1 unit represents 0.25 inch.

21. Give the printout for the following partial March inventory with the DATA shown. See answer section.

```
10    REM    MARCH INVENTORY PROGRAM
20    REM    I = ITEM NUMBER, H = NO. IN STOCK, MAR 1, A = NO. ADDED
30    REM    S = NO. SOLD, R = REMAINING INVENTORY, APR 1
40    PRINT "ITEM", "IN STOCK, MAR 1","SOLD IN MAR","IN STOCK,APR 1"
50    FOR I = 1 TO 3
60    READ H, A, S
70    LET R = H + A - S
80    PRINT I, H, S, R
90    NEXT I
100   DATA 60, 0, 42, 110, 50, 120, 21, 2, 16
110   END
```

22. Change the March inventory program to also print a column for A, the number added in March. Give a computer heading for the new column. Give the printout. See answer section.

23. Add a fourth item of inventory to the program. Add DATA for the new item. Give the added new line of the printout.

23. 50 FOR I = 1 TO 4
    105 DATA 100, 30, 64
      4   100 64 66

24. Give the three input amounts and the printout for the checkbook balance program.

24. example:
BALANCE FORWARD? 256.48
AMOUNT OF DEPOSIT? 67.73
AMOUNT OF THIS CHECK? 23.91
NEW BALANCE IS $300.3

```
10    REM    CHECKBOOK BALANCE PROGRAM
20    REM    B = BALANCE FORWARD, D = AMOUNT OF DEPOSIT,
             C = AMOUNT OF THIS CHECK
30    PRINT "BALANCE FORWARD";
40    INPUT B
50    PRINT "AMOUNT OF DEPOSIT";
60    INPUT D
70    PRINT "AMOUNT OF THIS CHECK";
80    INPUT C
90    LET B = B + D - C
100   PRINT "NEW BALANCE IS $"; B
110   END
```

12
USING STATISTICS

GRAPHS

Graphs can be effectively used to communicate data about changes and comparisons.

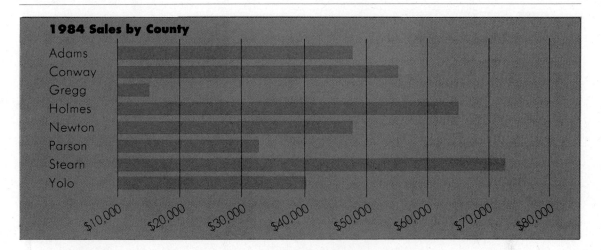

1984 Sales by County

Bill Denning, the book salesman, uses graphs to show his sales record. He uses different types of graphs to show different things. Bar graphs are used to show comparison. Bill uses the bar graph above to compare his sales in different counties.

EXAMPLE 1. Find his total sales in Adams County.

PLAN: **Step 1.** Find Adams County on the vertical scale.

Step 2. Find the amount on the horizontal scale.

The total in Adams County was $ 47,500.

EXAMPLE 2. Find the difference in sales between Gregg County and Holmes County.

PLAN: **Step 1.** Find the sales for Gregg County. $ 15,000

Step 2. Find the sales for Holmes County. $ 65,000

Step 3. Subtract to find the difference.
$ 65,000 − 15,000 = $ 50,000

TRY THIS

1. Find the sales in Parson County. $32,500
2. Which county had the greatest sales? Stearn County
3. Find the difference in sales between Conway County and Yolo County. $15,000

Line graphs show change. Bill uses line graphs to show changes in monthly sales.

Book Sales for 2 Years

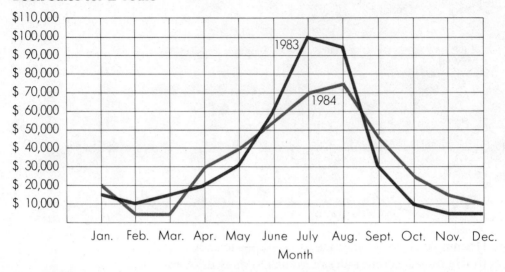

EXAMPLE 3.   Find the difference in June sales between 1983 and 1984.

PLAN: **Step 1.**   Find the June sales for 1983 and 1984.

1983 sales were $ 60,000.
1984 sales were $ 55,000.

Step 2.   Subtract to find the difference.

$ 60,000 − $ 55,000 = $ 5000

TRY THIS

4. Find the March sales in 1983. $15,000
5. Find the total August and September sales in 1984. $120,000
6. Find the difference in July sales for 1983 and 1984. $30,000 decrease

EXERCISES

Use the bar graph on page 405.

1. Find the sales in Holmes County. $65,000

2. Find the sales in Newton County. $47,500

3. Which county had the least amount of sales? Gregg County

4. What county had the second highest amount of sales? Holmes County

5. Find the total sales in Stearn and Holmes counties. $137,500

6. Find the total sales in Conway, Gregg, and Newton counties. $117,500

7. Find the difference in sales between Stearn and Gregg counties. $57,500

8. Find the difference in sales between Gregg and Parson counties. $17,500

Use the line graph on page 406.

9. Find the April sales in 1983. $20,000

10. Find the October sales in 1984. $25,000

11. Which month had the greatest sales in 1983? July

12. Which months had the least sales in 1984? Feb. & Mar.

13. Find the difference in November sales between 1983 and 1984. $10,000 increase

14. Find the difference in February sales between 1983 and 1984. $5,000 decrease

15. Between which two months in 1983 was there the greatest increase? June to July

16. Which year had the most total sales? Both years had $395,000.

People give campaign money to state legislators. The graph shows the patterns of giving.

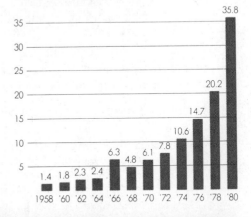

Legislative Campaign Spending In millions

17. When did the amount given first become more than 6 million dollars? 1966

18. In what year was there a decrease in the amount of money given? What was the decrease? 1968, 1.5 million dollars

19. In which years was there the greatest increase? What was the increase? 1978 to 1980, 15.6 million dollars

20. What was the amount of increase between 1964 and 1966? 3.9 million dollars

ON YOUR OWN

21. Find the total daily attendance at your school for the last 10 days. Make a bar or line graph showing the information.

MEAN, MEDIAN, AND MODE

Point out that the mean, median, and mode are called measures of central tendency. Mean is sometimes called the arithmetic mean, since it is an average found by simple arithmetic.

City governments and businesses use statistics in many ways to plan for the needs of people who work and visit every day.

When analyzing data, an important question is "What single number best represents the set of data as a whole?" The mean, median, and mode are numbers that are used to answer this question.

The *mean* is the average of a set of numbers.

EXAMPLE 1. Find the mean of these scores on a quiz with 15 problems.
8, 6, 7, 6, 15, 8, 8, 11, 10, 9, 8, 7, 10, 9, 5, 11, 12, 6, 9

Step 1. Find the sum of the scores.

The sum is 165.

Step 2. Divide by the number of scores.

$165 \div 19 \approx 8.7$

The mean is 8.7.

The mean of this set of scores would be useful for a teacher who wants to assign grades on this quiz.

Find the mean.

1. Test scores: 93, 88, 76, 91, 68, 75, 90, 93, 77 **83.4**
2. Annual salaries: $ 10,200, $ 7,800, $ 12,600, $ 15,800, $ 9,425, $ 16,500 **$12,054**
3. Pulse rates: 67, 73, 77, 59, 91, 82, 76, 75 **75**
4. Heights: 5'3", 6'0", 5'2", 5'5", 5'7", 6'2", 5'4". **5'8"**

The *median* of a set of numbers is the middle number when the numbers are arranged in order. **The median may or may not be a member of the set of data.**

EXAMPLE 2. Find the median of the quiz scores from Example 1. Arrange the scores in order from least to most.

5, 6, 6, 6, 7, 7, 8, 8, 8, 8, 9, 9, 9, 10, 10, 11, 11, 12, 15

The middle score 8 is the median.

Jerry Cohen's quiz score was 10. Because the median is 8, he knows that his score was in the upper half of the class.

EXAMPLE 3. Find the median number of children in the following families.

Family A, 3 children; Family B, 2 children; Family C, 0 children; Family D, 4 children.

PLAN: **Step 1.** Arrange the number of children in order from least to most.

0, 2, 3, 4

Step 2. Find the average of the two middle numbers.

$$\frac{2 + 3}{2} = 2.5$$

The median number of children is 2.5.

TRY THIS

Find the median.

5. Test scores: 93, 88, 76, 91, 68, 75, 90, 93, 77 **88**
6. Annual salaries: $ 10,200, $ 7,800, $ 12,600, $ 15,800, $ 9,425, $ 16,500 **$11,400**
7. Pulse rates: 67, 73, 77, 59, 91, 82, 76, 75 **75.5**
8. Heights: 5'3", 6'0", 5'2", 5'5", 5'7", 6'2", 5'4" **5'5"**

The *mode* of a set of numbers is the number which occurs most often. The mode would be important in a retail clothing store where it would be helpful to know which size sold most often.

The mode of the set of data, if it exists, is always a member of the set.

EXAMPLE 4. Sal's Shoe Shop sold these shoe sizes on Monday. Find the mode.

7A, 8B, 7C, 6A, 8B, $6\frac{1}{2}$B, 7A, 8B, 9A, 8B, 9B, 8B, 8A

The size 8B occurs five times. It is the mode.

A set of data may have more than one mode. If no number occurs more than once, there is no mode.

TRY THIS

Find the mode.

9. Plant heights (in cm): 63, 71, 64, 68, 72, 71, 73, 71, 62, 71 71

10. Baseball cap sizes: 7, $7\frac{1}{2}$, $7\frac{1}{8}$, $6\frac{7}{8}$, $7\frac{1}{2}$, $6\frac{1}{2}$, 7, $7\frac{1}{2}$, 7 7, $7\frac{1}{2}$

EXERCISES

1. Here is the number of traffic violations on a highway for ten days. Find the mean number of violations. 2, 3, 5, 0, 1, 4, 6, 0, 1, 2 2.4

2. In five successive gymnastic meets, Erin had the following scores on the uneven parallel bars: 6.2, 6.8, 7.1, 7.0, and 6.5. Find the mean score. 6.72

3. Samples of 20 computer chips were taken once a day for ten days and tested. Here is the number of defective chips found each day. Find the mean number of defective chips. 2, 0, 1, 0, 3, 1, 4, 0, 2, 1 1.4

4. Dan Sides recorded his systolic blood pressure for a week: 137, 142, 135, 140, 148, 139, 136. Find his mean systolic blood pressure for the week. 141

5. Following is a set of evacuation times in minutes for a series of monthly fire drills in a school. Find the median evacuation time. 2.3, 3.5, 2.8, 2.9, 3.2, 3.0, 3.1, 2.4, 2.6 2.9

6. The Eisenhower dollar was minted from 1971–1978. During 1976 a special bicentennial version was minted. This chart shows the types of dollars minted. Find the mean number minted. 29, 644, 519

Type	Number Minted
1976, variety 1	4,019,000
1976, variety 2	113,318,000
1976D, variety 1	21,048,710
1976D, variety 2	82,179,564

7. Here is a list of attendances for six basketball games. Find the median attendance. 629, 703, 526, 796, 423, 630 629.5

8. The number of points scored by a football team in each of its games is given below. Find the median score. 17, 24, 6, 35, 27, 0, 10 17

9. Here is a list of ring sizes which were sold in a day. Find the mode. 6, 7, 6, 8, 6, 7, 7, 7, 5, 6 6 and 7

10. This chart shows a record of ice cream flavors sales. Find the mode. 10

Flavor	Tally	Frequency
Chocolate	ЈHT I	6
Vanilla	ЈHT UHT	10
Strawberry	HHT	5
Other	III	3

11. Find the mode of this set of test scores. 90, 83, 79, 64, 84, 96, 77, 95 no mode

12. Here are the salaries for the employees at the Princeton Sports Shop. Find the mean, median, and mode. $ 55,000, $ 10,000, $ 12,000, $ 22,250, $ 18,500, $ 8,000, $ 12,000, $ 20,000, $ 15,500
$19,250, $15,500, $12,000

ON YOUR OWN

13. Collect data within your school, such as class enrollment. Find the mean, median, and mode for each set of data.

COUNTING PROBLEMS

Students may be interested to know that the study of probability such as those shown here is called "Combinatorics."

Two kinds of cones, 20 kinds of ice cream and three kinds of toppings mean there can be 120 different ice cream cones!

Joan Kozlovsky is a clothing designer. After high school she went to work for a clothing manufacturer. She also has taken several courses at a design school.

Joan is working to design articles of clothing that can be coordinated into a variety of outfits.

EXAMPLE 1.   Joan designs the following coordinating articles.

Jackets	**Trousers**	**Shirts**
Navy (N)	Navy (N)	White (W)
Plaid (P)	Grey (G)	Blue (B)
	Tan (T)	

To find all possible outfits, Joan can use a tree diagram.

Jackets	Trousers	Shirts	Outfits

```
Jackets     Trousers      Shirts          Outfits
                           W ——————— N — N — W
                N
                           B ——————— N — N — B

                           W ——————— N — G — W
    N           G
                           B ——————— N — G — B

                           W ——————— N — T — W
                T
                           B ——————— N — T — B


                           W ——————— P — N — W
                N
                           B ——————— P — N — B

                           W ——————— P — G — W
    P           G
                           B ——————— P — G — B

                           W ——————— P — T — W
                T
                           B ——————— P — T — B
```

TRY THIS

1. Joan designs the following matching skirts and jackets. Use a tree diagram to find how many outfits can be formed. **See answer section.**

Skirts	Jackets	Blouses
Blue	Blue	Pink
Striped	Striped	Light Blue
Grey		White

2. You have the following choices on a menu. Use a tree diagram to find how many combinations can be ordered. **See answer section.**

Soups	Main Dish	Vegetables
Vegetable	Roast Beef	Potatoes
Chowder	Veal Chops	Rice
	Leg of Lamb	Green Beans
	Crab	Carrots

From the tree diagram of Example 1, we see that for each shirt there are three choices for trousers, and for each kind of trousers, there are two jackets. To find the number of outfits without using a tree diagram, we can multiply.

Jackets	Trousers	Shirts
2	× 3	× 2	= 12

THE COUNTING PRINCIPLE

Mention that the tree diagrams yield the actual possibilities, whereas the counting principle gives only the number. For a large number the tree diagram is impractical.

If a first thing can be done in m different ways and, after it is done, a second thing can be done in n different ways, and after it is done, a third thing can be done in p different ways and so on, then all the things together can be done in $m \times n \times p \times \ldots$ different ways.

EXAMPLE 2.   Joan designs 4 different sport coats, 2 pairs of slacks, and 3 shirts. Use the counting principle to find how many different matching outfits can be formed.

Using the counting principle we have

Coats		**Trousers**		**Shirts**		
4	$\times$	2	$\times$	3	=	24

24 different outfits can be formed.

EXAMPLE 3.   On a dinner menu there are 6 choices for the main dish, 5 choices of vegetable, 3 salad dressings, and 4 desserts. Use the counting principle to find how many different dinner choices are possible.

Main Dish		**Vegetable**		**Dressing**		**Dessert**		
6	$\times$	5	$\times$	3	$\times$	4	=	360

There are 360 different dinner choices.

TRY THIS

Use the counting principle to solve the following.

3. At a restaurant there were 2 choices of appetizers, 3 choices of main dishes, and 2 choices of dessert. How many different combinations are possible? 12

4. On a trip from Baltimore to Pittsburgh to San Francisco, there are 2 possible flights from Baltimore to Pittsburgh and 3 possible flights from Pittsburgh to San Francisco. How many possible combinations of flights are there from Baltimore to San Francisco via Pittsburgh? 6

5. Mark works in a camera store. They carry two film sizes (20 exposures or 36 exposures), six film speeds and a choice of color print or slides. How many different kinds of film does the store have? 24

EXERCISES

1. You have the following matching trousers and shirts. Use a tree diagram to find how many outfits can be formed. **See answer section.**

Trousers	Shirts
Brown	White
Black	Blue
	Green

2. You have the following choices on a menu. Use a tree diagram to find how many combinations can be found. **See answer section.**

Appetizer	Main Dish	Vegetable
Salad	Fish	Baked potatoes
Soup	Beef	French fries
	Pork	Mashed potatoes

3. You have the following choices for pizza. You only get one choice of topping. Use the counting principle to find how many possible combinations there are. **48**

Size	Crust	Topping
Small	Regular	Cheese
Medium	Thick	Mushrooms
Large		Peppers
Jumbo		Sausage
		Olives
		Pepperoni

4. You go to an ice cream parlor for a sundae. You have a choice of 24 flavors of ice cream and 12 toppings. How many possible sundae combinations are there? **288**

5. In a certain state the automobile license plates have 2 letters followed by 4 digits. How many different license plates are possible? (Assume that any of the 26 letters and any of the 10 digits can be used.) **6,760,000**

ON YOUR OWN

6. Investigate the combination of numbers and letters on the automobile license plates of your state.

PROBABILITY AND ODDS

Keep in mind that in this lesson events discussed are equally likely to occur.

What is the probability of setting a record? of competing in a snowstorm? of serious injury? of winning a gold medal?

Lou Di Pietro is a life insurance actuary. He attended college and received special training. Lou calculates risks and premiums for his insurance company. He uses probability in his work.

Lou says that probability tells us how likely it is that an event will occur. The probability of an event is always a number from 0 to 1. It is the ratio of the number of favorable outcomes to the total number of outcomes.

$$\text{PROBABILITY OF AN EVENT} = \frac{\text{Number of favorable outcomes}}{\text{Total number of outcomes}}$$

EXAMPLE 1.   Find the probability of an event happening when there are 3 favorable outcomes out of 12 tries.

$$\text{Probability} = \frac{\text{No. of favorable outcomes}}{\text{Total no. of outcomes}} \frac{3}{12}$$

$$= \frac{3}{12} = \frac{1}{4}$$

The probability is $\frac{1}{4}$.

EXAMPLE 2.   Fred Reinhart has a key ring with five keys on it. One of the keys opens a padlock. He picks one key at random. What is the probability that he picks the key that opens the lock?

$$P \text{ (right key)} = \frac{\text{No. of favorable outcomes}}{\text{Total no. of outcomes}} \quad \frac{1}{5}$$

Probability can be expressed as a percent. So, in Example 2, the probability of picking the right key is 20%.   **Stress that probability as a ratio can always be expressed as a percent.**

The probability is $\frac{1}{5}$. ($\frac{1}{5} = 0.20 = 20\%$)

EXAMPLE 3.   Joyce Phillips is a member of a computer class. Thirty programs had been submitted for publication in a newsletter. Joyce has submitted two programs. The name of each program is written on a slip of paper and put in a box. What is the probability that Joyce will have a program selected?

$$P \text{ (Joyce)} = \frac{2}{30}$$
$$= \frac{1}{15}$$

The probability that Joyce will have a program picked is $\frac{1}{15}$ or about 7%.

TRY THIS

Express the following probabilities as a percent.

1. There are 10 jellybeans, all different, in a closed box. Mary only likes red, green, and white. If she gets 3 tries to pick one of her choice, what is the probability she will get one she likes? $\frac{3}{10}$ **or 30%**

2. In Example 2, what is the probability that Fred will choose the wrong key? $\frac{4}{5}$ **or 80%**

3. In the computer class of Example 3, three programs are submitted by Tom. What is the probability that one of Tom's programs will be selected? $\frac{1}{10}$ **or 10%**

Lou says that an idea closely related to probability is *odds*. The odds in favor of an event is the ratio of the probability of the event occurring to the probability of its not occurring.

EXAMPLE 4.　In Example 2, what are the odds that Fred will pick the right key?

The probability of picking the right key is $\frac{1}{5}$.
The probability of picking the wrong key is $\frac{4}{5}$.

The odds in favor of picking the right key are the ratio
$\frac{1}{5}$ to $\frac{4}{5}$, which is written 1 to 4.

TRY THIS　**4.** In the computer class in Example 3, what are the odds in favor of Joyce Phillips' having a program selected? 1 to 14

EXAMPLE 5.　A bowl contains 5 apples and 3 oranges. Cheryl chooses a piece of fruit at random. State the probability as a fraction and a percent that Cheryl will choose an orange. Then give the odds in favor of choosing an orange.

The probability of choosing an orange is $\frac{3}{8}$ or $37\frac{1}{2}\%$.
The odds in favor of choosing an orange are 3 to 5.

TRY THIS　**5.** A drawer contains 3 red pencils and 2 blue pencils. Jim chooses one at random. State the probability as a fraction and percent that Jim will choose a red pencil. Then give the odds in favor of choosing a red pencil.
$\frac{3}{5}$ or 60%; odds are 3 to 2.

EXERCISES

1. Mark is in a class containing 32 members. A representative is to be chosen at random. What is the probability that Mark will be chosen? $\frac{1}{32}$

2. In the situation of Exercise 1, there are two girls named Carol in the class. What is the probability that a girl named Carol will be chosen? $\frac{1}{16}$

3. In Juan's stamp collection there are 28 stamps in the Famous Americans Series. Four of these stamps contain a portrait of George Washington. Juan selects one stamp at random for an exhibit. What is the probability that he will select a George Washington stamp? $\frac{1}{7}$

4. A board game uses a spinner like this.

On a given spin what is the probability of getting a number which is prime? $\frac{5}{9}$

5. A bookshelf contains 4 history books, 3 math books, and 3 novels. Sheila chooses one at random. What are the odds in favor of choosing a novel? **3 to 7**

6. A T.V. weatherman says there is a 20% chance of rain. What are the odds against rain? **4 to 1**

7. A newspaper weather map shows an 80% chance of snow for a ski area. What are the odds that it will snow? **4 to 1**

8. A restaurant serves these cereals: Cream of Rice, Wisps of Wheat, Wheaty Flakes, Bran Flakes, and Rice-O-Bits. Phyllis chooses a cereal at random. State the probability, as a fraction and a percent, that Phyllis will choose a rice cereal. Then give the odds in favor of choosing a rice cereal. $\frac{2}{5}$ **or 40%, 2 to 3**

9. A jar contains jellybeans: 50 black, 70 orange, 80 yellow, and 48 red. Ron chose a jellybean at random. State the probability, as a fraction and a percent, that Ron chooses a black jellybean. Then give the odds in favor of choosing a black jellybean. $\frac{25}{124} \approx$ **20.2%, 25 to 99**

ON YOUR OWN

10. Contact your local weatherperson and find out how the probability of rain is determined.

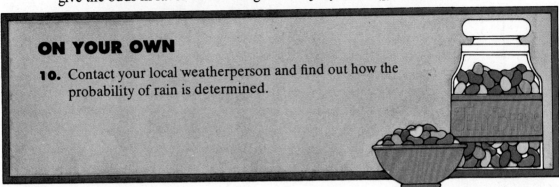

UNDERSTANDING STATISTICS

Stress the importance of being able to correctly interpret statistical data in daily life.

It has been said, "Statistics can prove anything." Wise or clever usage of statistics and graphs can lead the reader to different conclusions. Study these graphs.

Graph A

Georgia's Math Scores

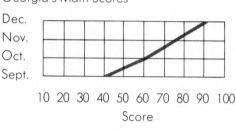

Graph B

Georgia's Math Scores

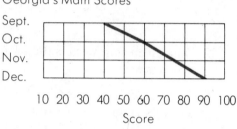

1. What does Graph A show for Georgia's score in September? **40**

2. What does Graph B show for Georgia's score in September? **40**

3. Compare the other months on both graphs. Are the identical scores shown? **Yes.**

4. What is the difference between Graph A and Graph B? **See answer section.**

5. Which graph gives a more positive impression of Georgia's work? Why? **Graph A. It has an upward curve.**

Study these graphs.

Graph C

Robert's Math Scores

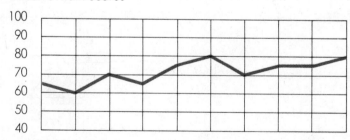

Graph D

Robert's Math Scores

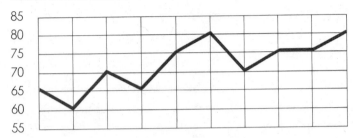

Month

6. What does Graph C show for Robert's score in Sept.? 65

7. What does Graph D show for Robert's score in Sept.? 65

8. Compare the other months on both graphs. Are identical scores shown? Yes.

9. What is the difference between Graph C and Graph D?
See answer section.

10. Which graph gives a more positive impression of Robert? Why? Graph D. It appears to show greater improvement.

Five students took a quiz. The scores were 100, 80, 75, 55, and 0. The mean (average) score is 62.

11. Did any student actually score a 62?

12. How many students scored higher than the mean? 3

13. How many students scored lower than the mean? 2

The median score for the quiz was 75.

14. Must at least one student get this median score? Yes.

15. How many students were above the median? 2

16. How many students were below the median? 2

17. If you had scored 75 on the quiz, would you like to be compared to the mean or median? Why?
Mean; There is a greater difference between 75 and the mean.

18. If you had scored 55 on the quiz, would you like to be compared to the mean or median? Why?
Mean; There is a lesser difference between 55 and the mean.

CHAPTER REVIEW

Airline Passengers

Moore Terminal   Key: ■ 1984 ■ 1985

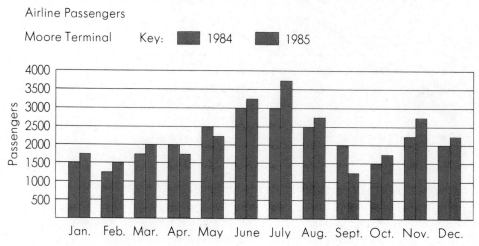

Use the graph above for exercises 1–10.

1. In which months of 1984 did the most passengers travel? **June, July**

2. In which month of 1985 did the fewest passengers travel? **September**

3. How many passengers were there in April 1984? **2000**

4. How many passengers were there in September 1985? **1250**

5. What was the passenger total for June, July, and August of 1984? **8500**

6. What was the passenger total for October, November, and December of 1985? **6750**

7. How many more passengers were there in January 1985 than in January 1984? **250**

8. How many more passengers were there in April 1984 than in April 1985? **250**

9. Which month in 1985 had the greatest increase in passengers compared with the same month in 1984? **July**

10. Which year had the highest passenger total? **1985**

Find the mean, median, and mode for each set of data. Round to the nearest tenth.

11. Test scores: 50, 40, 20, 100, 40 **mean, 50; median, 40; mode, 40**

12. Times (in seconds) for the 100-meter dash: 11.2, 10.9, 11.5, 11.4, 12.8, 11.4, 11.7, 10.9 **mean, 11.5; median, 11.4; mode,10.9 and 11.4**

13. Distance (meters) for the long jump: 6.2, 5.7, 6.2, 5.9, 7.1, 6.8
mean, 6.3; median, 6.2; mode, 6.2

14. Students per math class: 15, 18, 12, 27, 36, 20, 25
mean, 21.9; median, 20; no mode

15. Books sold to schools: 700, 2, 100, 2, 70, 12, 60, 2, 25
mean, 108.1; median, 25; mode, 2

16. Use the counting principle to find the number of possible combinations of rings. **24**

Size	Metal	Mounting
6	Gold	Diamond
7	Silver	Sapphire
8		Ruby
9		

17. Use the counting principle to find the number of possible combinations of shirts. **30**

Size	Color	Sleeve
12	Red	Long
$12\frac{1}{2}$	White	Short
13	Blue	
$13\frac{1}{2}$		
14		

18. There are 3 apples and 9 peaches in a bowl. Aaron picks a piece of fruit at random. State the probability, as a fraction and a percent, of Aaron picking an apple. Give the odds in favor of picking an apple. $\frac{1}{4}$ **or 25%, 1 to 3**

19. There are 10 dimes and 4 pennies in a jar. Cherie picks a coin at random. State the probability, as a fraction and a percent, of picking a dime. Give the odds *against* picking a dime. $\frac{5}{7}$ $\approx$ **71.4%, 2 to 5**

20. Marion got a 52 on her chemistry test. The mean was 50, the median was 48 and the mode was 45. Did Marion pass or fail? **pass**

APPENDIX

MEASUREMENT TABLES AND FORMULAS

METRIC MEASURES

Length

1 kilometer (km) = 1000 meters (m)
1 meter (m) = 100 centimeters (cm)
1 centimeter (cm) = 10 millimeters (mm)

Capacity

1 liter (L) = 1000 milliliters (mL)

Mass

1 metric ton (t) = 1000 kilograms (kg)
1 kilogram (kg) = 1000 grams (g)
1 gram (g) = 1000 milligrams (mg)

Temperature

0°C = freezing point of water
37°C = normal body temperature
100°C = boiling point of water

CUSTOMARY MEASURES

Length

12 inches (in.) = 1 foot (ft)
3 feet = 1 yard (yd)
36 inches = 1 yard
5280 feet = 1 mile (mi)
1760 yards = 1 mile

Capacity

8 fluid ounces (fl oz) = 1 cup (c)
2 cups = 1 pint (pt)
2 pints = 1 quart (qt)
4 quarts = 1 gallon (gal)

Weight

16 ounces (oz) = 1 pound (lb)
2000 pounds = 1 ton

Temperature

32°F = freezing point of water
98.6°F = normal body temperature
212°F = boiling point of water

FORMULAS

Perimeter of a rectangle	$P = 2l + 2w$	Area of a circle	$A = \pi r^2$
Perimeter of a square	$P = 4s$	Volume of a rectangular prism	$V = lwh$
Circumference of a circle	$C = \pi d$ or $C = 2\pi r$	Volume of a cube	$V = s \times s \times s$
Area of a rectangle	$A = lw$	Volume of a cylinder	$V = \pi r^2 h$
Area of a square	$A = s \times s$	Volume of a pyramid	$V = \frac{1}{3}lwh$
Area of a parallelogram	$A = bh$	Volume of a cone	$V = \frac{1}{3}\pi r^2 h$
Area of a triangle	$A = \frac{1}{2}bh$	Volume of a sphere	$V = \frac{4}{3}\pi r^3$
Area of a trapezoid	$A = \frac{1}{2}h(b_1 + b_2)$	Interest	$I = Prt$

SKILLS BANK

SKILL 1. Date Notation

Use the number of each month to write the date. Write the month first.

EXAMPLE   January 15, 1983 is written 1–15–83 or 1/15/83

---

1. February 7, 1982 **2–7–82**   **2.** October 18, 1985 **10–18–85**
3. June 10, 1984 **6–10–84**   **4.** March 20, 1986 **3–20–86**
5. May 27, 1983 **5–27–83**   **6.** November 19, 1990 **11–19–90**

Write the date indicated.

7. 5–4–84   **8.** 3–10–90   **9.** 6–6–86   **10.** 2–3–88
May 4, 1984   **March 10, 1990**   **June 6, 1986**   **February 3, 1988**

SKILL 2. Time Notation

Use colons to write time notation.

EXAMPLES   4 hours 27 minutes is 4:27
7 minutes after 6 o'clock is 6:07
6 hours 12 minutes 5 seconds is 6:12:05

---

1. 8 hours 10 minutes **8:10**   **2.** 15 minutes 30 seconds **0:15:30**
3. 25 minutes after 4 o'clock **4:25**   **4.** 1 hour 10 minutes 4 seconds **1:10:04**

Write the time.

5. 12:15:04   **6.** 2:08:37 **2 hr 8 min 37 sec or 8 min 37 sec after 2 o'clock**
12 hr 15 min 4 sec or 15 min 4 sec after 12 o'clock

SKILL 3. Place Value: Whole Numbers

Give the place and value of the underlined digit.

EXAMPLE   3<u>7</u>8,194. The 7 is in the ten-thousands' place. The value is 70,000.

---

1. Thousands' place 5000   2. Hundreds' place 800   3. Hundred-thousands' place 300,000

1. <u>5</u>,397   **2.** 1,<u>8</u>76   **3.** <u>3</u>45,940   **4.** 9,<u>2</u>87,164
5. 3<u>9</u>,278,176,400   **6.** 948,2<u>7</u>6,149,124   **4. Millions' place 9,000,000**
5. Billions' place 9,000,000,000   6. Ten-millions' place 70,000,000

SKILL 4. Word Names for Whole Numbers

Write word names.

EXAMPLE   4276 is four thousand, two hundred seventy-six.

1. eighty-four   2. three hundred seventy-five   3. four thousand one hundred fifty-nine

1. 84   **2.** 375   **3.** 4159   **4.** 7004   **5.** 8080   **6.** 4700

4. seven thousand four   5. eight thousand eighty   6. four thousand seven hundred

SKILL 5. Standard Notation

Write standard notation.

EXAMPLES   Eight thousand, two hundred fifteen is 8215.
28 million, 764 thousand, 86 is 28,764,086.

1. five hundred seventy-three **573**   **2.** eight thousand, eighty **8080**
3. 97 thousand, 479 **97,479**   **4.** 381 million, 4 thousand, 145 **381,004,145**

SKILL 6. Money Notation

Write money notation.

EXAMPLES   four cents is 4¢ or $0.04
forty dollars is $40 or $40.00
five dollars and six cents is $5.06

1. five cents **$0.05**   **2.** fourteen cents **$0.14**
3. twelve dollars **$12**   **4.** fifty-one dollars and nineteen cents **$51.19**

SKILL 7. Writing Checks

Write the dollar amount in words and the cents amount as a fraction
of a dollar.

EXAMPLES $86.05—Eighty-six and $\frac{05}{100}$ dollars

$7.00—Seven and $\frac{00}{100}$ dollars

$0.87—Zero and $\frac{87}{100}$ dollars

1. Nine and $\frac{84}{100}$ dollars   2. Four hundred thirty-seven and $\frac{59}{100}$ dollars   3. Eight and $\frac{07}{100}$ dollars

1. $9.84   **2.** $437.59   **3.** $8.07   **4.** $6.00   **5.** $0.07

4. Six dollars   5. Zero and $\frac{07}{100}$ dollars

SKILL 8. Decimal Place Value

Give the place and value of the underlined digit.

EXAMPLE   7.34<u>7</u>9. The 7 is in the thousandths' place. Its value is 0.007.

1. 4.<u>5</u>983	**2.** 58.5<u>7</u>	**3.** 1.07<u>9</u>	**4.** 7.642<u>9</u>
5. 3.4<u>2</u>7	**6.** 0.<u>4</u>387	**7.** 7.0<u>5</u>7	**8.** 0.<u>3</u>

SKILL 9. Decimal Word Names

Write short word names.

EXAMPLES   7.6 is 7 and 6 tenths
8.731 is 8 and 731 thousandths
0.0041 is 41 ten-thousandths

1. 4.8	**2.** 84.39	**3.** 0.327	**4.** 1.3492
5. 0.49	**6.** 4.006	**7.** 0.4	**8.** 12.002

SKILL 10. Decimal Notation

Write decimal notation.

EXAMPLES   4 and 7 tenths is 4.7
8 and 84 thousandths is 8.084
5 hundredths is 0.05

1. 8 and 26 hundredths **8.26**   **2.** 96 and 8 tenths **96.8**
3. 17 and 8 hundredths **17.08**   **4.** 4 and 4 thousandths **4.004**

SKILL 11. Rounding Whole Numbers

Round to the underlined place. If the digit to the right is 5 or more, round up. If the digit is less than 5, keep the underlined digit as is.

EXAMPLES   4<u>2</u>8 becomes 430   8 is more than 5, so we round up to 3.
7<u>2</u>19 becomes 7200   1 is less than 5, so the 2 is kept.

1. <u>7</u>9 **80**   **2.** 8<u>4</u>3 **840**   **3.** <u>8</u>79 **900**   **4.** 4<u>3</u>99 **4400**
5. <u>6</u>249 **6000**   **6.** 8<u>7</u>,548 **88,000** **7.** <u>8</u>1,824 **80,000** **8.** <u>8</u>16,248 **800,000**

SKILL 12. Rounding: Decimals and Money

Round to the underlined place. After rounding decimals, you may
drop digits to the right of the decimal point.

EXAMPLES 8.7 becomes 9   Round 8 up to 9.
            7.41 becomes 7.4   Keep 4. Drop digit to the right.
            $6.50 becomes $7   Round 6 up to 7. Drop digits to the right.

---

1. 7.7 **8**   **2.** 9.71 **9.7**   **3.** 8.254 **8.3**   **4.** 9.72 **10**
5. 0.78 **0.8**   **6.** 9.4172 **9.42**   **7.** 6.1234 **6.123**   **8.** 6.074 **6.07**

SKILL 13. Comparing Decimals

Use =, >, or < to compare decimals. First write 0's to make the
number of decimal places the same.

EXAMPLE   0.7 and 0.675 become 0.700 and 0.675
            Write 0.7 > 0.675 because 0.700 is greater than 0.675.

---

1. 0.4 and 0.40 =   **2.** 0.5 and 0.4 >   **3.** 0.83 and 0.8 >
4. 0.428 and 0.482 <   **5.** 0.427 and 0.43 <   **6.** 0.56 and 0.560 =

SKILL 14. Adding Whole Numbers

Be sure the digits line up vertically. Begin adding with the column on the right.

EXAMPLE   7284 + 948 + 86

$$\begin{array}{r} {\scriptstyle 1\,2\,1} \\ 7284 \\ 948 \\ +86 \\ \hline 8318 \end{array}$$

---

1. 16 + 83 **99**   **2.** 375 + 426 **801**   **3.** 893 + 44 **937**   **4.** 799 + 6 **805**

5. $\begin{array}{r} 74 \\ +39 \\ \hline \textbf{113} \end{array}$ **6.** $\begin{array}{r} 4927 \\ +8644 \\ \hline \textbf{13,571} \end{array}$ **7.** $\begin{array}{r} 18,739 \\ +65,891 \\ \hline \textbf{84,630} \end{array}$ **8.** $\begin{array}{r} 376,498 \\ +38,141 \\ \hline \textbf{414,639} \end{array}$

9. $\begin{array}{r} 96 \\ 29 \\ 34 \\ +8 \\ \hline \textbf{167} \end{array}$ **10.** $\begin{array}{r} 8427 \\ 896 \\ 429 \\ +6 \\ \hline \textbf{9758} \end{array}$ **11.** $\begin{array}{r} 5938 \\ 2716 \\ +4948 \\ \hline \textbf{13,602} \end{array}$ **12.** $\begin{array}{r} 764,289 \\ 19,476 \\ 25,487 \\ +3,965 \\ \hline \textbf{813,217} \end{array}$

SKILL 15. Adding Money

Line up decimal points. Add. Place decimal points in the sum.

EXAMPLE $89.28 + $6.47

$$\begin{array}{r} \overset{1}{}\overset{1}{} \\ \$\,89.28 \\ +\;\;6.47 \\ \hline \$\,95.75 \end{array}$$

1. $0.87 + $0.75 **$1.62** **2.** $7.48 + $0.99 **$8.47** **3.** $3.49 + $8.85 **$12.34**

4.
$$\begin{array}{r} \$\,0.87 \\ 0.05 \\ +\,0.18 \\ \hline \$1.10 \end{array}$$

5.
$$\begin{array}{r} \$\,9.05 \\ 0.86 \\ +\,9.38 \\ \hline \$19.29 \end{array}$$

6.
$$\begin{array}{r} \$\,357.08 \\ 680.34 \\ +\;\;\;1.88 \\ \hline \$1039.30 \end{array}$$

7.
$$\begin{array}{r} \$\,1429.48 \\ 3754.18 \\ 426.30 \\ +\;\;\;48.95 \\ \hline \$5658.91 \end{array}$$

SKILL 16. Adding Decimals

Line up decimal points. Write 0's to fill places. Add. Place decimal point in the sum.

EXAMPLE 7.4 + 0.75 + 16.498

$$\begin{array}{r} \overset{1}{}\overset{1}{} \\ 7.400 \\ 0.750 \\ +16.498 \\ \hline 24.648 \end{array}$$

1. 0.8 + 0.1 **0.9** **2.** 0.9 + 0.5 **1.4** **3.** 8.7 + 9.4 **18.1** **4.** 7.3 + 8.95 **16.25**

5.
$$\begin{array}{r} 14.878 \\ 5.493 \\ +\,8.798 \\ \hline 29.169 \end{array}$$

6.
$$\begin{array}{r} 4.5 \\ 0.7 \\ +8.4 \\ \hline 13.6 \end{array}$$

7.
$$\begin{array}{r} 0.9 \\ 20.5 \\ 0.08 \\ +\,6.9 \\ \hline 28.38 \end{array}$$

8.
$$\begin{array}{r} 985.2 \\ 98.52 \\ 9.852 \\ +\;\;0.9852 \\ \hline 1094.5572 \end{array}$$

SKILL 17. Estimating Sums

Round to the highest place. Then add the rounded numbers.

EXAMPLES

$$\begin{array}{rcr} 748 &\rightarrow& 700 \\ 296 &\rightarrow& 300 \\ +355 &\rightarrow& \underline{400} \\ && 1400 \end{array}$$

$$\begin{array}{rcr} 7.98 &\rightarrow& 8 \\ 2.149 &\rightarrow& 2 \\ +3.2 &\rightarrow& \underline{3} \\ && 13 \end{array}$$

$$\begin{array}{rcr} \$\;8.75 &\rightarrow& \$\;9 \\ 10.26 &\rightarrow& 10 \\ +\;4.07 &\rightarrow& \underline{\;\;4} \\ && \$23 \end{array}$$

1. 38 40
   +43 40
   ——— 80

2. 5,398,647
   +6,649,800
   ——————— 5,000,000
              7,000,000
             12,000,000

3. 8.7 9
   +3.4 3
   ——— 12

4. 15.672 16
   + 7.931 8
   ———— 24

5. 3.79   4
   8.1   8
   +9.543 10
   ———— 22

6. $4.75 $5
   8.99   9
   + 6.98 7
   ——— $21

7. $14.06 $10
   10.79 10
   + 26.48 30
   ——— $50

8. $ 6.98 $7
   10.15 10
   + 5.05   5
   ——— $22

SKILL 18. Subtracting Whole Numbers

EXAMPLE 7291 − 3428

$$\begin{array}{r} {\scriptstyle 6\ 12\ 8\ 11} \\ 7\,2\,9\,1 \\ -\ 3\,4\,2\,8 \\ \hline 3\,8\,6\,3 \end{array}$$

Start on the right.
Rename when necessary.

1. 86
   −21
   —— 65

2. 91
   −26
   —— 65

3. 80
   −19
   —— 61

4. 748
   −129
   —— 619

5. 876
   −299
   —— 577

6. 400
   − 75
   —— 325

7. 6294
   −1995
   —— 4299

8. 37,286
   −29,148
   —— 8138

SKILL 19. Subtracting Money

Line up decimal points. Subtract. Place decimal point in the answer.

EXAMPLE $26.49 − $19.75

$$\begin{array}{r} {\scriptstyle 1\ 15} \\ {\scriptstyle \ \ 5\ \ 14} \\ \$\,2\,6\,.\,4\,9 \\ -\ 1\,9\,.\,7\,5 \\ \hline \$\ \ \ 6\,.\,7\,4 \end{array}$$

1. $8.29
   − 6.48
   —— $1.81

2. $10.98
   − 6.99
   —— $3.99

3. $14.00
   − 12.75
   —— $1.25

4. $37.48
   − 29.50
   —— $7.98

5. $427.50
   − 125.49
   —— $302.01

6. $87.48
   − 6.90
   —— $80.58

7. $275.00
   − 86.50
   —— $188.50

8. $10.07
   − 0.98
   —— $9.09

9. $60.00
   −5.98
   —— $54.02

10. $59.80
   −5.98
   —— $53.82

11. $8.55
   −2.75
   —— $5.80

12. $100.00
   −54.50
   —— $45.50

SKILL 20. Subtracting Decimals

Line up decimal points. Write 0's to fill places. Subtract. Place decimal point in the answer.

EXAMPLES $8.75 - 1.9$

$$\begin{array}{r} \overset{7\ \ 17}{8}.\overset{}{7}5 \\ -\ 1.90 \\ \hline 6.85 \end{array}$$

$3.7 - 1.246$

$$\begin{array}{r} \overset{6\ \ 9\ \ 10}{3}.\overset{}{7}\cancel{0}\cancel{0} \\ -\ 1.246 \\ \hline 2.454 \end{array}$$

1. $8.9 - 1.7$ **7.2**   **2.** $6.75 - 1.8$ **4.95**   **3.** $9.7 - 3.873$ **5.827**   **4.** $7 - 2.4$ **4.6**

5.
$$\begin{array}{r} 9.87 \\ -3.9 \\ \hline \mathbf{5.97} \end{array}$$

6.
$$\begin{array}{r} 4.749 \\ -3.7 \\ \hline \mathbf{1.049} \end{array}$$

7.
$$\begin{array}{r} 7.8 \\ -1.47 \\ \hline \mathbf{6.33} \end{array}$$

8.
$$\begin{array}{r} 8.3 \\ -2.644 \\ \hline \mathbf{5.656} \end{array}$$

SKILL 21. Estimating Differences

Round to the highest place. Then subtract the rounded numbers.

EXAMPLES

$$\begin{array}{r} 7249 \rightarrow\ \ 7000 \\ -3387 \rightarrow -3000 \\ \hline 4000 \end{array}$$

$$\begin{array}{r} 8.79 \rightarrow\ \ 9 \\ -3.8\ \rightarrow -4 \\ \hline 5 \end{array}$$

$$\begin{array}{r} \$8.94 \rightarrow\ \ \$9 \\ -\ 6.03 \rightarrow -\ 6 \\ \hline \$3 \end{array}$$

1.
$$\begin{array}{r} 89\ \ \mathbf{90} \\ -21\ \ \mathbf{\underline{20}} \\ \mathbf{70} \end{array}$$

2.
$$\begin{array}{r} 478\ \ \mathbf{500} \\ -189\ \ \mathbf{\underline{200}} \\ \mathbf{300} \end{array}$$

3.
$$\begin{array}{r} 7011\ \ \mathbf{7000} \\ -1990\ \ \mathbf{\underline{2000}} \\ \mathbf{5000} \end{array}$$

4.
$$\begin{array}{r} 8.1\ \ \mathbf{8} \\ -1.95\ \ \mathbf{\underline{2}} \\ \mathbf{6} \end{array}$$

5.
$$\begin{array}{r} 3.48\ \ \mathbf{3} \\ -1.69\ \ \mathbf{\underline{2}} \\ \mathbf{1} \end{array}$$

6.
$$\begin{array}{r} \$8.79\ \ \mathbf{\$9} \\ -4.85\ \ \mathbf{\underline{5}} \\ \mathbf{\$4} \end{array}$$

7.
$$\begin{array}{r} \$3.07\ \ \mathbf{\$3} \\ -1.94\ \ \mathbf{\underline{2}} \\ \mathbf{\$1} \end{array}$$

8.
$$\begin{array}{r} \$9.73\ \ \mathbf{\$10} \\ -8.84\ \ \mathbf{\underline{9}} \\ \mathbf{\$1} \end{array}$$

SKILL 22. Multiplying Whole Numbers

EXAMPLES

$$\begin{array}{r} \overset{2\,1}{876} \\ \times\ \ 3 \\ \hline 2628 \leftarrow (\times 3) \end{array}$$

$$\begin{array}{r} 876 \\ \times\ 23 \\ \hline 2628 \leftarrow (\times 3) \\ 17520 \leftarrow (\times 20) \\ \hline 20,148 \leftarrow \text{Add} \end{array}$$

$$\begin{array}{r} 876 \\ \times 123 \\ \hline 2628 \leftarrow (\times 3) \\ 17520 \leftarrow (\times 20) \\ 87600 \leftarrow (\times 100) \\ \hline 107,748 \leftarrow \text{Add} \end{array}$$

1.
$$\begin{array}{r} 87 \\ \times\ 5 \\ \hline \mathbf{435} \end{array}$$

2.
$$\begin{array}{r} 679 \\ \times\ \ 6 \\ \hline \mathbf{4074} \end{array}$$

3.
$$\begin{array}{r} 86 \\ \times 70 \\ \hline \mathbf{6020} \end{array}$$

4.
$$\begin{array}{r} 49 \\ \times 52 \\ \hline \mathbf{2548} \end{array}$$

	5. 678	**6.** 4285	**7.** 895	**8.** 6749
	× 35	× 53	×321	× 705
	23,730	227,105	287,295	4,758,045

SKILL 23. Multiplying Money

Multiply. Mark off 2 decimal places in the product.

EXAMPLE $7.45 × 32 = $238.40

1. $1.85	**2.** $3.78	**3.** $4.77	**4.** $12.42
× 12	× 25	× 50	× 100
$22.20	$94.50	$238.50	$1242

SKILL 24. Special Products

Count 0's in both factors. Place the same number of 0's in the product. Multiply non-zero digits.

EXAMPLE   700   two 0's
            × 60   one 0
            42,000   three 0's

1. 80	**2.** 50	**3.** 800	**4.** 900
× 9	×40	× 50	×900
720	2000	40,000	810,000

5. 3000	**6.** 600	**7.** 2000	**8.** 400
× 50	× 20	× 100	×500
150,000	12,000	200,000	200,000

SKILL 25. Estimating Products: Whole Numbers

Round each factor if there is more than one digit. Use Skill 11.

EXAMPLES   48 → 50   798 → 800
            × 7   × 7   × 32   × 30
                  350   24,000

1. 87 90	**2.** 503 500	**3.** 39 40	**4.** 415 400
× 9 __9__	× 8 __8__	×39 __40__	× 87 __90__
810	4000	1600	36,000

5. 698	**6.** 8748	**7.** 7486	**8.** 249 200
×102 700	× 38 9000	× 198 7000	×251 __300__
100	40	200	60,000
70,000	360,000	1,400,000	

SKILL 26. Estimating Products: Money

Estimate the product by multiplying rounded factors. Use Skill 12.

EXAMPLES

$\$7.06 \rightarrow \$7$
$\times \quad 8 \rightarrow \times 8$
$\$56$

$\$3.98 \quad \$4$
$\times \quad 21 \quad \times 20$
$\$80$

$\$87.50 \rightarrow \quad \$90$
$\times \quad 42 \rightarrow \times 40$
$\$3600$

1. $\$7.95$ $\$8$
$\times \quad 6$ $\dfrac{6}{\$48}$

2. $\$3.64$ $\$4$
$\times \quad 9$ $\dfrac{9}{\$36}$

3. $\$61.30$ $\$60$
$\times \quad 7$ $\dfrac{7}{\$420}$

4. $\$49.50$ $\$50$
$\times \quad 6$ $\dfrac{6}{\$300}$

5. $\$7.88$ 30
$\times \quad 31$ $\dfrac{\$8}{\$240}$

6. $\$1.87$ 30
$\times \quad 28$ $\dfrac{\$2}{\$60}$

7. $\$6.07$ 200
$\times \quad 198$ $\dfrac{\$6}{\$1200}$

8. $\$7.89$ 300
$\times \quad 287$ $\dfrac{\$8}{\$2400}$

9. $\$39.90$ $\$40$
$\times \quad 51$ $\dfrac{50}{\$2000}$

10. $\$61.25$ $\$60$
$\times \quad 77$ $\dfrac{80}{\$4800}$

11. $\$88.25$ 100
$\times \quad 107$ $\dfrac{\$90}{\$9000}$

12. $\$40.98$ 300
$\times \quad 279$ $\dfrac{\$40}{\$12000}$

SKILL 27. Multiplying Decimals

Multiply. Count decimal places in the factors. Place the same number of decimal places in the product. Write 0's in the product, as needed, to obtain the correct number of places.

EXAMPLES

0.01 2 places
$\times \quad 3$ $+0$ places
0.03 2 places

7.69 2 places
$\times \quad 8.5$ $+1$ place
3845
61520
65.365 3 places

1. 9.7
$\times \quad 8$
77.6

2. 74
$\times 0.05$
3.70

3. 43.7
$\times \quad 17$
742.9

4. 4.85
$\times \quad 0.5$
2.425

5. 54.8
$\times \quad 0.9$
49.32

6. 0.8
$\times 0.8$
0.64

7. 0.09
$\times \quad 0.9$
0.081

8. 0.007
$\times \quad \quad 1$
0.007

SKILL 28. Estimating Products: Decimals

Estimate the products.

EXAMPLES

$4.7 \rightarrow \quad 5$
$\times 2.19 \rightarrow \times 2$
10

$81.47 \rightarrow \quad 80$
$\times \quad 19.9 \rightarrow \times 20$
1600

1. 5.9 **6**	2. 8.153 **8**	3. 9.11 **9**	4. 7.75 **8**
$\times 6.34$ $\frac{6}{36}$	$\times\ 6.88$ $\frac{7}{56}$	$\times\ 6$ $\frac{6}{54}$	$\times 7.75$ $\frac{8}{64}$

5. 69.8 **70**	6. 10.19 **10**	7. 19.76 **20**	8. 81.2 **80**
$\times\ \ 31$ $\frac{30}{2100}$	$\times\ 41.4$ $\frac{40}{400}$	$\times\ \ 68$ $\frac{70}{1400}$	$\times 79.9$ $\frac{80}{6400}$

SKILL 29. Special Products: Decimals

Multiply. Move the decimal point to the right when multiplying by special whole numbers. Move the decimal point to the left when multiplying by a special decimal.

EXAMPLES $100 \times 8.7 = 870$

Two 0's   Move decimal point
              to the right
              two places.

$0.01 \times 8.7 = 0.087$

Two   Move decimal point
decimal   to the left
places   two places.

78.5	**842**	**8753**	**120**
1. 10×7.85	2. 100×8.42	3. 1000×8.753	4. 100×1.2
8.71	**0.782**	**0.1382**	**0.051**
5. 0.1×87.1	6. 0.01×78.2	7. 0.001×138.2	8. 0.01×5.1

SKILL 30. Fractions Mean Division

EXAMPLE $\dfrac{6}{2} \rightarrow 2\overline{)6}^{\,3}$ Divide the numerator 6 by the denominator 2.

$\dfrac{6}{2} = 3$ Read 6 divided by 2 is 3.

1. $\frac{0}{3}$ **0**	2. $\frac{4}{2}$ **2**	3. $\frac{10}{5}$ **2**
4. $\frac{12}{3}$ **4**	5. $\frac{6}{6}$ **1**	6. $\frac{10}{10}$ **1**
7. $\frac{18}{1}$ **18**	8. $\frac{12}{4}$ **3**	

SKILL 31. Equal Fractions

Cross multiply to tell whether the fractions are equal. If the cross products are equal, the fractions are equal.

EXAMPLE $\frac{2}{3} \diagdown \frac{4}{6}$ $2 \times 6 = 12$ and $3 \times 4 = 12$ The fractions are equal.

1. $\frac{1}{2}, \frac{1}{3} \neq$ **2.** $\frac{1}{2}, \frac{2}{4} =$ **3.** $\frac{3}{4}, \frac{2}{3} \neq$ **4.** $\frac{4}{8}, \frac{2}{4} =$

5. $\frac{0}{3}, \frac{0}{2} =$ **6.** $\frac{5}{5}, \frac{6}{6} =$ **7.** $\frac{9}{6}, \frac{3}{2} =$ **8.** $\frac{5}{6}, \frac{6}{7} \neq$

SKILL 32. Comparing Fractions

Use $=$, $>$, or $<$ to compare fractions. Begin with the first numerator to find cross products. The fractions have the same comparison symbol as the cross products, if you begin with the first numerator.

EXAMPLE Compare $\frac{2}{3}$ and $\frac{3}{4}$.

$2 \times 4 = 8$ and $3 \times 3 = 9$

$8 < 9$, and so, $\frac{2}{3} < \frac{3}{4}$.

1. $\frac{1}{4}$ and $\frac{3}{4} <$ **2.** $\frac{1}{2}$ and $\frac{1}{3} >$ **3.** $\frac{3}{4}$ and $\frac{4}{5} <$ **4.** $\frac{2}{3}$ and $\frac{6}{9} =$

5. $\frac{7}{8}$ and $\frac{3}{4} >$ **6.** $\frac{6}{12}$ and $\frac{1}{2} =$ **7.** $\frac{4}{7}$ and $\frac{7}{4} <$ **8.** $\frac{9}{10}$ and $\frac{10}{12} >$

9. $\frac{1}{7}$ and $\frac{1}{8} >$ **10.** $\frac{8}{1}$ and $\frac{1}{8} >$ **11.** $\frac{7}{1}$ and $\frac{8}{1} <$ **12.** $\frac{4}{6}$ and $\frac{8}{12} =$

SKILL 33. Writing Decimals as Fractions

Multiplying a decimal by a factor of 1 does not change the decimal.

EXAMPLES $1.7 = \frac{17}{10}$ $\frac{1.7}{1} \times \frac{10}{10} = \frac{17}{10}$ Multiply by a factor of 1. The numerator must become a whole number.

$0.02 = \frac{2}{100}$ $\frac{0.02}{1} \times \frac{100}{100} = \frac{2}{100}$ Multiply by a factor of 1.

1. $0.1 \frac{1}{10}$ **2.** $0.5 \frac{5}{10}$ **3.** $1.4 \frac{14}{10}$ **4.** $3.7 \frac{37}{10}$

5. $0.01 \frac{1}{100}$ **6.** $0.15 \frac{15}{100}$ **7.** $1.15 \frac{115}{100}$ **8.** $2.37 \frac{237}{100}$

9. $0.001 \frac{1}{1000}$ **10.** $0.037 \frac{37}{1000}$ **11.** $0.148 \frac{148}{1000}$ **12.** $2.407 \frac{2407}{1000}$

SKILL 34. Writing Fractions as Decimals

Convert the fraction to a decimal. Divide the numerator by the denominator. Round to the nearest hundredth if necessary.

EXAMPLES

$$\frac{7}{8} \to 8\overline{)7.000} = 0.875$$

$$\begin{array}{r} 0.875 \\ 8\overline{)7.000} \\ \underline{6\,4} \\ 60 \\ \underline{56} \\ 40 \\ \underline{40} \end{array}$$

$$\begin{array}{r} 0.666 \approx 0.67 \\ 3\overline{)2.000} \\ \underline{1\,8} \\ 20 \\ \underline{18} \\ 20 \\ \underline{18} \\ 2 \end{array}$$

1. $\frac{1}{2}$ 0.5 **2.** $\frac{1}{3}$ 0.33 **3.** $\frac{1}{4}$ 0.25 **4.** $\frac{1}{5}$ 0.2

5. $\frac{1}{6}$ 0.17 **6.** $\frac{1}{8}$ 0.125 **7.** $\frac{1}{10}$ 0.1 **8.** $\frac{1}{12}$ 0.08

9. $\frac{3}{4}$ 0.75 **10.** $\frac{4}{5}$ 0.8 **11.** $\frac{5}{10}$ 0.5 **12.** $\frac{6}{100}$ 0.06

SKILL 35. Writing Mixed Numbers as Fractions

Convert the mixed number to a fraction. Use the same denominator. To find the new numerator, multiply the denominator and the whole number, then add the numerator.

EXAMPLE $5\frac{2}{3}$ $(3 \times 5) + 2 = 17$ So, $5\frac{2}{3} = \frac{17}{3}$.

1. $1\frac{1}{2}$ $\frac{3}{2}$ **2.** $1\frac{1}{3}$ $\frac{4}{3}$ **3.** $1\frac{2}{3}$ $\frac{5}{3}$ **4.** $3\frac{1}{2}$ $\frac{7}{2}$

5. $1\frac{1}{4}$ $\frac{5}{4}$ **6.** $1\frac{3}{4}$ $\frac{7}{4}$ **7.** $2\frac{3}{4}$ $\frac{11}{4}$ **8.** $3\frac{4}{5}$ $\frac{19}{5}$

9. $4\frac{3}{5}$ $\frac{23}{5}$ **10.** $1\frac{7}{8}$ $\frac{15}{8}$ **11.** $2\frac{5}{12}$ $\frac{29}{12}$ **12.** $3\frac{7}{16}$ $\frac{55}{16}$

SKILL 36. Writing Fractions as Mixed Numbers

Convert the fraction to a mixed number. Divide the numerator by the denominator.

EXAMPLE $\dfrac{9}{4} \rightarrow 4\overline{)9}\;\;\begin{array}{c}2\frac{1}{4}\\ \underline{8}\\ 1\end{array}$ So, $\dfrac{9}{4} = 2\dfrac{1}{4}$.

1. $\dfrac{3}{2}$ $1\frac{1}{2}$ **2.** $\dfrac{4}{3}$ $1\frac{1}{3}$ **3.** $\dfrac{7}{2}$ $3\frac{1}{2}$ **4.** $\dfrac{10}{3}$ $3\frac{1}{3}$

5. $\dfrac{5}{4}$ $1\frac{1}{4}$ **6.** $\dfrac{11}{4}$ $2\frac{3}{4}$ **7.** $\dfrac{7}{5}$ $1\frac{2}{5}$ **8.** $\dfrac{14}{5}$ $2\frac{4}{5}$

9. $\dfrac{11}{8}$ $1\frac{3}{8}$ **10.** $\dfrac{19}{8}$ $2\frac{3}{8}$ **11.** $\dfrac{13}{10}$ $1\frac{3}{10}$ **12.** $\dfrac{29}{10}$ $2\frac{9}{10}$

SKILL 37. Writing Decimals as Mixed Numbers

Convert the decimal to a mixed number. The number of decimal places is the same as the number of 0's in the denominator of the mixed number.

EXAMPLES $1.2 = 1 + 0.2 = 1 + \dfrac{2}{10} = 1\dfrac{2}{10}$

$27.35 = 27 + 0.35 = 27 + \dfrac{35}{100} = 27\dfrac{35}{100}$

$1.035 = 1 + 0.035 = 1 + \dfrac{35}{1000} = 1\dfrac{35}{1000}$

1. 2.3 $2\frac{3}{10}$ **2.** 4.8 $4\frac{8}{10}$ **3.** 12.2 $12\frac{2}{10}$ **4.** 72.5 $72\frac{5}{10}$

5. 8.98 $8\frac{98}{100}$ **6.** 2.12 $2\frac{12}{100}$ **7.** 3.07 $3\frac{7}{100}$ **8.** 15.01 $15\frac{1}{100}$

9. 3.135 $3\frac{135}{1000}$ **10.** 4.750 $4\frac{750}{1000}$ **11.** 8.075 $8\frac{75}{1000}$ **12.** 1.001 $1\frac{1}{1000}$

SKILL 38. Writing Mixed Numbers as Decimals

Convert the mixed number to a decimal. Use Skill 34 to write the fraction part as a decimal.

EXAMPLE $1\dfrac{1}{2} = 1 + \dfrac{1}{2} = 1 + 0.5 = 1.5$

1. $1\frac{4}{10}$ 1.4   **2.** $3\frac{8}{10}$ 3.8   **3.** $2\frac{1}{2}$ 2.5   **4.** $3\frac{3}{4}$ 3.75

5. $2\frac{1}{4}$ 2.25   **6.** $10\frac{1}{2}$ 10.5   **7.** $11\frac{1}{4}$ 11.25   **8.** $12\frac{3}{4}$ 12.75

9. $5\frac{5}{100}$ 5.05   **10.** $7\frac{35}{100}$ 7.35   **11.** $7\frac{1}{5}$ 7.2   **12.** $8\frac{5}{10}$ 8.5

SKILL 39. Finding Equal Fractions

Find a fraction equal to the one given, but with the indicated new denominator. Divide the new denominator by the given denominator. Multiply to find the new numerator.

EXAMPLE Write $\frac{2}{3}$ as a fraction with a denominator of 12.

$$\frac{2}{3} = \frac{?}{12} \qquad 12 \div 3 = 4 \text{ and } 4 \times 2 = 8 \qquad \frac{2}{3} = \frac{8}{12}$$

1. $\frac{1}{2}(8)$ $\frac{4}{8}$ **2.** $\frac{1}{3}(9)$ $\frac{3}{9}$ **3.** $\frac{3}{4}(36)$ $\frac{27}{36}$ **4.** $\frac{3}{4}(8)$ $\frac{6}{8}$

5. $\frac{3}{4}(12)$ $\frac{9}{12}$ **6.** $\frac{2}{3}(21)$ $\frac{14}{21}$ **7.** $\frac{2}{3}(15)$ $\frac{10}{15}$ **8.** $\frac{5}{6}(18)$ $\frac{15}{18}$

9. $\frac{3}{8}(24)$ $\frac{9}{24}$ **10.** $\frac{2}{5}(10)$ $\frac{4}{10}$ **11.** $\frac{1}{2}(10)$ $\frac{5}{10}$ **12.** $\frac{1}{2}(12)$ $\frac{6}{12}$

SKILL 40. Simplifying Fractions

Divide the numerator and denominator by their greatest common factor. Change to a whole or mixed number when possible.

EXAMPLES $\frac{6}{12} = \frac{6 \div 6}{12 \div 6} = \frac{1}{2}$

$\frac{6}{4} = \frac{6 \div 2}{4 \div 2} = \frac{3}{2} = 1\frac{1}{2}$

1. $\frac{3}{6}$ $\frac{1}{2}$ **2.** $\frac{9}{12}$ $\frac{3}{4}$ **3.** $\frac{4}{6}$ $\frac{2}{3}$ **4.** $\frac{6}{8}$ $\frac{3}{4}$

5. $\frac{10}{6}$ $1\frac{2}{3}$ **6.** $\frac{12}{10}$ $1\frac{1}{5}$ **7.** $\frac{10}{8}$ $1\frac{1}{4}$ **8.** $\frac{12}{8}$ $1\frac{1}{2}$

9. $\frac{15}{3}$ 5   **10.** $\frac{8}{2}$ 4   **11.** $\frac{10}{5}$ 2   **12.** $\frac{12}{3}$ 4

SKILL 41. Reciprocals

Find the reciprocal for each number.

EXAMPLES The reciprocal of $\frac{1}{2}$ is 2.

$\frac{1}{2}\diagup\frac{2}{1}$ Interchange the numerator and the denominator.

The reciprocal of 6 is $\frac{1}{6}$.

$\frac{6}{1}\diagup\frac{1}{6}$ Write 6 as $\frac{6}{1}$.

---

1. $\frac{1}{3}$ 3   **2.** $\frac{2}{3}$ $\frac{3}{2}$ **3.** $\frac{1}{4}$ 4   **4.** $\frac{3}{4}$ $\frac{4}{3}$ **5.** $\frac{7}{8}$ $\frac{8}{7}$ **6.** 8 $\frac{1}{8}$

SKILL 42. Least Common Denominator

Find the least common denominator (LCD). Compare multiples of each denominator.

EXAMPLE $\frac{1}{2}, \frac{1}{3} \rightarrow$ Multiples of 2: 2, 4, ⑥, 8, 10, 12, . . .

Multiples of 3: 3, ⑥, 9, 12, 15, . . .

The LCD of 2 and 3 is 6.

---

1. $\frac{1}{2}, \frac{1}{4}$ 4   **2.** $\frac{1}{2}, \frac{1}{5}$ 10   **3.** $\frac{1}{2}, \frac{1}{8}$ 8   **4.** $\frac{1}{2}, \frac{1}{10}$ 10

5. $\frac{1}{3}, \frac{1}{4}$ 12   **6.** $\frac{1}{3}, \frac{1}{6}$ 6   **7.** $\frac{1}{3}, \frac{1}{10}$ 30   **8.** $\frac{1}{4}, \frac{1}{5}$ 20

SKILL 43. Ratios

Write the ratio as a fraction. Simplify when possible.

EXAMPLES

	Ratio	Simplify	Read
10 problems done in 2 minutes	$\frac{10}{2}$	$\frac{5}{1}$	5 to 1
7 hits in 24 times at bat	$\frac{7}{24}$		7 to 24

---

1. 100 miles in 2 hours $\frac{50}{1}$ **2.** 3 buses for 120 people $\frac{1}{40}$

3. 2 eggs per 5 servings $\frac{2}{5}$ **4.** 2 teachers for 48 students $\frac{1}{24}$

SKILL 44. Converting Percents to Decimals

Convert the percent to a decimal. Move the decimal point 2 places
to the left. Drop the % sign.

EXAMPLES $12\% = 12. = 0.12$ $8\frac{1}{3}\% = 08.\frac{1}{3} = 0.08\frac{1}{3}$ $5.5\% = 05.5 = 0.055$

1. 16% **0.16**   **2.** 6% **0.06**   **3.** 3.7% **0.037**   **4.** 1% **0.01**

5. 250% **2.5**   **6.** $6\frac{1}{2}\%$ **0.065**   **7.** $9\frac{2}{3}\%$ **0.09$\frac{2}{3}$**   **8.** 150% **1.5**

SKILL 45. Converting Decimals to Percents

Convert the decimal to a percent. Move decimal point 2 places to the
right. Write the % sign.

EXAMPLES $0.18 = 0.18 = 18\%$

$0.7 = 0.70 = 70\%$ Add 1 zero.

$6 = 6.00 = 600\%$ Add 2 zeros.

1. 0.98 **98%**   **2.** 1.73 **173%**   **3.** 0.82 **82%**   **4.** 2.03 **203%**
5. 0.01 **1%**   **6.** 0.08 **8%**   **7.** 0.09 **9%**   **8.** 0.15 **15%**

SKILL 46. Converting Percents to Fractions

Convert to a fraction, mixed number, or whole number. Replace %
with $\times \frac{1}{100}$, since $n\%$ means $n \times \frac{1}{100}$.

EXAMPLES $20\% = 20 \times \frac{1}{100} = \frac{20}{100} = \frac{1}{5}$ Change % to $\times \frac{1}{100}$, multiply, and simplify.

$150\% = 150 \times \frac{1}{100} = \frac{150}{100} = 1\frac{1}{2}$

$33\frac{1}{3}\% = \frac{100}{3} \times \frac{1}{100} = \frac{100}{300} = \frac{1}{3}$ First change mixed number to a fraction (Skill 35).

$12.5\% = 0.125 = \frac{125}{1000} = \frac{1}{8}$ First convert percent to a decimal (Skill 44), then convert the decimal to a fraction (Skill 33).

1. 10% $\frac{1}{10}$ **2.** 30% $\frac{3}{10}$ **3.** 50% $\frac{1}{2}$ **4.** 75% $\frac{3}{4}$

5. $12\frac{1}{2}\%$ $\frac{1}{8}$ **6.** $16\frac{2}{3}\%$ $\frac{1}{6}$ **7.** $66\frac{2}{3}\%$ $\frac{2}{3}$ **8.** $87\frac{1}{2}\%$ $\frac{7}{8}$

SKILL 47. Converting Fractions to Percents

Convert each fraction to a percent. Begin by changing the fraction or mixed number to a decimal (Skills 34 and 38). Then change the decimal to a percent.

EXAMPLES $\frac{7}{8} \rightarrow \underset{8\overline{)7.000}}{0.875} \rightarrow 87.5\%$

$1\frac{1}{4} \rightarrow 1 + \frac{1}{4} \rightarrow 1 + 0.25 \rightarrow 1.25 \rightarrow 125\%$

$\frac{2}{3} \rightarrow \underset{3\overline{)2.00}}{0.66\frac{2}{3}} \rightarrow 66\frac{2}{3}\%$ For repeating decimals, use a fraction after hundredths.

1. $\frac{1}{10}$ **10%** 2. $\frac{1}{5}$ **20%** 3. $\frac{3}{10}$ **30%** 4. $\frac{2}{5}$ **40%**

5. $\frac{3}{20}$ **15%** 6. $\frac{7}{25}$ **28%** 7. $\frac{9}{50}$ **18%** 8. $\frac{79}{100}$ **79%**

9. $1\frac{1}{2}$ **150%** 10. $2\frac{3}{4}$ **275%** 11. 1 **100%** 12. 5 **500%**

SKILL 48. Multiplying Money and Fractions

Multiply. Use Skill 54. Round to the nearest cent.

EXAMPLES $\frac{2}{3} \times \$17.48 = \frac{2}{3} \times \frac{\$17.48}{1} = \frac{\$34.96}{3}$

$\underset{3\overline{)\$34.96}}{\$11.653} \approx \$11.65$

$\$4.99 \times \frac{3}{4} = \frac{\$4.99}{1} \times \frac{3}{4} = \frac{\$14.97}{4}$

$\underset{4\overline{)\$14.97}}{\$3.7425} \approx \$3.74$

1. $\frac{1}{2} \times \$0.85$ **$0.43** 2. $\frac{2}{3} \times \$1.45$ **$0.97** 3. $\frac{3}{4} \times \$98.50$ **$73.88**

4. $\frac{4}{5} \times \$128.42$ **$102.74** 5. $\$0.75 \times \frac{2}{3}$ **$.50** 6. $\$7.84 \times \frac{1}{3}$ **$2.61**

7. $\$88.50 \times \frac{1}{4}$ **$21.13** 8. $\$289.90 \times \frac{9}{10}$ **$260.91** 9. $\frac{7}{8} \times \$8.49$ **$7.43**

10. $\$16.47 \times \frac{1}{2}$ **$8.24** 11. $\$28.47 \times \frac{2}{3}$ **$18.98** 12. $\frac{7}{12} \times \$148.57$ **$86.67**

SKILL 49. Translating to Number Sentences

Translate. Convert each % to a decimal or fraction (Skills 44 and 46).
Use n for "what," "what number," or "what percent."

EXAMPLES   What is 20% of 50?   *What % of 50 is 5?*

$\quad\quad\quad\quad \downarrow \quad \downarrow \;\; \downarrow \quad\quad \downarrow \quad\quad\quad \downarrow \quad\quad \downarrow \quad \downarrow$

$\quad\quad\quad\quad n \quad = 0.20 \times 50 \quad\quad\quad n \quad\quad \times 50 = 5$

$\quad\quad\quad\quad$ or

$\quad\quad\quad\quad n = \frac{1}{5} \times 50$

1. What is 50% of 75?
$\quad\quad n = 0.50 \times 75$

2. 10% of what number is 5?
$\quad\quad 0.10 \times n = 5$

3. What % of 12 is 3?
$\quad\quad n \times 12 = 3$

4. 62 is 75% of what number?
$\quad\quad 62 = 0.75 \times n$

5. 40% of 26.7 is what number?
$\quad\quad 0.40 \times 26.7 = n$

6. 16 is 25% of what number?
$\quad\quad 16 = 0.25 \times n$

7. $33\frac{1}{3}$% of 18 is what number?
$\quad\quad 0.33\frac{1}{3} \times 18 = n$

8. 60 is 10% of what number?
$\quad\quad 60 = 0.10 \times n$

9. $12\frac{1}{2}$% of 16 is what number?
$\quad\quad 0.125 \times 16 = n$

10. What % of 100 is 49?
$\quad\quad n \times 100 = 49$

SKILL 50. Dividing: 1-Digit Divisors, Remainders

Divide. Write the remainder over the divisor as a fraction. If a
decimal point appears in the dividend, put a decimal point directly
above it in the quotient.

EXAMPLES

$$
\begin{array}{r} 57 \\ 9\overline{)516} \\ 45 \\ \hline 66 \\ 63 \\ \hline 3 \end{array}
$$

The quotient is
$57\frac{3}{9}$ or $57\frac{1}{3}$.

$$
\begin{array}{r} 6. \\ 6\overline{)36.54} \\ 36 \\ \hline 0 \end{array}
$$

$$
\begin{array}{r} 6.0 \\ 6\overline{)36.54} \\ 36 \\ \hline 05 \\ 0 \\ \hline 54 \end{array}
$$

$$
\begin{array}{r} 6.09 \\ 6\overline{)36.54} \\ 36 \\ \hline 05 \\ 0 \\ \hline 54 \\ 54 \\ \hline \end{array}
$$

1. $2\overline{)78}$ **39**

2. $3\overline{)78}$ **26**

3. $4\overline{)78}$ **19$\frac{2}{4}$**

4. $9\overline{)78}$ **8$\frac{6}{9}$**

5. $5\overline{)397}$ **79$\frac{2}{5}$**

6. $6\overline{)499}$ **83$\frac{1}{6}$**

7. $7\overline{)8248}$ **1178$\frac{2}{7}$**

8. $8\overline{)8248}$ **1031**

9. $2\overline{)14,942}$
7471

10. $4\overline{)89,276}$
22,319

11. $6\overline{)48,192}$
8032

12. $8\overline{)79,000}$
9875

SKILL 51. Dividing: 2- and 3-Digit Divisors

Divide. Use the steps, estimate, multiply, subtract, and bring down.

EXAMPLES $1974.00 \div 25$

$$\begin{array}{r} \$\ \ 78.96 \\ 25\overline{)\$1974.00} \\ \underline{175} \\ 224 \\ \underline{200} \\ 240 \\ \underline{225} \\ 150 \\ \underline{150} \end{array}$$

$$\begin{array}{r} 0.15 \\ 640\overline{)96.00} \\ \underline{640} \\ 3200 \\ \underline{3200} \end{array}$$

1. $91 \div 13$ **7**　　2. $30 \div 22$ **1.36**　　3. $178 \div 50$ **3.56**　　**$249.21** 4. $\$4735 \div 19$

5. $32\overline{)100}$ **3.125**　6. $12\overline{)1000}$ **83.33**　7. $50\overline{)\$2.50}$ **$0.05**　8. $40\overline{)10}$ **0.25**

SKILL 52. Dividing a Decimal by a Decimal

Divide. Round to the nearest hundredth when necessary. Multiply divisor by 10 or 100 or 1000 to make it a whole number. Multiply dividend by the same number. Write 0's in the dividend as needed.

EXAMPLE $7.13 \div 0.3$

$$\begin{array}{r} 23.766 \approx 23.77 \\ 0.3\overline{)7.1300} \end{array}$$

1. $12.2 \div 0.2$ **61**　　2. $7.6 \div 0.4$ **19**　　3. $9 \div 1.2$ **7.5**　　4. $9.7 \div 0.02$ **485**

5. $0.1\overline{)8.7}$ **87**　　6. $0.2\overline{)9.5}$ **47.5**　　7. $0.04\overline{)6}$ **150**　　8. $0.07\overline{)8}$ **114.29**

9. $1.2\overline{)6}$ **5**　　10. $2.5\overline{)10}$ **4**　　11. $0.01\overline{)8.4}$ **840**　　12. $0.15\overline{)6}$ **40**

SKILL 53. Multiplying Fractions

Multiply fractions by multiplying numerators and multiplying denominators.

EXAMPLES $\frac{1}{2} \times \frac{3}{4} = \frac{3}{8}$　　$3 \times \frac{4}{13} = \frac{3}{1} \times \frac{4}{13} = \frac{12}{13}$

1. $\frac{1}{2} \times \frac{1}{3}$ **$\frac{1}{6}$**　　2. $\frac{1}{5} \times \frac{2}{3}$ **$\frac{2}{15}$**　　3. $\frac{1}{2} \times \frac{3}{4}$ **$\frac{3}{8}$**　　4. $\frac{1}{3} \times \frac{1}{3}$ **$\frac{1}{9}$**

5. $6 \times \frac{1}{7}$ **$\frac{6}{7}$**　　6. $\frac{1}{14} \times 5$ **$\frac{5}{14}$**　　7. $\frac{3}{19} \times 7$ **$\frac{21}{19}$**　　8. $5 \times \frac{3}{19}$ **$\frac{15}{19}$**

SKILL 54. Multiplying Fractions-Simplifying

Multiply. Simplify if possible. Use Skill 40.

EXAMPLES $\frac{4}{5} \times \frac{5}{6} = \frac{20}{30}$ $\qquad \frac{20}{30} = \frac{20 \div 10}{30 \div 10} = \frac{2}{3}$ $\qquad 6 \times \frac{4}{5} = \frac{6}{1} \times \frac{4}{5} = \frac{24}{5} = 4\frac{4}{5}$

1. $\frac{1}{2} \times \frac{2}{3}$ $\frac{1}{3}$ $\qquad$ **2.** $\frac{1}{5} \times \frac{5}{6}$ $\frac{1}{6}$ $\qquad$ **3.** $\frac{3}{6} \times \frac{2}{3}$ $\frac{1}{3}$ $\qquad$ **4.** $\frac{4}{8} \times \frac{2}{6}$ $\frac{1}{6}$

5. $\frac{3}{2} \times \frac{2}{3}$ 1 $\qquad$ **6.** $5 \times \frac{2}{6}$ $1\frac{2}{3}$ $\qquad$ **7.** $\frac{3}{4} \times 4$ 3 $\qquad$ **8.** $\frac{2}{3} \times \frac{1}{4}$ $\frac{1}{6}$

SKILL 55. Multiplying Mixed Numbers

Multiply and simplify. Begin by converting mixed numbers to fractions (Skill 35).

EXAMPLE $2\frac{1}{2} \times 3\frac{1}{5} = \frac{5}{2} \times \frac{16}{5} = \frac{80}{10} = 8$

1. $1\frac{1}{2} \times 1\frac{1}{3}$ 2 $\qquad$ **2.** $3\frac{1}{2} \times 4$ 14 $\qquad$ **3.** $5 \times 1\frac{3}{4}$ $8\frac{3}{4}$ $\qquad$ **4.** $10 \times 4\frac{1}{2}$ 45

5. $1\frac{1}{4} \times 3\frac{1}{2}$ $4\frac{3}{8}$ $\qquad$ **6.** $2\frac{1}{3} \times 3$ 7 $\qquad$ **7.** $1\frac{3}{4} \times 1\frac{1}{2}$ $2\frac{5}{8}$ $\qquad$ **8.** $6\frac{2}{3} \times 2$ $13\frac{1}{3}$

SKILL 56. Dividing Fractions

To divide by a fraction, multiply by the reciprocal of the divisor. (See Skill 41).

EXAMPLES $\frac{3}{4} \div \frac{1}{2} = \frac{3}{4} \times \frac{2}{1}$ $\qquad$ The reciprocal of $\frac{1}{2}$ is $\frac{2}{1}$.

$\qquad\qquad\qquad = \frac{6}{4} = \frac{3}{2} = 1\frac{1}{2}$

$\qquad\quad \frac{3}{4} \div 2 = \frac{3}{4} \times \frac{1}{2}$ $\qquad$ The reciprocal of 2 or $\frac{2}{1}$ is $\frac{1}{2}$.

$\qquad\qquad\qquad = \frac{3}{8}$

1. $\frac{2}{3} \div \frac{1}{3}$ 2 $\qquad$ **2.** $\frac{3}{4} \div \frac{1}{4}$ 3 $\qquad$ **3.** $\frac{7}{8} \div \frac{1}{8}$ 7 $\qquad$ **4.** $\frac{9}{10} \div \frac{1}{10}$ 9

5. $\frac{3}{4} \div \frac{2}{3}$ $1\frac{1}{8}$ $\qquad$ **6.** $\frac{4}{5} \div \frac{1}{2}$ $1\frac{3}{5}$ $\qquad$ **7.** $\frac{7}{8} \div 3$ $\frac{7}{24}$ $\qquad$ **8.** $\frac{4}{5} \div 2$ $\frac{2}{5}$

9. $8 \div \frac{1}{2}$ 16 $\qquad$ **10.** $12 \div \frac{1}{3}$ 36 $\qquad$ **11.** $6 \div \frac{2}{3}$ 9 $\qquad$ **12.** $\frac{1}{2} \div 2$ $\frac{1}{4}$

SKILL 57. Dividing Mixed Numbers

Divide and simplify. Begin by converting mixed numbers to fractions (Skill 35).

EXAMPLE $2\frac{1}{2} \div 1\frac{1}{4} = \frac{5}{2} \div \frac{5}{4} = \frac{5}{2} \times \frac{4}{5} = \frac{20}{10} = 2$

1. $1\frac{1}{2} \div \frac{1}{2}$ 3   **2.** $2\frac{2}{3} \div 1\frac{1}{3}$ 2   **3.** $\frac{7}{8} \div 1\frac{1}{2}$ $\frac{7}{12}$ **4.** $6 \div 1\frac{1}{2}$ 4

5. $4\frac{2}{3} \div \frac{1}{3}$ 14   **6.** $4\frac{2}{3} \div 3$ $1\frac{5}{9}$ **7.** $5 \div 2\frac{1}{2}$ 2   **8.** $7\frac{1}{2} \div 1\frac{1}{2}$ 5

SKILL 58. Adding Fractions with Same Denominator

Add and simplify. When the denominators are the same, the sum has that same denominator. The new numerator is the sum of the numerators.

EXAMPLE $\frac{3}{8} + \frac{3}{8} = \frac{6}{8} = \frac{3}{4}$

1. $\frac{1}{5} + \frac{1}{5}$ $\frac{2}{5}$ **2.** $\frac{1}{2} + \frac{1}{2}$ 1   **3.** $\frac{2}{3} + \frac{2}{3}$ $1\frac{1}{3}$ **4.** $\frac{1}{4} + \frac{1}{4}$ $\frac{1}{2}$

5. $\frac{3}{8} + \frac{4}{8}$ $\frac{7}{8}$ **6.** $\frac{5}{10} + \frac{1}{10}$ $\frac{3}{5}$ **7.** $\frac{6}{8} + \frac{1}{8}$ $\frac{7}{8}$ **8.** $\frac{4}{3} + \frac{5}{3}$ 3

SKILL 59. Adding Fractions, Different Denominators

Add. Simplify when possible. Begin by finding lowest common denominators (LCD) (Skill 42). Then write equivalent fractions (Skill 39).

EXAMPLE $\frac{3}{4} + \frac{5}{6}$ $\frac{3}{4} = \frac{9}{12}$ The LCD of 4 and 6 is 12.

$$+ \frac{5}{6} = \frac{10}{12}$$
$$\frac{19}{12} = 1\frac{7}{12}$$

1. $\frac{1}{2} + \frac{1}{4}$ $\frac{3}{4}$ **2.** $\frac{1}{2} + \frac{1}{3}$ $\frac{5}{6}$ **3.** $\frac{1}{2} + \frac{3}{4}$ $1\frac{1}{4}$ **4.** $\frac{1}{2} + \frac{7}{10}$ $1\frac{1}{5}$

5. $\frac{2}{3} + \frac{3}{4}$ $1\frac{5}{12}$ **6.** $\frac{1}{3} + \frac{5}{6}$ $1\frac{1}{6}$ **7.** $\frac{3}{8} + \frac{1}{2}$ $\frac{7}{8}$ **8.** $\frac{1}{5} + \frac{9}{10}$ $1\frac{1}{10}$

SKILL 60. Adding Mixed Numbers

Add. Simplify when possible.

EXAMPLES

$$3\frac{7}{10}$$
$$+4\frac{5}{10}$$
$$\overline{7\frac{12}{10}} = 7\frac{6}{5}$$
$$= 7 + 1\frac{1}{5}$$
$$= 8\frac{1}{5}$$

$$4\frac{1}{2} = 4\frac{3}{6}$$
$$+6\frac{2}{3} = 5\frac{4}{6}$$
$$\overline{\phantom{+6\frac{2}{3} = }9\frac{7}{6}} = 9 + 1\frac{1}{6}$$
$$= 10\frac{1}{6}$$

---

1. $3\frac{1}{3} + 1\frac{1}{3}$ $4\frac{2}{3}$ **2.** $4\frac{7}{8} + 3\frac{5}{8}$ $8\frac{1}{2}$ **3.** $8\frac{6}{10} + 7\frac{4}{10}$ 16

4. $9\frac{5}{6} + 9\frac{5}{6}$ $19\frac{2}{3}$ **5.** $2\frac{1}{2} + 2\frac{1}{3}$ $4\frac{5}{6}$ **6.** $3\frac{2}{3} + 4\frac{1}{6}$ $7\frac{5}{6}$

7. $5\frac{3}{4} + 7\frac{3}{8}$ $13\frac{1}{8}$ **8.** $3\frac{1}{2} + 4\frac{6}{10}$ $8\frac{1}{10}$ **9.** $8 + 7\frac{2}{3}$ $15\frac{2}{3}$

10. $5\frac{5}{6} + 8$ $13\frac{5}{6}$ **11.** $3\frac{4}{5} + 5\frac{1}{5}$ 9 **12.** $9\frac{1}{2} + 6\frac{2}{3}$ $16\frac{1}{6}$

SKILL 61. Subtracting Fractions

Subtract. Simplify when possible.

EXAMPLES   Same denominators   Different denominators

$$\frac{7}{12}$$
$$-\frac{5}{12}$$
$$\overline{\frac{2}{12}} = \frac{1}{6}$$

$$\frac{3}{4} = \frac{6}{8}$$
$$-\frac{1}{8} = \frac{1}{8}$$
$$\overline{\phantom{-\frac{1}{8} = }\frac{5}{8}}$$

---

1. $\frac{4}{6} - \frac{1}{6}$ $\frac{1}{2}$ **2.** $\frac{4}{3} - \frac{2}{3}$ $\frac{2}{3}$ **3.** $\frac{6}{7} - \frac{1}{7}$ $\frac{5}{7}$ **4.** $\frac{9}{10} - \frac{4}{10}$ $\frac{1}{2}$

5. $\frac{1}{2} - \frac{1}{3}$ $\frac{1}{6}$ **6.** $\frac{3}{4} - \frac{2}{3}$ $\frac{1}{12}$ **7.** $\frac{7}{8} - \frac{2}{3}$ $\frac{5}{24}$ **8.** $\frac{4}{5} - \frac{1}{2}$ $\frac{3}{10}$

9. $\frac{2}{3} - \frac{2}{9}$ $\frac{4}{9}$ **10.** $\frac{5}{8} - \frac{5}{8}$ 0 **11.** $\frac{7}{12} - \frac{1}{3}$ $\frac{1}{4}$ **12.** $\frac{9}{10} - \frac{1}{5}$ $\frac{7}{10}$

SKILL 62. Subtracting Mixed Numbers

Simplify when possible.

EXAMPLES Same denominators

$$4\frac{7}{8}$$
$$-3\frac{1}{8}$$
$$\overline{1\frac{6}{8} = 1\frac{3}{4}}$$

Different denominators

$$7\frac{1}{2} = 7\frac{2}{4}$$
$$-3\frac{1}{4} = 3\frac{1}{4}$$
$$\overline{\qquad 4\frac{1}{4}}$$

1. $7\frac{8}{10} - 4\frac{3}{10}$ $3\frac{1}{2}$ **2.** $6\frac{2}{3} - 1\frac{1}{3}$ $5\frac{1}{3}$ **3.** $8\frac{7}{8} - 2\frac{3}{8}$ $6\frac{1}{2}$ **4.** $5\frac{2}{3} - 1\frac{2}{3}$ 4

5. $5\frac{1}{2} - 1\frac{1}{3}$ $4\frac{1}{6}$ **6.** $7\frac{3}{4} - 1\frac{3}{8}$ $6\frac{3}{8}$ **7.** $7\frac{4}{10} - 3\frac{1}{5}$ $4\frac{1}{5}$ **8.** $8\frac{11}{12} - 8\frac{2}{3}$ $\frac{1}{4}$

SKILL 63. Subtracting Mixed Numbers with Renaming

Simplify when possible. Sometimes the fractions cannot be subtracted without renaming.

EXAMPLES

$$12 \quad = 11\frac{2}{2}$$
$$- \ 3\frac{1}{2} = \ 3\frac{1}{2}$$
$$\overline{\qquad 8\frac{1}{2}}$$

$$4\frac{1}{2} = 4\frac{4}{8} = 3\frac{12}{8}$$
$$-1\frac{7}{8} = 1\frac{7}{8} = 1\frac{7}{8}$$
$$\overline{\qquad\qquad 2\frac{5}{8}}$$

1. $7 - 1\frac{1}{2}$ $5\frac{1}{2}$ **2.** $5 - 3\frac{2}{3}$ $1\frac{1}{3}$ **3.** $8 - 3\frac{3}{4}$ $4\frac{1}{4}$ **4.** $10 - 3\frac{6}{10}$ $6\frac{2}{5}$

5. $8\frac{1}{4} - 7\frac{3}{4}$ $\frac{1}{2}$ **6.** $9\frac{1}{3} - 6\frac{2}{3}$ $2\frac{2}{3}$ **7.** $5\frac{2}{5} - 3\frac{4}{5}$ $1\frac{3}{5}$ **8.** $9\frac{3}{10} - 6\frac{7}{10}$ $2\frac{3}{5}$

SKILL 64. Solving Proportions

Solve. The "·" means times ($\times$).

EXAMPLE $\frac{4}{5} = \frac{10}{x}$ $4 \cdot x = 5 \cdot 10$ Cross multiply to get a simple equation.

$$4x = 50$$

$$x = \frac{50}{4}$$ Since 50 is 4 times x, we find x by dividing by 4.

$$x = 12\frac{1}{2} \quad \text{or} \quad 12.5$$

1. $\frac{1}{2} = \frac{x}{8}$ **4**   **2.** $\frac{1}{2} = \frac{8}{x}$ **16**   **3.** $\frac{1}{3} = \frac{12}{x}$ **36**   **4.** $\frac{1}{3} = \frac{x}{12}$ **4**

5. $\frac{x}{2} = \frac{8}{16}$ **1**   **6.** $\frac{x}{3} = \frac{4}{12}$ **1**   **7.** $\frac{3}{x} = \frac{9}{10}$ **3$\frac{1}{3}$**   **8.** $\frac{2}{x} = \frac{9}{12}$ **2$\frac{2}{3}$**

SKILL 65. Solving an Equation by Dividing

To solve an equation in which the multiplier of x is a whole number
or a decimal, divide both sides by the number.

EXAMPLES $8x = 32$

      $\frac{8}{8}x = \frac{32}{8}$ Divide both sides by 8.

      $1x = 4$ or $x = 4$ $1x$ is the same as x.

      $0.5x = 9$

      $\frac{0.5x}{0.5} = \frac{9}{0.5}$ Divide both sides by 0.5.

      $x = 18$

---

           6   **5**   **27**   **20.33**
1. $4x = 24$ **2.** $7x = 35$ **3.** $5x = 135$ **4.** $12x = 244$

5. $0.3x = 9$ **30**   **6.** $0.7x = 35$ **50**   **7.** $0.1x = 12$ **120**   **8.** $0.75x = 150$

9. $36 = 9x$ **10.** $48 = 0.6x$ **11.** $120 = 60x$ **12.** $200 = 0.2x$

       4   **80**   **2**   **8. 200**

                                                       12. 1000

SKILL 66. Solving an Equation by Multiplying

To solve an equation in which the multiplier of x is a fraction,
multiply both sides by the reciprocal of the fraction (Skill 41).

EXAMPLES $\frac{1}{4}x = 11$ $\frac{3}{4}x = 12$

     $4 \cdot \frac{1}{4}x = 4 \cdot 11$ $\frac{4}{3} \cdot \frac{3}{4}x = \frac{4}{3} \cdot 12$

         $1x = 44$ $1x = \frac{4}{3} \cdot 12$

           $x = 44$ $x = \frac{48}{3}$ (Skill 54)

                           $x = 16$

                                                      9.33

1. $\frac{1}{2}x = 12$ **24**   **2.** $\frac{1}{3}x = 19$ **57**   **3.** $\frac{2}{3}x = 20$ **30**   **4.** $\frac{3}{4}x = 7$

                                                       50

5. $15 = \frac{2}{3}x$ **22.5**   **6.** $24 = \frac{1}{4}x$ **96**   **7.** $76 = \frac{2}{3}x$ **114**   **8.** $10 = \frac{1}{5}x$

                                                       200

SKILL 67. Finding a Percent of a Number

First, translate to a number sentence (Skill 49). Solve.

EXAMPLES

Using decimals

37% of 50 is what number?

$0.37 \times 50 = n$

$18.5 = n$

Using fractions

What is 25% of 50?

$n = \frac{1}{4} \times 50$

$n = 12.5$ or $12\frac{1}{2}$

---

1. 1% of 84 is what number? **0.84**   **2.** What is 80% of 70? **56**

3. 75% of 40 is what number? **30**   **4.** 8.6% of 30 is what? **2.58**

5. What is 7% of 34? **2.38**   **6.** What is 12.5% of 24? **3**

7. $66\frac{2}{3}$% of 24 is what? **16**   **8.** 50% of 60 is what number? **30**

9. 125% of 40 is what? **50**   **10.** 200% of 65 is what? **130**

SKILL 68. Finding What Percent One Number Is of Another

First, translate into a number sentence (Skill 49), then use Skill 65 to solve.

EXAMPLES

9 is what percent of 12?

$9 = n \times 12$

$\frac{9}{12} = n$

Use Skill 47 to change $\frac{9}{12}$ to 75%. So, $n = 75\%$.

What percent of 8 is 16?

$n \times 8 = 16$

$n = \frac{16}{8}$

Use Skill 47 to change 2 to 200%. So, $n = 200\%$.

---

1. 3 is what percent of 10? **30%**   **2.** 2 is what percent of 100? **2%**
3. 5 is what percent of 25? **20%**   **4.** What percent of 100 is 75? **75%**
5. What percent of 10 is 12? **120%**   **6.** What percent of 20 is 10? **50%**
7. 25 is what percent of 75? **33$\frac{1}{3}$%**   **8.** 16 is what percent of 10? **160%**
9. What percent of 1 is 4? **400%**   **10.** 1 is what percent of 2? **50%**

SKILL 69. Finding a Number Given a Percent

First translate into a number sentence (Skill 49). Then use Skill 65 or Skill 66 to solve.

EXAMPLES

Using decimals

4 is 50% of what number?

$$4 = 0.50 \times n$$

$$\frac{4}{0.50} = n \qquad 0.50\overline{)4.00}$$
$$\underline{4\,00}$$
$$8 = n$$

Using fractions

4 is 25% of what number?

$$4 = \frac{1}{4} \times n$$

$$\frac{4}{1} \times 4 = \frac{4}{1} \times \frac{1}{4} \times n$$

$$16 = n$$

1. 4 is 20% of what number? **20**

2. 9 is 25% of what number? **36**

3. 21 is 15% of what number? **140**

4. 30 is 150% of what number? **20**

5. 8 is 75% of what number? **10$\frac{2}{3}$**

6. 5 is 33$\frac{1}{3}$% of what number? **15**

7. 17 is 50% of what number? **34**

8. 60 is 80% of what number? **75**

SKILL 70. Finding Percent of Increase or Decrease

To find the percent of increase or decrease, first find the *amount* of increase or decrease. Then divide this amount by the starting number.

EXAMPLES What is the percent of increase from 8 to 10?

$10 - 8 = 2$, the amount of increase

$$\frac{\text{amount of increase} \rightarrow 2}{\text{starting number} \quad \rightarrow 8} \rightarrow 25\%$$

What is the percent of decrease from 10 to 8?

$10 - 8 = 2$, the amount of decrease

$$\frac{\text{amount of decrease} \rightarrow 2}{\text{starting number} \quad \rightarrow 10} \rightarrow 20\%$$

1. Increase from 10 to 15 **50%**

2. Decrease from 15 to 5 **66$\frac{2}{3}$%**

3. Increase from 20 to 25 **25%**

4. Decrease from 50 to 40 **20%**

5. Increase from 75 to 100 **33$\frac{1}{3}$%**

6. Decrease from 75 to 50 **33$\frac{1}{3}$%**

7. Increase from 35 to 70 **100%**

8. Decrease from 100 to 60 **40%**

SKILL 71. Rounding to the Nearest Percent

Round the decimal to the nearest percent. First round to the nearest hundredth (Skill 12), then change to a percent (Skill 45).

EXAMPLE $0.8724 \approx 0.87$
$0.87 \rightarrow 87\%$

1. 0.984 **98%**   **2.** 0.876 **88%**   **3.** 0.129 **13%**
4. 0.645 **65%**   **5.** 0.1234 **12%**   **6.** 0.2398 **24%**
7. 0.8171 **82%**   **8.** 0.3456 **35%**   **9.** 0.9193 **92%**
10. 0.28764 **29%**   **11.** 0.19567 **20%**   **12.** 0.27849 **28%**

SKILL 72. Changing Metric Units

Multiply to change larger units to smaller. Divide to change smaller units to larger. If necessary, look up units in Table of Measures, page 425.

EXAMPLES   Larger units to smaller units   Smaller units to larger units

8.5 m = _____ cm   375 mL = _____ L
1 m = 100 cm   1000 mL = 1 L
8.5 × 100 = 850 cm   375 ÷ 1000 = 0.375 L

1. 6 km = __**6000**__ m   **2.** 7 m = __**700**__ cm
3. 875 mm = __**87.5**__ cm   **4.** 6248 m = __**6.248**__ km
5. 7 L = __**7000**__ mL   **6.** 3742 mL = __**3.742**__ L
7. 260 mg = __**0.26**__ g   **8.** 750 kg = __**750,000**__ g

SKILL 73. Changing Customary Units

Multiply to change larger units to smaller. Divide to change smaller units to larger. If necessary, look up units in Table of Measures, page 425.

EXAMPLES   Larger units to smaller units   Smaller units to larger units

4 ft = _____ in.   11 qt = _____ gal

1 ft = 12 in.   4 qt = 1 gal

4 ft = 4 × 12 in. = 48 in. $11 \div 4 = 2\frac{3}{4}$, so 11 qt = $2\frac{3}{4}$ gal

1. 6 ft = __**72**__ in.   **2.** 4 yd = __**144**__ in.

3. 2 mi = __**10,560**__ ft   **4.** 6 pt = __**12**__ cups

5. 4 qt = <u> 8 </u> pt   **6.** 3 tons = <u> 6000 </u> lb

7. $6\frac{1}{3}$ yd = <u> 19 </u> ft   **8.** $6\frac{1}{4}$ gal = <u> 25 </u> qt

9. $1\frac{3}{4}$ lb = <u> 28 </u> oz   **10.** 10 ft = <u> $3\frac{1}{3}$ </u> yd

11. 15 qt = <u> $3\frac{3}{4}$ </u> gal   **12.** 18 in. = <u> $1\frac{1}{2}$ </u> ft

13. 54 in. = <u> $1\frac{1}{2}$ </u> yd   **14.** 7 cups = <u> $3\frac{1}{2}$ </u> pt

SKILL 74. Adding Measures

Add each unit separately. Rename if the smaller unit can be changed to the larger unit (Skills 72 and 73).

EXAMPLES

$$\begin{array}{r} 9\text{ m }\ \ 75\text{ cm} \\ +\ 8\text{ m }\ \ 65\text{ cm} \\ \hline 17\text{ m }140\text{ cm} = 18\text{ m }40\text{ cm} \end{array}$$

$$\begin{array}{r} 8\text{ lb }\ 15\text{ oz} \\ +\ 9\text{ lb }\ 10\text{ oz} \\ \hline 17\text{ lb }25\text{ oz} = 18\text{ lb }\ 9\text{ oz} \end{array}$$

---

1. $\begin{array}{r} 5\text{ km }900\text{ m} \\ +6\text{ km }600\text{ m} \\ \hline \textbf{12 km 500 m} \end{array}$ **2.** $\begin{array}{r} 3\text{ m }725\text{ mm} \\ +5\text{ m }800\text{ mm} \\ \hline \textbf{9 m 525 mm} \end{array}$ **3.** $\begin{array}{r} 4\text{ L }180\text{ mL} \\ +5\text{ L }600\text{ mL} \\ \hline \textbf{9 L 780 mL} \end{array}$

4. $\begin{array}{r} 8\text{ kg }700\text{ g} \\ +10\text{ kg }850\text{ g} \\ \hline \textbf{19 kg 550 g} \end{array}$ **5.** $\begin{array}{r} 6\text{ ft }10\text{ in.} \\ +5\text{ ft }\ \ 9\text{ in.} \\ \hline \textbf{12 ft 7 in.} \end{array}$ **6.** $\begin{array}{r} 4\text{ gal }5\text{ qt} \\ +9\text{ gal }2\text{ qt} \\ \hline \textbf{14 gal 3 qt} \end{array}$

7. $\begin{array}{r} 7\text{ yd }19\text{ in.} \\ +6\text{ yd }25\text{ in.} \\ \hline \textbf{14 yd 8 in.} \end{array}$ **8.** $\begin{array}{r} 27\text{ lb }10\text{ oz} \\ +39\text{ lb }12\text{ oz} \\ \hline \textbf{67 lb 6 oz} \end{array}$ **9.** $\begin{array}{r} 9\text{ yd }2\text{ ft} \\ +6\text{ yd }2\text{ ft} \\ \hline \textbf{16 yd 1 ft} \end{array}$

SKILL 75. Subtracting Measures

Subtract. Rename first, if the smaller unit cannot be subtracted.

EXAMPLES

$$\begin{array}{r} 9\text{ m }25\text{ cm} \\ -3\text{ m }65\text{ cm} \end{array} \rightarrow \begin{array}{r} 8\text{ m }125\text{ cm} \\ -3\text{ m }\ \ 65\text{ cm} \\ \hline 5\text{ m }\ \ 60\text{ cm} \end{array}$$

$$\begin{array}{r} 8\text{ yd }10\text{ in.} \\ -6\text{ yd }28\text{ in.} \end{array} \rightarrow \begin{array}{r} 7\text{ yd }46\text{ in.} \\ -6\text{ yd }28\text{ in.} \\ \hline 1\text{ yd }18\text{ in.} \end{array}$$

---

1. $\begin{array}{r} 8\text{ m }800\text{ cm} \\ -5\text{ m }815\text{ cm} \\ \hline \textbf{2 m 985 cm} \end{array}$ **2.** $\begin{array}{r} 10\text{ kg }440\text{ g} \\ -\ 6\text{ kg }784\text{ g} \\ \hline \textbf{3 kg 656 g} \end{array}$ **3.** $\begin{array}{r} 15\text{ L }150\text{ mL} \\ -\ 9\text{ L }625\text{ mL} \\ \hline \textbf{5 L 525 mL} \end{array}$

4. $\begin{array}{r} 4\text{ km }325\text{ m} \\ -1\text{ km }886\text{ m} \\ \hline \textbf{2 km 439 m} \end{array}$ **5.** $\begin{array}{r} 7\text{ ft }\ \ 9\text{ in.} \\ -2\text{ ft }11\text{ in.} \\ \hline \textbf{4 ft 10 in.} \end{array}$ **6.** $\begin{array}{r} 5\text{ gal }1\text{ qt} \\ -3\text{ gal }3\text{ qt} \\ \hline \textbf{1 gal 2 qt} \end{array}$

SKILL 76. Perimeter

Perimeter is the sum of the lengths of the sides of a figure. For a rectangle, $P = 2 \times$ length plus $2 \times$ width. For a square, $P = 4 \times$ length of a side. Find the perimeter of each figure.

EXAMPLE

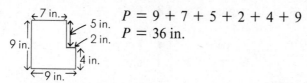

$P = 9 + 7 + 5 + 2 + 4 + 9$
$P = 36$ in.

1. 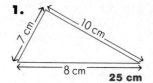 **25 cm**

2. **20 in.**

3. 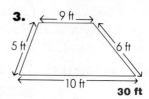 **30 ft**

4. A six-sided figure with sides of 3 yd, 3 yd, 7 yd, 3 yd, 3 yd, and 7 yd **26 yd**

5. A triangle with sides of 6 m, 8 m, and 9 m **23 m**

6. A square with each side of 4 ft **16 ft**

7. Rectangle

$l = 8.2$ m

$w = 7.3$ m **31 m**

8. Square

$s = 12.6$ m

50.4 m

9. Rectangle

$l = 2\frac{1}{2}$ ft

$w = 1\frac{1}{4}$ ft **7$\frac{1}{2}$ ft**

SKILL 77. Circumference

Circumference (C) is the distance around a circle. $C = \pi \times$ diameter or $2\pi \times$ radius. Use 3.14 for π. Find the circumference.

EXAMPLES

$C = \pi d$
$C = 3.14 \times 10$
$C = 31.4$ in.

$C = 2\pi r$
$C = 2 \times 3.14 \times 2.9$
$C = 18.212$ m

1. 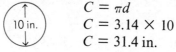 **18.84 ft**

2. **125.6 in.**

3. 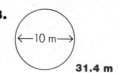 **31.4 m**

4. A circle with radius of 3 yd **18.84 yd**

5. A circle with diameter of 19.2 cm **60.3 cm**

6. A circle with radius of 8.7 m **54.6 m**

SKILL 78. Area: Rectangles, Squares

For the area of a rectangle, use the formula $A = \text{length} \times \text{width}$.
For the area of a square, $A = \text{side} \times \text{side}$. The answer is in square
units (unit²). Find the area.

EXAMPLES

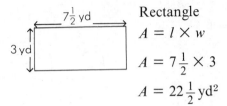

Rectangle
$A = l \times w$
$A = 7\frac{1}{2} \times 3$
$A = 22\frac{1}{2} \text{ yd}^2$

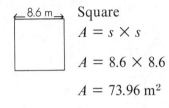

Square
$A = s \times s$
$A = 8.6 \times 8.6$
$A = 73.96 \text{ m}^2$

1.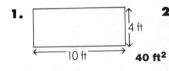
40 ft²

2.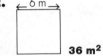
36 m²

3.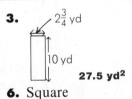
27.5 yd²

4. Square

$s = 5.3 \text{ m}$ **28.09 m²**

5. Rectangle

$l = 420 \text{ cm}$ **126,000 cm²**

$w = 300 \text{ cm}$

6. Square

$s = 2\frac{1}{2} \text{ yd}$ **6.25 yd²**

SKILL 79. Area: Parallelograms, Triangles

To find the area of a parallelogram use the formula, Area = base × height.
For a triangle, Area $= \frac{1}{2} \times$ base × height. Find the area.

EXAMPLES

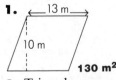

Parallelogram
$A = bh$
$A = 3 \times 7$
$A = 21 \text{ ft}^2$

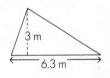

Triangle
$A = \frac{1}{2}bh$
$A = \frac{1}{2} \times 6.3 \times 3$
$A = 9.45 \text{ m}^2$

1.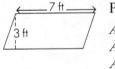
130 m²

2.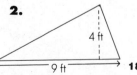
18 ft²

3.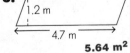
5.64 m²

4. Triangle

$b = 8 \text{ ft}$ **16 ft²**

$h = 4 \text{ ft}$

5. Parallelogram

$b = 10 \text{ ft}$ **45 ft²**

$h = 4\frac{1}{2} \text{ ft}$

6. Triangle

$b = 6.5 \text{ m}$ **26 m²**

$h = 8 \text{ m}$

SKILL 80. Area: Circles

For a circle, the area formula is $A = \pi r^2$, where r^2 means radius $\times$ radius. Use 3.14 for π.

EXAMPLES

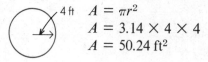

$A = \pi r^2$
$A = 3.14 \times 4 \times 4$
$A = 50.24 \text{ ft}^2$

Radius is $\frac{1}{2}$ the diameter, so, $\frac{1}{2}$ of 10 is 5.

$A = \pi r^2$
$A = 3.14 \times 5 \times 5$
$A = 78.5 \text{ cm}^2$

1. 8 in.

201 in.²

2. 20 ft

314 ft²

3. 3.5 cm

38.5 cm²

4. Circle

$r = 8.6$ in. **232 in.²**

5. Circle

$d = 12$ ft **113 ft²**

6. Circle

$r = 1.8$ m **10.2 m²**

SKILL 81. Volume: Rectangular Prisms, Cubes

Volume is measured in cubic units (unit³). For a rectangular prism, $V = \text{length} \times \text{width} \times \text{height}$. For a cube, $V = \text{side} \times \text{side} \times \text{side}$. Find the volume.

EXAMPLES

 6 m, 4 m, 3 m

Rectangular prism
$V = l \times w \times h$
$V = 4 \times 3 \times 6$
$V = 72 \text{ m}^3$

 5.2 cm

Cube
$V = s \times s \times s$
$V = 5.2 \times 5.2 \times 5.2$
$V = 140.608 \text{ cm}^3$

1. 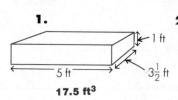 1 ft, 5 ft, $3\frac{1}{2}$ ft

17.5 ft³

2. 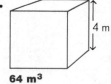 4 m

64 m³

3. 3.5 cm, 5.6 cm, 2.7 cm

52.92 cm³

4. Cube

$s = 2\frac{1}{2}$ ft **15.6 ft³**

5. Rectangular prism

$l = 3.6$ m **180 m³**
$w = 5$ m
$h = 10$ m

6. Cube

$s = 4.3$ cm **79.507 cm³**

SKILL 82. Volume: Cylinders

For a cylinder, volume = area of the base × height. Area of base = πr^2, so $V = \pi r^2 h$. Use 3.14 for π. Find the volume.

EXAMPLE

$V = \pi r^2 h$
$V = 3.14 \times 3 \times 3 \times 10$
$V = 282.6 \text{ in.}^3$

10 in.

3 in.

1.
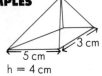
5 ft

2 ft **62.8 ft³**

2.
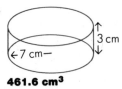
3 cm

←7 cm—

461.6 cm³

3.

8 in.

5 in. **628 in.³**

4. Cylinder
$r = 2 \text{ yd}$
$h = 4 \text{ yd}$ **50.24 yd³**

5. Cylinder
$r = 14 \text{ cm}$
$h = 12 \text{ cm}$ **7385.28 cm³**

6. Cylinder
$r = 6 \text{ m}$
$h = 2.7 \text{ m}$ **305.208 m³**

SKILL 83. Volume: Rectangular Pyramids, Cones

For a pyramid, $V = \frac{1}{3} \times$ length × width × height, so $V = \frac{1}{3} lwh$. For a cone, $V = \frac{1}{3}$ area of base × height, so $V = \frac{1}{3} \pi r^2 h$. Use 3.14 for π. Find the volume.

EXAMPLES

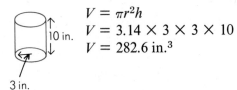

Rectangular pyramid

$V = \frac{1}{3} lwh$

$V = \frac{1}{3} \times 5 \times 3 \times 4$

$V = 20 \text{ cm}^3$

5 cm
3 cm
h = 4 cm

Cone

h = 10 m

$V = \frac{1}{3} \pi r^2 h$

$V = \frac{1}{3} \times 3.14 \times 3 \times 3 \times 10$

$V = 94.2 \text{ m}^3$

3 m

1.
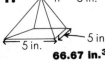
h = 8 in.
5 in.
5 in. **66.67 in.³**

2.
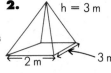
h = 3 m
6 m³
2 m
3 m

3.
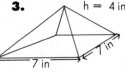
h = 4 in
7 in
7 in
65.33 in.³

4. Cone
$r = 1.5 \text{ m}$
$h = 2 \text{ m}$ **4.71 m³**

5. Pyramid
$l = 16 \text{ ft}$
$w = 14 \text{ ft}$
$h = 13 \text{ ft}$ **970.67 ft³**

6. Cone
$r = 19.7 \text{ m}$
$h = 18 \text{ m}$ **7311.62 m³**

SKILL 84. Volume: Spheres

For a sphere, volume $= \frac{4}{3} \times \pi \times r \times r \times r$.

So, $V = \frac{4}{3}\pi r^3$. Find the volume.

EXAMPLE

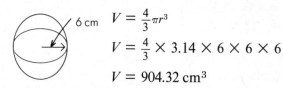

6 cm

$V = \frac{4}{3}\pi r^3$

$V = \frac{4}{3} \times 3.14 \times 6 \times 6 \times 6$

$V = 904.32$ cm³

1. 5 in.

523.3 in.³

2. 85 in.

2,571,137 in.³

3. 102 mm

4,442,924 mm³

4. Sphere

$r = 7.4$ ft **1696.5 ft³**

5. Sphere

$r = 19.7$ ft **32,009 ft³**

6. Sphere

$r = 220$ cm **44,579,627 cm³**

SKILL 85. Finding Means (Averages)

Add the numbers and divide by the number of addends. Mean and average are the same.

EXAMPLE 27, 48, 63

$27 + 48 + 63 = 138$

$138 \div 3 = 46$

1. 19, 24, 38 **27**
2. 5, 6, 7, 8, 9 **7**
3. 100, 121, 157 **126**
4. 11.2, 11.7, 12.3, 12.2 **11.85**
5. 0, 2, 100 **34**
6. 1, 4, 9, 16, 25, 36, 49 **20**

SKILL 86. Finding Medians

Arrange the numbers in order. The middle number is the median.

EXAMPLE 29, 36, 19, 40, 11
11, 19, <u>29</u>, 36, 40

If there are two middle numbers, the median is the number halfway between them.

EXAMPLE 16, 25, 5, 4, 7, 50
4, 5, 7, 16, 25, 50
7 + 16 = 23
23 ÷ 2 = 11.5 median

1. 7, 8, 9 **8**   **2.** 0, 1, 2, 3 **1.5**

3. 12, 19, 7, 8, 2, 23 **10**   **4.** 14, 18, 16, 12, 22, 8 **15**

5. 17.2, 18.2, 3.6, 4.8 **11**   **6.** 13, 19, 25, 14, 8, 6, 24 **14**

SKILL 87. Evaluating Formulas

Substitute the given values into each formula. Evaluate the formula by simplifying the expression.

EXAMPLES $F = \frac{9}{5}C + 32$, $C = 25°$ $P = 2l + 2w$, $l = 22$, $w = 15$

$F = \frac{9}{5} \times 25 + 32$ $P = 2 \times 22 + 2 \times 15$

$= 45 + 32$ $= 44 + 30$

$= 77°$ $= 74$

1. $A = lw$, $l = 12$, $w = 15$ **180**

2. $C = 2\pi r$, $r = 33$, $\pi = 3.14$ **207.24**

3. $D = rt$, $r = 55$, $t = 3.5$ **192.5**

4. $I = Prt$, $P = \$1400$, $r = 8\%$, $t = 2$ yr **$224**

5. $C = \frac{5}{9}(F - 32)$, $F = 212°$ **100°**

6. $A = \frac{1}{2}bh$, $b = 75$, $h = 10.5$ **393.75**

7. $P = 2l + 2w$, $l = 17.3$, $w = 15$ **64.6**

FINDING A JOB

How can you find a job?
Every high-school age person has asked that question.

LEARN ABOUT YOURSELF

Think about yourself. Think about your education, experience,
interests, and needs. Both you and your employer are better
off when the job is one that you can do, would like, and that will
fill your needs.

Begin by answering these questions:

1. How many years of school have you completed?
2. List courses you liked. Why?
3. List courses you didn't like. Why?
4. List jobs (including nonpaid) you have liked and not liked.
   Why?
5. List hobbies, sports, etc., you have liked and not liked.
   Tell why.
6. List skills (mental, social, or physical) you have learned (in or
   out of school).
7. List personal traits (good and bad) you have.
8. Why do you want a job? How long do you want to work? How
   much money do you expect to make?
9. List some jobs you might consider. Tell whether each one is
   one that you want to do, are willing to do, or would do if
   nothing else is available.

Do you see a pattern that indicates you would be happier working
with people than with things? That you would rather work
outdoors than indoors? That you prefer a closely supervised job
rather than one in which you work on your own?

Your school counselor and your local State Employment Office
have tests that will help you pinpoint your abilities and your
interests.

TELL ABOUT YOURSELF

A *resume* is a typed page that tells about your education and work experience. You can send it to places where you would like to work, or you can include it when you apply for a job. A neat resume shows that you care about yourself, that you want to make a good impression, and that you would make a serious employee. You should especially make sure you have not made any spelling errors.

Should be typed, short, and neat

Make yourself look good

Be specific, but not too limiting

Courses specific to this job

Don't leave gaps of time unaccounted for

By law you need not give age, sex, race, or health

```
                          RESUME


                    Alvin R. Heath
                    2851 Hampton Street
                    Dallas, Texas 47216
                    Home phone:  555-6543


Objective:  To get a job as a clerk-typist.

Education:  South High School; graduated 1984

            Accounting:  2 years

            Typing:  2 years

Experience:         Ace Bookstore
7-80 to present     4212 Maple Avenue
                    Dallas, Texas  47820

          Sales clerk.  Waited on customers; summer and
                        part-time.



Personal:  Age 20; unmarried; height - 5 feet, 11 inches;

           weight 169 pounds; excellent health.



References:

Mrs. C. Walters      Mr. John Beecher      Mr. James Paul
4212 Maple Avenue    968 Wicker Lane       2803 Hampton St.
Dallas, Texas 47829  Dallas, Texas 49122   Dallas, Texas 47216

Employer             Teacher               Neighbor
Ace Bookstore        South High School
```

A work reference   A school reference   A personal reference

WHERE TO LOOK FOR JOBS

There are many places to look for news about jobs. Some are

your local State Employment Office
school counselors
bulletin boards
classified ads in newspapers
help wanted signs in store windows
relatives or friends who are employed
private employment agencies

MANAGEMENT TRAINEE

Aunt Em's Olde Tyme Cookies, seeks a responsible person to train for Asst. Manager's position at Main St. Store. Counter sales/fast food exp. required. Please call Bob 555-9875.

ESTIMATOR Trainee to be trained by Atlanta subcontractor to do construction take-off & estimating. Must have expertise in gen. math, knowledge of elementary geometry & mech. drawing or drafting, prefer some college. Send brief resume to this paper Ad No. 3305103.

RECEPTIONIST: Job training center. Greet & register students, aid teachers w/seminars & lessons. Promotable beginner with some typing & real interest in dealing with people, to $1050/mo. Call 555-1212. Mary Weeks Placement Agency. 9 Embarcadero Center, Suite 1000.

MAIL/INVENTORY CLERK For corp. headquarters located at 155 Bovet Road, Rockille, HS grad; prefer 1–2 yrs. office exper. Valid Texas driver's lic. Neat, well-groomed & courteous. $9,500/year + company-paid benefits. Call Sue, 555-5000. EOE by choice!

Typist/Word Processing Trainee

Train on Wang. Type 60 wpm, Dictaphone exper. Good salary & benefits. Other positions available. Call Rick 555-5333 **FIRST PERSONNEL**

SECRETARY

Major computer peripheral manufacturer has an opening in its district office for a dependable, self starting individual. Candidate will perform general clerical duties including typing (60wpm) and filing. A pleasant phone voice is a must. No shorthand is required.

Our salary/benefits package is very attractive, and the small office atmosphere makes this a pleasant office in which to work. If interested, send resume or call:

Computer Corporation
200 Union Street
Chicago, Ill.
555-2824   An Equal Opportunity Employer M/F

POLICE OFFICER

$1653–2109/mo.

The City of Manchester is seeking lateral entry police officers. Applications are accepted on a continual basis. Officers receive the following benefits: $330 uniform allowance, educational incentive pay. "CHP" PERS retirement, dental plan, Blue Cross.

Completion of POST basic training is required and recent law enforcement experience is desired. The department is interested in hiring competent officers including women and minorities. Apply immediately to: City of Manchester, Personnel Office, 835 E. 14th St., Manchester, VA or call 555-3396. An Equal Opportunity Employer.

City of Manchester

PAINTER Foreman (m/f). Min. 5 yrs. paint exp. & 2 yrs. supr. exp. Pay dep. on exp. & ability. Monthly bonus plan. Call Jim, 777-1430

Mailroom Messenger

We are a world leader in marine transportation services, headquartered in Minneapolis, and we'd like to talk with you about our opening for a Mailroom Messenger. This position will entail deliveries in the downtown area and St. Paul as well as maintenance of company automobile.

We offer an excellent benefits package, including an educational assistance program, opportunity for advancement, and a great work environment!

If you have a valid Minnesota Driver's License and have a good driving record with 1 year's office experience, please come to our Personnel Department, 1 Market Plaza, St. P, between 1:30–5PM. EOE/MFH

ADDISON MARITIME CORPORATION

What can you tell about a job from these ads? Are you qualified? How much does it pay? What hours do they want you to work? Can you get there without a car? Does the job sound interesting?

APPLYING FOR A JOB

When you find a place looking for employees, you may be asked
to fill out a job application form. Fill out the form neatly. If some
question does not relate to you, write N/A—not applicable.

EMPLOYMENT APPLICATION FORM

NAME _____   SOCIAL
           LAST   FIRST   MIDDLE   SEC. NO. _____

                                                     TELEPHONE

ADDRESS _____   NO. _____
            NUMBER AND STREET   CITY   STATE   ZIP

_____

EDUCATION

HIGH
SCHOOL _____   LOCATION _____

      YEAR   COURSE OF
      GRADUATED _____   STUDY _____

COLLEGE 1. _____   LOCATION _____

      NO. OF   YEAR
      YEARS _____   GRADUATED _____   DEGREE _____   MAJOR _____   MINOR _____   G.P.A. _____

      2. _____   LOCATION _____

      NO. OF   YEAR
      YEARS _____   GRADUATED _____   DEGREE _____   MAJOR _____   MINOR _____   G.P.A. _____

OTHER DEGREES: AREA OF
COLLEGE _____   DEGREE _____   SPECIALIZATION _____

_____

EMPLOYMENT RECORD

NAME OF   KIND OF
EMPLOYER _____   BUSINESS _____

TITLE OF YOUR   EMPLOYMENT   SALARY AT
POSITION _____   DATES: FROM _____ TO _____   TERMINATION _____

DESCRIPTION OF
WORK PERFORMED _____

REASON FOR
LEAVING _____

NAME OF   KIND OF
EMPLOYER _____   BUSINESS _____

TITLE OF YOUR   EMPLOYMENT   SALARY AT
POSITION _____   DATES: FROM _____ TO _____   TERMINATION _____

DESCRIPTION OF
WORK PERFORMED _____

REASON FOR
LEAVING _____

I CERTIFY THAT THE ABOVE INFORMATION IS CORRECT TO THE BEST OF MY KNOWLEDGE AND BELIEF, AND I AM AWARE
THAT PROOF OF FALSIFICATION OF THIS APPLICATION ON MY PART MAY BE CAUSE FOR DISMISSAL.

                       SIGNED _____

TAKING A TEST TO GET A JOB

Some employers will ask you to take an aptitude test. The test
helps the employer decide whether you will be able to do the kind
of work that needs to be done. Here are some sample parts.

APTITUDE TEST

A. VERBAL

Find two words that are most nearly the SAME in meaning or
OPPOSITE in meaning.

1. a. dreary b, d; same
   b. loyal
   c. ancient
   d. faithful

2. a. begin a, c; opposite
   b. amiable
   c. cease
   d. helpful

B. NUMERICAL

1. Multiply $78 \times 24 =$ c

   a. 468
   b. 1342
   c. 1872
   d. None of these

2. A customer buys one item for $1.98 and
another item for $3.75. How much change
should be given for a 10-dollar bill? a

   a. $4.27
   b. $5.73
   c. $4.26
   d. None of these

C. SPATIAL

What can be made from the object on the left? 3

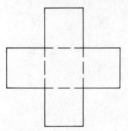   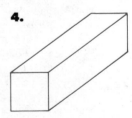

1. **2.** **3.** **4.**

D. FORM PERCEPTION

Which is exactly the same as the figure on the left? 4

1. **2.** **3.** **4.**

464   FINDING A JOB

E. CLERICAL PERCEPTION

Which names are exactly the same? **3**

1. Smith & Co.—Smith, Inc. **2.** Long Inc.—Long Icn.

3. Jones, A.C.—Jones, A.C. **4.** Albert Lang—Albert Long

F. MOTOR COORDINATION

Do the same as is shown as quickly as possible.

Start
Here

G. FINGER DEXTERITY

Put a rivet on each washer as fast as you can.

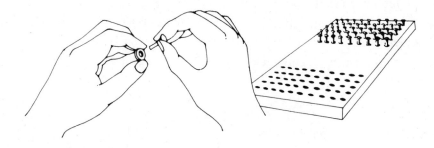

H. MANUAL DEXTERITY

Move the pegs to the lower part of this board as fast as you can.

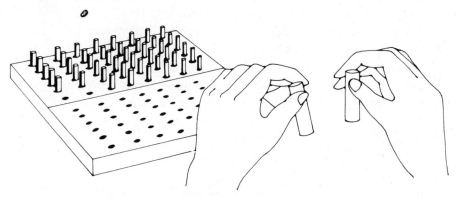

Do parts A–E. Think about parts F–H. Which parts do you think you would do the best? What kinds of jobs does this imply?

MEETING THE EMPLOYER

The last step in getting a job is meeting the employer—a job interview. In this interview, you want to find out about the job and what is expected of you. The employer wants to find out if you can do the job that needs to be filled.

The job interview should stick to these two main issues.

Here are some tips on having a successful interview.

BEFORE THE INTERVIEW

1. **Know yourself.** Review your interests. Also, recall what you said in your resume and in your application. These papers will be on the interviewer's desk.

2. **Know the employer.** Find out something about the place where you hope to work—its products or services. This shows you really are interested in the job.

3. **Dress properly.** Wear clothes that seem to fit with the job. Be neat and clean.

4. **Be on time.** Make sure you know where you are going and get there on time.

AT THE INTERVIEW

1. **Be yourself.** Do not try to act a role.

2. **Be positive.** Emphasize your strengths and what you can do. Do not make excuses for lack of experience.

3. **Ask questions.** Find out what you are expected to do on the job and what the hours are. Be ready to talk about money when the interviewer brings it up. However, if the interviewer doesn't mention money, you should.

4. You may be offered a job at the interview. You can accept immediately, or you may ask for some time to think about it—no more than one day. Respond promptly with a firm answer. Remember, the employer wants the job filled so that work will go on as usual as soon as possible.

AFTER THE INTERVIEW

If the employer is planning to interview several people and does not offer you a job at the interview, it is a good idea to send a letter. In it, supply any further information that was asked for or say that you are still interested in the job.

SOCIAL SECURITY NUMBER

Before you are hired, you must obtain a *Social Security number.*
You can get this form at the local Social Security Office. You also
will need proof showing your date of birth, your identity, and
whether you are a U.S. citizen (or your immigration status).

APPLICATION FOR A SOCIAL SECURITY NUMBER

DEPARTMENT OF HEALTH AND HUMAN SERVICES
SOCIAL SECURITY ADMINISTRATION

FORM APPROVED
OMB NO. 72-S79002

FORM SS-5 — APPLICATION FOR A
SOCIAL SECURITY NUMBER CARD
(Original, Replacement or Correction)

MICROFILM REF. NO. (SSA USE ONLY)

Unless the requested information is provided, we may not be able to issue a Social Security Number (20 CFR 422.103(b))

INSTRUCTIONS TO APPLICANT ▶ Before completing this form, please read the instructions on the opposite page. You can type or print, using pen with dark blue or black ink. Do not use pencil.

NAA 1 NAME TO BE SHOWN ON CARD — First / Middle / Last

NAB FULL NAME AT BIRTH (IF OTHER THAN ABOVE) — First / Middle / Last

ONA OTHER NAME(S) USED

STT 2 MAILING ADDRESS (Street/Apt. No., P.O. Box, Rural Route No.)

CTY STE ZIP — CITY / STATE / ZIP CODE

CSP 3 CITIZENSHIP (Check one only)
☐ a. U.S. citizen
☐ b. Legal alien allowed to work
☐ c. Legal alien not allowed to work
☐ d. Other (See instructions on Page 2)

SEX 4 ☐ Male ☐ Female

SEX ETB 5

RACE/ETHNIC DESCRIPTION (Check one only) (Voluntary)
☐ a. Asian, Asian American or Pacific Islander (Includes persons of Chinese, Filipino, Japanese, Korean, Samoan, etc., ancestry or descent)
☐ b. Hispanic (Includes persons of Chicano, Cuban, Mexican or Mexican-American, Puerto Rican, South or Central American, or other Spanish ancestry or descent)
☐ c. Negro or Black (not Hispanic)
☐ d. North American Indian or Alaskan Native
☐ e. White (not Hispanic)

DOB 6 DATE OF BIRTH — MONTH / DAY / YEAR

7 AGE / PRESENT AGE

PLB 8 PLACE OF BIRTH — CITY / STATE OR FOREIGN COUNTRY

MNA 9 MOTHER'S NAME AT HER BIRTH — First / Middle / Last (her maiden name)

FNA FATHER'S NAME — First / Middle / Last

PNO 10 a. Have you or someone on your behalf applied for a social security number before? ☐ No ☐ Don't Know ☐ Yes
If you checked "yes" complete items "b" through "e" below, otherwise go to item 11

SSN PNS PNY b. Enter social security number

c. In what State did you apply? / What year?

NLC d. Enter the name shown on your most recent social security card

e. If the birth date you used was different from the date shown in item 6, enter it here. MONTH / DAY / YEAR

DON 11 TODAY'S DATE — MONTH / DAY / YEAR

12 Telephone number where we can reach you during the day — HOME / OTHER

ASD WARNING: Deliberately providing false information on this application is punishable by a fine of $1,000 or one year in jail, or both.

13 YOUR SIGNATURE

14 YOUR RELATIONSHIP TO PERSON IN ITEM 1
☐ Self ☐ Other (Specify) _____

WITNESS (Needed only if signed by mark "X")

WITNESS (Needed only if signed by mark "X")

DO NOT WRITE BELOW THIS LINE (FOR SSA USE ONLY)

DTC SSA RECEIPT DATE _____

☐ SUPPORTING DOCUMENT—
☐ EXPEDITE CASE
☐ DUP ISSUED

SSN ASSIGNED OR VERIFIED

SSN

NPN

BIC

SIGNATURE AND TITLE OF EMPLOYEE(S) REVIEWING EVIDENCE AND/OR CONDUCTING INTERVIEW.

DOC / NTC / CAN

TYPE(S) OF EVIDENCE SUBMITTED

☐ MANDATORY IN PERSON INTERVIEW CONDUCTED

DATE

DATE

IDN / ITV / DCL

TRY THIS ANSWERS

CHAPTER 1

Page 2

1. 1825 **2.** 2850 **3.** 112.42 **4.** 86.33 **5.** 113
6. 169 **7.** 36.8 **8.** 503.16

Pages 4–5

1. 52,000 **2.** 26,000 **3.** 7,000 **4.** 24 **5.** 8
6. 30 **7.** $5 **8.** $62 **9.** $740 **10.** 670
11. 3080 **12.** 33 **13.** $31

Page 9

1. 1932 **2.** 3960 **3.** 152 **4.** $25.68 **5.** 13.25
6. 23.41 **7.** 0.36 **8.** 60.63

Pages 12–14

1. 400 **2.** 48,000 **3.** 2,500,000 **4.** 1000
5. $56 **6.** $3500 **7.** 1500 **8.** $3 **9.** 50

Pages 17–18

1. 80% **2.** 94% **3.** 63% **4.** 64% **5.** 73%
6. 78% **7.** $940 **8.** 2.7 **9.** $84.48 **10.** 600

Pages 21–22

1.

Interval	Tally	Frequency
16–18	IIII	4
19–21	IIII I	6
22–24	IIII	4
25–27	II	2
28–30	IIII I	6
31–33		0
34–36	IIII	4
37–39	I	1
40–42	II	2
43–45	IIII	4
46–48	I	1
49–51	I	1
52–54	II	2
55–57	II	2
58–60	I	1

2.

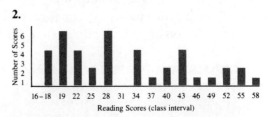

3. 70, C **4.** 91, A **5.** 66, D **6.** 83, B

Pages 25–26

1. 13.1 meters per second **2.** 1.6 miles
3. 272.2 gallons **4.** 166.5 cm^2 **5.** 104 cm^2
6. 210 in.^{2}

CHAPTER 2

Pages 34–35

1. Job B pays $608 more. **2.** Job A pays $15.54
more. **3.** Job A provides more money.
4. Job A, $12,570; Job B, $15,450

Pages 39–40

1. $278.10 **2.** $180, $72, $252 **3.** $208, $39,
$247

Pages 43–45

1. $15.30 **2.** $19 **3.** $25.10 **4.** $31.80
5. $9.21 **6.** $6.14 **7.** $17.12 **8.** $14.17
9. $132.21 **10.** $204.77

Page 47

1. $166.00 **2.** $224.75 **3.** $132.90 **4.** $168.80
5. $291.71 **6.** $329.83

Pages 51–52

1. $166.21 **2.** $198.00 **3.** $348.00 **4.** $331.25
5. $455.50

Page 55

1. $33.75 **2.** $5981.50 **3.** $150 **4.** $350
5. $725

Page 59
1. $79.36   2. $162.54   3. $391.25

CHAPTER 3

Pages 68–69
1. $37.19, $35.00   2. Fourteen and $\frac{82}{100}$
3. One hundred nineteen and $\frac{16}{100}$ 4. Sixty-four and $\frac{97}{100}$ 5. $25.00   6. $520.88

Pages 73–75
1. $14.87   2. Give Eleanor $14.00 in cash.
3. $820.25   4. $509.54

Page 80
1. $426.93, $381.67

Pages 83–85
1. $32   2. $28.50   3. $484.38   4. $895.40
5. $1292.18   6. $573.51   7. $840.53
8. $4512.38   9. $6102.65   10. $25,262.62

Pages 89–90
1. $10,850   2. $869.06

Pages 93–94
1. $0.90, $88.25   2. $9.25, $716.53   3. $16.00

Pages 97–98
1. $0.50   2. 50   3. $9.75   4. $4   5. $48
6. $8062.50   7. 3.2%, 2.0%   8. $3692.07
9. $108   10. $37.50

Pages 101–103
1. $790   2. $56.50   3. 6.4%   4. 10%   5. $100
6. $60.13

CHAPTER 4

Page 110
1. $46.86   2. $374.88   3. $406.12   4. $343.64
5. 18%   6. 10%   7. 12%   8. 6%

Pages 113–114
1. $39.91   2. $62.79   3. $49.41   4. $48.19
5. $49.47   6. $47.63   7. $2.18   8. $1.38
9. $1.22   10. $2.38   11. $0.76   12. $0.16

Pages 117–119
1. $0.089 per oz   2. $0.045 per oz
3. $0.021 per oz   4. $0.001 per gram
5. $0.098 per oz   6. Store C at $0.068 per oz
7. Store B at $0.0595 per oz   8. Brand A at
$0.049 per oz   9. Brand C at $0.023 per oz
10. Brand B at $0.055 per oz   11. $1.41
12. Store B at $7.88

Pages 123–125
1. $9   2. $8   3. $9   4. $5   5. $1.00   6. $3.30
7. $1.60   8. $0.90   9. $1.50   10. $8.90   11. $5.80

Pages 127–128
1. $17.21   2. $20.77   3. 33%   4. $1.32   5. $1.68

Page 132
1. $1.99   2. $2.20   3. $77.48   4. $40.28
5. $146.23   6. $123.70

Pages 135–136
1. $20.15   2. $6.25   3. $51.10   4. $5.11

Pages 139–141
1. 20 times   2. 40 times   3. 250 times   4. $30
5. $30   6. $2.40   7. $45   8. $40   9. $435

CHAPTER 5

Pages 148–149
1. $312   2. $381.50   3. $1059.77   4. $54,750
5. yes

Pages 151–152
1. $467.50   2. $571   3. $630   4. $1430

Pages 155–156
1. $10,312.50   2. $20,562.50   3. $5375
4. $1615   5. yes   6. no

Pages 159–160

1. $758.50 2. $1514.70 3. $914.30
4. $74,977.32, $74,954.41 5. 97% 6. 3%
7. $901.41

Pages 163–165

1. $115,616 2. $223,674 3. $3501.60
4. $75,949.20 5. $47,557.20 6. $110,701.20
7. $51,660 8. $30,740

Pages 167–168

1. 58915 2. 59502 3. $36.34 4. $89.60
5. $7.78 6. $89.76 7. $89.70 8. $66.12

Page 171

1. $57.60 2. 74 months

Pages 175–176

1. 20 yd² 2. 12 yd² 3. 6 yd² 4. $7\frac{1}{3}$ yd²
5. $8\frac{5}{9}$ yd² 6. 42 yd² 7. 70 ft 8. 51 ft 4 in.
9. 78 ft 4 in. 10. $307 11. $2968.75

Pages 179–180

1. 4 rolls 2. 7 rolls 3. 10 rolls 4. 17 rolls
5. $140.85 6. $163.80

CHAPTER 6

Page 188

1. $81,900 2. $30,720

Pages 193–194

1. $\frac{2}{5}$ 2. 12.02 ft 3. $7\frac{3}{4}''$, $11\frac{1}{2}''$

Pages 197–198

1. $1452 2. $420

Pages 201–202

1. $2500 2. $3900 3. 54 ft 4. $\frac{1}{2}$ in.

Pages 205–207

1. $1080 2. $208 3. 26 bags

Page 209

1. 2 cartons 2. $293.75

Pages 213–214

1. 3 gal 3 qt 2. 1 gal 1 qt 3. $656 4. $787.20

Pages 217–219

1. $1100 2. $960

CHAPTER 7

Pages 226–227

1. $0.44 2. $1.50 3. $0.95 4. $1.19
5. $3.91 6. $5.24 7. $6.01 8. $15.02
9. $1.79 10. $5.04

Pages 230–231

1. $10,886.15 2. $14,495 3. $2404 4. $1921
5. $1681 6. $2378 7. $210 refund
8. $83 balance due

Pages 235–236

1. $466.82 2. $576.50 3. $209.80 4. $218.37

Pages 239–240

1. $16,100; $805 2. $18,500; $740
3. $50,000; $250 4. $28,800; $576
5. $18,000; $648 6. $37,500; $843.75
7. $24,500; $490

Pages 243–245

1. $230 2. $240 3. $315 4. $380 5. $272
6. $254 7. $641

Pages 249–250

1. $20.25 2. $35.42 3. $6900 4. $8200
5. $280 6. $206.67

Page 253

1. $1126.25, $248.75 2. $690.90, $296.10

Page 257

1. $165 2. $257.96 3. $332.15 4. $18.63

CHAPTER 8

Pages 264–265
1. $8761 **2.** $9507

Page 269
1. $2181.88

Pages 271–272
1. $29.80, $119.20 **2.** $2982, $5964
3. $1882.08, $382.08, $2482.08 **4.** $630.36

Pages 275–276
1. $67.59 **2.** $194.97 **3.** $264.24

Pages 279–280
1. 68 ft **2.** 45 mph

Pages 283–284
1. 132 miles **2.** 203 miles **3.** 87 miles
4. 6 hr, 9.6 gallons **5.** $955, $119.38 per day

Page 287
1. $237.77 **2.** $148.16 **3.** $346.30 **4.** $163.44
5. $127.53 **6.** $194.88 **7.** $186.46 **8.** $165.79

Pages 291–292
1. $468 **2.** $450 **3.** 33 gal **4.** 250 gal
5. $480

Pages 295–296
1. $265.74, $21.26 **2.** $262.96, $21.04
3. $271.30, $21.70 **4.** $281.48, $22.52
5. $188.32, $15.07 **6.** $131.95, $10.56
7. $231.33, $18.51 **8.** $178.44, $14.28
9. $21.63 **10.** $21.11 **11.** $26.67 **12.** $16.83

CHAPTER 9

Pages 304–305
1. Maris, 53 **2.** Gehrig, 823 **3.** Montgomery,
0:13.41 **4.** Borckink, 0:41.25 **5.** Schlaak,
96 ft 5 in. **6.** Fosbury, 1 ft 5 in.

Pages 309–312
1. 6, 15 **2.** 136, 143, 160 **3.** 194 **4.** 138
5. 32 **6.** 8 **7.** 0 **8.** The Duck Pins won by a
score of 567 to 566.

Page 315
1. 1.303 atm **2.** 2.176 atm **3.** 30 min
4. 14 min

Pages 319–320
1. 41 yd **2.** 40 yd **3.** 16 yd **4.** 3.8 yd
5. 5.3 yd **6.** 5.8 yd **7.** 60% **8.** 58.3%
9. 56.8%

Pages 323–325
1. .400 **2.** .333 **3.** .311 **4.** 9 hits **5.** 3.6
6. 4.6 **7.** 6 games back

Page 327
1. 23 points **2.** 17 points **3.** 73% **4.** 56%
5. 45%

Pages 331–332
1. 5 strokes **2.** 3 strokes **3.** 7 strokes
4. 73 strokes **5.** 96 strokes **6.** 67 strokes
7. 75 strokes **8.** 74 par course **9.** 68 par course

Pages 335–337
1. 2.5 nautical miles **2.** 6.8 nautical miles
3. 7.6 knots **4.** 218 minutes or 3.6 hr

Pages 338–339
1. 142 beats per min **2.** 67.5 lb **3.** 112 lb

CHAPTER 10

Page 346
1. 15.1%, Average **2.** 2.6 L

Pages 349–350
1. Yes **2.** quadriceps: 67.5–82.5 ft-lb,
hamstring: 37.8–46.2 ft-lb **3.** 37.5 lb
4. 53.56 kg; 55.17 kg

Pages 352–354

1. 1.7 m²   2. 0.27 mL   3. 18.28 mL
4. 19.87 mL

Pages 357–358

1. 7.7 vehicles   2. 37 sec   3. 30 sec   4. 2.3 sec

Page 361

1. 31 panels   2. $840

Pages 365–367

1. 5, 4, and 3   2. 250,000 ohms
3. 6100 ± 610 ohms   4. 31.6 ohms

Page 369

1. $100   2. $134   3. $165   4. $330

Pages 372–374

1. $H = M - 97$ 2. $X = Q + 32$ 3. $G = \frac{A}{T}$
4. $R = \frac{T}{P}$ 5. $M = 2(Q - G)$ 6. 1320 volts
7. 60 miles per hour   8. 30 hits

CHAPTER 11

Pages 382–383

1. 5   2. 20   3. 272   4. 8.5   5. 80   6. 400
7. 192   8. 340

Pages 385–386

1. 10   Read values for D and N from DATA
   statement
   20   Multiply the number of dimes, D, by 10
   cents. Multiply the number of nickels, N,
   by 5 cents. Add the cents. Assign the total
   to C.
   30   Print the total cents, C.
   40   Accept 6 for D and 11 for N.
   50   Program is finished.
2. 115
3. 10   Read a value for S from DATA statement.
   20   Multiply the length of a side, S, by 4.
   30   Print THE PERIMETER IS and the value
   of P, 104.
   40   Accept 26 for P.
   50   Program is finished.
4. THE PERIMETER IS 104

Pages 388–389

1. $I = P * R * T$ 2. $D = S \uparrow 2 / (30 * F)$
3. $D = R * T$ 4. $A = H * (B * SB)/2$
(Do not use the same letter for B and b.)

5. ex:
   10   READ N
   20   LET G = 2.1 * N + 3.7
   30   PRINT "G = "G
   40   DATA 25, 18
   50   GO TO 10
   60   END
   G = 56.2
   G = 41.5

6. ex:
   10   READ V
   20   LET Y = 0.05 * V + 1
   30   PRINT "Y = "Y
   40   DATA 50, 55
   50   GO TO 10
   60   END
   Y = 3.5
   Y = 3.75

Pages 391–392

1. x + 1.5, y − 0.75
2. x − 1.5, y − 0.75
3. x − 1.5, y + 0.75
4.–7.

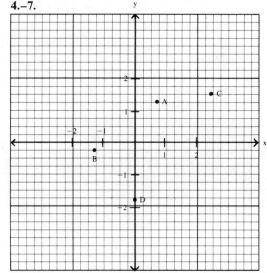

Pages 395–396

1. 68, $110.40; 140, $2848   **2.** $952, $197.45

Page 399

1. $149.28   **2.** $443.28   **3.** $24.67

CHAPTER 12

Pages 405–406

1. $32,500   **2.** Stearn County   **3.** $15,000
4. $15,000   **5.** $120,000   **6.** $30,000 decrease

Pages 408–410

1. 83.4   **2.** $12,054   **3.** 75   **4.** 88   **5.** $11,400
6. 75.5   **7.** 71   **8.** 7, $7\frac{1}{2}$

Pages 413–415

1. Skirts   Jackets   Blouses   Outfits

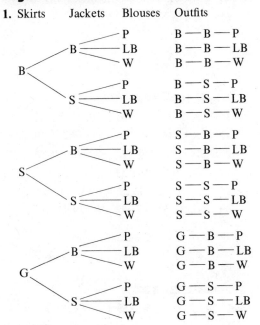

18 outfits total
3. 12   **4.** 6   **5.** 24

Pages 418–419

1. $\frac{3}{10}$ or 30%   **2.** $\frac{4}{5}$ or 80%   **3.** $\frac{1}{10}$ or 10%
4. 1 to 14   **5.** $\frac{3}{5}$ or 60%; odds are 3 to 2

Pages 413–415

2. Soups   Main   Veg   Comb.
          Dish

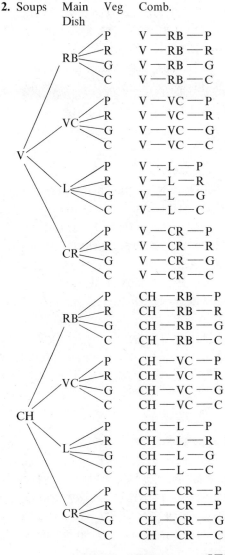

SKILLS REVIEW ANSWERS

CHAPTER 2

Pages 30–31
1. 196 **3.** 16,187 **5.** $16.07 **7.** $40.13
9. 12.6 **11.** 18.90 **13.** 22.56 **15.** 8194
17. 383,040 **19.** 4000 **21.** 54,000
23. $5.04 **25.** $128.88 **27.** 655.2 **29.** 0.0006
31. 15.2 **33.** 430 **35.** 50 **37.** 19,000 **39.** 4
41. 16 **43.** 5.03 **45.** 14.80 **47.** $1.81
49. $5.19 **51.** $0.37 **53.** $0.03 **55.** $\frac{1}{12}$ **57.** $\frac{3}{16}$
59. $5\frac{1}{3}$ **61.** 75 **63.** $2.08 **65.** $2.72
67. $4.66 **69.** $3.75 **71.** 0.15 **73.** 0.2
75. 10

CHAPTER 3

Pages 64–65
1. $0.08, or 8¢ **3.** $15 **5.** $200.16 **7.** $28
9. $59 **11.** 6 **13.** $800 **15.** 0.8
17. 0.875 or 0.88 **19.** 0.17 **21.** 0.57 **23.** 5.9
25. 78.7883 **27.** 9.6 **29.** 10.75 **31.** 0.44
33. 1.30 **35.** 0.09 **37.** 0.078 **39.** $45.95
41. $15.36 **43.** $305.20 **45.** $16.08
47. $10.38 **49.** $14.28 **51.** 20.3 **53.** 7.76
55. $\frac{35}{8}$ or $4\frac{3}{8}$ **57.** $\frac{8}{15}$ **59.** $\frac{27}{40}$ **61.** $\frac{1}{4}$ **63.** $\frac{3}{4}$
65. 26 **67.** $1\frac{3}{10}$ **69.** $6 **71.** $10.30
73. $37.50

CHAPTER 4

Pages 106–107
1. $5 **3.** $1.77 **5.** $\frac{3}{2}$ or $1\frac{1}{2}$ **7.** $\frac{11}{6}$ or $1\frac{5}{6}$
9. 0.16 **11.** 0.05 **13.** $19.11 **15.** $11.56
17. $29.08 **19.** $22.19 **21.** 6.7 **23.** 1.803
25. 1 **27.** 9 **29.** $715.76 **31.** $3487.50
33. 149.6 **35.** 46.428 **37.** $0.19 **39.** $1.50

41. $0.43 **43.** 10.58 **45.** $\frac{4}{5}$ **47.** $\frac{4}{15}$ **49.** $1\frac{1}{3}$
51. $3\frac{9}{16}$ **53.** $485 **55.** $0.73 **57.** $18
59. $26.25 **61.** $21 **63.** $18.48

CHAPTER 5

Pages 144–145
1. 8.73¢ **3.** $48.30 **5.** $\frac{3}{2}$ **7.** $\frac{15}{8}$ **9.** 0.18
11. 3.16 **13.** 86% **15.** 200% **17.** $123.66
19. $16.60 **21.** $6.88 **23.** $23.76 **25.** $580.37
27. $3467.61 **29.** 8 **31.** 25 **33.** 21 **35.** 86
37. 15 **39.** $4\frac{1}{2}$ **41.** $2\frac{1}{2}$ **43.** $6\frac{1}{2}$ **45.** $56.70
47. $24 **49.** $0.225 **51.** 87.5% **53.** 64%
55. 9 ft 4 in. **57.** 15 ft 5 in.

CHAPTER 6

Pages 184–185
1. 7 **3.** $22 **5.** $\frac{1}{2}$ **7.** $\frac{3}{5}$ **9.** $\frac{5}{1}$ **11.** $\frac{7}{2}$
13. $8.69 **15.** $267.66 **17.** $4.24 **19.** $43.75
21. 720 **23.** 2176 **25.** $22.80 **27.** $71.76
29. $40 **31.** $200 **33.** 3.1 **35.** 3.9 **37.** 73
39. 23 **41.** 30 **43.** 4.08 **45.** 14 **47.** 8
49. 16 in.² **51.** 48 yd² **53.** 39.69 m²

CHAPTER 7

Pages 222–223
1. 50 **3.** 600 **5.** 32,900 **7.** 428,000 **9.** 9
11. 10 **13.** $17 **15.** $7.90 **17.** 0.43 **19.** 0.08
21. $\frac{49}{100}$ **23.** $1\frac{9}{20}$ **25.** 170 **27.** 11,080
29. $15.85 **31.** $32.00 **33.** 17.9 **35.** 7.860
37. 69 **39.** 779 **41.** 3592 **43.** 325.424
45. $1.74 **47.** $217.50 **49.** $49 **51.** $1200
53. 44.94 **55.** 10.488 **57.** 6 **59.** 5 **61.** 4
63. $\frac{4}{9}$ **65.** 83

CHAPTER 8

Pages 260–261

1. 5 **3.** $7.90 **5.** $\frac{9}{10}$ **7.** $\frac{107}{100}$ **9.** 0.73 **11.** 0.06
13. $\frac{27}{100}$ **15.** $\frac{4}{5}$ **17.** 770 **19.** 568,050 **21.** $8.01
23. $13.15 **25.** 12.6 **27.** 9.689 **29.** 230
31. 2112 **33.** $52.43 **35.** $823.20 **37.** 655.2
39. 76.08 **41.** 65r3 **43.** 1177r2 **45.** 27.6
47. 31.22 **49.** 62.5 **51.** 52.27 **53.** 140
55. 0.31 **57.** 165

CHAPTER 9

Pages 300–301

1. 16 **3.** 20 **5.** $115 **7.** $190.00 **9.** 0.4
11. 0.38 **13.** 0.29 **15.** 0.55 **17.** $3\frac{2}{3}$ **19.** $5\frac{4}{5}$
21. 15 **23.** 4 **25.** 18 **27.** 12 **29.** 0.16
31. 0.08 **33.** 14.556 **35.** 20.238 **37.** 4349
39. 38,938 **41.** 2.75 **43.** 4.872 **45.** 27
47. 6.25 **49.** 2.4 **51.** 48.0 **53.** $\frac{3}{4}$ **55.** $\frac{1}{10}$
57. $\frac{5}{12}$ **59.** $\frac{29}{60}$ **61.** 60% **63.** $66\frac{2}{3}$% **65.** 72 in.
67. 4 ft **69.** 2 ft 2 in. **71.** 6 ft 7 in.

CHAPTER 10

Pages 342–343

1. $5 **3.** $139 **5.** 1.6 **7.** 318.10
9. $18.96 **11.** $16,767 **13.** 25.838 **15.** 35.38
17. $52.09 **19.** $355.89 **21.** 1.65 **23.** 0.599
25. 1.97 **27.** 623 **29.** 346,761 **31.** 8500
33. 9,460,000 **35.** 584.56 **37.** 2.7872 **39.** 5r1
41. 23 **43.** 501r4 **45.** 6002r3 **47.** 89.7
49. 40.37 **51.** 2.5 **53.** 117.55 **55.** $71.28
57. $2.20 **59.** 608.88 **61.** $60 **63.** $24
65. $66

CHAPTER 11

Pages 378–379

1. n = 0.18 × 63 **3.** n × 10 = 8
5. n × 16 = 12 **7.** 14,269 **9.** 477,798
11. 7.873 **13.** 35.472 **15.** 208 **17.** 17,258
19. 0.36 **21.** 3.764 **23.** 7470 **25.** 786,480
27. 3600 **29.** 160,000 **31.** 5.88 **33.** 28.45
35. 3r6 **37.** 67r5 **39.** 6531r4 **41.** 42
43. 60 **45.** 7.16 **47.** 0.2 **49.** 3.48 **51.** 2.10
53. 4000 mL **55.** 8.605 kg **57.** 31.4

SKILLS BANK ANSWERS

SKILL 1.
1. 2–7–82 **3.** 6–10–84 **5.** 5–27–83
7. May 4, 1984 **9.** June 6, 1986

SKILL 2.
1. 8:10 **3.** 4:25 **5.** 12 hr 15 min 4 sec or
15 min 4 sec after 12 o'clock

SKILL 3.
1. Thousands' place 5000 **3.** Hundred-
thousands' place 300,000 **5.** Billions' place
9,000,000,000

SKILL 4.
1. eighty-four **3.** four thousand one hundred
fifty-nine

SKILL 5.
1. 573 **3.** 97,479

SKILL 6.
1. $0.05 **3.** $12

SKILL 7.
1. Nine and $\frac{84}{100}$ dollars **3.** Eight and $\frac{07}{100}$ dollars

SKILL 8.
1. tenths' place 0.5 **3.** thousandths' place 0.009
5. hundredths' place 0.02

SKILL 9.
1. 4 and 8 tenths **3.** 327 thousandths
5. 49 hundredths **7.** 4 tenths

SKILL 10.
1. 8.26 **3.** 17.08

SKILL 11.
1. 80 **3.** 900 **5.** 6000 **7.** 80,000

SKILL 12.
1. 8 **3.** 8.3 **5.** 0.8 **7.** 6.123

SKILL 13.
1. = **3.** > **5.** <

SKILL 14.
1. 99 **3.** 937 **5.** 113 **7.** 84,630 **9.** 167
11. 13,602

SKILL 15.
1. $1.62 **3.** $12.34 **5.** $19.29 **7.** $5658.91

SKILL 16.
1. 0.9 **3.** 18.1 **5.** 29.169 **7.** 28.38

SKILL 17.

1.
$$\begin{array}{r} 40 \\ +40 \\ \hline 80 \end{array}$$
3.
$$\begin{array}{r} 9 \\ +3 \\ \hline 12 \end{array}$$
5.
$$\begin{array}{r} 4 \\ 8 \\ +10 \\ \hline 22 \end{array}$$
7.
$$\begin{array}{r} \$10 \\ 10 \\ +30 \\ \hline \$50 \end{array}$$

SKILL 18.
1. 65 **3.** 61 **5.** 577 **7.** 4299

SKILL 19.
1. $1.81 **3.** $1.25 **5.** $302.01 **7.** $188.50

SKILL 20.
1. 7.2 **3.** 5.827 **5.** 5.97 **7.** 6.33

SKILL 21.

1.
$$\begin{array}{r} 90 \\ -20 \\ \hline 70 \end{array}$$
3.
$$\begin{array}{r} 7000 \\ -2000 \\ \hline 5000 \end{array}$$
5.
$$\begin{array}{r} 3 \\ -2 \\ \hline 1 \end{array}$$
7.
$$\begin{array}{r} \$3 \\ -2 \\ \hline \$1 \end{array}$$

SKILL 22.
1. 435 **3.** 6020 **5.** 23,730 **7.** 287,295

SKILL 23.
1. $22.20 **3.** $238.50

SKILL 24.

1. 720 3. 40,000 5. 150,000 7. 200,000

SKILL 25.

1. $90 \atop \underline{\times 9} \atop 810$ 3. $40 \atop \underline{\times 40} \atop 1600$ 5. $700 \atop \underline{\times 100} \atop 70{,}000$ 7. $7000 \atop \underline{\times 200} \atop 1{,}400{,}000$

SKILL 26.

1. $\$8 \atop \underline{\times 6} \atop \$48$ 3. $\$60 \atop \underline{\times 7} \atop \$420$ 5. $30 \atop \underline{\times \$8} \atop \$240$ 7. $200 \atop \underline{\times \$6} \atop \$1200$ 9. $\$40 \atop \underline{\times 50} \atop \$2000$

11. $100 \atop \underline{\times \$90} \atop \$9000$

SKILL 27.

1. 77.6 3. 742.9 5. 49.32 7. 0.081

SKILL 28.

1. $6 \atop \underline{\times 6} \atop 36$ 3. $9 \atop \underline{\times 6} \atop 54$ 5. $70 \atop \underline{\times 30} \atop 2100$ 7. $20 \atop \underline{\times 70} \atop 1400$

SKILL 29.

1. 78.5 3. 8753 5. 8.71 7. 0.1382

SKILL 30.

1. 0 3. 2 5. 1 7. 18

SKILL 31.

1. $\neq$ 3. $\neq$ 5. $=$ 7. $=$

SKILL 32.

1. $<$ 3. $<$ 5. $>$ 7. $>$ 9. $>$ 11. $<$

SKILL 33.

1. $\frac{1}{10}$ 3. $\frac{14}{10}$ 5. $\frac{1}{100}$ 7. $\frac{115}{100}$ 9. $\frac{1}{1000}$ 11. $\frac{148}{1000}$

SKILL 34.

1. 0.5 3. 0.25 5. $\sim$0.17 7. 0.1 9. 0.75
11. 0.5

SKILL 35.

1. $\frac{3}{2}$ 3. $\frac{5}{3}$ 5. $\frac{5}{4}$ 7. $\frac{11}{4}$ 9. $\frac{23}{5}$ 11. $\frac{29}{12}$

SKILL 36.

1. $1\frac{1}{2}$ 3. $3\frac{1}{2}$ 5. $1\frac{1}{4}$ 7. $1\frac{2}{5}$ 9. $1\frac{3}{8}$ 11. $1\frac{3}{10}$

SKILL 37.

1. $2\frac{3}{10}$ 3. $12\frac{2}{10}$ 5. $8\frac{98}{100}$ 7. $3\frac{7}{100}$ 9. $3\frac{135}{1000}$
11. $8\frac{75}{1000}$

SKILL 38.

1. 1.4 3. 2.5 5. 2.25 7. 11.25 9. 5.05
11. 7.2

SKILL 39.

1. $\frac{4}{8}$ 3. $\frac{27}{36}$ 5. $\frac{9}{12}$ 7. $\frac{10}{15}$ 9. $\frac{9}{24}$ 11. $\frac{5}{10}$

SKILL 40.

1. $\frac{1}{2}$ 3. $\frac{2}{3}$ 5. $1\frac{2}{3}$ 7. $1\frac{1}{4}$ 9. 5 11. 2

SKILL 41.

1. 3 3. 4 5. $\frac{8}{7}$ 7. $\frac{1}{36}$

SKILL 42.

1. 4 3. 8 5. 12 7. 30 9. 12 11. 12

SKILL 43.

1. $\frac{50}{1}$ 3. $\frac{2}{5}$

SKILL 44.

1. 0.16 3. 0.037 5. 2.5 7. $0.09\frac{2}{3}$ 9. 0.1
11. 0.15

SKILL 45.

1. 98% 3. 82% 5. 1% 7. 9% 9. 30%
11. 700%

SKILL 46.

1. $\frac{1}{10}$ 3. $\frac{1}{2}$ 5. $\frac{1}{6}$ 7. $\frac{2}{3}$ 9. 2 11. $\frac{3}{8}$

SKILL 47.

1. 10% 3. 30% 5. 15% 7. 18% 9. 150%
11. 100% 13. $16\frac{2}{3}$% 15. 37.5%

SKILL 48.

1. $0.43 3. $73.88 5. $.50 7. $21.13
9. $7.43 11. $18.98

SKILL 49.
1. $n = 0.50 \times 75$ 3. $n \times 12 = 3$
5. $0.40 \times 26.7 = n$ 7. $0.33\frac{1}{3} \times 18 = n$
9. $0.125 \times 16 = n$

SKILL 50.
1. 39 3. $19\frac{2}{4}$ 5. $79\frac{2}{3}$ 7. $1178\frac{4}{7}$ 9. 7471
11. 8032

SKILL 51.
1. 7 3. 3.56 5. 3.125 7. $0.05 9. 6.29
11. 0.13

SKILL 52.
1. 61 3. 7.5 5. 87 7. 150 9. 5 11. 840

SKILL 53.
1. $\frac{1}{6}$ 3. $\frac{3}{8}$ 5. $\frac{6}{7}$ 7. $\frac{21}{19}$ 9. $\frac{1}{15}$ 11. $\frac{20}{37}$

SKILL 54.
1. $\frac{1}{3}$ 3. $\frac{1}{3}$ 5. 1 7. 3 9. 1 11. 8

SKILL 55.
1. 2 3. $8\frac{3}{4}$ 5. $4\frac{3}{8}$ 7. $2\frac{5}{8}$

SKILL 56.
1. 2 3. 7 5. $1\frac{1}{8}$ 7. $\frac{7}{24}$ 9. 16 11. 9

SKILL 57.
1. 3 3. $\frac{7}{12}$ 5. 14 7. 2 9. $\frac{2}{9}$ 11. 1

SKILL 58.
1. $\frac{2}{3}$ 3. $1\frac{1}{3}$ 5. $\frac{7}{8}$ 7. $\frac{7}{8}$ 9. $\frac{3}{4}$ 11. $\frac{3}{5}$

SKILL 59.
1. $\frac{3}{4}$ 3. $1\frac{1}{4}$ 5. $1\frac{5}{12}$ 7. $\frac{7}{8}$

SKILL 60.
1. $4\frac{2}{3}$ 3. 16 5. $4\frac{5}{6}$ 7. $13\frac{1}{8}$ 9. $15\frac{2}{3}$ 11. 9

SKILL 61.
1. $\frac{1}{2}$ 3. $\frac{5}{7}$ 5. $\frac{1}{6}$ 7. $\frac{5}{24}$ 9. $\frac{4}{9}$ 11. $\frac{1}{4}$

SKILL 62.
1. $3\frac{1}{2}$ 3. $6\frac{1}{2}$ 5. $4\frac{1}{6}$ 7. $4\frac{1}{5}$ 9. $2\frac{3}{4}$ 11. 4

SKILL 63.
1. $5\frac{1}{2}$ 3. $4\frac{1}{4}$ 5. $\frac{1}{2}$ 7. $1\frac{3}{5}$ 9. $4\frac{3}{4}$ 11. $2\frac{1}{2}$

SKILL 64.
1. 4 3. 36 5. 1 7. $3\frac{1}{3}$ 9. $7\frac{1}{2}$ 11. 3

SKILL 65.
1. 6 3. 27 5. 30 7. 120 9. 4 11. 2

SKILL 66.
1. 24 3. 30 5. 22.5 7. 114 9. 30
11. 26.67

SKILL 67.
1. 0.84 3. 30 5. 2.38 7. 16 9. 50

SKILL 68.
1. 30% 3. 20% 5. 120% 7. $33\frac{1}{3}$% 9. 400%

SKILL 69.
1. 20 3. 140 5. $10\frac{2}{3}$ 7. 34 9. 1000

SKILL 70.
1. 50% 3. 25% 5. $33\frac{1}{3}$% 7. 100% 9. 20%

SKILL 71.
1. 98% 3. 13% 5. 12% 7. 82% 9. 92%
11. 20%

SKILL 72.
1. 6000 3. 700 5. 0.4 7. 87.5 9. 0.53
11. 6.248 13. 7000 15. 3.742 17. 0.576
19. 0.26 21. 0.00824 23. 750,000

SKILL 73.
1. 72 3. 10,560 5. 8 7. 19 9. 28 11. $3\frac{3}{4}$
13. $1\frac{1}{2}$ 15. $1\frac{1}{4}$

SKILL 74.
1. 12 km 500 m 3. 9 L 780 mL 5. 12 ft 7 in.
7. 14 yd 8 in. 9. 16 yd 1 ft

SKILL 75.
1. 2 m 985 cm   3. 5 L 525 mL   5. 4 ft 10 in.
7. 2 yd 34 in.   9. 2 yd 2 ft

SKILL 76.
1. 25 cm   3. 30 ft   5. 23 m   7. 31 m   9. $7\frac{1}{2}$ ft

SKILL 77.
1. 18.84 ft   3. 31.4 m   5. 60.3 cm

SKILL 78.
1. 40 ft²   3. 27.5 yd²   5. 126,000 cm²

SKILL 79.
1. 130 m²   3. 5.64 m²   5. 45 ft²

SKILL 80.
1. 201 in.²   3. 38.5 cm²   5. 113 ft²

SKILL 81.
1. 17.5 ft³   3. 52.92 cm³   5. 180 m³

SKILL 82.
1. 62.8 ft³   3. 628 in.³   5. 7385.28 cm³

SKILL 83.
1. 66.67 in.³   3. 1465.33 in.³   5. 970.67 ft³

SKILL 84.
1. 523.3 in.³   3. 4,442,924 mm³   5. 32,009 ft³

SKILL 85.
1. 27   3. 126   5. 34

SKILL 86.
1. 8   3. 10   5. 11

SKILL 87.
1. 180   3. 192.5   5. 100°   7. 64.6

INDEX

carpenter, 192
carpet installer, 174
cashier, 225
catalog sales supervisor, 130
claims adjuster, 252
clothing designer, 412
computer programmer, 381
counselor, 147
data processor, 42
electrician, 53
electronics technician, 364
employment counselor, 33
energy specialist, 170
exercise technician, 345, 388
farmer, 88
financial counselor, 109
general contractor, 187
highway patrol officer, 278
insulation installer, 204
insurance agent, 242, 252
insurance broker, 248
lab technician, 352
life insurance actuary, 416
loan officer, 158
meter reader, 166
motorcycle salesperson, 261
numerical control programmer, 390
painter, 212
paper hanger, 178
payroll clerk, 38
physical fitness director, 338
physical therapist, 348
pieceworkers, 58–61
plumber, 200
real estate agent, 154
record keeper, 308, 318, 326
referee, 318
restaurant owner, 124
roofer, 196
salespeople, 50, 54–55, 135, 263, 268, 398
scorekeeper (basketball), 326

shop owner, 134
skycap, 48
solar heat installer, 360
sportswriter, 322
stockbroker, 96
store manager, 126, 394
tax assessor, 238
taxi driver, 47
tile installer, 208
traffic engineer, 356
travel agent, 294
umpire, 318
waitress, 46
Carpenter, 192
Carpentry, 192–194
Carpet
  installing, 176
  measuring for, 174–175
  total cost, 176
Carpet installer, 174
Cashier, 225
Catalog sales supervisor, 130
Catalog shopping, 130–132
Ceiling, area of, 204, 206, 213, 217
Certificate (stock), 96
Changing
  metric units, 452
  customary units, 452
Check
  register, 75, 79
  stub, 74, 79
  writing a, 72–74
Checking account
  balancing with computer, 400
  reconciling, 78–80
  recordkeeping for, 74–75
  statement of, 78
  writing checks on, 72–74
Circle graph, 109–110
Circumference, 201, 389, 454
City income tax, 235–236
Claims adjuster, 252
Closing costs, 155–156
Clothing designer, 412
Collision coverage, 242
Commission
  on airline tickets, 294, 296
  on art, 368
  on automobile sale, 263

  on stock, 98
  straight, 54–55
  and wages, 50–51
Commuting, cost of, 34
Comparing
  decimals, 429
  fractions, 436
Comprehensive coverage (insurance), 242
Computer
  and balancing checkbook, 400
  and formulas, 388–389
  hints, 385
  home, 398–400
  and inventory, 394–396
  language (BASIC), 381–383
  programs, 384–386
Computer programmer, 381
Consumer hints, 73, 79, 116
Converting
  decimals to percents, 441
  fractions to percents, 442
  percents to decimals, 441
  percents to fractions, 441
Cosigner of loan, 90
Cost factor, 187–188
Counselor, 147
Counting, 412–414
  principle, 413
Credit cards, 92–94
Current yield (bond), 101

Data
  averaging, 22
  graphing, 21, 109
  organizing, 20
  table of, 20–21
Data processor, 42
Date notation, 426
Decimal
  notation, 428
  place value, 428
  word names, 428
Decimals
  addition of, 2
  division of, 9
  estimating products, quotients of, 13, 329, 363